BECOMING INDIAN

Publication of this book and the fellowship from which it resulted were made possible
with the generous support of the National Endowment for the Humanities and
The Brown Foundation, Inc., of Houston, Texas.

School for Advanced Research
Resident Scholar Series

James F. Brooks
General Editor

BECOMING INDIAN

The Struggle over Cherokee Identity
in the Twenty-first Century

Circe Sturm

SAR
PRESS

School for Advanced Research Press

Santa Fe

School for Advanced Research Press
Post Office Box 2188
Santa Fe, New Mexico 87504-2188
www.sarpress.org

Managing Editor: Lisa Pacheco
Editorial Assistant: Ellen Goldberg
Designer and Production Manager: Cynthia Dyer
Manuscript Editor: Amanda A. Morgan
Proofreader: Kate Whelan
Indexer: Catherine Fox

Library of Congress Cataloging-in-Publication Data

Sturm, Circe, 1967-
    Becoming Indian : the struggle over Cherokee identity in the twenty-first century / Circe Sturm.
        p. cm.
    Includes bibliographical references and index.
    ISBN 978-1-934691-44-1 (alk. paper)
    1. Cherokee Indians—Ethnic identity. 2. Cherokee Indians—Mixed descent. 3. Cherokee Indians—
Politics and government. 4. Tribal government—Oklahoma. 5. Self-determination, National—
Oklahoma. 6. United States—Race relations. 7. United States—Politics and government. I. Title.
    E99.C5S878 2011
    975.004'97557—dc22

                                2010042355

Library of Congress Catalog Card Number: 2010042355
International Standard Book Numbers: paperback 978-1-934691-44-1, ebook 978-1-938645-54-9
First edition 2011. Third printing 2021.

Cover illustration: Stephan Balkenhol, "Untitled (Man with Indian Feather)." © 2018 Artist Rights Society
(ARS), New York / VG Bild-Kunst, Bonn.

To my daughter, Miranda Lewis, and my husband, Randolph Lewis,
who bring me such joy and who always help me to carry
the possibility of a better world in my heart.

I have an idea that some men are born out of their due place. Accident has cast them amid certain surroundings, but they have always a nostalgia for a home they know not. They are strangers in their birthplace, and the leafy lanes they have known from childhood or the populous street in which they have played, remain but a place of passage. They may spend their whole lives aliens among their kindred and remain aloof among the only scenes they have ever known. Perhaps it is this sense of strangeness that sends men far and wide in the search for something permanent, to which they may attach themselves. Perhaps some deep-rooted atavism urges the wanderer back to lands which his ancestors left in the dim beginnings of history. Sometimes a man hits upon a place to which he mysteriously feels that he belongs. Here is the home he sought, and he will settle amid scenes that he has never seen before, among men he has never known, as though they were familiar to him from his birth. Here at last he finds rest.

—*W. Somerset Maugham,* The Moon and Sixpence

At the heart of America's history of Indian hating is an unmistakable yearning to be Indian.

—*Louis Owens summarizing D. H. Lawrence,* Other Destinies: Understanding the American Indian Novel

Contents

Figures

Tables

Acknowledgments

Writing a book is a long and challenging journey. When at times along the way I strayed from my path, I counted on friends, family, and colleagues to call me back. They did, repeatedly, and for that I am immensely grateful. I take great pleasure in putting the finishing touches on this book and finally having the opportunity to thank all of the people who sustained it, and its author, over these many years.

First and foremost, this book owes its existence to the generosity of Cherokee people, who have kindly tolerated my intermittent presence in their lives over the past seventeen years. I thank them for putting up with me, for answering my questions with such candor and insight, and for always helping me to see the humor in any situation. Although the need to preserve anonymity prevents me from acknowledging each of them by name, I hope that they will find comfort in seeing their words reflected in these pages. They are part of a long tradition of Cherokee intellectuals, of both the formally educated and grassroots varieties, who have taught outsiders about Cherokee society and politics—and I count myself lucky to have been on the receiving end of that wisdom. On a more practical level, I am also indebted to all the Cherokee and other American Indian scholars—working in tribes, at universities, and simply out there in the world—who mailed newspaper articles, pointed out resources, shared research files, and provided written and spoken feedback on my work in progress.

I also want to extend my appreciation to the Cherokee Nation proper in Tahlequah, Oklahoma, and the Eastern Band of Cherokee Indians in Cherokee, North

Carolina, for granting me permission to conduct research among their citizens. The United Keetoowah Band of Cherokee Indians had a less formal role in the project, but interviews with some of their leaders and citizens provided important points of comparison as well. I also thank all the members of the state-recognized and self-identified Cherokee tribes who participated in this project. Your honesty and kindness allowed me to add an important dimension to this study.

The support of friends, mentors, and colleagues has meant a great deal to me, and I have a deep appreciation for all those who patiently slogged through rough drafts and provided their thoughts, criticisms, and suggestions. Though I am sure I will not recall every individual who deserves mention, let me at least give it a try: to Carol A. Smith for her support and encouragement and for being the first person to recognize the seeds of a book in this topic; to Norman Stolzoff, Deborah Cahalen Schneider, and Patricia Erikson, members of my dissertation writing group, for reading the first, very rough stab at writing a chapter on this subject; to my former colleagues at the University of Oklahoma, Jason Jackson, Margaret Bender, Morris Foster, Loretta Fowler, Dan Swan, Joshua Piker, Ari Kelman, Julia Ehrhardt, Francesca Sawaya, Karl Rambo, Robert Warrior, Clara Sue Kidwell, Barbara Hobson, and Jerry Bread, for their support and critical engagement, and especially to the members of my writing group, Misha Klein, Sean O'Neill, Peter Cahn, Katherine "Tassie" Hirschfeld, Amanda Minks, Kristin Dowell, and Marc David, for helping me to get over the final hump of drafting the entire manuscript; to my former graduate students, Candessa Teehee Morgan, Abigail Wightman, Brian J. Gilley, Jessica Walker Blanchard, Kristy Feldhousen-Giles, Rhonda S. Fair, and Brice Obermeyer, for bravely offering their own critical insights; to colleagues at other universities and in other settings, including Valerie Lambert, Michael Lambert, Les Field, Matthew Bokovoy, and Tiya Miles, who all supported this book in different ways; and to my new colleagues at the University of Texas at Austin, especially Shannon Speed, Polly Strong, Ted Gordon, Samuel Wilson, Kathleen Stewart, and John Hartigan, who have made me feel welcome while also listening to my ideas and giving me space to see this project through to the end—I thank you each and every one. I wish to especially acknowledge J. Kehaulani Kauanui, who was often a first reader of early drafts, whose sharp intellect has added so much to this work, and whose loyalty and friendship have so enriched my life. I also want to thank Eva Marie Garroutte for her insights as a Cherokee citizen and a sociologist. We had several helpful exchanges over the years, and each time, her perceptiveness pushed my work in new directions. Though I may not have incorporated every suggestion or done justice to all of these individuals' collective wisdom, I know that this book is greatly improved because of their efforts on my behalf.

I am grateful, as well, to the many colleagues at universities around the country (and abroad) who invited me to lecture at their home institutions and who gave me an opportunity to present parts of this book to a fresh audience. In particular, I would like to thank Jace Weaver and Claudio Saunt at the University of Georgia, the Native American Studies Committee and the Vice Provost for Diversity Initiatives at

Columbia University, Maria Vittoria D'Amcio at the Universitá degli Studi di Catania, James Clifford and Donna Haraway at the University of California–Santa Cruz, J. Kehualani Kauanui at Wesleyan University, Les Field at the University of New Mexico, and Orin Starn at Duke University. In addition, my dear old friend Richard Allen at the Cherokee Nation invited me to present my research at the State of Sequoyah Commission Conference, sponsored by the Cherokee Nation, before a largely Cherokee audience. I was also invited to participate in three advanced seminars in Native American studies. The first, "Doing Indigenous Research," was organized by Jennifer Nez Denetdale and took place at the School for Advanced Research in Santa Fe, New Mexico; the second, "Native American Identity," also took place at the School for Advanced Research and was organized by Suzan Shown Harjo; the third, "Comparative Indigeneities of the Americas," was organized by M. Bianet Castellanos and Lourdes Gutiérrez Nájera and was held at the University of Minnesota. All of these opportunities to engage in meaningful and sustained dialogue with advanced students and colleagues have had a significant impact on this book's final version.

A special word of thanks to Jessica Walker Blanchard, my graduate research assistant during spring and summer 2003. During these months, she conducted interviews when I could not, wrote up notes based on her own observations in the field, transcribed interviews, and logged many hours driving from one community to another, often out of state. The data she contributed were fundamental to the completion of this project, and I greatly appreciate all of her careful and painstaking work.

For financial support at various stages of research and writing, I gratefully acknowledge the National Endowment for the Humanities and the American Council of Learned Societies, who supported a yearlong residential fellowship at the School of American Research (now known as the School for Advanced Research) in Santa Fe. The School was a remarkable place in many respects, with its scenic beauty and intellectually stimulating environment. While there, I had the good fortune to share my fellowship year with an extraordinary group of scholars, many of whom have become my close friends. My heartfelt thanks to J. Kehaulani Kauanui, Jessica Cattelino, Lawrence Cohen, Jason Yaeger, Bruce Knauft, Suzan Show Harjo, Catherine Cocks, Richard Leventhal, James Brooks, Rebecca Allahyari, Nancy Owen Lewis, and Noah Zatz for providing support and critical feedback. I also wish to thank the University of Oklahoma's Office of the Vice President for Research and the College of Arts and Science for two summer fellowships and additional funds to hire a graduate research assistant, and the National Science Foundation for first funding my research in the Cherokee Nation in 1995–1996 with a Dissertation Improvement Grant. Without the data and insights from those early years in the field, and all these various sources of support, this project would never have come to fruition.

An earlier version of chapter 7 appears as "States of Sovereignty: Race Shifting, Recognition, and Rights in Cherokee Country," in *Beyond Red Power: New Perspectives on Twentieth-Century American Indian Political History*. This material is copyrighted by the School for Advanced Research (SAR) Press and is used by permission. Publishing this book has been a long but surprisingly pleasant process because of the good people at SAR Press. In this regard, let me note my gratitude to James Brooks for his support over the years and for first acquiring my manuscript when he was still the director of SAR Press, before assuming the role of president of the entire institution. Though I never got to work directly with my old friend, his successor was another friend, Catherine ("Cam") Cocks, whom I also knew from my graduate school days at the University of California at Davis. Cam is a brilliant historian with an incisive mind. She always kept faith in my work, even when I waffled. She called repeatedly to check in and always offered encouragement. She also read drafts of my writing, and I feel lucky for having had the chance to work with an editor of her caliber. She has since left the Press, and I am now working with Lisa Pacheco, who has also been nothing but supportive and kind in ushering the book through its final stages. SAR Press found two wonderful reviewers, who remain anonymous but whose imprint on the book is lasting. I thank them all for challenging me to make it better, and I hope that I have done justice to their suggestions.

Finally, I wish to thank my family for putting up with a wife, mother, sister, and daughter who was sometimes absent as she struggled to bring this book to life. Thank you, Mom, Dad, Chris, and Eddie, for your loving support and encouragement. Thank you, too, Miranda, my precious daughter, for your patience and understanding. You are a remarkable child with wisdom beyond your years, and you always make me proud. I hope that in some small way this book will also make you proud of me. And last but not least, to my beloved husband, Randy Lewis, who has been my life partner for twenty-four years: you have labored so hard behind the scenes to make this book happen, providing food, child care, editorial skills, intellectual feedback, and emotional support. More importantly, you loved me and stuck by my side through it all, and I am so lucky and grateful to have you in my life. Thank you is not enough, but it will have to do—at least for now.

o n e
Opening

Often when we are about to leave a place, we find out what really matters, what people care about, what rattles around inside their hearts. So it was for me at the end of fourteen months of ethnographic fieldwork in Tahlequah, Oklahoma—the heart of the Cherokee Nation—where I lived in 1995 and 1996 and where I have returned on a regular basis ever since. On the eve of my first departure, a number of Cherokee people, particularly tribal employees, started directing my attention toward an intriguing and at times disturbing phenomenon. This is how in late April 1996 I found myself screening a video with five Cherokee Nation employees, two of whom worked in the executive offices, the others for the *Cherokee Advocate*, the official tribal newspaper.[1] Several of them had insisted that if I was going to write about Cherokee identity politics,[2] I needed to see this particular video. A woman from the Eastern Band of Cherokee Indians in North Carolina had shot the original footage, having traveled all the way to Portsmouth, Ohio, in July 1987 to record the unusual proceedings. The images she captured were so powerful that tribal employees in Oklahoma and North Carolina were still expressing confusion and resentment almost a decade later.

Though it was in terrible shape from repeated dubbing, the video gripped our attention. Not only had it been shot surreptitiously, with the novice filmmaker and her companion posing as news reporters, but also our version was a copy of a copy of a copy that had been passed hand to hand, like some weird Grateful Dead bootleg, making its way through Indian country from the eastern seaboard to the lower Midwest. I recall asking myself why these two Cherokee women felt the need to engage in guerilla-style filmmaking and hide their identities as Eastern Band tribal members—and what subject could have so captivated Cherokee audiences around the country and had such staying power that they still found it meaningful, even critically so. The answers were not simple. Sitting on uncomfortable office furniture in the tribal complex, we watched an effort at repatriation that took place in 1987, three years prior to the passage of the Native American Graves Protection Repatriation Act in 1990. During this event, the five-thousand-year-old remains of forty-seven Native Americans were handed over for reburial to a group of amateur genealogists who had decided to form a Cherokee Indian tribe.[4]

Who were these people? This was the great mystery of the video. My viewing companions had their own answers: fake Indians, New Age poseurs, "wannabes." Though the terms made me wince, it seemed that everyone in the room expected me to share their perspective and to do something about it—they assumed that I would write some sort of anthropological exposé. Instead, I found myself wondering how we could tell whether these people were really Indian, or Cherokee, or not, and on what basis such decisions should be made.

The prelude to this seemingly bizarre turn of events had taken place only a year before the tape was made. In fall 1986, David Kuhn, a lawyer and an avid amateur archaeologist who was working under the auspices of the Scioto County Board of Commissioners, had unearthed an archaic Indian village in an area near present-day Portsmouth, Ohio. When the news became public, a local man named Oliver Collins began to lobby the commissioners, arguing that the remains were a part of his people's history and needed to be reinterred. Collins was and is a local leader of the Tallige Fire Cherokee Nation, a group of self-identified Cherokees that is not federally recognized but has been acknowledged by the state of Ohio in a state senate proclamation. According to Collins, the Tallige Fire community claimed kinship with the remains, not as direct descendants but as ostensible Cherokees. Because they identified themselves as American Indians, they felt that they had a right not only to possess the remains but also to rebury these in whatever manner they saw fit. Skeptical of these assertions, a Scioto County commissioner said, "I don't know who [the remains] belong to. They don't belong to me and they don't belong to the tribe that's here. I guess, like us, they were children to God and that's where He wanted them, back in the ground" (*Dayton Daily News*, July 20, 1987). In what appeared to be a goodwill gesture toward Native American concerns, the Scioto County Board of Commissioners granted the Tallige Fire community its request. The remains of the forty-seven individuals were handed over for reburial in a large, media-driven spectacle with nearly two hundred people in attendance. This was the event that the two amateur filmmakers documented.

Several things struck me as I sat there watching this video, hearing the groans and laughter of my friends and acquaintances in the Cherokee Nation offices. First were the very public nature of what would normally be a private event and the way in which the media and crowd eagerly gathered to watch the exotic display. The tape began with what seemed to be a representative clip from the local news, with the reporter describing in reverential tones the four-day ritual reburial, but the images that followed were a little off. I was struck by the odd regalia—hospital smocks for the men and Pocahontas-style, off-the-shoulder dresses for the women—that were worn during the ritual. This uniform style of dress among the forty or so Tallige Fire community members must have been part of a deliberate plan, for they stood in sharp relief to the gathered crowd in cutoff jeans and sleeveless Whisky River T-shirts, trying to beat the midday summer sun. Without the differences in dress, it would have been hard to tell who was who, because all of the participants, including the Tallige Fire Cherokees, appeared at least on the surface to be working-class whites, given their skin color, clothing, and mannerisms and the long line of beat-up Dodge pickups and Pontiac sedans parked at the side of the road.

Although their complicated histories and identities lay far beneath what might be gleaned from an old videotape or a casual observation, it was clear that Tallige Fire community members viewed the repatriation as an opportunity to validate their kinship claims to Indian ancestors. After the initial news clip, the video showed the reburial ceremony in all of its elaborate detail, with step-by-step explanations from Oliver Collins and other Tallige Fire leaders, who wanted the crowd to know what was going on and why it had larger cultural significance. I watched as each of the senior women of the tribe carried a small wooden casket to the edge of a large hole, approximately 15 feet deep and 20 feet in diameter. As they gingerly lowered the caskets to the men, who smudged them with burning sage, cedar, and tobacco and placed them carefully in a circle around a central fire, Oliver Collins would say something cryptic like this: "The ceremony in front of you is very old...lost to history, it's been going on so long."[5] At times he was a bit less mysterious: "We are sanctifying this ground. The sacred fire will burn the entire time we are reinterring the bodies and then be put out, but the coals will remain here forever." Regardless of the specific language he used and his clarity or lack thereof, this seemed to me, and to most of the people watching the video with me, to be some kind of performance in which the Tallige Fire members were "playing Indian" in an effort to authenticate their status as a Native American community and that they did so in a manner that was inconsistent—at times, seeming secure in their identity claims and at others, more tentative.[6]

At one point, when pressed about the origins of the group, Collins told the news media, "These people [gathered here] are of Cherokee descent.... We are in association with the Cherokee Nation. That's the first step. We want to belong, if we can prove our bloodlines. We are amateur genealogists. That's what we are."[7] But only moments later, he said that the group was "bringing [its] forefathers and foremothers back to their home" and that his people needed "to say prayers to [their] deceased." Though I noted the many inconsistencies in his statements, it was clear that Collins held fast to the belief that he and other members of the Tallige Fire community had Cherokee ancestry, despite not being able to prove it. What had begun as a genealogical association of people interested in documenting their Indian ancestry seemed to be morphing before my eyes into a tribe, or at least into a group of people who wanted to belong to a tribe and who seemed comfortable with performing that moment of desire as Cherokees.

Although these contortions were disorienting to watch and raised many questions, for me what was most striking was the great number of children who were innocently participating in the day's events—babies in their mothers' arms, young children and teenagers, sweltering away in the late July heat, patiently helping to stoke fires and lower tiny caskets, meant only to hold a handful of bones, down ladders. I kept thinking to myself that these children would grow up believing that these were their Indian ways and more specifically their Cherokee ways, though little about the ceremony bore any resemblance to Cherokee funerals or other ceremonies I had attended.[8] Regardless of whether the ritual was "authentically" Cherokee—after all, culture is what people say, think, and do, not some fixed abstraction—I was watching enculturation in process. These children were experiencing a sense of community through ritual and were now part of a distinctive subculture, even if it was one of their own parents' making. Would they develop a growing sense of themselves as Indians, Cherokees, and members of a tribe? It seemed quite possible, at least if the behavior of their parents and community leaders was any indication.

By 1988, only a year after this ceremony took place, Oliver Collins had become much more confident in asserting his community's Cherokee identity. Gone was any ambiguity about who he and the Tallige were. He wrote to his constituents in the *Tallige Cherokee Nation Newsletter*, urging the following:

> I believe we should have a monthly Sweat Bath and I believe we should purify all the Blood in our Nation's citizens to be truly Native American—and Cherokee—and SOON. We must start calling ourselves Cherokees in today's society. It is time to come out of the closet and make our selves known to the dominant society—OUT IN PUBLIC! In 1990 when the next U.S. Census is taken, we must say on the forms that we are Cherokee. We must change our Race on all documents, such as Driver's Licenses, Social Security Numbers, Birth Certificates, etc.[9]

To me, this quote is fascinating because it captures a moment of racial movement in which people who previously had identified as descendants of Indians, but not as Indians or tribal citizens,[10] jumped over some imaginary line toward a new level of Native American identity, one that manifested itself in an overtly public way. Maybe their original public performance, the four-day ritual reburial itself, was somehow responsible for solidifying their sense of identity—like a race renegade's version of the Stonewall riots:[11] We are here. We are Cherokee. But this same public performance filled my viewing companions at the Cherokee Nation with frustration and contempt, for when they looked at the video, what they saw were not distant Cherokee kin but "wannabes"—white people appropriating the Cherokees' name and misrepresenting

Table 1.1 American Indian Population Growth, 1960–2000

Census Year	Population	Increase
1960	551,700	—
1970	827,300	50%
1980	1,420,400	72%
1990	1,959,200	38%
2000 (one race)*	2,476,000	26%
2000 (one or more races)*	4,119,300	110%
2000 (combined total)*	6,595,300	237%

Sources: Passel 1997:11, Thornton 1990:197, and U.S. Bureau of the Census 2000

*The 2000 census was the first to allow the option of choosing more than one racial identity. The combined total includes all American Indian respondents, meaning those identifying as solely American Indian and those identifying as American Indian and at least one other race.

their culture. Though I recognized their concerns and shared some of their frustrations, I did not want to rush to judgment. Emotions were running high on all sides, and many questions still needed to be answered.

* * *

The shifting racial identity expressed by Oliver Collins and the Tallige Fire community is not an aberration in the racial and political landscape of this country but part of a growing demographic trend. According to U.S. census figures taken between 1960 and 2000, the Native American population has grown at a phenomenal rate—from 551,700 to 2,476,000, an increase of 349 percent. If we also include multiracial individuals from the 2000 census, people who identified as American Indian and at least one other race, then the total American Indian population jumps to 4,119,300, representing a startling growth of 647 percent over the same forty-year period (table 1.1).

Demographers say that such rapid growth is impossible without immigration and cannot possibly result from natural processes such as an excess of Native American births over deaths (Gonzales 1998; Nagel 1995:947; Passel 1997:11–12; Thornton 1990:197). Instead, this population increase appears to be dominated by what I term "racial shifters," individuals who have changed their racial self-identification on the U.S. census from non-Indian to Indian in recent years (Gonzales 1998; Nagel 1995; Passel 1997).[12] Although what people report on the census can vary dramatically from their everyday lived experiences, I believe that the census data offer a window onto a much broader process of racial and social transformation, a process that we can more fully understand when we turn to the ethnographic data.

In part because of the sheer numbers of people involved, racial shifting is an extremely diverse phenomenon. Many racial shifters are people who, in the course of looking for their roots, have only just discovered their Native American ancestry. Others are people who have family stories, oral histories, of an Indian great-great-grandmother or grandfather that they have not been able to document. Still others have long known that they were of Native American descent, including their specific tribal affiliation, and often have some documentation to this effect. For whatever reason they either have ignored or suppressed this fact and are only now becoming interested in reclaiming this aspect of their family history. Despite their differences, these people share a firm belief that they have Indian blood and that this means something significant about who they are and how they should live their lives.

But others have garnered quite a bit of attention in tribal communities and the scholarly literature for professing a Native American identity that seems dubious and instrumental. These include sentimental New Agers who simply feel an affinity with what they imagine to be native culture and who may even go so far as to appropriate a Native American identity as a way of marking their difference from mainstream society (Deloria 1998; Green 1988; Huhndorf 2001). Others commit outright ethnic fraud, asserting a false Native American identity in an effort to gain some symbolic or material advantage.[13] Muddying these waters, some individuals even appear to create an American Indian identity as a cover for criminal activity and have had charges levied against them. Probably the most notorious of these involved the Sovereign Cherokee Nation of Tejas, the brainchild of a retired U.S. Air Force officer. In July 1991, this "tribe" was accused of "a variety of massive business frauds" in a U.S. Senate subcommittee hearing (Garroutte 2003:26). Members were accused of selling phony insurance policies to corporations, creating a bogus offshore tax haven, and carrying illegally concealed weapons—the idea being that if they fashioned themselves as an American Indian tribe, they could get away with all of this in the name of tribal sovereignty (Garroutte 2003:26).

This book does not explore these more extreme examples of racial appropriation, fraud, and criminality—all of which have received much attention in the academic literature, particularly among American Indian scholars (Allen 1995; Cook-Lynn 1993, 2001; Gonzales 1998, 2002; Green 1988; Pewewardy 2004). Instead, I explore the deeper social and cultural values that lie behind this racial movement and why so many Americans, from so many different walks of life, are now reinscribing their autobiographies and finding such deep personal and collective meaning in the process of reclaiming Indianness. This is not something people were so willing to do forty years ago, and the fact that they do so now reveals much, I believe, about the shifting politics of race and indigeneity in the United States.

Some useful explanations have been put forth for this racial reinscription and the dramatic shifts in the demographic data that have resulted (Cornell 1988; Nagel 1996; Thornton 1990).[14] Perhaps the most insightful work on this topic is that of Joan Nagel, a sociologist. In her book *American Indian Ethnic Renewal: Red Power and the Resurgence of Identity and Culture* (1996), Nagel suggests that the trend toward reindigenization is the result of broad political forces in the latter decades of the twentieth century. She, like sociologist Stephen Cornell (1988), argues that federal Indian policies intended to assimilate Native Americans—such as relocation and termination—actually backfired, in that they created a largely urban and somewhat deracinated American Indian population primed for ethnic renewal. When the civil rights movement hit the scene in the early 1960s, it inspired the feminist and Red Power movements that followed shortly thereafter. American Indians were just one of many ethnic groups that responded to this new political atmosphere with increased political consciousness, community pride, and mobilization, often taking the form of pan-tribal organizations. In sum, Nagel suggests that in the wake of this sea change in U.S. racial politics, more and more people found meaning in celebrating their tribal roots and reclaiming their indigenous identities. The motivations were both symbolic and material as Indian identities were given new political and cultural value and as the federal government responded to activist demands with new programs such as affirmative action, educational funding, and increased health care services.

Nagel's work does an excellent job of accounting for ethnic renewal among urban Indians and those whose families had maintained tribal ties until only a generation or two back, but her answers are less satisfying when applied to other "new Indians," such as those whose families have not identified as Native American for several generations or whose tribal ties go back to the nineteenth century. My ethnographic research suggests that many racial shifters readily admit that their siblings and parents do not identify themselves as American Indians and that their last Indian-identified relative may have been a great-great-great-grandparent. In addition, many live in states with relatively small Native American populations and in rural areas and small towns rather than large urban cities. Given this geographic and generational isolation from other Native Americans, it seems that political changes—which are always fundamentally social processes—provide only a partial explanation for the renewed sense of American Indian identity among racial shifters. To fill in the remaining gap, I suggest that we stay attuned to overarching political processes while focusing on the meanings and values that have come to be attached to racial and cultural differences, specifically to indigeneity, in contemporary American society.

Among American Indians, one of the more potent idioms of racial and cultural difference is that of blood. More than just a metaphor for lineage, descent, or kinship, blood is often imagined as a shared biogenetic substance that links all the people of a tribe to one another. Relatives and, by extension, tribal members share common blood in both the past and present, and it is believed that tribal descendents literally have some of the same blood substance as their forebears. Moreover, blood is also commonly described as the bearer of indigenous cultural and racial difference, because race and culture are seen as being carried in the blood. This conflation of blood with race, culture, and kinship is common among American Indians because blood—the stuff of life and death—is a rich part of our human imaginary, but also because blood has been enshrined as a measure of Indian identity for well over a century in the laws and policies of tribal, state, and federal governments (Sturm 2002).

Most racial shifters firmly believe that they have Native American blood. If we take them at their word that they are Indian descendants who have long thought of themselves and their families as non-Indian, then the question remains as to what motivates their shift in self-identification. Although many observers are quick to dismiss race shifters as political and economic opportunists, I suggest that deeper desires are at work. While trying to find a respectful way to explore those desires as something more than greed or self-aggrandizement, I also have questions for those with less plausible connections to indigeneity. Given the sheer numbers of people making these claims, I think we have to consider the possibility that a small percentage of them may be inventing a Native American heritage where none exists, rather than connecting with a previously hidden branch of the family tree. If that is the case, why would someone without indigenous ancestry want to be seen as a Native American? Even for those who can document their indigenous forebears, how does this fact of genealogy get translated into an indigenous identity claim, and why would this sort of kinship claim be privileged as the key to "being Cherokee" over those of self-ascription, social relationship, or even citizenship? What has Indian blood come to mean in the past forty years that would make it so desirable?

A fundamental task for this book is to show how indigenous ancestry and identity have been revalued and what the overall demographic movement that results from this process says about the changing nature of racial politics in this country. Clearly, some of this revaluing took place as a result of political struggles in the 1960s and 1970s. But why did this population explosion continue in the more politically conservative climate of the 1980s and 1990s, with well over four million individuals identifying themselves as American Indian in terms of race on the 2000 census, while an even larger number identified themselves as having American Indian ancestry, even though their primary racial identity was non-Indian? Why have so many people moved from claiming family ties or tribal descent to asserting a more explicitly Native American identity? Is this an intentional adaptation of indigenous identity for economic purposes, as some critics suggest? Or is it a more subtle process, a romanticized longing for spiritual and cultural regeneration, reconnection, and reinvention?

The answers to these questions, I believe, can be found at the intersection of race, culture, and indigeneity, in the meanings and values these terms evoke in our national imagination, and in the power that these different identities have in our social and political landscapes. In the course of this book, using ethnographic and archival data collected over the past fourteen years with racial shifters in Oklahoma, Arkansas, Missouri, Texas, and Alabama and with federally recognized Cherokees in Oklahoma and North Carolina, I provide some answers to these questions and point to some areas for future consideration and debate. Some of the answers will be found in the power relations embedded in race shifting, which unfold in unexpected ways that challenge our ideas not only about racial "passing"—consciously striving to belong to a different racial category than the one into which one is born—but also about racial, cultural, and political identity more generally. Although some aspects of race privilege may be maintained within this process, the interplay of racial, cultural, and political identities within race shifting is much more complex than we might initially expect, based on common assumptions about who wields power in our societies and how this intersects with the color of their skin. Some of these assumptions need to be reevaluated in light of this new social movement.

Questions of race, identity, and political power are critical for Indian country, as they are for indigenous peoples around the world.[15] Because Native Americans in the United States are defined not only by federal and tribal policy but also by public and scholarly discourse, competing definitions of indigenous identity spark conflicts between federally recognized, state-recognized, and self-identified Indians. All of these groups are forced to wrestle with controversial questions concerning who is really Indian and who should have the power to decide. These are important concerns for tribal, state, and federal governments and for our society as a whole. By exploring the meaning of racial ideas and practices in this unique but revealing situation, we learn more about the process of racial formation, as well as the dangers in linking racial, cultural, and national identities. These issues affect not only Native American people in the United States but also the citizens of nation-states around the world, where questions of national identity and racial belonging continue to be fiercely debated.

Whiteness and Authenticity

Racial shifters provoke a variety of responses in Indian country, a fact that highlights the social, political, cultural, and even racial diversity of Native American communities. Some Native Americans find this recent surge in Indian self-identification baffling. Others find it amusing or even flattering. Still others fear that it poses a threat to their cultural integrity and political sovereignty and are critical of racial shifters who for whatever reason adopt a Native American identity later in life. However, these different camps are united by one thing: their strongest invective is aimed at white racial shifters.[16] Most Native Americans believe that whites, more than any other ethnic or racial group, want to be Indian. This perception accounts for the ubiquity in Indian communities of the term "wannabe," a derisive term that usually refers to white people fitting this profile.[17] For some Native Americans, however, the term also includes Indian descendants with a racially white physical appearance who do not have community or cultural ties. Federally recognized tribal members are not the only ones who use the term as an insult. Ironically, even racial shifters who might be called "wannabes" themselves use the term to describe those who fail to meet their standards of Indianness. For the purposes of this book, I try to avoid the term "wannabe" because of its derogatory connotations, except when exploring how Indian people use it in everyday discourse as a way of signaling their social and political critiques. Unpacking this racialized discourse is fundamental to the goal of better understanding what Native American identity politics is all about.

The oft-spoken perception that racial shifting is a migration away from whiteness and toward Indianness seems to be borne out by demographic statistics, again taken from U.S. census data, showing that the vast majority of racial shifters previously identified themselves as white rather than as some other race (Gonzales 1998:202; Passel 1976:397, 403). For me, it is the whiteness of this phenomenon that raises some of the most interesting social and theoretical questions. For instance, why would such a large number of individuals want to move out of whiteness and into Indianness, given that whiteness has long been a privileged racial position within the social structure of this country? In essence, race shifters are trying to reclaim or create something they feel they have lost, and in doing so, they often try to opt out of mainstream white society, a place their multiracial ancestors either chose or were forced to call home. The desire to move from a powerful social position (that of the settler colonial subject) to a seemingly less powerful one (the indigenous subject) is significant because it challenges our theoretical understanding of racial passing as being an effort to move up in the social and political hierarchy. Obviously, race relations and indigenous politics are now much more complicated than this type of simplistic assumption would have us believe.

A second related question is why whites, or at least people who have for generations passed as white, would specifically want to reclaim Indianness and not some other aspect of their identity. If it is true that many Americans have some combination of white, black, and Indian ancestry—as historians and demographers have argued—then why this shift toward Indianness and not, say, blackness (Hollinger 2003; Williamson 1995)? Is the specific allure of Indianness simply its nativist claim, meaning that indigenous people are unique because they have special rights as the original inhabitants of this land, or does Indianness offer something even more?

In general, Native American scholars (both Cherokees and others) have suggested that the impetus for this social movement into Indianness can be easily found at the intersection of race and class (Allen 1995; Gonzales 1998; Green 1988; Pewewardy 2004; Quinn 1990). They argue that race shifters are mostly poor or working-class whites trying to access economic benefits from a federally recognized tribe or a government agency. Such interpretations are also found outside academia, such as among federally recognized Cherokees in Oklahoma and North Carolina. For example, Fergus Beech, an elderly Cherokee man in Oklahoma, explained to me, "Money attracts outside elements just like honey does flies" (January 23, 1996), and Barbara Stevens, a middle-aged Cherokee woman, said, "They're just using that [identity] to make money. Those people aren't Cherokee" (January 29, 1996).[18] Ben Dreadfulwater, another middle-aged Oklahoma Cherokee, was more specific when he said that "a lot of what is motivating these people is fear. With the high cost of health and all, they want to get free services from the IHS [Indian Health Service]—freebies, you know" (January 29, 1996). I heard remarkably similar comments when I visited the Eastern Band of Cherokee Indians in North Carolina in fall 2003. Speaking with several tribal employees, I asked them their opinion about what kind of person is typically drawn to race shifting. Melissa Hunter, a woman in her late thirties, answered right away: "Lower- and middle-class Caucasians that are in search of a…self. I don't see any rich white people coming in. It's the lower and middle class, not even the upper middle class." Betty Baker, her feisty mother, who also worked for the tribe, quickly added, "They don't want to be white trash anymore, so they decide they want to be Cherokee.... That's just the way I look at it" (October 22, 2003).

Though some of the comments may seem harsh, these scholars and Cherokee citizens raise an important point, particularly given the tendency of many people to overgeneralize and assume that the experience of white identity is one of class privilege rather than race privilege.[19] Because white people are differentiated in class terms, economic instrumentalism may motivate some individuals to shift their racial identity to Cherokee or Indian. But this is, I think, only a small part of the story that I have seen unfolding for many years. I say this, in part, because I found quite a bit of class diversity among the many racial shifters interviewed for this project. Certainly, the majority were working class, but there was also a sizeable number of professionals, including teachers, nurses, doctors, lawyers, engineers, and even state legislators.[20] If we limit our understanding of the effort to reclaim an indigenous identity to its strictly economic motivations, then we miss the larger picture and the deeper meanings beneath this demographic movement. For instance, how would we account for the large number of celebrity Cherokees—extremely wealthy individuals within the entertainment industry who find value in professing a Cherokee identity to the public? Examples include Cher, Tommy Lee Jones, Rita Coolidge, Willie Nelson, Quentin Tarantino, Elvis Presley, and Johnny Depp, to name but a few, all of whom could pass as white but have chosen to offer a more complex self-identification.[21] Even more telling is that former President Bill Clinton publicly claimed to have a Cherokee grandmother at a time when he was one of the most powerful people on the planet.[22]

Clearly, people from widely divergent class backgrounds, with different access to social power, have claimed an American Indian identity in general and Cherokeeness in particular, even in the face of considerable skepticism from Indians and non-Indians alike. Many race shifters are aware that much of Indian country believes that their reclamations of Cherokee identity are purely instrumental and generally illegitimate. In response to such stinging criticisms, race shifters argue just the opposite, insisting at every turn that money has nothing to do with their quest. For example, in an interview, Principal Chief Joe Perry of the Tsalagi Nvdagi, or Texas Cherokees, said the following: "When people find out what tribe they are, a lot of the federally recognized tribes are really against that in a lot of ways. They don't want these people…and I don't know why. I guess they think we might take some money from them. Hell, we don't want their money! We've been out here working all our lives. We don't need their money" (July 8, 2003). Another man wrote to me and said, "No, I do not receive any benefits from being Native American and never have. If I were offered any, I would probably spit in their eye to show my contempt!" (March 13, 1996).

Seeing Heart Stevens, a sixty-five-year-old man who has retired to Florida but is still the chief of a self-identified Cherokee tribe in Virginia, gave this thoughtful response:

We probably could get benefits under the Arts and Crafts law and some others, but this is contrary to our purpose and sincerity. Real Indians are fiercely independent, and Indian rights are notoriously unstable. Entitlements are here today, gone tomorrow. The underlying political process really doesn't want to help Indians, because someone with political power is benefiting from all the tax breaks, getting around pollution laws, casinos, grants, etc. In the long run, these hurt Indians more than help them, and Indians should help each other instead of fighting one another. Independence and education have always been the Cherokee way, and it is the reason we have survived for so long. We don't expect others to pay our way.[23] (March 11, 1996)

Brent Stephens, an officer in the Southern Cherokee Nation, made a similar observation: "I keep hearing about ulterior motives. They want this or they want that. But you know, there aren't benefits floating around out there that I'm aware of that just fall on you because you're an Indian. I think it could easily be outweighed by the prejudice that you face, at least when you get outside the Indian territory" (June 25, 2003).

In keeping with these assertions, most race shifters are not able to access any direct financial benefits based on their self-proclaimed Cherokee identity, largely because none of them are federally recognized as Cherokee citizens. Only that small number of people who are members of the fifteen state-recognized Cherokee communities are able to receive federal and state funds on a consistent basis or to legally sell their wares under the Indian Arts and Crafts Act of 1990.[24] To my mind, these facts make it unlikely that money is the key motivation, leading me to look in other directions for answers to questions such as Why claim indigeneity? Why Cherokee? And why now?

To answer these questions, I look beyond mere economic instrumentalism to the deeper meanings and motivations that underlie race shifting. One of my main concerns is with how racial shifters and federally recognized Cherokee citizens assign value, as both a symbolic and material property, to different racial identities. For instance, how do they assign whiteness or Indianness with certain social, cultural, and political valences? And how do these different racial evaluations both reproduce and challenge those of the broader U.S. society? The answers to these questions are numerous and complex, as I have learned in the course of researching this book. In asking these questions, much of what I am trying to understand is the broader "field of opinion"—what is said as much as what is not said but implied—in public discourses about Cherokee identity (Bourdieu 1977:167–168). Of course, both Cherokee and non-Cherokee people participate in and come to subjectively identify themselves within such discourses of racial value. My hope is that, with closer scrutiny, these discourses of Cherokeeness and whiteness will reveal not only their particular histories but also the various stakes for their speakers and that we will then be better able to see and understand how these different racial values are socially and politically constructed, internalized, and challenged by different kinds of people.

To assert that the vast majority of racial shifters are white is not meant to deny their blood ties to Indian ancestors or to question the validity of their desire to reindigenize themselves. As an increasing number of multiracial celebrities (for example, Mariah Carey, Keanu Reaves, Halle Berry, and Russell Crowe) have made clear, people who are racialized as white can have nonwhite ancestry, just as those who are racialized as black, Hispanic, or Indian can have white ancestry. Instead, emphasizing the white-ness of race shifters is meant to acknowledge the social, historical, and political space of racial privilege that is maintained when one is perceived as being white, even if that perception flies in the face one's own self-identification or genealogical records. Racial identity is not simply a question of ancestry—though this is a critical issue for many people—but of social ascription and, increasingly, achievement. More often than not, we ascribe racial identities to one another based merely on superficial observations of skin color, facial features, hair texture, and overall mannerisms. These initial ascriptions of race may be challenged and reassigned over time as we get to know one another better and learn about one another's life experiences, particularly about kinfolk, communities of origin, and cultural differences. In this way, multiracial people may achieve a form of social recognition that is more in line with their own self-perceptions. At the same time, racial first impressions have power in that they shape the vast majority of our day-to-day lived experiences, including whether the grocery clerk will ask for identification when we write a check, the security guard will tail us through Banana Republic, or the old lady down the street will leave her porch and go inside when we walk by her house, simply because our perceived difference makes her nervous. These things happen. Despite our complicated racial histories and ancestries, we still make snap judgments about who others are and react accordingly.

Despite the everyday significance of physical appearance in assessing Indianness, a book of this nature needs to look beyond the obvious and take seriously the question of ancestry. Doing so sheds light on differences of social position among race shifters. For instance, if a race shifter has known Indian ancestry, then arguably his or her family has been passing as white, maybe even for generations, for reasons often related to racial discrimination. In such cases, we see the legacies of colonization and assimilation, both forced and chosen, in which individuals and families have had to endure the pain of severing their community and kinship ties in order to achieve a higher social status.[25] Here, race shifting would be an effort to reclaim a racial identity that was either forsaken or lost. If they do not have Indian ancestry, then their effort to pass as Indian is often seen as a form of appropriation, an expression of a desire to be something they are not. However, this distinction can also be troubled if we consider the different ways that people reckon ancestry, even within the same community. Because ancestry is socially constructed and subject to contested interpretations, it does not automatically confer racial or indigenous status. Thus, even the racial shifting of those with American Indian ancestors can be subject to accusations of appropriation.

Although questions of ancestry are critical to debates about reclamation and appropriation, I cannot provide definitive answers in the chapters ahead as to whether individual race shifters have indigenous ancestors. In general, most of what we know and learn as cultural anthropologists is limited to what people tell us, and as some scholars have argued, it is this reliance on human discourse as data that moves our discipline away from the social sciences and closer to the humanities. Even if we can cross-check what people say with what they do, there really is no way that we can verify or authenticate the vast majority of their assertions. Certainly, we can make sure that we got the basic historical facts right, such as when someone held political office, started a war, or wrote a letter. But how would I go about verifying a statement about kinship? To do so would require that I transport myself back in time to see who had sex with whom and what children resulted. Even if I could engage in some ethically absurd form of anthropological time travel, how would I know that a particular act of intercourse led to a particular birth? Even the dry documentation of the paper trail is often deceptive when it comes to racial histories. Let us say that I had been able to find genealogical documentation on fifty individuals. How would I know that the documents I had uncovered were not doctored or manipulated in some way at the time they were created? How would I know that a parent—or a nurse—told the truth (the whole truth) or even was privy to it? If we go down this road, questions regarding truth, authenticity, and even science are endless.

I suggest that we travel in a different direction. I believe that we can learn far more about the social and political construction of Native American identity by asking not whether these claims of kinship are true or false but under what conditions others accept them. When trying to determine whether or not someone is Indian in daily life, most people do not go looking for a literal paper trail. Instead, they measure such claims against their own internalized standards of community belonging, which may or may not put a premium on genealogical verification. Their initial questions are rarely about documentation of blood and ancestry to the exclusion of all else. More common is a line of inquiry that emphasizes social, political, and cultural belonging, such as "Can you name a family member?" or "You know your tribe, but does your tribe know you?"

Although information about ancestry might reveal critical differences of social location, particularly regarding histories of colonial incorporation, it may be less relevant to our overall understanding of contemporary Native American identity politics than the motivations behind race shifting and its many trajectories. Unlike some more skeptical observers, I believe that most racial shifters are operating in good faith on the firm conviction that they have Indian ancestors. For me, then, the point is not whether their ancestors are real or imagined but how these beliefs about ancestry shape and even alter racial self-identification in ways that have profound effects on the broader American Indian population. My own goal is not to wield power as a "scientific" observer to sort out the "wannabes" from the "real" Indians. Anthropologists have tried to do this in the past, often with disastrous political effects.[26] Instead, my goal is to listen to what people have to say and then, in the words of Clifford Geertz (2000:58), "to figure out what the devil they think they are up to." In doing so, I hope to shed light on a world of discourse swirling around and through what it means to be Indian—or not—in this country today.

Cherokee Neotribalism: Questions and Collaborations

My interest in racial shifting originates in my ongoing research collaborations with the Cherokee Nation and the United Keetoowah Band of Cherokee Indians, both head-quartered in northeastern Oklahoma, and more recently with the Eastern Band of Cherokee Indians in North Carolina—all three of which are federally recognized tribes. For Cherokee citizens of these tribes, racial shifters are a particular source of consternation because racial shifters tend to identify themselves as Cherokee more than as any other tribe, making Cherokees the butt of many jokes in Indian country (Nagel 1996:101–105; Thornton 1990:172–175). I have often heard people say things like "Put sixteen Cherokees in a room, what do you get? A full blood"; "If that Cherokee nicks himself shaving, he'll turn into a white man"; "Have you ever seen the Cherokee Barbie doll? Yeah, it's the blonde one that's already on the shelf"; and "My friend just discovered she was an Indian...must be another Cherokee princess."[27] These jokes usu-ally jab at the whiteness, mixedness, and newness that have come to be associated with Cherokee identity. This association is, in part, due to the fact that Cherokee tribes have relatively open enrollment policies, but it also reflects a growing awareness about widespread racial shifting into Cherokeeness and its potential effect on the three tribes with federal recognition.

Racial shifters are laying claim to Cherokeeness at an astonishing rate because, more often than not, racial shifting is a migration not just from whiteness to Indianness, but to a particular tribal identity—the most popular happens to be Cherokee. Racial shifting is about claiming not just racial alterity but also a particu-lar form of indigeneity that is interpreted as being Cherokee. Because of the surge in Cherokee self-identification and reclamation that has taken place over the past thirty years, the overall growth of the Cherokee population has been nothing short of phe-nomenal. In the 1970 U.S. census, 66,150 individuals identified themselves as Cherokee; only a decade later, the number had grown to 232,344—representing a stunning population growth of 251 percent (Thornton 1990:199). The 1990 census reveals a somewhat slower growth rate of 58 percent for the preceding decade, with 369,035 people identifying as Cherokee. By 2000, however, that number had almost doubled, reaching just under three-quarters of a million people. In the three decades from 1970 to 2000, the Cherokee population increased by more than 1,000 percent, a pace far outstripping that of the broader American Indian population (table 1.2).

The Cherokees were by far and away the largest tribal grouping on the 2000 cen-sus, with the Navajos a distant second (U.S. Bureau of the Census 2000).[28] But of the total Cherokee population, only a little more than one-third (35 percent) are registered members of one of three federally recognized Cherokee tribes, which means that close to half a million individuals claim to be Cherokee despite federal, tribal, and even anthropological definitions to the contrary.[29] And this is only the tip of the iceberg because these figures are limited to individuals who are willing to assert their Cherokee ancestry on U.S. census documents. Many more cases go unrecorded in federal statistics

Table 1.2 Cherokee Population Growth, 1970–2000

Census Year	Population	Increase
1970	66,150	–
1980	232,344	251%
1990	369,035	58%
2000 (one race) *	281,069	-24%
2000 (one or more races)*	448,464	22%
2000 (combined total)*	729,533	98%

Sources: Thornton 1990:197; U.S. Bureau of the Census 2000.

*The 2000 census was the first to allow the option of choosing more than one racial identity. The combined total includes all American Indian respondents who specified a Cherokee tribal affiliation, meaning those identifying as solely American Indian by race and also those identifying as American Indian and at least one other race.

yet make an impression around the office water cooler, in the local newspaper, or at a regional powwow.

What accounts for this gravitation toward Cherokeeness and not some other tribal identity, particularly among individuals who previously identified as white? Although this is a question I address at greater length in the next several chapters, I would like to suggest three reasons up front. First, the Cherokee people's long-term reputation for cultural syncretism and for readily adopting white standards of civilization might make being a member of one of the Five Civilized Tribes appealing to many white-Indian descendants. Second, the tendency among Cherokees toward higher rates of exogamy than other Native American tribes means that many Cherokee citizens and descendants have a white appearance (Thornton 1990:173). Finally, the current administrative policies regarding tribal enrollment for the Cherokee Nation and the Eastern Band of Cherokee Indians in North Carolina have affected the general public's interpretation of what a Cherokee tribal citizen looks like, so they assume that most Cherokees look racially white.[30] In the case of the Eastern Band, tribal enrollment requires 1/16 degree of Cherokee blood that can be traced to an ancestor on the 1924 Baker Roll.[31] For the Cherokee Nation, Cherokee ancestry is determined via the Dawes Roll, but there is no minimum blood-quantum requirement for tribal citizenship. As a result, the Cherokee ancestry of enrolled members varies from full-blood to 1/4096, which "raises questions about the symbolic significance of blood and the degree to which blood connections can be stretched and still carry any sense of legitimacy" (Sturm 2002:3).[32]

The collective implication of these enrollment policies, exogamy rates, and cultural stereotypes is that Cherokees are understood as being potentially white—both in physical appearance and culturally—in ways that set them apart from most other tribes. Many Native American communities suffered colonialism at a later date and intermarried with whites at a somewhat lower rate than Cherokees. Many of these same tribes have reputations for traditionalism and stricter policies on tribal enrollment. Perhaps as a consequence, they are somehow perceived as more rigidly Indian, their boundaries less pervious to race shifting. This does not mean that no racial shifters claim Lakota, Hopi, or Inupiaq identities—such claims do occur, but less frequently. In making this observation, I do not mean to suggest that all Cherokees are white or that Cherokees are not culturally conservative—far from it—only that being a white, or light-skinned, nontraditional Cherokee falls within the realm of possibility.[33]

Given the impact of race shifting on public perceptions of Cherokeeness, many federally recognized Cherokees are concerned, even alarmed, about this situation. In fact, the Cherokee Nation and the Eastern Band of Cherokee Indians in North Carolina seem to view this demographic trend as a growing problem. In the early 1980s, both tribes started to collect information, documents, and videos like the one described at the start of this chapter, on what they refer to somewhat ominously as "entities using the Cherokee name."[34] Let me make clear an important point: the tribes are not hostile to newcomers or reluctant to reconnect with long-lost kin. Nor are they particularly concerned about individual claims of Cherokee identity that race shifters might express, with or without genealogical documentation. What concern the tribes are people like Oliver Collins and his friends: race shifters who have coalesced into organized social and political groups, particularly those asserting tribal status and seeking federal or state recognition. For example, in the summer of 2003, Troy Wayne Poteete, a former Cherokee Nation tribal council member then working in the tribe's office of legal affairs, said to me, "Even if they have an ancestor on some roll—join the historical society, chart it all out, study about it, but don't start a damn tribe!" (August 1, 2003). Richard Allen, a policy analyst in the executive branch of the Cherokee Nation, was even more forceful when he told me that groups who suggest they are Cherokee are in it for commercial reasons. He added, "To me, not only is that an insult, but it's also an attack on our sovereignty as Cherokee people, as the Cherokee Nation" (July 31, 2003). Because of such concerns, the Cherokee Nation's tribal registrar had amassed several file drawers on the subject by the time I first arrived in Tahlequah, Oklahoma, in summer 1995.[35] It is a remarkable cache of materials, but I hardly had to seek it out. Cherokee Nation employees did not merely provide me with access to these materials; they actively directed me to them, wanting someone with the necessary time and energy to dive into the looming mass of papers and clippings.

What did I encounter? Arranged by state, the files contained a wealth of information on racial shifting. To get a better sense of the size and scope of this phenomenon, I read and collated these materials to create a master list of self-identified and state-recognized Cherokee organizations.[36] I then cross-checked my list with three other lists. One was provided by the Eastern Band of Cherokee Indians in North Carolina in March 1995. Another was compiled by the Cherokee Nation and presented a few months later to the U.S. Senate Committee on Indian Affairs in a hearing concerning proposed changes in the federal recognition process. The third was an overview of Cherokee groups engaged in the federal recognition process, created in 2001 by Virginia DeMarce, a historian working for the Office of Federal Acknowledgment at the Bureau of Indian Affairs in Washington, D.C. I have also added to these lists, on the basis of extensive Internet searches, a mail survey I conducted in 1996 and ethnographic fieldwork from the past fourteen years. Combining these sources, I have been able to find information on more than 250 self-identified and state-recognized Cherokee tribes scattered throughout the United States. All of these groups and communities are what the Eastern Band of Cherokee Indians and Cherokee Nation refer to as "entities using the Cherokee name." None of these are federally recognized, yet fifteen of them have acquired some form of state recognition. At least thirty-one have made contact with the Office of Federal Acknowledgment and are seeking federal recognition.

Now, for the first time, we can see the geographic distribution of these organizations. They tend to cluster in the southeastern United States, in and around the original homelands of the Cherokee people.[37] More than mere geographical continuity is at work here. Historically, Native American populations have been decimated or pushed out by state policies in the Southeast, leaving a presumed void of Indianness into which these new groups can assert themselves (Passel 1997:25). For example, Georgia alone has forty-three such groups, three of which are state-recognized, a bitterly ironic fact, given that Georgia is largely responsible for Cherokee removal on the infamous Trail of Tears in 1838. Florida is the runner-up with twenty-three groups, and Alabama, Arkansas, and Tennessee each have between sixteen and twenty. On the flip side, race shifters tend to avoid states with a large Native American population either historically or at present—such as South Dakota, New Mexico, and Montana. That Cherokee race shifters have not coalesced in these states is not simply due to the fact that they are far removed from Cherokee homelands. In fact, Cherokee-identifying entities appear all over the U.S. map; they are not confined to the Southeast, as some historians and anthropologists have suggested (Brewton 1963; Quinn 1990). Thirty-six states have at least one Cherokee entity within their boundaries, and some states outside the Southeast, such as California, Texas, and Ohio, have as many as thirteen. Racial shifters are everywhere, and the specific migration from whiteness to Indianness to Cherokee neotribalism can be found all across the United States from Alaska to Vermont (figure 1.1), with international echoes in Mexico and Germany.[38]

This explosion in the number of self-identified and state-recognized Cherokee tribes means that for a significant number of racial shifters, claiming indigeneity is not simply about being Indian, being Cherokee, or honoring native roots. It is also about being tribal in a collective sense. The underlying logic of race shifting and neotribalism often goes something like this: if your tribe of origin will not have you, either because you cannot document your Cherokee ancestry or because you fail to meet the standards for citizenship in some other way, then it is better to have a tribe of your

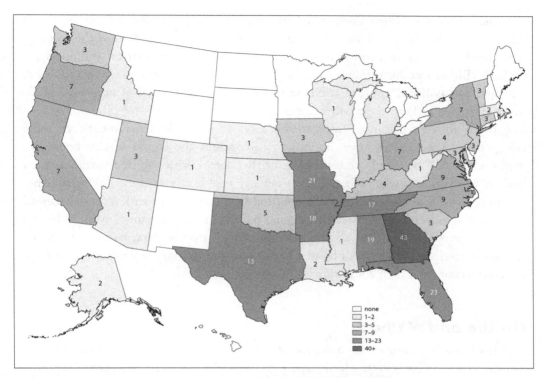

Figure 1.1 Self-identified and state-recognized Cherokee communities by state

own. For most racial shifters involved in this process of collectivizing their identity, the creation of a tribe provides them with a sense of community belonging, including a time and place in which they can simply "be Cherokee." For some, this sense of belonging extends into forms of civic engagement that deeply influence the rhythm of their daily lives. Others organize for explicitly political purposes, such as achieving federal or state recognition as a Native American tribe, usually because they seek the specific legal rights associated with that status or the dignity that such recognition might afford.

For many scholars, as well as for the citizens of the three federally recognized Cherokee tribes, these collective expressions of neotribalism raise larger, more pressing questions: What kinds of political rights or sovereign entitlements should these individuals, as Cherokee descendants, be able to access? Should they have the right to organize as separate tribal polities, or did their ancestors give up that right when they left the tribal fold all those years ago? Even if members of these new tribal entities do not seek political recognition and simply want to be left in peace to do their own thing, does their mere existence—given the sheer numbers involved—somehow cloud the issue of what Indian identity and tribal citizenship mean in this country? Or to put it in the starkest of terms, do these new entities somehow pose a threat to federally recognized and even existing state-recognized tribes?

The answers to these questions have profound implications for native North America. In the conversations I have had with Cherokee people around the country, there tend to be two main ways of responding to the issue, one critical and one sympathetic. Either race shifters are white "wannabes" who create tribes in an act of racial, cultural, and political appropriation for dubious ends, or they are Cherokee descendants trying to reclaim their political rights as Indian people.

Although the truth often lies somewhere in between, the tension between these two perspectives surfaces again and again throughout the course of this book. No doubt, there will be people on either side of this debate who will be frustrated that I bothered to listen to what others had to say. My goal is not to come down on either side or to provide some false sense of resolution but instead to provide a more balanced and nuanced view of the social, cultural, and political stakes at hand. I want to let the various arguments unfold in all their complexity so that readers, particularly those who are American Indians, will be in a better position to grapple with these issues in the contexts of their own communities.

On Life and Methods

This book has been more than a decade in the making, and both the amount of time and the variety of sources that have gone into its production deserve a note of explanation. I first started thinking about racial shifting as a research topic in the summer of 1995, just after I moved to Tahlequah, Oklahoma, to begin ethnographic research in the Cherokee Nation. Although I had encountered racial shifters as a graduate student living in Northern California, I did not arrive in Tahlequah with them in mind. Instead, I had come to explore the discourses and policies of Indian blood and to see how these played out among Oklahoma Cherokees, or at least among those who were citizens of the Cherokee Nation, a large and diverse tribe with a reputation for inclusiveness. As I started my fieldwork, I noticed that the issue of racial shifting regularly surfaced in my conversations with Cherokee people. Soon it became apparent that this issue played a central role in local understandings of Cherokee identity and that I needed to address it in a much more systematic way. From that point forward, I began to ask a standard set of questions about the topic in my interviews with citizen Cherokees, as well as race shifters (people who were not enrolled as Cherokee Nation citizens but nonetheless identified themselves as Cherokee). I listened carefully to their stories and asked follow-up questions that would help me understand the complexity of the subject.

Within a few months of my arrival, tribal employees at the Cherokee Nation led me to their small archive of materials concerning self-identified and state-recognized Cherokees. The archive included published sources such as newspaper clippings, tribal newsletters, court documents, and Bureau of Indian Affairs records, as well as unpublished materials such as personal and professional correspondence, tribal records, enrollment cards, tribal histories, genealogies, and photographs. All of the materials were filed according to state, so if I wanted to know what was happening in Georgia or Louisiana, the relevant materials were located in a single folder. In fall 1995, I spent more than a week reading everything in the files, copying the documents that I thought were particularly significant, and compiling a master list of self-identified and state-recognized Cherokee tribes. Over the years, I continued to add to that list from information that was forwarded to me by contacts throughout Indian country.

Even though I had discovered a wealth of new information about racial shifting in this small archive and through my own research, I wanted to get a broader picture of what was happening around the country and to ask some specific questions that were not addressed in the documents I was reading. So in spring 1996 I conducted a small mail survey of these new self-identified and state-recognized Cherokee tribes. Of the total number I was familiar with at the time, I mailed surveys to one hundred (about half), selecting them based on their geographic location and sociopolitical characteristics. I was particularly curious about tribes located outside the Southeast, because some of the scholarly literature had described Cherokee neotribalism as a strictly southeastern phenomenon. I was also curious about the size of tribal memberships, the longevity of these organizations, their activities, and their perceptions of federally recognized Cherokees.

I addressed the survey to tribal officers, asking that it be freely circulated among their membership as a whole and inviting anyone who was interested in answering the questions to complete the survey and mail it back to me. The survey was ambitious, overly so, with ten questions asking for basic demographic information and another twenty-eight that were open-ended and much more substantial, covering ideas about race, culture, tribalism, spirituality, Indianness, Cherokeeness, and sovereignty. I asked questions such as, What does membership in your tribal organization mean to you? What do you consider to be the characteristics of a Cherokee person? What do you consider to be the basis of tribal sovereignty? Where does it originate? Because the survey was so lengthy and could not be completed in less than an hour, I received only fifteen completed questionnaires (a 15 percent response rate), mostly from people who were past retirement age and who had plenty of time on their hands (their average age was sixty; see appendix 4). Although the surveys are not representative in that they are skewed toward an older demographic, they proved useful in providing a historical perspective on the phenomenon, because many of the respondents had been involved with self-identified Cherokee organizations for several decades.

Originally, I had intended to use the data from the survey, as well as the archival materials, fieldwork, and interviews, to include a chapter on racial shifting in my dissertation on Cherokee identity politics (which would eventually become my first book). When I returned to California in 1996, I made a first attempt at writing up my findings. However, the topic was so variable and complex and so interesting in its own right that I could not do it justice in fifty pages—it demanded book-length treatment. I filed my dissertation without including the material on racial shifting and decided to return to it when I could give it my full attention.

Much to my surprise, that moment of return did not arrive until fall 2002. In the intervening five years, I had moved back to Oklahoma, joined the faculty at the University of Oklahoma, learned how to be a professor, published my first book, gone up for tenure, and had a baby. Although much of my attention was consumed by these activities, I never abandoned the idea that I would return to the subject of racial shifting for my next book. I continued to read anything that seemed relevant to the topic, drawing from scholarly sources outside my own discipline and from popular culture and mainstream literature. I continued to gather data from personal interviews, especially when I did fieldwork in Tahlequah, most notably in summer 1998. I also applied for external grants in the hope of being able to fund extensive ethnographic fieldwork among race-shifter communities. However, I had little luck in securing external research money for this portion of the project, perhaps because external reviewers often look askance at a proposal for multi-sited ethnographic research, especially if it is to be conducted by a single individual. Between 1997 and 2002, I was mostly on my own in terms of figuring out how to do the legwork of gathering data, and much of what I was able to learn came from being in the right place at the right time, from living in Oklahoma and socializing with Indian people, and occasionally from serendipity rather than intention.

Fortunately, the type of knowledge that comes from informal interactions is just as valuable to anthropologists as what we might get from recorded interviews, because it provides qualitatively different insights about what people think, say, and do in everyday settings. For almost a decade and a half, I lived in Oklahoma and was known as someone working on the topic of racial shifting. News of my research interests circulated widely among citizen Cherokees and racial shifters alike, who contacted me when they wanted to ask questions, exchange information, or simply talk about racial shifting. Even as I went about my life, raising my daughter and working, I spent countless hours in phone and e-mail conversations with racial shifters, as well as citizen Cherokees and other American Indians, about the topic of racial shifting. I have also had these conversations at powwows, conferences, meetings, and other American Indian–related events over the years. Like the formal components of the research that I have been doing since 1995, all of these informal exchanges inform my overall understanding of the subject.

In addition to the everyday encounters that happened as a part of living in Oklahoma and traveling in American Indian circles, I conducted fifty-four face-to-face, formal, recorded interviews with fifty individuals, all of whom were citizens of the Cherokee Nation, the Eastern Band of Cherokee Indians, or the United Keetoowah Band of Cherokee Indians (see appendix 6). These interviews all dealt with the topic of racial shifting, in whole or in part, and coincided with three main periods of fieldwork. The first was fourteen months in Tahlequah between summer 1995 and 1996 and was the ethnographic component of my dissertation research; the second, also in Tahlequah, was a three-month stint in summer 1998 when I gathered data needed to revise the dissertation into a book; and the last was in summer and fall 2003, when I began to do follow-up interviews with citizens of the Cherokee Nation. In October of that same year, I also traveled to Cherokee, North Carolina, the home of the Eastern Band of Cherokee Indians, so that I could include Eastern Band perspectives in this project. Although the Eastern Band determined that my research was exempt under their Institutional Review Board guidelines, they asked that I limit my interviews to tribal employees, a request that I honored. However, all of the tribal employees and leaders whom I interviewed specifically stated that the insights they offered were not official tribal positions but rather their own opinions.

Although I was never able to secure external funding for the research component of this project, in fall 2002 I was awarded a substantial research grant from the University of Oklahoma. I used that money to hire a graduate student research assistant named Jessica Walker Blanchard, who had an excellent reputation among my colleagues for her fieldwork skills. In figuring out how to make best use of her time and abilities, I had to make some tough choices in terms of maximizing the breadth of the data without sacrificing its depth or quality. I was already such a familiar face among Oklahoma Cherokees that it made sense for me to continue working with a community where I already had a strong sense of rapport, while relying on my assistant for fieldwork in other locations. In the spring of 2003, she started conducting research in four communities located in Alabama, Arkansas, Texas, and Oklahoma. I selected these communities for several reasons. The first was a large, state-recognized tribe in Alabama that had a long history and relatively cohesive sense of community. I wanted to see how a large, state-recognized tribe might differ from a self-identified one, and although there were other possibilities to choose from, I chose this one because my assistant was from Alabama and had known some of the members of this tribe in her youth. We both felt that her familiarity with the people and the place would be an asset in the interviewing process.[39]

I chose the second tribe because it was located in Arkansas, a place that has seen a firestorm of race-shifting activity, with numerous Cherokee tribes coming into being, factionalizing, dissolving, and re-forming over the past several decades. All of these groups claim to be descendants of the Old Settlers, the early Cherokee migrants to the West who settled in Arkansas in the first three decades of the nineteenth century. Of the many possibilities, I selected a tribe that was fairly well organized and sizable but that was not state-recognized, so that it could serve as a basis for comparison with the one in Alabama. In addition to my usual questions, I wanted to know more about the contested history of these groups in Arkansas and why they had not been able to gain recognition at the state level.

The third group was located in Texas, where, as in Arkansas, bands of Cherokee people had settled in the early decades of the nineteenth century. I had heard from citizen Cherokees in Oklahoma that this particular group had hosted a regular stomp dance, had traveled back and forth between a ceremonial ground in Texas and the ones in Oklahoma, and included some tribal members who spoke enough Cherokee to make basic conversation. These social and cultural connections intrigued me, and I wanted to see why this group was engaged in practices that even Oklahoma Cherokees recognized as being specifically Cherokee, whereas most race shifter groups were involved in powwow dancing and other pan-Indian activities. I chose the final group because it was located in Oklahoma and was trying to claim the same land base, treaties, and political rights as the two federally recognized Cherokee tribes in the area. This presented a unique opportunity to see how these claims were being challenged at the local level and on what basis.

As I continued working with people, mostly in Oklahoma, my assistant set out with her notebook and tape recorder. In all her interactions with the four groups, she made it clear that she was doing research on my behalf, an arrangement that was reinforced when she obtained informed consent. Between February and July 2003, she conducted twenty-eight formal interviews, almost all of which were tape-recorded (see appendix 5). She asked a standard set of open-ended questions that I provided, a slightly revised version of what I had initially asked in the mail surveys, and then she followed these questions with her own spontaneous ones. We always talked at length before she went to do fieldwork, and I provided her with guidance about the issues that most concerned me. She also wrote extensive descriptive and analytic field notes about people and events and gave these to me shortly after she returned, at which point we talked about her experiences and impressions and I asked follow-up questions as needed. Later, she provided me with transcriptions of all her interviews. However, as I started writing, I also listened to these tapes on my own to double-check the transcriptions and to get a sense of people's affect and tone of voice. The direct quotations I cite from race shifters are taken mostly from my assistant's interviews or the earlier mail surveys and only in a few instances from interviews I conducted. In two places within the book, which are clearly identified, I describe an event that my assistant recorded in her field notes. I wrote these scenes based on her eyewitness accounts of them and then gave them to her to make certain that my interpretations of these events dovetailed with her memories of them.

As should be obvious by now, the topic of racial shifting was far too complex, varied, and geographically dispersed for me to get at it by concentrating my energies on understanding a single community such as the Eastern Band of Cherokee Indians or the Echota Cherokee of Georgia. Such an approach has value in its own right and certainly would have provided additional insights that are missing here, but I wanted to see the big picture and to learn what people in radically different contexts thought about racial shifting. My assistant's work enabled me to broaden my perspective to multiple field sites and to answer the questions that I first set for myself in my survey. Although she was in the field for only thirty days over a six-month period and I had logged many years with the topic, she was a valued collaborator in that her field notes and our many conversations helped to shape my thoughts on this project. While I want to give her credit for her contributions, I do not want to assign her any of the responsibility for what in the end are my own choices and interpretations.

Because of the way in which the data were gathered, there are certain biases in this work beyond what anthropologists typically bring to the table. For example, I do not have the same long-term relationship with self-identified and state-recognized Cherokee communities as I do with the Cherokee Nation. Nor do I have as long a relationship with the United Keetoowah Band of Cherokee Indians or the Eastern Band of Cherokee Indians as I have with the Cherokee Nation, with whom I have worked on an ongoing basis for fourteen years. Because I have a rich history with this community, my formal interviews with Cherokee Nation citizens included good friends and old acquaintances, as well as people I had just met. In contrast, the interviews I conducted with citizens of the United Keetoowah Band and Eastern Band and with occasional race shifters were usually our first and only meeting. These different relationships and histories color the quality of the interview data, but not, I believe, in a way that compromises the fundamental insights of the book.

One other fact affected how people interacted with me in the field: my own status as a Mississippi Choctaw descendant, which was not information I volunteered unless someone asked me directly whether I had tribal ties. In these instances, I identified myself as having primarily Sicilian and German ancestry, but also Mississippi Choctaw ancestry through my father's mother. I was always quick to add that I was not a tribal citizen and had not been raised in Mississippi within the context of a tribal community. Despite these important caveats, I soon realized that I had little control over other people's readings of my ancestry and identity. I felt sort of like a Rorschach test in that people would see in me whatever they wished to see. For example, the race shifters with whom I interacted on an informal basis tended to view me as someone who would be sympathetic to their interests because I, too, had American Indian ancestry and was not formally recognized as a tribal citizen. At the same time, Cherokee Nation citizens saw me as being sympathetic to their interests, not so much because of my ancestry (they tended to put me in the "descendant" category) but rather because they knew me to be a champion of tribal sovereignty and other political goals of the tribe, as well as a long-term friend to a good number of them. I am not sure how citizens of the United Keetoowah Band or Eastern Band of Cherokee Indians viewed me, but I imagine that I benefited from having other Cherokees vouch for me in a way that facilitated the interview process.

In noting these different relationships, histories, and personal details, I am trying to provide readers with additional context that will help them understand, evaluate, and even challenge my own interpretations of the data. I welcome those challenges and hope that people will read against the grain, pushing the analysis in new directions. In this regard, I have also provided additional demographic and contextual information about each of the ninety-five individuals who participated in formal interviews or surveys (appendices 4–6). Someone with a different scholarly orientation than my own could use this information to develop a statistical analysis; others might wonder why I did not put more effort into controlling the variables of the research. The fact of the matter is that, as an interdisciplinary scholar working at the nexus of the social sciences and the humanities, I never intended to carry out that type of definitive project.

My goals have always been more modest: to convey something about what is being said and not being said in public discourses on Cherokee identity and to better understand the political ramifications of that discourse on Cherokee people and their communities. Taken together, I believe that the primary sources I have gathered—the interviews, ethnographic observations, field notes, and archival documents—along with the more standard secondary sources mentioned in the reference list, tell us a great deal about the discursive terrain of racial shifting. My hope is that my work will raise new questions and concerns, spark additional debate, and lay the groundwork for future research.

A final word about proper names and pseudonyms: as I noted in the acknowledgments, I am deeply indebted to the many people in Cherokee country, broadly defined, who offered their time and counsel on the subject of racial shifting. I wish that I could give each and every one of these individuals credit for their contributions, but anthropologists work in a new era of institutional review boards and informed consent and our code of ethics requires that we protect the privacy of individuals with whom we collaborate, whether or not they want their identities protected. The topic of racial shifting is so volatile and politically heated that, although most people agreed to be identified by name when signing their consent forms, I have chosen to protect their anonymity in almost all cases. The few actual names I included belong to individuals who formally consented and repeatedly requested to be named and were either old friends, public figures, or people who had a chance to read an earlier draft of the material. I have also used names that have already appeared in published sources. Quotations taken from interviews and survey responses are followed in the text by complete dates in parentheses.

Because the topic of this book is so controversial and people have such radically different opinions about it, the book is divided into two parts, each of which represents an equally important position within the overall phenomenon. Part 1 focuses on the stories that racial shifters tell about their lives as they rename themselves and their communities as Cherokee, and part 2 focuses on citizen Cherokees and their perspectives on racial shifting. I use the term "citizen Cherokee" to describe people who are citizens of one of the three federally recognized Cherokee tribes and to distinguish them from those who are enrolled members of nonrecognized and state-recognized Cherokee tribes. This usage is not meant to make a fetish of federal recognition, nor is it meant to question other forms of indigenous identification. Rather, it is intended to clarify historical, political, and legal differences that are important to interpretations of tribal politics and sovereignty, something that will become increasingly apparent over the course of this book.[40] (Some people will be dismayed that I placed state-recognized tribes in a category alongside nonrecognized tribes, but I did so because states usually have less stringent standards for tribal recognition than the federal government. The differences between these two forms of external recognition is discussed in greater detail in chapter 7).

Part 1 begins by describing and analyzing the most common narrative elements within race shifters' accounts of indigenous reclamation. Chapter 2 shows how certain framing devices and tropes permeate the discourse of race shifters living throughout the country, so much so that they have taken on an archetypical quality. Chapter 3 unpacks this discourse further and shows that whiteness is another important element underlying these stories. It examines how race shifters define their own newly reclaimed Cherokee identities in terms of whiteness, both implicitly and explicitly, and how they do so to such an extent that it makes movement between the two categories a possibility. Finally, chapter 4 argues that the all-encompassing personal transformation that race shifters experience is actually a form of conversion in which Cherokee identity is linked to new spiritual ideals and practices in the context of a more intense community engagement.

Part 2 begins by exploring, in chapter 5, how citizen Cherokees use the term "wannabe" and a few related terms to define racial shifters as fundamentally "other" or non-Cherokee. I also focus on how they make sense of this movement, casting it as an effort to access a higher social status that depends, in part, on changes in the value of particular racial identities. Chapter 6 considers much more ambiguous terms such as "outtaluck," "descendant," and "Thindian" and how they reveal when citizen Cherokees are willing to cede ground to racial shifters and when they are not. It also describes the overall culture of assessment that now permeates Cherokee country and the privileged role that genealogical documentation is playing within it. Chapter 7 examines more directly the political and legal consequences of racial shifting, especially when it takes a more collective form. In particular, I show how state recognition of newly self-identified Cherokee tribes has complicated the nature and meaning of contemporary tribal sovereignty. Chapter 8 concludes the book by exploring the various racial and cultural logics that underpin debates about racial shifting and what they say about race and indigenous identity in America today. In dividing the book thus, I have done my best to tell a complex and controversial story in a way that is fair and accurate to all the parties involved.

PART ONE
Racial Shifters

What I see is an awakening, an awakening to the difference within them…that sets them apart and makes them feel like they're not like anyone else. What's going on here? Almost everybody I speak to, without exception, within the last ten years [has] had a spiritual experience of some sort that has begun an awakening within them to their native heritage. And it is an awesome thing to see. It's not random. I may talk to a person in Seattle and then an hour later a person from Ocala, Florida, and it's the same thing—they've had this spiritual experience awakening them to their ancestors, their heritage, their blood.

—Self-identified Cherokee woman, small town in Alabama, May 21, 2003

t w o
What Lies Beneath
Hidden Histories and Racial Ghosts

Brent Stephens is a fifty-three-year-old trial lawyer from Indiana now living in Oklahoma. He has a striking face, light blue eyes, olive skin, and a long gray ponytail reaching down his back. In his free time, he is an official of the Southern Cherokee Nation, a self-identified Cherokee tribe located in Webbers Falls, just south of Tahlequah, Oklahoma. For Stephens, being Cherokee has grown increasingly important over the course of his life, and he responds openly when asked about his experiences as a Cherokee-identified person. It seems to be a subject he wants, or perhaps needs, to talk about.

When asked whether there was ever a time when he did not see himself as Cherokee, at first Stephens responds by playing up the Cherokeeness of his family, even painting them as the objects of anti-Indian scorn. "It's kind of hard, when you grow up in rural, southern Indiana, where you and your family are known as the half breed or whatever, it's kind of hard not identifying," he says. "It's not something that you could hide, or it's not something that I avoided anyhow. Quite frankly, I was proud of that fact." Though he may have been proud of his Cherokee ancestry even in the face of social prejudice, the rest of his comments seem to complicate his claim to a straight-forward Indian identity in a family known as "half breeds." Indeed, the more he talks, the more intricate and confusing his story becomes.

Stephens has always identified as Cherokee, he says, despite external pressure to repress his Cherokee connections. Most of his relatives, for example, "don't want to recognize the fact that they're Indian." The older ones even tried to obscure their Cherokee origins. "Both my parents were Cherokee, my father and my mother," he says, though he did not discover his mother's Cherokee ties until he was in his twenties. His parents were not the only ones who refused to talk about their Cherokee ancestry. Stephens recalls going to a family reunion with old photographs of relatives he was hoping to identify and encountering resistance from older kinfolk. "I don't want to look at those," one great-aunt said when confronted with the photographs. "Get those out of here. I don't want to talk about that." Stephens remembers pleading, "Well, then tell me about Grandpa Stephens," or "Tell me about your dad," asking for information about anybody in the family, but his great-aunt cut him off: "No, we don't wanna talk about that." In the way Stephens relates the story, his great-aunt's sense of shame about being Indian is the essential point. With some sadness, he explains that her behavior is typical of the older generations because "it was instilled in them actually not to talk about being Indian."

Because of his family's collective silence on the topic, Stephens learned far more about his connections to Cherokee history after he grew up and moved away from home. "What I found," he says, "is that the area that I grew up in was an area where a large number of Cherokee had ended up settling at various times, starting maybe as late as the late 1700s but clearly by the early 1800s." Describing the lay of the land is no mere exercise in geography; for Stephens, it helps to establish the plausibility of his Cherokee story, rooting it in a particular place and time: "It's on a wide river in southern Indiana. I've since found that there were several different settlements starting in the late 1700s on the White River 'cause it empties into the Wabash, right above the Ohio. It's basically a direct route on the Ohio River in southern Indiana."

Although these historical and geographic details intrigue him, they are not enough to satisfy his curiosity. He still yearns for more information, but like many people researching their family history, Stephens has come up against a problem of documentation, in particular a lack of records in the rural community where he was raised. "For some reason, all these Cherokee ended up here, and there was a lot of inter-marrying over the years, and we all lived out in the country, and nobody talked about anything. In fact, nobody had any records on anyone either. Like the first documentation on my dad's side that I can find is when my great-grandmother applied for a birth certificate so she could get Social Security in the 1940s." With his relatives falling into the gaps of the bureaucratic record, he is left without the paperwork that could help him answer his fundamental question—Who am I?

As he describes the various obstacles to his self-discovery, Stephens finally arrives at what seems to be the key point for him—the reason family members felt enough fear and shame to hide their Cherokee identity. "Around 1900, I don't know the exact year (I've not researched it), but Indiana had laws like most states that if you were 1/32 or 1/16 [Indian blood quantum], or I don't know what the cutoff was here, but if you were part-Indian, you couldn't own land, you couldn't vote, couldn't use the courts, couldn't testify in court, and you couldn't marry a white person, so it behooved them not to be an Indian." This explanation for going underground circulates widely among race shifters, not just in Indiana and Oklahoma but all across the country. Stephens explains that the older generation, "the ones above [him] anyhow, that they didn't talk about [their Cherokee identity] because of the discrimination and because of the legal aspects when you go back a couple of generations. That's why they denied that part of it." He says that some of these issues affect the younger generations as well. "The ones of my generation, I think it's more a matter of shame. I mean there's still stigma applied to being an Indian in many parts of Indiana. This isn't the most tolerant state. So, you know, I guess that's the reason why there's some that don't talk about it or deny it actually. They don't want to hear about it, that's for sure."

Given that there was so much resistance to identifying as Cherokee in his family, community, and state, maybe the real question that Stephens's story raises is how he ever came to see himself as a Cherokee person to begin with. How, in the face of so much repression—and so little information—has he maintained a sense of Cherokee identity and seen it grow in importance over the years as he has moved from rural Indiana to small-town Oklahoma and become an active part of a fledgling Cherokee community?

Stephens sees his reclamation as part of his tendency to go against the grain. "I'm the first one in my family to have a high school education," he says, "let alone a college degree, and at least from the male line, the first one that was nonalcoholic." He laughs, adding, "Broke that pattern as well!" Stephens also sees himself as a rebel who broke the silence about his Cherokee ancestry by embracing his family's hidden Indian history. In telling of his racial journey into Indianness, he paints himself as a lone figure who only wanted to know the truth, even if it is one that his family fought hard to hide. He sounds as if he was determined—and willing to face the possibility of alienating his kinfolk—to proudly reclaim his Cherokee identity. Even if his family does eventually reject him, Stephens will not be alone, for he is one of many thousands of Americans who have found redemption, hope, and meaning in connecting with their hidden Cherokee histories and with others like themselves.

* * *

Though we may not know all the reasons that motivate Stephens's racial reclamation, what we can see from these snippets of his interview (June 25, 2003) is that race shifting is always a narrative act. In the stories that racial shifters tell about their lives, they express a changing sense of self that comes alive in the telling, in the very act of naming themselves and their histories as Cherokee. As Stephens's story makes clear and as I show over the course of this chapter, the most common element in these narratives is a painful sense of hidden history, the notion that at one point in time, often long ago, an authentic racial self had to be denied and obscured from public view to protect an Indian person from social discrimination and the force of law.[1]

As I heard these stories many times over the past decade, I noticed that they are almost always set in the nineteenth century and concern grandparents, great-grandparents, and even more distant kin. These stories often describe a family history of public disavowal of Cherokee identity combined with some level of private preservation, though the latter often proved more difficult than the former. The collective drama of racial reclamation is rooted in the tragedy of racial denial—somewhere, someplace, hiding one's identity from the public was an act of necessity, and its significance was passed down through the generations, with parents and grandparents warning their offspring about the dire consequences if they should ever let slip their real identity, or so the story goes.

Almost always, these are sad stories told in a wistful or angry tone. Race shifters might now look back and see an ancestor's hiding as a necessary part of a survivor's art, particularly in the rural South in a meaner epoch, but the tale has still come to be imbued with tragedy for most of them. Again and again, as people described relatives who were forced to deny kith and kin, I heard what struck me as a fear of racial erasure, and I sensed that they clung all the more tenaciously to their own tribal identity because it had almost slipped away irretrievably. It was as if they were unwilling to let go of something they had almost lost but now found, something once secret but now revealed.

Because Cherokeeness has become so important to their sense of self, many race shifters seem to mourn the decades of racial hiding that bleached the family tree from a certain point onward. For instance, Luanne Helton, a genealogist for a state-recognized tribe in Alabama, described her feelings on the topic:

> Many of those who are members of the tribe have a hidden history. I mean…
> they're descendants of people who had to hide who they were just to live, who
> had to hide who they were to be able to stay in their place that they loved.
> Everyone descends from…has blood in their veins that had to be hidden in
> order to survive, and…because of that, of course, well, when I got my [tribal
> enrollment] card, the tears flowed because I was able to say what my ancestors
> had to hide. I was able to proclaim what they had to lie about just to stay alive
> and stay in their homeland. (May 21, 2003)

For Luanne, the repression of what she believes to be her authentic self was a source of pain, as it was for other tribal members she knew. But by obtaining the genealogical documents needed for tribal enrollment in a state-recognized tribe, she and other tribal members are able to bring these stories to light and use them to create a community in which they can experience a shared sense of recovered history, social acceptance, and racial belonging. These are stories of redemption, of a racial self being made whole, of wandering in the desert of prejudice before finding the healing salvation of "truth" in the records of some county courthouse. It is little wonder that these narratives have such appeal in much of America, where Christian allegories remain potent and omnipresent and where our media culture encourages the recovery and confession of much that is hidden, buried, and repressed.

Being Black Dutch

According to the familiar stories of race shifters, hiding one's indigenous origins could involve outright denial, simple omission, or complex strategies of reclassification. One of the most common strategies was to camouflage Indian ancestry with designations like Black Dutch or Black Irish, slippery terms that allow for whiteness while also accounting for a darker complexion. What surprised me was the great consistency I heard in such stories: of the forty-five racial shifters interviewed or surveyed, twenty-two said that their families had called themselves Black Dutch to hide their Cherokee background.

I had never heard the term growing up in the South and wanted to know its origins, but there appears to be no authoritative definition, only some assorted rumblings whose vagueness must have suited those shifting out of Cherokeeness at the time. Some genealogists believe that the term Black Dutch originated as a reference for dark-skinned German speakers who descended from Roman soldiers or Spanish sailors or for Sephardic Jews who had intermarried with Dutch Protestants to escape the Spanish Inquisition, but little evidence supports either of these propositions. The more likely interpretation is that by the mid-nineteenth century, Black Dutch had come to refer to any dark-complexioned individual of European descent and had in fact become a colloquial expression, a slightly derogatory term for anyone of small stature, swarthy complexion, foreign extraction, or working-class status.[2]

Despite its varied meanings in the nineteenth century, the term Black Dutch has come to have very specific connotations for contemporary race shifters, many of whom believe that their family members once claimed it as a way of obscuring their Native American roots.[3] Today, these stories are ubiquitous in race-shifting communities; the term Black Dutch has become a kind of code word for Indianness, one that signals a history of racial obscurity even as it reveals this history in the present. For instance, David "Deerwalker" Madison told how his family history of being Black Dutch led him to discover his Cherokee ancestry and laid the groundwork for his later movement from whiteness into Indianness. He described a teasing exchange with a friend, a fellow racial shifter with whom he was close. "My friend…said, 'What are you?' and I said, 'I'm part Irish, part English, and part Black Dutch.' 'Ha ha ha. There's no such thing as Black Dutch!' I said, 'Oh yes there is. My mother told me so.' And he said, 'That's Indian!'" (May 18, 2003). Madison went on to explain that this exchange spurred him to rediscover his actual family history and why it had been buried: "I found that I actually did have Cherokee roots…that I had a cousin that had hid out from the Trail of Tears on a ridge that's not very far from our house and had literally lived in some caves for a couple of years to stay away from it…. I found out my grandmother was born in 1884 and…that her four brothers was taken aside after the Trail of Tears and was told, you know, 'Don't say anything to anybody. If anybody asks who you are, you tell 'em you're Black Dutch or, you know, you're not Indian'" (May 18, 2003). Other racial shifters echo Madison's words. Whether the details of these oral histories are fiction or truth is not the point here. What matters is that racial shifters have come to understand that being Black Dutch signals a common history of racial repression in which Indianness, and in this case, specifically Cherokeeness, was out of necessity secreted away behind a veneer of dark-skinned "whiteness" and purposefully imprecise terminology.

Some federally recognized Cherokees are troubled by these stories of racial hiding, because they imply that those who hid had a choice whether to be Indian. They seem to take offense at the notion that detribalization or assimilation was a viable option for some Cherokees, presumably due to intermarriage and somewhat lighter complexions, because they feel that Cherokeeness is not something that could or should be shed in a pinch. Certainly, their relatives either did not have that option or, if they did, chose not to exercise it, as federally recognized Cherokees have sometimes pointed out to me with a whiff of contempt. So it is perhaps with a hint of defensiveness that racial shifters often respond that racial hiding was a strategic choice born of necessity, a savvy move to protect one's family in the face of social persecution. For example, Principal Chief Joe Perry of the Tsalagi Nvdagi, or Texas Cherokees, described his grandmother's reaction when he asked her why she denied her Cherokee heritage and said that she was Black Dutch instead:

> She said, "Sit down there, boy!" So I sat down. She always had a stool right
> past the hottest place in the kitchen, right next to a wood stove. So I sat down
> there, and she said, "I wanna tell you something. Smith County, Texas," she
> said, "the government men came out in 1900. I was seventeen years old. We
> had some people working for us out there, living with my grandfather, that
> were Tsalagi people, Cherokee people. And they come up and ask you and say,
> 'What are you, black or white?' 'I'm not white. I'm Indian,' he said. 'You sure
> you're not black or white?' and he said, 'No.' 'Well, how 'bout your wife? Is
> she black or white?' 'Oh, she's Indian just like me, same thing.' They said,
> 'Are you sure you're the same thing?' and he says, 'Yes.' They did not say
> a word."
>
> My grandmother says that when school started, the U.S. marshals came
> out, picked the kids up, and took them to Indian Territory. Mama and Daddy
> followed. She said, "Now do you understand why?" I said, "Yes, ma'am. It's
> the law." She said, "That is correct." She said, "We were always scared to death
> that they're going to come and get us." Can you imagine that? When she said
> that, she was ninety-four years old.... When I talk to her, I'm Cherokee. If
> anybody else talked to her, I'm Black Dutch." (July 8, 2003)

According to Perry, his family members made the choice to pass into whiteness and out of Cherokeeness in order to protect themselves from losing land and kin. Yet, the choice was a situational one in that his family maintained the ruse only in front of outsiders; among themselves and with their kin in Indian Territory, which became the state of Oklahoma in 1907, they continued to identify as Cherokee.

Victimization and Racial Persecution

In sharing these stories of racial hiding to escape persecution, race shifters create a common narrative of victimization that helps them forge new social bonds with others like themselves. Where once they were forced to take their racial identities underground, now they create contexts in which repression and recovery are the lingua franca, where they can openly lament and reclaim their Cherokee histories and identities. For some self-identified tribal communities, these stories of victimization have common elements tied to the law and politics of their specific social and geographic locations. For instance, various members of the Cherokee Tribe of Northeast Alabama told me that until the mid-1970s, it was against the law for Indians to own land in the state. One woman, Jessica Gates, explained that "1949 was the last documented case of somebody being removed from Alabama that was native…1972 was when the rules got changed about land. Up until '72, you couldn't own land in Alabama if you were Indian. If you had more than one-eighth Indian in you, you couldn't own land" (March 29, 2003). Another member of the tribe, a middle-aged man, recalled a somewhat more extreme version when he said, "We don't run around saying, you know, 'We're Cherokee.'… I don't know about anybody else, but in Alabama up 'til about 1975, it was illegal to be a Cherokee, so…no wonder people kept their mouth shut about it" (May 18, 2003). Most members of the Cherokee Tribe of Northeast Alabama have local origins, and thus their racial narratives are relatively consistent in describing laws on the books in Alabama up until the mid-1970s that discriminated against native people and caused many to opt out of Indianness for the relative security of whiteness.[4]

In other self-identified Cherokee communities, such stories might differ in detail though not in overall content. For instance, the Southern Cherokee Nation is located in Webbers Falls, Oklahoma, just south of two federally recognized Cherokee tribes in Tahlequah, Oklahoma—the Cherokee Nation and the United Keetoowah Band. Because members of the Southern Cherokee Nation hail from different parts of the country, their stories bear the traces of many different geographic contexts, while still sharing similar narrative elements. Darren Nixon, who is a Southern Cherokee Nation marshal, tells a story about his family's situation in Missouri that is remarkably similar to Brent Stephens's story about Indiana, recorded at the start of this chapter: "You take up home in Missouri. Reason people here would say, 'Oh, I'm Portuguese or Black Dutch' and they would be half-blood Cherokees or a quarter, in Missouri, it was a state law. In fact, it's still on the books until 1970-something. They'd run you out of town, if you was an Indian and you walk through or linger about. So that tells you something. That's why if you asked 'em if they was Indian, they'd say no" (May 24, 2003). George Richey, the current chief of the Southern Cherokee Nation, also said that laws that discriminated against Indians were "peppered all over the county," including where his family lived in North Carolina. "A lot of those Cherokees even claimed to be Black Dutch and Irish and everything they could," he said, "because if you were an Indian, you could not own land, you could not vote" (July 22, 2003).

Although each of theses stories took root in a different part of the country, they share common narrative elements, so much so that they seem to have taken on an archetypical quality. Whether they originate in northern Alabama or central Missouri, such stories of racial hiding are bookended by the same set of historical events, the period of Indian removal in the mid-nineteenth century (which includes the Trail of Tears in the 1830s)⁵ and the Red Power movement for Native American civil rights in the 1970s. Although these are historical events that happened at a national level, what interests me is the way in which they have been made local, reread and re-created in terms of local meanings and understandings. Race shifters identify the source of their oppression not in the federal government but in the faces of local officials and the legislation they enacted. Likewise, liberation came not in the wake of something called Red Power, a phrase that few would use, but in local acts of reclamation and recognition made by their own friends and families and by state Indian commissions. The details of the telling seem to say, "This is personal."

Subverting Racial Classifications and Hierarchies

While Cherokee race shifters often highlight local laws and practices as the reason their ancestors had to reject Indianness in favor of whiteness, most allude at the same time to the wider racial system in which their families lived in Alabama, Georgia, Missouri, Arkansas, and Texas. This system, they maintain, had no room for Indians who did not live with their tribe or who chose to remain in their eastern homelands in the post–Indian removal era. Because the federal legislation surrounding removal made it more difficult for Native Americans to remain in the East, unless their tribal nations had negotiated some other arrangement with the federal government, racial shifters believe that maintaining an American Indian identity was not a viable option for many who stayed behind.

Consider, for example, the story of Jessica Gates, an enrolled member of the Eastern Band of Cherokee Indians in North Carolina. A forty-five-year-old woman who was raised in Alabama, Gates is somewhat unusual in that she has spent the past two decades participating in the social and ceremonial life of two state-recognized Cherokee tribes in Alabama, rather than in the federally recognized tribal community in Cherokee, North Carolina. She described how the post-removal period affected her family in North Carolina, saying that when an Indian midwife delivered her aunts and uncles during the Depression, her grandparents paid a white doctor to issue birth certificates listing the infants as white "once [her grandfather] knew, three days old, that they were pretty close to being acceptable [in appearance] by the white community." Sweeping back the blonde hair that reached to her waist, she went on, "Now if they had been black or real dark, then he would have issued a black certificate at birth, because you either had to have a black certificate or a white certificate in the South to go to school, to own land, to do anything. So everything was hidden [in regard to Indianness]" (March 29, 2003).

Most racial shifters described a similar experience of having to choose between whiteness and blackness rather than being able to claim their "true" identity and said that it was extremely painful for their families. Instead of perhaps seeing it as a case of fortuitous physiognomy that could then be exploited for social gain or financial necessity, race shifters described the experience in sorrowful and angry terms. For instance, one elderly woman who lives in Arkansas and goes by the name of Heart of the Wolf told this story:

> There were a group of Indians in that area that the military…had orders to kill every Indian they seen, shoot 'em down. So there was a very large group of Indians that ran up in the hills. That's how they got up in the Ozarks, Missouri and Arkansas, and hid. They would hide and one of the members that did not look Cherokee would go into town and do the shopping and come back.… The government put the fear of God in them. And at that time, I forget the year, are you aware that there was a law in Missouri, it was against the law a few years back for Indians to live in Missouri?… Well, they had to start thinking and living as a white person. They forced us to be white, act white, live white…and that is a very, very degrading feeling. (April 22, 2003)

This perception of degradation and painful loss in the process of passing as white is critical to the narratives of racial shifters, for it inoculates them—or so they seem to hope—against charges that their ancestors were irresponsible to their tribal brethren or, even worse, not really Cherokee in a significant way.[6] Their account of the act of hiding seems to require echoes of Anne Frank or the Underground Railroad—indicating that it was the product of grim necessity, not cowardice or lack of caring—lest their current efforts at Cherokee reclamation be called into question.

Most racial shifters recount that when forced into hiding, their families opted out of Indianness and into whiteness rather than blackness—a choice that reflects their negotiation of racial hierarchy. If their only options in the second half of the nineteenth century were to be black, white, or mulatto, then better to pass out of dark-skinned prejudice and into white-skinned privilege, if at all possible. Nonetheless, a small but significant number of racial shifters describe a hidden history of Cherokeeness obscured by blackness rather than whiteness. In these stories, relatives chose to describe themselves as black or mulatto to obscure their native ancestry, in much the same way that other racial shifters had described themselves as quasi-white Black Dutch or Black Irish. For example, Morris Carter, a tall, elderly man with gray hair and glasses, described how his relatives in Georgia responded to U.S. census takers when asked about their racial identities. "My granddad was white, my great-great-granddad was white, and then they go to my great-granddad. He was scared of being killed, so he was black! They didn't say he was a Negro—he was black.… He just labeled himself as black" (May 24, 2003). Morris, unlike a fair number of racial shifters, looks very much like someone with Cherokee ancestry; he physically appears to be Indian. He went on, laughing out loud, "So I went from white to black, and now I'm red! Ha ha ha! Now I'm red!" (May 24, 2003). Maybe Morris's darker, Indian appearance provides some clue as to why his relatives opted for blackness rather than whiteness. Maybe they were too dark to pass as white and access white-skinned privilege.

Even more interesting is the shared perception among racial shifters like Morris that blackness was a better option than Indianness, the idea being that although African Americans had their own demons to face in U.S. society, particularly in the violent prejudice of their white Southern neighbors, at least they could own land and reside in the post-Reconstruction South without the constant fear of deportation to Indian Territory.[7] Such stories of hiding under the mantle of blackness rarely extend back into the antebellum period during which removal occurred; instead, they describe situations in the late nineteenth and early twentieth centuries. Thus, in narrating their complex family histories and in making the choice to identify openly as Cherokee rather than white, racial shifters seem to gently subvert the standard racial hierarchies that place African Americans and Native Americans beneath whites.

Ancestral Callings and Racial Essentialism

Racial shifters offer other subversions as well. In their narratives of racial reinscription, racial shifters challenge the material and epistemological bases of Cherokeeness at the very same moment that they reproduce dominant understandings of race, culture, and tribal community. Where we most hear this tension between resistance and reproduction is in the dynamic interplay of race and culture that is embedded in these stories. For instance, in many interviews, racial shifters mentioned specific aspects of Cherokee and pan-Indian culture in discussions of their own identities, such as open-mindedness, spiritual integrity, and generosity, just as I had expected. More surprising was the degree to which they also utilized essentialist understandings of race in their very acts of racial reconstruction. On numerous occasions, racial shifters would focus on various physiological markers of racial identity—high cheekbones, straight hair, dark olive skin, brown eyes, or even shovel-shaped incisors—that they may or may not have had. Often with some imagination, they would see any one of these features as a physical manifestation of their own Cherokee identity or as biological proof of their kinship claims. For instance, at one meeting of the Northern Cherokee Nation of Old Louisiana Territory in Arkansas, when a handsomely chiseled but quite pale young man walked through the front door of the Western Sizzlin steak house, the entire room erupted with cries of "It's the reincarnation of Attakullakulla! He's come back to us, here in the flesh."[8] It mattered not a whit that this young man bore little if any resemblance to the great eighteenth-century Cherokee leader. The power of these statements lay not in their truth or falseness but in their ability to forge social connections. This was the collective imagination at work, linking the members of the room to one another and to Cherokee history.

Because shared kinship creates a powerful sense of social connectedness, racial shifters tend to seize on particular ancestors, real or imagined, as touchstones when they rewrite their autobiographies. Not only are these figures traced through elaborate oral histories so that they can then be imagined and inscribed in the physiognomy of other tribal members, but also they are marshaled in ways that seem to defy common Euro-American notions of genealogical distance (Schneider 1980). For race shifters, these particular ancestors have the power to define their descendants in essential ways, in large part because they are racial others. Many describe their shift in identity as a spiritual awakening to their ancestral heritage. Many even insist that their ancestors are literally embodied within them—as an essential, biogenetic, cultural, and racial substance—and, if listened to, will guide them toward their true path and identity. One middle-aged woman described this as "an ancestral calling to people to come back home," with her friend chiming in, "Yeah, it's an ancestral calling...because one of our prophecies says the seventh generation will come back" (April 26, 2003). On another occasion, a woman from a completely different community said that people were identifying themselves as Cherokees because "their ancestors were calling them from the dust" (May 21, 2003).

Sometimes these folk theories are buttressed by scientific interpretations of a sort. For example, Luanne Helton described how when she first visited the original Cherokee homeland in North Carolina, she experienced waves of overwhelming sorrow due to her "genetic memory." "I'm just thinking that in my DNA, I know we carry the DNA of our ancestors, literally," she said, "and somehow this was impressed in those genes, the sorrow of leaving the homeland" (May 21, 2003). Another man who identified himself as Cherokee but had no tribal affiliation explained that DNA accounted for the blood integrity and racial distinctiveness of Native Americans, saying, "We're all peoples of the turtle's back. It's been proven through your anthropology and DNA testing that the native peoples of this continent have no blood ties to what they call the original man [to whom Europeans and other non-native people might be traced]" (March 29, 2003). Yet another man, named Arlo Davis, went so far as to say that genetic memory could account for why Native Americans knew their distant kin and their culture:

> There was people that I could walk into a room and scare the daylights out of
> 'em 'cause I would know who they were. And never would speak a word to
> 'em. I knew their kids. I knew their family.... And that is scary. I'm going to
> tell you, it's scary because the thing about it is that, until I learned a little
> more, until I got to researching why this is happening, that the native Indians
> of America...we are the only ones that have blood memories of our family.
> Most Indians can speak their language before or at birth. It's scary. It can be
> proven. (February 22, 2003)

On numerous occasions, racial shifters linked mystical experiences of knowing—whether it was ancient kin, culture, or their own Indian ancestry—with a quite literal racial and cultural essentialism. According to this logic, their ancestors call to them from the past to fulfill their destinies in the present. They are inscribed on their bodies and located in their DNA and blood. From the moment of birth, ancestral memories and culture are lurking beneath the surface of their own consciousness, even though they may not recognize this until later in life when there is a moment of racial awakening.

If we follow this same line of thought to its logical conclusion, then Cherokee ancestors have unique powers not usually attributed to Spanish or Irish ancestors—even small traces of their ancient blood can redefine their multiracial descendants as Indians. Much like the laws and logic of hypodescent that have long been at work in African American communities, it is almost as if there is a type of racial homeopathy at work here, such that a tiny fraction of blood, or better yet, Cherokee ancestral substance, has the power to remake one's entire racial, cultural, and social body.[9] Sarah Glory, a member of a state-recognized tribe in northeast Alabama, explained it like this: "One drop of [Cherokee] blood.... If you have it in your heart, you live that, you feel that. Then, you know, nobody should judge you" (May 18, 2003). In this case, blood is powerful indeed. Not only does it stand for the conflation of race, culture, and kinship, but it also is the actual vehicle that carries Cherokee identity from one generation to the next, even protecting the bearer from the skepticism she has surely faced. Similarly, because the heart is the organ responsible for the circulation of blood, many racial shifters extend this metaphor of blood to locate their Cherokee identity in or at the heart, like this middle-aged woman in Alabama: "All my life, I knew I was different. I was not like everybody else. I felt it inside. I didn't know what to call it.... I don't look Cherokee, unfortunately...but my heart is Cherokee, and it's hard to describe that to someone who is not Cherokee. They can't feel...it's your blood. It's who you are! You know, the tribe is not something I do. It's not a social outlet, though there's lot of social activity. It's who I am" (May 21, 2003).

The concern in these examples is not with how much blood one has, whether one is full blood, mixed blood, or any particular degree of relatedness to a Cherokee ancestor. In fact, race shifters refuse such notions of genealogical distance and quantifications of racial kinship, in no small measure because such logic would surely work against them. Instead, their concern is whether someone has Cherokee ancestry in a looser sense and whether they honor that ancestry by being or becoming "Cherokee at heart." They focus on the shared belief that if they have any degree of Cherokee blood, then this is all that matters—they are Cherokee, end of story. But there is a flip side to this perspective, for when race shifters gloss over their own multiracial histories by privileging their Cherokee ancestry over their white ancestry, they fail to acknowledge the power that attends whiteness and the ways that this might also be embedded in their own histories, life experiences, and bodies.

Why this interpretive leap to Indianness among racial shifters? Why is Indianness the one form of ancestry that has such staying power for them? I imagine that it is because native cultures have long encouraged such metaphorical and literal connections to ancient kin. Indeed, although essentialist discourses of blood kinship are common throughout the United States, they are particularly potent in native North America. For instance, in a 1997 interview with literary scholar Larry Evers, Pulitzer Prize–winning author N. Scott Momaday (Kiowa/Cherokee) described the deep-seated relationship between indigenous people and their ancestral kin as something linked to "memory in the blood": the ability of descendants to know even the very distant past because of a "racial memory that leaps across generations" (Garroutte 2003:120).

Cherokee sociologist Eva Garroutte uses this example to explain that there is a broad understanding among American Indians that physical relatedness is "heritable, fundamental and effectual" and that blood is seen to literally connect tribal members to one another and to "something beyond the individual" (Garroutte 2003:119–120). Garroutte (2003:120–121) also points out that non-Indian scholars have been quick to dismiss such claims as racist but that these need to be understood within the context of tribal philosophies of knowledge. If we take Garroutte's suggestion seriously, then such essentialist understandings of blood kinship may not be about race at all, at least in any social scientific sense, but about sacred understandings of kinship and tribal belonging that are rooted in tribal epistemologies. Yet, even if we recognize how these essentialisms may have radically different meanings for different subjects in different contexts, whether in a scholarly treatise or the divination of a traditional healer, we also need to acknowledge their racial effects. Defining who is Cherokee and who is not is really about the social construction of both racial and indigenous difference, and essentialism plays a key role in that process.

Whether essentialism is linked to the mysticism of tribal kinship or to more widespread understandings of race and indigeneity, a remarkably similar discourse characterizes the social construction of Cherokee identity in both federally recognized and race-shifting communities. Such similarity may reflect a degree of cultural continuity between the two groups or the ubiquity of essentialist understandings of race and indigeneity in U.S. society. A more likely explanation is that it reflects not coincidence or continuity but much more recent social interactions, as well as a tendency for race shifters, perhaps unconsciously, to borrow essentialist understandings of kinship and identity from other native people and their published writings. Surely race shifters do so, in part, because essentialism is a powerful narrative for establishing political rights, particularly for people who are often excluded from those rights and who have few ways to authenticate their claims in the eyes of dominant society. Such strategic uses of essentialism are common among the disenfranchised, not so much because they challenge dominant understandings of identity but because they have a powerful ability to create community, to inextricably bind together groups of what are often quite diverse individuals.

I want to be careful not to reduce these essentialist ideas and practices to sheer tactical posturing rather than some more heartfelt motivation. Clearly, in their narratives of racial redemption, racial shifters are feeling and experiencing something quite deeply, something that appears to be linked more to emotions and mysticism than instrumental designs, even unconscious ones. Yet, social scientific frameworks have tended to misconstrue any and all essentialist philosophies as racist or as convenient mythologies for securing vested interests and, as a result, offer limited insights into the discourses and experiences of Native American identity.[10] I believe that we need to respect the mystical quality of this transformation and that we can do so by making room in our analyses for essentialist philosophies, whether local or tribal, not as mere objects but as knowledge systems that constitute subjects in powerful ways.

Out of Hiding

When race shifters respond to what they perceive as an ancestral calling and reclaim their hidden histories of Indianness, they often describe the process as one of "coming out of the closet," a metaphor that they seem to have unintentionally borrowed from the gay, lesbian, bisexual, and transgender community (Sedgwick 1992). I mention this point in passing in chapter 1, when I describe the way in which Oliver Collins urged his community in Ohio, the Tallige Fire Cherokee Nation, to go public and reassert its Indian identity: "It is time to *come out of the closet* and make our selves known to the dominant society" (Allen 1995:8; italics added). Collins seemed to suggest that today's society has entered a new age in which previously hidden aspects of one's racial self need no longer be shut away behind closed doors. According to Collins, contemporary American society either has become more tolerant of racial difference or at least can be made more tolerant if enough people "come out" as racial "others." If you've got it, Collins seemed to suggest, then it's time to flaunt it.

Members of the Northern Cherokee Nation of Old Louisiana Territory also used the metaphor of the closet to allude to a broader shift toward greater racial tolerance. For instance, when asked why people were increasingly willing to identify themselves as Cherokee, one tribal member responded, "'Cause they quit hiding. They've quit looking to hide." Another chimed in, "Because some began to *come out* and say, 'Hey, I'm Cherokee.' So, that encouraged others to do it" (April 26, 2003; italics added). More explicit was the following dialogue between Arlo Davis, the group's deputy chief, and Robby Giles, its Arkansas district representative, in which they equated non-Indian society with "straight society":

RG: I don't think you can learn to be Cherokee. Cherokee is in the heart.

AD: You can learn traditions and things like that, but as far as I can see, we lost all our traditions, all of our heritage you might say, through two hundred years of oppression with the white government, the dominant race, the white race. Our people were not allowed to talk about it. The federal troops would have been there, shipping them out.

RG: Or killed 'em, one or the other.

AD: Or killed them on the spot rather than moving them out. It was that critical. Sometimes they didn't even give them a chance. They'd just shoot them on the spot when they found 'em and knew they was Cherokee.

RG: Any other Cherokee, not just our tribe, but any [Cherokee] tribe, they hold
        their head up proud. And I think that in this day and age, there's a lot of
        people in the *straight society* that has lost this part. So everybody is looking
        for that anchor, whether they're white, black, green, purple, or whatever.
        They're looking for that foundation. (February 22, 2003; italics added)

According to Giles and Davis, non-Indian society is "straight" in that it has lost its
social and emotional moorings. Racial shifters, in contrast, are full of pride, an attitude tied to the pleasure they take in their recently reclaimed tribal identity. For them,
being Cherokee implies having culture and community and a sense of self that though
once closeted is now openly embraced.

What I believe we may hear in the words of Giles, Davis, and other race shifters
is an unintended "queering" of Cherokee discourses and identities. Although the term
"queer" is often used simply to denote same-sex desire and sexuality, whether lesbian,
gay, or bisexual, in this instance I borrow Eve Sedgwick's (1993:8) definition: "the
open mesh of possibilities, gaps, overlaps, dissonances and resonances, lapses and
excesses of meaning when the constituent elements of anyone's gender, of anyone's sexuality aren't made (or can't be made) to signify monolithically." If we apply this definition to the case of racial shifters and examine the way in which they narrate and
construct their own Cherokee identities, then we can see how their very refusal of normative definitions of Cherokeeness might be considered queer.[11] By using the term
"queer" to describe these racial processes, my intention is not to deny the linkages
between "queerness" and same-sex sexuality, to deny the different material, social, and
political bases of Native American identities, or to deny racial shifters the possibility
of their own queer sexualities. Instead, I offer the term as a description not of an identity but of a process of self-representation and as a way to explore parallels and distinctions in the making of race and sexuality.

Although the broader metaphor of the closet has become a common way of
describing previously hidden lifestyles and identities among all kinds of people, for
racial shifters it has particular resonance. By the very act of openly identifying themselves as Cherokees, they both celebrate and terminate their hidden history of
Indianness—what was once private and individual becomes public and communal.
Where once they experienced a sense of individual racial misrecognition and erasure—
the feeling that they did not quite fit in the world around them—now they find a
sense of wholeness, community belonging, and racial redemption.

In the process of coming out as Cherokees, racial shifters announce to the world that
they are special and more specifically that they are indigenous people with a unique
relationship to the territory and history of this country. In doing so, they also challenge
monolithic understandings of Cherokeeness and expand ideas of racial and cultural
identity so that these are tied much more explicitly to "performative acts of experi-
mental self-perception and filiation," as Sedgwick (1993:9) would have it. As I see it,
this performative aspect of identity making is critical, for it is in the performance of

narrating their hidden histories, of evoking images of racial victimhood, longing, and desire, of refusing whiteness, of creating new tribes and kin networks—whether fictive or not—that racial shifters not only name themselves as Cherokee but also challenge the possibilities of what it means to be Cherokee in the contemporary world. However, these public challenges are not necessarily cause for celebration, because they can sometimes obscure the workings of power, an issue I turn to in the next chapter as I explore another hidden dimension of racial shifting.

t h r e e
Racial Choices and the Specter of Whiteness

Dark green hills stretch across the horizon and bump up against a heavy, gray sky.[1] Intermittent showers, so characteristic of late May in the heartland of the old South, still manage to swell the streams and muddy the ground, and every once in a while a lone thunderclap sends a family of white-tailed deer and a small herd of buffalo scattering. Despite the threatening weather, which includes a tornado watch, the Sequoyah Cavern campground is full to capacity on this Friday evening, with about twenty motor homes and thirty-five tents circling the grassy dance arena. The people who have come together for this weekend's powwow, hosted by a state-recognized Cherokee tribe in northeastern Alabama, are doing much like the animals that inhabit this neck of the woods: waiting it out and trying to make the best of a soggy, even sorry, situation.

To better pass the time, some people start gathering for what they call "a pickin' an' a grinnin'" at a small recreational area near the center of the campground. A small crowd listens to a young woman named Dancing Eyes as she sings a heartfelt rendition of "Amazing Grace" in Cherokee. As the day wears into the evening, more people join in the fun. Eventually, they relocate their impromptu jamboree to a weathered cabin in the middle of a field not far from the dance grounds. When the rain lets up enough for some musicians to set up a small public address system on the cabin's front porch, the music takes off into the night and the crowd swells. Some are playing spoons, others fiddles and guitars. Others take to the mike to tell funny stories. Two

47

men in particular, from Cherokee, North Carolina, are good at slinging insults and anecdotes about well-known Cherokees on the national powwow circuit, and they quickly have everyone in stitches. The butt of the joke might be from Oklahoma, North Carolina, California, or just down the street, but it does not seem to matter to the audience. Whether they are local or not, officially recognized or not, everyone appears to know the characters in the stories—at least well enough to get the punch lines. Much later in the evening, the music and the laughter start to settle down, and the pickers begin to head to their Army-issue tents, Coleman campers, and a nearby motel in the small town of Fort Payne, the sock capital of the world.

By 10:30 the next morning, those who spent the night socializing are finally on their feet and are bringing the powwow to life. Though previously they had sworn never to have contest dancing at their annual powwow, the Cherokee Tribe of Northeast Alabama decided to give it a try this year. Partly, they hoped to attract more visitors and generate prize money for the dancers, but the real goal may have been to add to a pot of money that one day would be used to buy a choice tract of land—the idea being that if they could own land collectively and encourage tribal members to build homes in a residential cluster, then they might experience a more vibrant sense of Cherokee community as they envision it. But the $3 admission fees do not seem to add up very quickly, especially given that hardly anyone watches the entrance gate. As people mill about aimlessly, four drum groups arrive and begin to unload their gear. Only one of the drum groups "looks Indian," the one that is paid to be here. Its members are citizens of the Cheyenne, Creek, and Navajo nations who now live in Alabama or Tennessee. Another drum has mostly young boys, playing with their sticks and acting important, and the other two drums are made up of people who come to the annual powwow on a regular basis—some are members of the local tribe, others not.

When the various drums finally get set up, thirty or forty people begin to take their places for Grand Entry. The hired drummers strike the first beat of the day, filling the air with a southern-style song, in a lower register than that of their northern neighbors—a choice that seems appropriate, given that this gathering is in Alabama, though Lynyrd Skynyrd might seem appropriate too. The dancers begin to move, keeping time with the pounding rhythm, their feet echoing the drummers' every stroke. Only a few are able to keep time with the precision that comes from years of experience. Only a few have the kind of regalia that reflect how someone—perhaps a wife or grandmother—was willing to spend long hours beading and sewing or how an older male relative was able to honor the dancer with genuine eagle feathers.[2] Several of the dancers are adorned with soft, brown, pseudoleather getups, straight from the *Crazy Crow* catalogue. A few opt for Cherokee-specific garb rather than the more common Plains-style regalia of the pan-Indian powwow. One young woman wears a beautiful, traditional, red and white calico tear dress, styled after those that were worn on the Trail of Tears, and a middle-aged man wears a long, heavy, white tunic over buckskin breeches, with a red, white, and blue sash tied around his waist, a heavy silver medallion hanging from his neck, and a large red turban, graced with what appears to be a giant white ostrich feather. When the first song comes to an end and the dancers clear the arena, the announcer calls them back—not for a flag song, veterans' song, or prayer song that one might expect to hear at almost any powwow in the country but for an intertribal number, in the hope that even more people will participate.

I am not present to watch these events unfold. Instead, I read about them weeks later in the pages of my research assistant's field notes. According to her notes, the early intertribal number is not the only time that the powwow breaks with tradition and heads off in a surprising direction. Because the weather still is not cooperating, sticking to the official schedule of events becomes nearly impossible, and there are plenty of opportunities for the unexpected to happen. Intertribal and competition dances continue to take place throughout the day, but they are punctuated by brief intermissions during which members of the local tribe put on performances to entertain the restless crowd. Mostly, it is people like Dancing Eyes, a guy named Wolf, and someone's granddaughter on the flute, each taking a turn at the mike.

At one point, however, two teenage boys—grass dancers in fluorescent regalia— step into the arena. They wear serious expressions on their faces and try to stand tall. Suddenly, music comes over the intercom. It is not drum music, but someone playing a familiar lick on a banjo: "nene, ne ne, ne ne, ne ne, nee." One of the boys dances a few steps and pauses: "nene, ne ne, ne ne, ne ne, neee." The other dances in reply. Sure enough, to the crowd's shock and amusement, the boys are dancing a fully choreographed grass-dance number to the "Dueling Banjos" song from the movie *Deliverance*! Maybe "Sweet Home Alabama" will be next, or monster trucks counting coup? Whether the performance is meant to be playful or ironic, the boys certainly get the crowd's attention. People stand on their lawn chairs trying to get a better view, either because they are stunned that anyone would do such a thing or because they appreciate the familiar tune. As the music gets faster, the boys dance faster, and the crowd whips itself into a frenzy of appreciation, cheering the boys on, howling with laughter, taking the surreal and making of it a raucous good time.

* * *

No one could ignore the southern flavor of these events or the unique blending of southern white, Cherokee, and pan-Indian cultures. Sometimes, as in the case of the grass dancers, local tribal members seemed to play with the cultural possibilities, to create new ways of expressing what it means to be Indian and Cherokee in that particular time and place. At other times, such as when singing a traditional Cherokee hymn, they took a much more reverent approach. Regardless of the attitude or occasion, a key influence in these performances (and in the overall cultural mix at this powwow) was southern white culture, and more specifically that of the South's rural working class. No one was whistling "Dixie" or wearing hoop skirts, but the symbols of the rural, white, working-class South were everywhere apparent in the Cherokee Tribe of Northeast Alabama's language, clothing, style of play, and social interactions, even in their choice of music. I laughed when I first heard about the "Dueling Banjos" number and joked about Lynyrd Skynyrd, the quintessential 1970s southern rock band, because such music has been the sound track to life in the working-class South for several decades, something I know from my own family reunions and years of living in east Texas, where it is both cliché and fact.

The southern quality of this gathering might seem strange to some observers. When Indian people from other parts of the country visit these types of events that are less "fry bread" than "southern fried," I suspect that it fuels their assumption that race shifting is a poor, white, southern thing by definition. However, race shifters are quick to reject this interpretation and argue that whiteness has nothing to do with it. For them, reclaiming their Cherokee identity is deeply meaningful and is more about matters of the spirit than the trappings of racial appearance. Whether their reclamation takes place in the rural South or some other region of the country, race shifters are often so busy asserting their right to indigeneity that they do not acknowledge their own white skin privilege. Instead, where whiteness might otherwise have been, there are both an absence and a refusal, as if whiteness were the new hidden history, the new stigma.

That racial shifters often ignore and even at times deny their whiteness is not surprising, given that such "power-evasive" maneuvers (Frankenberg 1993) have long characterized U.S. race relations, at least among those who have generally lived white lives.[3] Historian Grace Hale writes: "Central to the meaning of whiteness is a broad, collective American silence. The denial of white as a racial identity, the denial that whiteness has a history, allows the quiet, the blankness to stand as the norm. This erasure allows many to fuse their absence of racial being with the nation, making whiteness their unspoken but deepest sense of what it means to be American" (Hale 1999:xi). In a similar fashion, by selectively emphasizing Cherokee rather than white histories and identities, race shifters gloss over (or intentionally ignore) the social privileges that attend whiteness, including how their own lived experiences might differ from those of Cherokees who have a markedly Indian physical appearance.[4] In doing so, they make a tacit assumption that whiteness can find a safe home within Cherokeeness, without ever questioning what effects this might have on the broader Cherokee population. Perhaps this reflects the usual zeal of the newly converted, but race shifters seem to minimize their whiteness at the very moment they begin to maximize their Indianness, as if one must replace the other instead of standing side by side.

Some race shifters may prefer to minimize their links to whiteness because, in asserting their Cherokeeness, they recognize that indigeneity is something distinct from race. However, even among those who recognize this distinction, race continues to haunt their narratives of indigenous reclamation in a variety of ways. Both implicitly and explicitly, race shifters define their Cherokeeness in terms of whiteness, and they do so to an extent that makes movement between the two possible. The rest of this chapter examines how Cherokeeness and whiteness intersect in the minds of race shifters and how their perceived differences and similarities enable their indigenous claims. In the first section, I explore how race shifters use the language of choice both to deny and to articulate their links to whiteness and white skin privilege—without realizing it, race shifters have the luxury of choice that comes with an "unmarked" appearance. In the second, I consider the values associated with whiteness—what it does and does not offer race shifters—and how these values might motivate specific forms of racial omission and desire. Conversely, I examine the values associated with Indianness, and specifically with Cherokeeness, to see how the virtues of indigeneity might make those of whiteness pale in comparison. In the last section, I look at the ways in which race shifters explicitly associate Cherokeeness with an "original whiteness," meaning their belief that Cherokees had a white physical appearance in the precolonial era, one that allows them to imagine a Cherokee past in which their present appearance would make sense.

Cherokee by Choice

One of the clearest examples of how race shifters privilege Cherokeeness at the expense of whiteness can be seen in their discourses and practices surrounding the U.S. census. For instance, when I asked race shifters how they had identified themselves on the 2000 census, the vast majority replied that they had checked only the American Indian box and then added that their tribal affiliation was Cherokee. Because so few acknowledged that they also had white ancestry, I often followed up my initial question by asking, "Why did you mark American Indian on the census as opposed to anything else?" or "Would you ever consider marking more than one box?" Though I never mentioned whiteness in the questions, it was nonetheless implied, or at least most race shifters seemed to read it that way. Often, despite having appearances that would be read as unambiguously white in most social contexts, most race shifters responded defensively with a quick denial that whiteness had anything to do with their own sense of racial history and identity. For instance, Charlene Hamilton, the second vice chief of the Cherokee Tribe of Northeastern Alabama, said that she would never consider marking more than one box: "Because I'm not white.... In my feelings, in my spirit...I am Cherokee in blood, in spirit, and *by choice*" (May 18, 2003; italics added).

Other race shifters were more willing to concede their white ancestry but would often, in the same breath, assert that their racial self-identification was solely Native American. For example, Marge Peterson, a fifty-six-year-old accountant who is also the principal chief of the Southeastern Cherokee Confederacy, stated, "Although I am Cherokee and Irish, as far as I am concerned, I am 100 percent Cherokee, both racially and ethnically," the implication again being that Lawson is exclusively Cherokee by choice (April 23, 1996).[5]

Why do race shifters prefer to talk about their Cherokeeness at the expense of their whiteness to such a degree? Why not claim both? My research suggests that for a variety of reasons, race shifters tend to name their histories selectively as Cherokee rather than Cherokee and white. In some cases, their moment of racial epiphany seems so intense as to blot out their white past. In others, they suggest that people would be foolish not to embrace their Cherokee heritage. For instance, when asked why some people with Cherokee ancestry do not identify themselves as Cherokee, Luanne Helton was somewhat dismissive: "Well, they always have a choice. Everyone has their free agency to do as they choose to do. But if they have this experience come to them and choose to ignore it, they will not be happy. I have seen this. And what it is…is you're not being true to yourself. And you have to be true to yourself if there's going to be happiness in your life" (May 21, 2003).

Another racial shifter, a man who goes by the name of Running Wolf, interviewed at the Circle of Friends Powwow in Arkansas, also stated that he was different from Cherokees who grew up on tribal land, because he had a choice whether to identify as Indian. When asked to clarify what he meant, he implied that being Cherokee was a matter of personal sentiment, saying, "How did I come to find this out [to identify as Cherokee]? I felt it inside that I was one of the people, not like the European, white man, you know. My heart is with the people, the Indian people. It's the way I've always felt" (March 29, 2003). Not only does the doctrine of choice conflict with the historical necessity of hiding their identities that many race shifters recount, but also their association of racial identification with choice and free will inadvertently signals white skin privilege. In other words, having a choice about how to racially identify implies a social power that only white-skinned or physically ambiguous individuals can access. This is an awkward fact that few race shifters are willing to concede.

Part of the reason race shifters rarely make the connection between choice and privilege is that for some of them, being Cherokee by choice can imply a kind of moral superiority vis-à-vis others who have a more obvious American Indian appearance. The idea here is that race shifters are somehow better Indians because they chose to be Cherokee rather than have that identity ascribed to them at birth, as if voluntary association is superior to accidents of love and history. The privileging of choice in these instances implies that racial identity is linked less to social ascription than to personal recognizance and intuition. To "know one's heart," to be "true to one's self," to hear the "calling of one's ancestors," and to respond "in the Cherokee way" are all common catchphrases in the conversations race shifters have about what it means to be Cherokee and become Cherokee again after a long period of disconnection.

According to race shifters, such a perspective places them in a social space far removed from (and implicitly above) potential Cherokees in their own families who fail to appreciate the significance of their Indian ancestry, as well as from physically identifiable Cherokees who have always been Cherokee because they had no other option. This attitude separates them from family members who lack the wisdom, insight, or courage to reclaim their Cherokeeness, foolishly preferring to let such a fecund identity lie fallow. It also distances them from phenotypically white Cherokee citizens in the three federally recognized tribes, most of whom express a sense of "race cognizance" (Frankenberg 1993) and are well aware that their perceived whiteness provides them with social privileges not so readily accessed by other members of their families and tribal communities. Race shifters differ from these Cherokee citizens because they hold up choice as a moral standard and, in doing so, evade powerful racial differences that give some people more choices than others.

In addition to the doctrine of choice and its associated meanings, the rhetoric of some race shifters includes an evasion of their own whiteness out of a fear that it might undermine their claims to indigeneity. In the U.S. national context, multiracial individuals were asked until 2000 to choose one racial option, the implication being that one could not have or identify with more than one race, at least in terms of federal documents like the census. This racial logic suggested that, regardless of the complexities of actual ancestry or lived experiences, race shifters who identified themselves as Cherokee and white raised the possibility that they were neither Cherokee nor white but something in between—a "mixed blood," a "white Indian," or in the more disturbing language of Cher's 1973 pop hit, a "half breed."

As that song suggests, multiracial ancestry is often associated with awkward racial ambiguity and illegitimacy. I had a conversation in Hulbert, Oklahoma, with a politically prominent Cherokee Nation citizen, a Cherokee Baptist who was also a fluent Cherokee language speaker, who had a strange but pragmatic rationale for either/or rather than both/and racial classifications. I was showing him old photographs that he had asked to see of my Mississippi Choctaw relatives, and he said, "You know, the question you need to ask yourself, Circe, is if there was to be a war between the Choctaw and the United States, on which side would you fight? That's a question we have had to ask ourselves before, that we might have to ask ourselves again, and that you should ask yourself now" (January 12, 1996). Of course, the implication of his question was that, regardless of what he saw in my family photographs or how I identified myself, he would know I was really Indian only by the way I answered the question, which would reveal something important about my political commitments and community loyalties. Similarly, on a federal census document before 2000, I had to choose one possibility and forgo all alternatives. I had to narrowly declare where my loyalties lay, for to do otherwise was unaccountable. The implication is that multiracial individuals like myself are either white or Indian—that we could not possibly be both—and that only in such a politically and socially loaded context would our true colors, so to speak, be revealed. Violence would beget truth, as he saw it, and separate the weekend warriors from the real thing. Ironically, most race shifters would probably embrace this line of reasoning because it also privileges choice—the decision to enlist, as it were—over racial markers about which they might feel some vulnerability.

Given these monolithic understandings of racial identity in both federal and (sometimes) tribal contexts, many race shifters express a sense of racial insecurity: a fear that their whiteness will undermine their Indianness, just as it may have done for some of their relatives in the past. Though most interviewees responded by simply evading their physical or cultural whiteness, others grappled with what whiteness means in a more immediate way. Whether by choice or necessity, race shifters who currently reside in the South or who have southern roots tended to express a greater degree of race cognizance than those living in other parts of the country. By this I mean that they were more willing to acknowledge and talk about racial discrimination against nonwhites, particularly against Cherokees and other Native Americans with whom they now expressed solidarity. But even as they expressed this sense of racial awareness and empathy, most failed to make the connection between systemic racial discrimination and their own life experiences. They might talk about antiblack and anti-Indian racism, but whiteness and white privilege were hardly ever mentioned, certainly not in a way that would suggest firsthand experience with white skin privilege.[6]

A case in point: one race shifter in northeast Alabama was so deeply ashamed of his father's anti-Indian racism that he decided to rename himself with a Cherokee name as a way of signifying his rejection of his father's racism and acceptance of his own Cherokee ancestry. "I kind of quit my past life and started a new one," he said, the idea being that his declaration would neutralize his whiteness and the way that it was attached to a history of race privilege and southern white racism (Haynes 2001:92).[7] To race shifters such as this young man, claiming indigeneity appears as voluntary and straightforward as finding a new job. In practice, race is not something that can be so easily left behind (as an entire literature on the challenges of racial passing suggests), and it is extremely difficult to defy widespread systems of social classification based largely on physical appearance—as many race shifters will attest.[8] Nonetheless, this particular individual made a conscious decision to reject the legacy of white racism in his family by reclaiming a Cherokee identity. With the simple act of renaming himself, his history could be retold in such a way as to blunt the sharp edges of southern white racism and racial erasure.

As individual race shifters like this man struggle with the meanings that race has in their lives, they reveal the contradictions and tensions that surround their multiracial histories. Though they would prefer to keep the specter of whiteness under wraps, it still manages to emerge in their narratives in a variety of ways, particularly in the language of choice that they use to describe their racial becoming—without realizing that choice itself is a subtle marker of whiteness. In reclaiming his Indianness, the young man described above never gave up his white skin privilege but instead relied on it, for whiteness was the mechanism that allowed him to reclaim one racial self over another. Only by being unmarked in terms of physical appearance could he make the choice to leave his old life behind and start anew. There is an even more powerful way in which whiteness defines race shifters' experiences and shapes their sensibilities. As recent scholars have shown, for many Americans, whiteness has come to be associated with blandness or tastelessness; because whiteness is racially and culturally unmarked (has no particular flavor), it is often perceived as a kind of racial and cultural void (Delgado and Stefancic 1997; Frankenberg 1993; Hill 1997; Perry 2002; Roediger 1991; Ware 1992; Weismantel 2001). Indeed, a common interpretation among U.S. citizens is that blacks, Asians, Latinos, American Indians, and other indigenous people, such as Native Hawaiians, have culture whereas whites do not (although this is certainly not the case—all people have culture in equal degrees).[9] Given that whiteness is associated with cultural blandness and emptiness and a lack of racial distinctiveness, how do the specific connotations of whiteness shape a collective desire among multiracial individuals to reclaim redness?

During my ethnographic fieldwork, I listened again and again to the assertion that whites were, in effect, human containers devoid of racial and cultural content, not only by racial shifters but also by citizens of the three federally recognized Cherokee tribes. The statements of the latter were often quite direct, describing not a markedly different white culture, as I had initially expected, but a complete absence of culture. For example, Andrew Ross, a Cherokee Nation citizen in his late thirties, told me, "U.S. people have no culture of their own. I mean, the white people of the U.S. are the ones that have no heritage or culture. Blacks have Africa. White people, if their family has lived here since the country began, then they have lost their heritage, so they borrow. They *wannabe*" (January 19, 1996; italics added).

Some racial shifters expressed a similar sentiment, though this association of whiteness with cultural emptiness was much more personalized because they had previously experienced the supposed cultural loss and longing of white identity. For instance, a woman in her mid-sixties who is a member of a state-recognized group in Missouri described what it meant for her to identify herself as Cherokee: "When my sisters and I were being raised...we did not know any of our family.... We were just raised by my mother, and we had an emptiness inside of us that we did not know who we were or what we were. But when I found out and I began to search, I'm getting a fulfillment. I'm getting that emptiness filled. It's...it's beyond what you could even express. It's hard to keep the tears back even when I'm talking, because it means so much to me" (February 22, 2003).

Another woman, from northeast Alabama, said that she joined her tribe because it gave her an overwhelming feeling of home. She went on to say, "I have always felt something was missing, and I've blamed it on me. I've blamed myself.... But the moment I received my acceptance letter that had my card from the tribe, that emptiness was gone. The very moment, yes. It's gone. It's not there" (May 21, 2003).

Racial shifters use many narratives to describe their life experiences, but one of the most common is to recall their white past as a time of racial and cultural discomfort, emptiness, and longing that could be satisfied only by something else entirely. This is what sets racial shifters apart from whites who have not had these experiences and who do not share these perceptions and from Cherokee descendants who choose not to reclaim an indigenous identity. If this particular experience of whiteness is the key motivation behind their racial transformation, then what is it about Indianness, and more specifically Cherokeeness, that fills this void, that satisfies the sense of racial desire and cultural longing, that provides an ideal destination in the desperate flight from cultural dissatisfaction? How did they go from the garden-variety, low-level angst that often accompanies modern American life to grass dancing to "Dueling Banjos?" To make sense of this process will require some culinary metaphors, for the language of race shifting is in many ways the language of hunger.

The Cultural Fulfillment of Racial Belonging

If whiteness is an empty plate, then Indianness is a gourmet meal. For a majority of racial shifters, becoming Cherokee provides a visceral sense of cultural nourishment and enrichment, one in which the painfully empty becomes satisfyingly full.[10] Heart of the Wolf, an elder of the Northern Cherokee Nation of Old Louisiana Territory, put it this way: "White men, they don't have history. They don't have culture. They don't have what we have. I am still learning about our beliefs and ways. I am still hungry for anything I can learn" (February 23, 2003). But what is it about the substance of Cherokee culture that is so meaningful, so satisfying at this particular moment in time? Why not return to their European roots and delight in tossing the caber at a Scottish heritage festival or wearing traditional Romanian clothing? Why not wear wooden shoes or a Celtic cross? Although race shifters might have explored these options, ultimately their experience of white culture left them hungry, whereas even small portions of Indianness stuck to their ribs.

Compared with white and nonwhite identities, there appears to be something more exotic, something almost magical about Indianness that draws these individuals in and leads them to explore, reclaim, and at times magnify any connection they might have to Cherokee history, culture, and kin. Part of the attraction is the many deeply romantic, stereotypical values that have long been associated with Native American identity and culture—gender equity, democracy, environmental stewardship, and an original relationship to the land, to name but a few. Although any one of these could motivate a feeling of racial and cultural desire, two stand out as the most widely evoked among racial shifters. First is a specific type of spirituality, tied to communal ritual experience, that provides a sense of connection with the natural world and with other members of a given racial body. The other stereotypical value is a feeling of community belonging, a tribal sensibility if you will, in which the sum is greater than the parts—something that is the near opposite of the anomic individualism many race shifters evoke when describing the modern condition of whiteness. In effect, both stereotypical values signal the way in which Indianness can re-enchant the social universe.[11] Individuals may place greater emphasis on one or the other, yet both are usually present and are fundamentally linked to each other in the broader discourse of racial shifting.

Race shifters expressed the way they associated spiritual and communal belonging with Indianness, and more specifically with Cherokeeness, in the language they used to describe what being Cherokee means: pride in having a culture, belonging to a race, having a tribal family, and gaining spiritual wisdom, for example. All of these cultural attributes are antithetical to what race shifters (and others) associate with whiteness, such as a feeling of emptiness, a lack of culture, no sense of extended family, being spiritually unmoored, and shame—the latter being something that seems to come up primarily in the South. In other words, the specific social and cultural values attached to race in these instances are motivating large-scale shifts in racial self-identification and are resulting in an unprecedented flight from whiteness toward Indianness. It is not simply that one racial identity is perceived as being culturally empty and the other full (though this is a significant part of the motivation) but that whiteness is associated with certain undesirable characteristics and Indianness with desirable ones and that these prove to be the near opposite of each other. This is why no process of reconnection to a European ancestry could provide the symbolic inversion that most race shifters are seeking: whiteness itself is the malady, Indianness the cure.

When race shifters establish or reestablish their identities as Indians, part of what they find desirable is that they suddenly feel they have the moral authority to learn and use certain American Indian cultural practices that may have been previously closed to them. In this instance, because race shifters now openly identify themselves as Cherokee, they feel able to claim rights to Cherokee culture as they understand it. Ironically, many race shifters fail in their quest to access such cultural knowledge (which is often ceremonial and ritual), because they lack the resources, skills, or drive to obtain it, not to mention a willing teacher and a community of practitioners. Many people who find themselves in this situation turn to books, articles, the Internet, or any source of information they can access to cobble together a new form of cultural expression, something that they often name as Cherokee and as Indian. It is too easy to dismiss this process as frivolous or, worse, as pitiful self-deception. After all, people around the world reinvent culture all the time, sometimes intentionally, sometimes not. That is the way culture works, changing in time and space according to some new whimsy or need. For race shifters at this particular moment in U.S. history, Indianness appears to fill the need—but why?

Indianness is particularly appealing to racial shifters because it is so open to this process of reinvention. For racial shifters, as well as much of the broader U.S. society, because of their historical, social, or geographic distance from Native American nations and communities, Indianness has come to stand for almost anything they choose, at least anything that resembles their stereotypical expectations about what Indians should think, say, and do—such as caring about fellow tribal members, living in harmony with nature, or having mystical insights. Indianness is still viewed as being rich with meaning and tradition, in comparison with the perceived emptiness of whiteness, but what constitutes Indianness is open to interpretation.[12] In this case, rather than being innate or essential, racial identity is largely a social and cultural construct, making it vulnerable to manipulation. However, essentialism and constructivism are mainly academic ways of talking about race. On the ground, across the United States, nobody talks about such abstractions, at least not with the clinical vocabulary of the social sciences. Yet, through the hidden histories and joyful reclamations of Cherokeeness, race shifters make it clear that for many contemporary Americans, race is an increasingly flexible concept and that Indianness is the most malleable of all. Through the medium of culture, race shifters borrow, learn, adopt, and even create new practices and in the process reinvent themselves as indigenous people.

The "Original Whiteness" of a Cherokee Identity

In the process of rejecting whiteness and reclaiming indigeneity, racial shifters must also reclaim a specific tribal identity, a choice that has important social and political ramifications. As I mention in the opening chapter, the vast majority of racial shifters identify themselves as Cherokee, and the reasons for this are both fascinating and complex. The Cherokees are one of the largest and most well-known tribes in the United States. Ask just about anyone, particularly non-Indians, to name three Native American tribes, and you are likely to hear the Cherokees mentioned. No surprise, given the ubiquity of Cherokee images and identities in U.S. society. In fact, one could argue that "Cherokee" has come to have the same relationship to "Indian" as "Mexican" has to "Hispanic" or "Anglo" to "white" in the minds of many Americans, so being part-Cherokee stands in for being part-Indian in classic metonymic fashion.

A case in point: a colleague at another university told me that because she writes about Cherokee history, she had been approached by a man who identified himself as a Cherokee descendant. The scholar queried him about various aspects of his family history, such as where his relatives had lived and their surnames, and on the basis of his responses suggested to this man that his people might not have been Cherokee. The man insisted that he was Cherokee, that he had always been told so by his family members, and that he had could even prove it—he had a list of Cherokee words written down by his great-great-grandfather. Some days later, the man brought in what turned out to be a perfectly good Muskogee (Creek) word list. In all likelihood, this was not a case of intentional misrepresentation, in which this man or his family made an active choice at some point in their history to be Cherokee rather than Muskogee. Instead, it was simply a case of mistaken identity, revealing the kind of confusion that can happen when memory stretches over time, reaching back for specific connections that have become vague and tenuous across the generations.

Memory and time are always at play in the discourse of race shifting. Even for racial shifters whose families have elaborate oral histories regarding their Native American ancestry, specific social and cultural details are often lost or changed over time. For example, did great-great-grandmother have a clan? Did she speak her native language? Did she marry the man with whom she had children? Such answers are often hard to come by, because multiracial families have often worked hard to obscure their origins, sometimes for well over a century. When coming out of racial hiding, some race shifters seem to have seized upon Cherokeeness erroneously, such as when their grandmother or grandfather tried to remember the tribal identity of an older relative and mistakenly came up with Cherokee as a default option. Sometimes when the path into genealogical accuracy is not clear, people might choose something familiar from popular culture that resonates at some level.

Size is not the only factor, however. Race shifters with vague genealogies are not simply laying claim to the first large, well-known tribe that comes to mind, because they almost never claim ties to the Navajo Nation, the only other tribe that is as large and as famous as the Cherokee. Cherokeeness seems open to whiteness in ways that

Navajoness does not. To my mind, Cherokeeness is an ideal destination for race shift-ing because the tribe has a history of cultural adaptation, tribal exogamy, and relatively open standards of tribal citizenship. For many decades, being Cherokee has come to be profoundly associated with the likelihood of having multiracial European and Native American ancestry—that is, with being racially mixed in a particular way. Because so many citizen Cherokees look as white as racial shifters, the choice to identify as Cherokee makes perfect sense. Of course, this association ignores the fact that most indigenous people in the United States—particularly those whose ancestors lived along the eastern seaboard and bore the brunt of European and Euro-American colonialism—have multiracial ancestry in one form or another. Perhaps if Micmacs, Narragansetts, or Seminoles were as numerous and well known from American films, television shows, and pulp fiction as Cherokees, then race shifters with tenuous tribal connections might have looked to them. The Cherokee combination of apparent openness to whiteness and familiarity through pop culture has inspired a virtual stampede of racial reclassifi-cation. No other tribe signifies so conveniently, plausibly, and productively for the well-intentioned race shifter fumbling in the dark for a tribal home. Nothing else provides such a seemingly persuasive (if at times unspoken) explanation for a racially ambiguous or even strictly European appearance.

When pressed, racial shifters can be quite explicit about the association of Cherokeeness with white physical appearance—as in this statement by Vera Sheppard, a woman in her late seventies living in San Diego County, California: "The Cherokee people did not look Indian or what most people thought an Indian should look like. As I understand it, the Cherokee were not as dark skinned and did not have the angu-lar features of the Plains Indians. Appearance seems to make a difference to most peo-ple, even other Native Americans.... I feel that if one feels like a Cherokee, the appearance is unimportant" (June 16, 1996). This woman's seventy-year-old brother, Homer Schumacher, expressed a similar sentiment when he said, "The Cherokee peo-ple did not look the same as many other American Indians looked. Of course, at a very early time in American history, the Cherokee intermarried with the European, and so many of us do not look like what people think we should look like" (June 25, 1996). These siblings have developed similar explanations for why their appearance fails to meet the expectations of others. They seem to suggest that there is what I term an orig-inal whiteness to Cherokee identity, that Cherokees were distinct in physical appear-ance from other Native Americans at the time of European contact, that they were lighter and less angular, and that this difference was further reinforced by European and Cherokee intermarriage.

Some race shifters push the argument for original whiteness even further. Consider, for instance, the following statements by George Richey, the principal chief of the Southern Cherokee Nation, a self-identified tribe in northeastern Oklahoma, in response to a question about what Cherokees tend to look like: "You need to go back to when De Soto arrived in the Cherokee Nation, back in the 1600s. He met blonde-haired and blue-eyed Cherokees...and red-headed Cherokees. People come up to me and say, 'Hey, I have high cheek bones. I'm Indian.' I go, 'Hey, I don't and I am' [*laughs*]. And you've got to remember we've been in-bred, out-bred, up-bred, and down-bred. So what is a Cherokee feature?" (July 22, 2003).

Although there is no historical evidence that Cherokees had classically European coloring at the time of contact, it is well documented that Native Americans varied in physical appearance not only across regions but also within tribes. At any rate, historical accuracy is not the point of such statements. Rather, race shifters offer these as elaborate justifications for the disconnect between their Indian identities and white appearances, with the intention of suggesting that because Cherokees have always been white in appearance, there is no significant difference of history or experience between race shifters and Cherokees who look Indian in terms of physical appearance. What Richey went on to say in the same interview is quite telling in this regard:

> I don't believe there's such a thing as a full-blood Indian in the United States, or especially Cherokee, because we've intermarried for so many years. And the term "full blood" is kind of a misnomer. They may be a full blood as far as an American Indian bloodline, but when the Cherokees went to war, they would adopt their captives into the tribe. So Shawnees, Delawares, Natchee, Creeks, Catawbas, and Wakama Siouxans, all of those tribes and all of those cultures, and every tribe in the Southeast, their blood flows through Cherokee veins, because we adopted our captives. So, in that sense is why I say there is no such thing as a full-blood Cherokee.... Actually, the melting pot is not the United States. It's the Cherokee Nation [*laughs*]. (July 22, 2003)

According to Richey, because Cherokee history has long been characterized by adoptions, cultural borrowings, marriages, and other kinds of alliances across tribal and racial lines, the Cherokee Nation is a melting pot of assimilation that renders moot the question of what a Cherokee looks like. In an additional twist, Richey implied that being Cherokee is a monolithic experience that puts all self-described Cherokees on an equal footing. Because all Cherokees are mixed, both biologically and culturally, they are all fundamentally the same. Richey's argument is an extreme example of symbolic inversion, in which apparent whites are considered real Cherokees and apparent real Cherokees are made into something vaguely Euro-American.

Much of what I have been describing could be written off as innocent or naive attempts to square the circle of newly reclaimed Indianness with apparent whiteness, but the defensiveness has a darker side as well, as Richey's comment suggests. When race shifters feel attacked for their lack of Cherokee "authenticity," one response, extreme but not entirely uncommon, is to cast aspersions on the racial and cultural authenticity of federally recognized Cherokees. When racial shifters like Richey conflate their histories and identities with those of Cherokees who physically appear to be Indians, they overlook powerful differences of social experience that are based in large part on perceptions and understandings of racial difference.

As I demonstrate throughout this chapter, whiteness is both a tacit and explicit trope that fundamentally shapes the discourse of racial shifting. On the one hand, whiteness is merely a suggestion—a ghost of itself—when race shifters describe how their own indigenous histories have been subjected to a painful process of racial, social, and cultural erasure. Whiteness also hides in the language of racial choice and marks the difference between those who have racial options and those who do not. On the other hand, whiteness is explicit (and explicitly explained away) when race shifters suggest that they are Cherokee, in part, because—as they see it—real Cherokees look and act white, are the product of a melting pot, and are in many ways no different from the larger Euro-American population.

In all of these allusions to whiteness, a fundamental tension is revealed between race shifters' desire for alterity and their perception of equivalence. Race shifters view Cherokees (and by extension themselves) as being both different from and the same as their former colonizers. As a result, a strange racial alchemy is at work in which being Cherokee encompasses a comfortable exoticism. What fascinates me are the specific ways in which Cherokeeness and whiteness are understood as collapsing into and differing from each other—at times at odds, at other times blurring into one haze of possibility. Beneath this discourse is a changing sense of what constitutes sameness and difference and of how the boundaries are drawn between self and other, as well as a meaningful if somewhat delirious interplay between race, culture, and indigeneity.

In the case of race shifters in flight from what they perceive as white "emptiness," Indianness presents an attractive solution to their dilemma, with Cherokeeness representing the ideal resolution of racial ambiguity and desire. Cherokeeness meets the needs of this desire better than other tribal identities because it is comfortably exotic yet plausibly open to white individuals, more so than almost any other tribal identity. Cherokeeness allows race shifters to remain racially unmarked and in the mainstream and to maintain the privileges of whiteness when necessary or convenient, at the same time offering the social and cultural fulfillment of elastic alterity.

Reclaiming indigeneity is largely a quest for meaningful difference, one that can be plausibly embraced but whose depth should not be underestimated. At times, it even takes on the qualities of conversion, an overlooked aspect of this phenomenon that bears further investigation. In the chapter ahead, I consider in greater detail the spiritual and communal values attributed to Cherokeeness and how these might motivate people to reclaim their indigenous roots in particular ways. In this case, what lies beneath are not hidden histories and racial ghosts but tales of redemption in the most literal sense.

f o u r
Racial Conversion
and Cherokee Neotribalism

On August 4, 1987, deep in the age of Reagan, a man named Steven Miller became a Cherokee named Lone Warrior. The drama of that day is mostly lost. What remains is a tribal membership certificate, a single sheet of parchment with a rough image at its center—an amateur rendering of a hand spiraling up out of a fire, reaching toward the heavens, that seems designed to mark the document as Indian. Other than the awkward drawing at its center, every square inch of the certificate is covered in print, with words that describe the weight of the occasion. In choosing to become Lone Warrior, Miller signed an oath to "revive his Cherokee heritage and come to the aid of his people." The document also suggests that Miller was not alone: two witnesses by the names of Seeing Heart and Freedom Spring conducted a ceremony in which he stood before a sacred fire and received his new Cherokee name and a tribal roll number. The number did not come from the Cherokee Nation, the Eastern Band of Cherokee Indians, or the United Keetoowah Band of Cherokee Indians but instead was issued by the Pan American Indian Association—a quasi-tribal organization of American Indian descendants who, because they were unable to enroll in their tribes of origin, decided to launch a tribe of their own.[1]

With the ceremony in the woods and the certificate from that evening, Lone Warrior had accepted considerable responsibilities. "Insofar as I am able," the certificate states, "I pledge to honor and respect the traditions and the authority of my ancestral or adopted peoples." Lone Warrior was swearing to uphold a dozen promises:

1. To study the history, language and customs of my tribe;
2. To live as simply and naturally as possible and to stay free of the commercial pressures that would enslave me if they could;
3. To furnish my home with beautiful objects that will constantly remind me of my heritage;
4. To instantly come to the aid of any Indian, especially those of my own tribe;
5. To at least once in my life visit the remnants of my people;
6. To acquaint myself with the needs of my people and render aid whenever possible;
7. To experience a VISION QUEST at least once in my life [capital letters in original];
8. To oppose the desecration and commercialization of the graves and other sacred places of all Indians, and to work towards the return of sacred objects in museums and private collections to their rightful owners, and to work for a decent burial of the Indian dead on public display or lying in exploited desecration;
9. To obtain for myself the highest educational standard that I can;
10. To work for the preservation and conservation of our environment;
11. And to keep myself free from alcoholism, narcotics addiction, and any activities that would dishonor my name and that of my People. (Pan American Indian Association 1987)

Lone Warrior was vowing to live as a Cherokee from that day forward. Not only did he have to learn about Cherokee culture and practice it, but he also had to orient his world toward other American Indians, both living and dead—certainly a tall order. Sitting at my desk in Norman, Oklahoma, with a copy of this document in hand almost twenty-one years later, I have to wonder what has become of Lone Warrior. Does he still honor his commitment to an American Indian life? Does he still see himself as a Cherokee man named Lone Warrior, or sometime in the past two decades did he revert to simply being Steven Miller again?

* * *

I tell this story with a sense of respect and curiosity, fully aware that the mysteries of his life will remain forever closed to me. Although I do not know whether his commitments were deep and lasting, what I do know is that Lone Warrior's story, at least the one that is documented in his tribal membership certificate, suggests the kind of all-encompassing personal and social transformation that lies at the heart of race shifting. In my years of listening to such stories, I have come to believe that they are best understood through the lens of racial conversion—meaning a profound change in racial identification that is driven by new systems of meaning and new social contexts, some of which are spiritual in both content and form.[2] Because this is a novel context for thinking about conversion, I want to offer some additional clarifications about how and why I am using the term.

Within the scholarly literature, conversion has typically been defined as a type of sweeping personal change that, as sociologist Richard Travisano notes, entails a "radical reorganization of identity, meaning and life," regardless of whether it takes place in a religious or secular context (Greil and Rudy 1983:5–6).[3] Sociologists David Snow and Richard Malachek (1984:170) argue that conversion is not simply a minor shift in one's personal identity, beliefs, or loyalties but rather something more profound—a fundamental shift in paradigm in which what was once peripheral to one's universe of discourse and meaning takes center stage. The description fits the case of racial shifters quite well, for in various ways they almost invariably say that their own sense of Cherokeeness moved out of the periphery of their awareness to become a central organizing principle of their lives.

The process of racial conversion typically begins with people identifying themselves as Cherokee descendants—a much more modest assertion than claiming outright to be Cherokee. With varying degrees of ethnic modesty or cultural caution, they acknowledge their Cherokee ancestry alongside other cultural and national branches of their family tree. During this stage, they may say, for example, that they are part French, Scots-Irish, English, and Cherokee. They do not see themselves as having any particular social or political rights attached to their Cherokee identity, nor do they feel that they should reorganize their lives accordingly. Then, those who choose to make the transition take a giant leap (often quite sudden) toward Cherokeeness in their self-conception. What almost all race shifters interviewed for this study described is a process in which their own sense of Cherokeeness moved from the margins of their identity—as a distant memory and vague acknowledgment of a tribal connection—to occupy a central role in shaping their personal sense of self and their social lives. Rather than simply be Cherokee descendants, they became Cherokee people who needed to live a certain type of Cherokee life in the company of other Cherokees, however defined.

Although it may not be apparent at first glance, these Cherokee converts have experienced a shift in their core sense of identity in the same manner as a born-again Christian or a newly converted Muslim. Like other converts, their change in racial identification affects not only their spiritual beliefs but also their choice of behavior and social interactions from that moment forward (Heirich 1977:674). However, there are several problems with conceptualizing racial conversion—or any sort of conversion, for that matter—primarily in terms of a radical change in personal beliefs. The first is that conversion does not necessarily entail a complete deviation from prior convictions (Gabbert 2001:292, 305). In most cases, new beliefs, practices, and meanings coexist alongside old ones, and these different "moral authorities," as anthropologist Wolfgang Gabbert (2001:292) puts it, can each have "local or situational validity." So it should come as no surprise that racial shifters practice new Cherokee religious forms while also continuing to attend Christian church services or that they grass dance to "Dueling Banjos" in the context of a community powwow. Despite the plurality of forms that these practices take, they continue to name them and themselves as Cherokee. These continuities with the past do not imply that Cherokee conversion is less dramatic than any other form of conversion, only that conversion needs to be understood in much less rigid and absolute terms.

Another problem with thinking about racial conversion primarily in terms of changes in individual belief states is that many scholars, particularly in sociology, have tended to develop what anthropologist Salvatore Cucchiari (1988:417) calls "deprivation-ideology" models of conversion. He argues that within these frameworks, conversion is almost always explained in terms of the psychological makeup of individual converts—whether they experience alienation, despair, or deprivation, there is an assumption that something must be wrong that causes them to deviate from their prior convictions. Although it is true that racial shifters often describe their prior lives as alienating and unfulfilling, such feelings are not unusual in contemporary America. What is unusual is the way that racial shifters make sense of these feelings and choose to respond to them. By relying on the concept of conversion, I do not mean to convey any of the old baggage associated with the term or to cast aspersions on any of the individuals with whom I have come in contact. Their creative response to the experience of conversion from whiteness to Cherokeeness should not be characterized in terms of individual pathology, nor should it be viewed as something that is necessarily brought on by a state of crisis. Instead, the semiotic, phenomenological, and pragmatic dimensions of this process need to be respected as having value in their own right.

A final concern, perhaps the most significant, is the way in which conversion seems to unplug the individual from the collective, as if nothing could create a sense of religious identity other than solitary will. I am aware that conceptualizing conversion in terms of radical changes in personal beliefs runs the risk of de-emphasizing the broader social context in which such changes take place (Gabbert 2001:292; Hanks 2010:5). Cherokee conversion is a much more collective and socially dynamic phenomenon than this narrow view of the concept suggests. Instead, I take pains to show how this shift in racial identity has far-reaching social, economic, and political consequences beyond the realm of personal belief systems. Although spiritual beliefs and moral codes have an important role in racial conversion, a better way of conceptualizing it is as a fundamentally social process that involves, as anthropologist Robert Hefner suggests, an "adjustment in self-identification through the at least nominal acceptance of religious actions or beliefs deemed more fitting, useful or true" (Gabbert 2001:292). Such a definition enables us to appreciate how spiritual ideas and ethical values, as they are formed and expressed in new communities of practice, might motivate a change in racial identification.

In the following pages, I clarify how the subjective experiences of individual race shifters have led to the creation of new Cherokee tribes and conversely how social interactions within these communities have encouraged people to shift race on such a large scale. I am experimenting with conversion as an analytic lens, despite critiques that it can "muddy the historical relationship between subjective experience and collective existence" (Comaroff and Comaroff 1991:251). I do so because I believe that the term provides insights into the racial shifting phenomenon that we would otherwise lack.

In this spirit, the rest of this chapter explores how racial shifters narrate their personal transformations in ways that correspond to, and at times challenge, conventional understandings of conversion, paying close attention to how racial shifters describe their experiences and when the typical rhetoric of conversion is present in their narratives of personal change.[4] I begin with a description of the overall meanings that racial shifters attribute to Cherokeeness and Cherokee community life and explore how a need for spiritual and social connection might motivate racial conversion. Then, I outline how the power of racial conversion lies in it ability to provide a resolution of meaning, allowing Cherokee converts to reconstruct and reinterpret their own life histories according to a new Cherokee worldview, at least as it is richly imagined in many individually nuanced visions of tribal identity. Next, I show how Cherokee conversion is a process that relies on racial and religious proselytizing, in which the already converted seek out new potential converts, helping them to share a new racial and religious vision. Finally, I argue that the process of racial conversion has been fueled by recent historical transformations in the contemporary United States, where racial shifting has become a logical and meaningful response for an expanding demographic.

Life as a Born-Again Cherokee: Sharing a Spiritual and Communal Vision

When race shifters describe their conversion experiences, two main themes quickly become evident: spirituality and community. The first is a holistic spirituality tied to mystical knowledge and collective ritual experience. The second theme, Cherokee community, derives from the first, for it is Cherokee spirituality that provides race shifters with a sense of connection to the divine, the natural world, and one another. These intertwined values are what race shifters most associate with being and becoming Cherokee and are what they say most motivates their racial reclamation. For example, consider the case of Marge Peterson, a fifty-six-year-old accountant who is the principal chief of a group in Georgia. She explained that she did not receive any monetary benefits from being Cherokee but the spiritual compensations were immeasurable: "There is no spiritual feeling to compare with the ones I get when our tribe is returning Native American remains to Mother Earth, that have lain in museums and universities and medical examiners' offices for decades. Nothing compares to the fellowship and camaraderie at a traditional gathering or the high I get from the music of the drum and flutes and the dancing of the Native Americans. Nothing is as satisfying to my soul as seeing that native children have warm clothing for the winter and food in their bellies" (April 23, 1996).

Cara Wesley, a seventy-three-year-old homemaker from Washington, described tribal membership as a religious experience that heals the soul. "We get together as a family of two hundred and have our ceremonies and share our heritage, our spiritualities, our dancing, drumming, and singing, our feasts in our Native American Indian ways," she said. "You should see our campouts on our reservation.[5] They are so spiritually and physically uplifting!" (March 29, 1996). For both of these people, spiritual experiences were a significant part of what fueled the shift in racial identity. Previously white-identified Cherokee descendants, who once felt like atomized individuals with little racial or cultural content, are now experiencing life as members of spiritually based, tribal communities.

Why is race shifting so explicitly tied to matters of the spirit? One of the main reasons is that race shifters define Cherokeeness as a certain spiritual orientation. When asked to describe the key characteristics of a Cherokee person, they almost always mentioned spirituality first, as if to imply that Cherokees are inherently spiritual people, above all else. Typically, they described an all-encompassing spirituality that colors their everyday experiences. For example, Darren Bounds, a middle-aged member of a state-recognized tribe in Alabama, said that the key characteristic of a "real Cherokee" was "reverence in whatever form it comes out. It's not adherence to a particular religion, or anything, but just a certain recognition that we're here for spiritual reasons" (May 18, 2003). Brent Stephens in Oklahoma said that what characterizes Cherokee people is

> a spirituality that goes to the core.... Balance and harmony, which is the respect of all things, that type of thing is what I identify as the true Cherokee more than anything else. Where you respect your environment, you respect others, and a strong belief in the Creator, and living your life towards that. Where you're thanking the Creator for all the things you're doing, for your gifts, before you do things, [such as] when you're upsetting the balance and harmony of things, whether it's digging a hole, cutting off the limb of a tree, or whatever. That's what I identify as a true Cherokee. (June 25, 2003)

Luanne Helton, living in Alabama, described Cherokee spiritual beliefs explicitly in terms of faith: "The faith of the people, their faith is so strong. It's not 'Well, I believe if I pray it will be answered.' It's 'I know if I pray....' And it's a marvelous thing. The Cherokee people, the Cherokee people have always had a tremendous relationship with Father, Creator, Grandfather, whatever you want. And, again, it's not something that they do, the Cherokee do. It's part of who we are" (May 21, 2003). Although some of these individuals live in different states and belong to different Cherokee tribes that have emerged in the past two decades, they all define Cherokeeness in spiritual terms. Thus, it makes perfect sense that if they wish to be or become more fully Cherokee, they must practice some form of Cherokee spirituality in their day-to-day lives.

Like converts in other religious contexts, racial shifters tend to see their Indian awakening as bringing them closer to their true selves. Race shifters often talk about their conversion experiences as a process of finally coming to live as they were meant to live, something that can only happen after they begin to understand their long-repressed or neglected racial identity and its associated spiritual needs. As newly invigorated Cherokees, they often see themselves as innately spiritual people who need to practice some form of Cherokee spirituality in the company of other Cherokees. Once again, the social dimension is essential to the process of racial transformation. Race shifters usually seek spiritual community within the context of existing self-identified Cherokee tribes, or they create new ones, so that Cherokee neotribalism is a by-product of racial shifting. The smallest of these new tribes have only twenty or thirty members; the largest have closer to thirty-five thousand (Crutchfield and Belanger 2006). Most self-identified Cherokee tribes have a formal membership that is roughly between five and ten thousand (*Indian Country Today*, October 30, 2006).[6]

These local tribal organizations provide different opportunities for community engagement and religious exploration, some of which might not sound familiar to federally recognized Cherokees in Oklahoma and North Carolina. For instance, one tribe in Tennessee has frequent dances, potlucks, and healing circles (member Alice Wolfhawk, March 26, 1996).[7] Another tribe, in Georgia, has regular rounds of road trash pickup, barbecue suppers, new moon ceremonies, and sweat lodges (member Lisa Warrior Heart, March 18, 1996). Still another, in Washington, is even more comprehensive in what it offers tribal members, with a monthly council and clan meetings and various talking circles, including one for elders and one for women (member Cara Wesley, March 29, 1996). Wesley said that the talking circles work like support groups in which members can talk openly with one another about their personal problems. She also said that her tribe has corn-planting ceremonies each spring, a green corn festival in the fall, and other festivals throughout the year. The tribe has a long house, a seven-sided council house, and land where tribal members regularly drum, sing, and dance, something they also do at many public schools during the academic year. They also hold Cherokee language lessons every month and all tribal members receive a monthly newsletter (March 29, 1996).

Although federally recognized tribes might doubt the authenticity or appropriateness of the new Cherokee groups and their behaviors, it is undeniable that race shifters find profound meaning in them on multiple levels, including the spiritual. These new Cherokee tribes function not only as social and political units but also as religious ones. They provide a context in which race shifters can not only be Cherokee but also act Cherokee among people who accept them as such, and a significant part of acting Cherokee is participating in various types of community-based, highly experiential, religious activities.

In attending powwows, healing circles, sweat lodges, or other ceremonial events, race shifters have opportunities to confirm their status as Cherokees in contexts that are often nonjudgmental. In behaving as Cherokees with like-minded people, they come to recognize one another as Cherokees and to internalize that experience within their sense of self. The following description of a "coming out" ceremony that took place in

Alabama provides a good example of how this process works. Luanne Helton described the event:[8]

> A little boy had his coming out at a gathering I went to one time. This is the first time that they enter the circle as an individual, from there on [out]. And this little boy.... First, they did an honor dance, where they went to the circle and danced around the circle in honor of this event for him, and then when the honor dance was over, here were all these men—tall, strong men—gathered around this little boy, shaking his hand, encouraging him, speaking to him. And I saw that and I said, "There's no way this child is going to grow up and not know who he is. He is surrounded by people who know and acknowledge who he is to him."
>
> Among the Cherokee people and native people in general, it's allowed to practice who they are. The children have a stronger knowledge, a stronger sense of their own being, of who they are. When you find a young native child who's struggling and having difficulties, it's because that child is out of the culture and not in touch with his culture, because the native culture helps a person identify who they are, and that is so priceless. (May 21, 2003)

What Helton described is a classic example of a demonstration event, in which the little boy publicly confirmed his status as a convert and which, if taken as an isolated incident, might have no enduring significance for him.[9] However, this ceremony and others like it are not isolated events for many race shifters, and they need to be understood as taking place within a much broader context of consistent social participation. In recent decades, race shifters have developed elaborate social networks, as well as a variety of new cultural forms within them, that provide ongoing opportunities for them to experience life as Cherokees.

Whether it takes place on a daily, weekly, or monthly basis, regular participation in community activities and religious ceremonies helps to solidify racial conversion. During these social interactions, race shifters develop common religious ideologies that transcend the boundaries of their particular community. They come to believe that, as Cherokee people, they have a heightened sense of spiritual awareness and need for religious community, as well as a special ability to access mystical forms of power and knowledge. Heart of the Wolf in Arkansas explained, "[There are] things that we know, that we have no way of knowing" (February 22, 2003). Though occasionally race shifters have mystical experiences within the context of community ceremonies, more often they described them as taking place in the course of their usual day-to-day activities, albeit in a way that binds them to other Cherokee people. For instance, Brent Stephens in Oklahoma described a feeling that came over him when he was having a conversation with someone he had just met: "I've had a feeling among the elders I have met in North Carolina with the Eastern Band, as well as the ones in Oklahoma. It's like you're with them, you're talking, you know, and [you think], 'I know this person. I've met them.' You have that feeling of déjà vu with them" (June 25, 2003).

He went on to say that he liked the experience because he had "always understood Cherokees," implying that these mystical connections not only are typical of Cherokees but also allow Cherokees to comprehend one another on some other mystical plane of existence (June 25, 2003).

Prior to conversion, race shifters might not associate these mystical abilities with being Cherokee, but during the process of their personal transformation, they come to do so. Consider, for example, a conversation that took place between my research assistant, Jessica Walker Blanchard, and two members of a state-recognized tribe in Alabama. My assistant began by asking May Bellflower and Sheryl Jones whether there ever was a time in their lives when they did not openly identify as Cherokee. Bellflower was the first to respond:

MB: Not after I found out.

JWB: Why did you choose to identify yourself that way?

SJ: Because I had always heard my dad talk about it and he was getting on in years and I wanted to bring him into it, and he got a tribal card before he passed away.

JWB: He did? Oh, oh good.

MB: I had always been drawn to the Indian culture ever since I was little bitty. I wanted to grow up and be an Indian [*laughs*]. Little did I know, you know! Everything, you know, the cowboys and Indians on TV, I always pulled for the Indians!

SJ: Me too [*laughs*]!

MB: And, you know, that just stuck with me all my life. I had that desire, you know, so it finally came to pass. (May 17, 2003)

In this exchange, Bellflower implied that her youthful desire for all things Indian was driven by some unconscious knowledge of her own lineage. Later, the conversation took a more explicitly mystical turn when Walker Blanchard asked where Bellflower and Jones learned about Cherokee culture. Jones answered first:

SJ: Bits and pieces from my father. Uh, reading. It's always fascinated me and sort of [*hesitates*]...I don't want to get into this [*laughs nervously*]. I have feelings that...well, what would it be? Not a sixth sense.... What would you call that?

JWB: Like an instinct or something?

SJ: Yeah! Yes, and I've always wondered about it, and you know what you know, what you know! We're getting into it deep [*apologetically*], but....

JWB: That's OK!

SJ: My sister, ever since she's been a little girl, she's always had these dreams, and...they would come true! And I always thought she was spooky [*laughs*]. "Don't go dreaming about me!" I said.... I don't know what you call it.

JWB: Do you think it's a thing that's related to being Cherokee?

SJ: Yes. [To Bellflower] Wouldn't you think so? The Indian in your blood com-
       ing out? (May 17, 2003)

By the end of the conversation, Jones was attributing her own intuition and her sister's ability to foretell the future to their Cherokee blood and looked to Bellflower for
confirmation. Like many racial shifters, she associated being Cherokee, or even being
a Cherokee descendant, with a ready ability to access mystical knowledge about oneself, other people, and events that have not yet transpired.

Among race shifters, the source of this mystical knowledge is always Cherokee
ancestry, often referred to with the idiom of Cherokee blood. Such references to having Cherokee blood are not simply about lineal kinship, as most contemporary
Americans understand it, but rather a direct and ongoing connection with Cherokee
forebears that carries with it a hint of mysticism. Race shifters often believe that their
Cherokee ancestors maintain an active presence in their lives and are calling them to
return to Cherokee ways of being. For instance, Heart of the Wolf in Arkansas described
the spiritual guidance she received from her Cherokee ancestors: "I believe my grandmother's spirit brought me here, because since I have been here I have found my family on my Dad's side. I have learned the truth of my true bloodline. I am now involved
with my people. I now have my roll card and number.... Since I have found out the
real truth of who I am, I have been able to be the real me. I can now make everything
I wear. My grandmother and my great-grandmother's spirits inspire me as to what to
do, because before, I knew nothing about making any of our clothes" (February 23,
2003). Heart of the Wolf celebrated her ongoing communion with the spirits of her
deceased Cherokee ancestors. However, her relationship with these spiritual guides is
a product of her racial shifting in that she began to recognize their influence in her life
only after she discovered her Cherokee bloodline.

Blood has its own spiritual qualities in the conversion stories of race shifters. Like
the women described above, most race shifters used the idiom of blood as a metaphor
for kinship, as a way of talking about their Cherokee heritage in broad symbolic terms.
However, they also use it to literally mean that they have the actual blood substance
of their Cherokee forebears coursing through their bodies and that this powerful substance is what causes them to have mystical experiences, even when they do not
actively seek them out. For many race shifters, these experiences are a significant part
of what motivates their racial conversion. Consider how these themes converge in the
following explanation from Luanne Helton in Alabama, who tried to explain why people like her are choosing to identify themselves as Cherokees:

> Well, I call it, for lack of a better terminology or phrase, I call it their ances-
> tors calling them from the dust. That's what I call it. I've had so many people
> come to me at these gatherings and say things like, "I don't know why I'm
> here. I just got out riding around and ended up here." And yet, while they
> were there, this awakening began.... And being a spiritual thing, it...I don't
> know how to say what I'm trying to say. Being a spiritual event, wherein they

have some sort of spiritual experience that causes them to find their heritage, it's hard to ignore that.

But there are those that make the choice to ignore it, and they're not happy. I know people, now, but by and large, those that feel that pull, answer to it. They may not know why they go by a powwow and heard the drums and felt they had to stop. They may not know why they get a certain feeling at certain times in the year.... When I was a kid, in the late fall I used to get so depressed, it was not funny, and my granny Bullard would say, "Honey, that's your Cherokee blood. Hard time coming up, winter's on its way."... You have these things. You just can't ignore them and feel any degree of content. (May 21, 2003)

Like most race shifters, Luanne believes that when Cherokee descendants reclaim their Cherokee identities, they are responding to a call from American Indian ancestors who are actively leading them through a process of racial and religious recovery. After decades of racial dormancy, they might suddenly solve a long-standing genealogical puzzle and find the name of a Cherokee relative in an obscure courthouse document. Or they might find themselves at a powwow of a local Cherokee tribe, feeling a sense of sacred connection to the music, dance, and people without knowing why. Or they might meet an all-too-familiar stranger or have a dream that comes true or feel sad at a particular time of the year. The details of how these mysteries unfold are infinitely variable, but they all point in the same direction: race shifters believe that their conversion has happened for a spiritual reason, that their Cherokee ancestors are working through them, and that these ancesters are connecting them to a mystical world filled with great spiritual power.

Almost as if their ancestors are summoning them to enter a new Indian realm, race shifters describe them as calling out to them, inviting them to reclaim their lost heritage. Like Paul's on the road to Damascus, it is a spiritual invitation that cannot be ignored. Once they hear this call and recognize it for what it is, race shifters believe that they have little choice but to respond if they wish to feel any contentment in their present lives. Ultimately, what race shifters share is a vision of Cherokeeness as the key to spiritual happiness—only in becoming more fully Cherokee do they access a greater sense of spiritual and social belonging. Pulling at them through their own blood, their ancestors have guided them to their Cherokee destiny, to a place that heals old wounds of loss and assimilation and forges new bonds of meaning and purpose.

White Before, Cherokee After: Racial Conversion as a Resolution of Meaning

When racial converts talked about their lives, they often described a complex feeling of emptiness and longing that motivated their indigenous reclamation. When asked what her tribal membership meant to her, Heart of the Wolf in Arkansas replied, "Everything. I have a proud fulfillment in my life and in my heart that I've never had in my life. I needed to fulfill what was never there and to fill that emptiness that I had

had all my life. Not knowing what the emptiness was, that was very confusing" (February 22, 2003). She conveyed a common sentiment among race shifters—the idea that her previous life as a white Cherokee descendant was not quite right and that only in fully reclaiming her Cherokee identity and tribal ties did it come to be more meaningful and fulfilling. This type of autobiographical reconstruction is typical of religious converts, who tend to make clear distinctions in the way they characterize their lives before and after their conversions (Snow and Malachek 1983:266–269).

In a new narrative of self, race shifters discover a new frame for making sense of their lives in a satisfying way. Some scholars suggest that when converts reconstruct their life histories in an effort to better understand their personal experiences, "the past is not only shattered, the disjointed pieces are reassembled in accordance with the new universe of discourse and its grammar. Some aspects of the past are jettisoned, others are redefined, and some are put together in ways previously inconceivable" (Snow and Malachek 1983:266). According to anthropologist Peter Stromberg, converts often refashion their personal narratives, employing a set of symbols and ideologies that help them to "resolve enduring problems of meaning in their lives" (Stromberg 1990:42). This semantic refashioning does not happen all at once but rather is part of an ongoing process with a specific history. As converts assign new meanings to their experiences, they begin to see themselves and their problems in a new light, often in ways that are marked by moments of emotional intensity and psychological insight (Stromberg 1990:42–46).

Race shifters are no different, for they, too, begin to apply a new set of meanings to the world around them. During their racial conversion, they often adopt a Cherokee-centered perspective and use it to interpret their feelings and behaviors, as well as those of others. Whatever was wrong with their past lives can now be explained in terms of their alienation from "the Cherokee way." Conversely, whatever is right about their new lives is attributed to having identified more fully as Cherokees and participating in the social and religious life of a Cherokee community. Cherokeeness becomes the holistic framework that gives new meaning to their past, present, and future.

Given that this type of autobiographical reinscription is one of the bedrocks of conversion in general, we might wonder what specific problems of meaning race shifters are attempting to resolve in reclaiming their ties to a Cherokee self and world. One answer to this question comes from Sarah Glory, who served as principal chief of a state-recognized tribe in Alabama. A petite woman in her sixties with dark brown hair and eyes, she said, "In the four years that I was chief, I met many, many wonderful people. But I also saw people that had no family life, no church life, no nothing, so they wanted to join and belong, and you could just see this. And it was sad in a way" (May 18, 2003). According to Glory, some of the people who sought tribal membership were so socially disconnected that they were eager to belong to any group that would have them. June Davis, a race shifter in Arkansas, mentioned the need for community when she said that more people wanted to identify themselves as Cherokee because "in today's world, they're looking for security. They're looking for a home. Not necessarily in a house or anything, or in a single community, but they're looking for a home" (April 26, 2003). Jessica Gates in Alabama linked this need for community to the sense of loss and isolation that is brought on by modern living:

> I think that's part of the reason that people join [Cherokee tribal] groups. I think they're looking for some of that loss. They're also looking for a community and an identity. Because they've been so scrambled and so isolated in so many ways, they're searching for that. They're searching for some of the understanding of the old ways, because the newness, the modern things are just not meeting people's needs. You have such violence. You have such drugs and alcohol that is out there, and people really want what's better for their children. Not saying that the old ways were that great. Listening to Grandmother talk about some of the things she does, I couldn't do that, in any shape or form. But you want to continue some of that heritage and not lose it, because we've lost so much. (March 29, 2003)

All three of these women echoed the idea that racial conversion is being driven by a basic desire for community belonging in an age of cultural fragmentation and alienation. For many race shifters, what characterizes contemporary American life is a sense of cultural loss, social isolation, and insecurity, even homelessness if you will. They attribute these feelings to "today's world," "modern things," and "newness." What they describe bears a remarkable resemblance to Durkheim's (1933) now classic model of anomie—the sense of isolation and despair that comes from feeling adrift in the swiftly changing tides of modernity.

Race shifters might be adrift in the chaos of modernity, but most are not nostalgic for some stereotype of the pre-Columbian good old days. For example, Jessica Gates made the point that life was difficult in the past, even for Cherokees, especially when people like her grandmother had to labor hard to meet their basic needs and often had to hide their Indian identity. Gates expressed a common sentiment among race shifters: they do not wish to return to the past in some naive way, but simply to escape the social isolation and stress of the present, and being Cherokee allows them to do so. June Red Wolf Jenks in Georgia implied much the same thing: "[T]ribal membership means having a family, a clan, *a safe haven from Euro-American culture*, a place where I can be me" (March 9, 1996; italics added). And Marge Peterson, who also lives in Georgia but is a member of a different community, stated, "Living one's culture is never easy in contemporary society, but it can be done.... Although I was raised a Cherokee, my grandparents lived in a state of denial to outsiders out of fear. And for a brief period in my life, I wanted what my white peers were getting. I was young and stupid. This organization gave me back my identity and returned me to my roots and gives me pride in who I am. *It gives me a sense of acceptance in a world that is alien*, to share my religion with others of my race. I am a half-breed by birth, but totally Cherokee in my everyday life" (April 23, 1996; italics added). For both women, the experience of living in contemporary American society is both alien and alienating, seemingly more so for these Cherokee descendants than other white Americans. Cherokee neotribalism provides a hopeful alternative—a sense of connection, a place of social, cultural, racial, and religious belonging, and an opportunity for self-realization. For many race shifters, the vision of Cherokeeness is less nostalgic than it is utopian, for they do not wish so much to return to an ideal past but rather to create a more idyllic and communal present.

For alienated contemporary Americans such as race shifters, the conversion experience brings with it a comforting sense of the familial—a brotherhood or sisterhood of indigeneity. Many race shifters described tribal membership as belonging to a large extended family that provides mutual support, understanding, and acceptance. Kristin Wilson, a woman in her mid-forties who is a district representative for her tribe in Alabama, expressed it this way: "I love this tribe. They're warm, and...you'll find that most of them are very loving people, very giving. It's kind of like a big family, this tribe is. But you'll find that within any family, we squabble, but you know, that's life. Anytime, I can call just about anybody in this tribe and they will come. That means a lot to me" (May 17, 2003). Brent Stephens, who lives in eastern Oklahoma, described his tribal membership in a similar fashion. "This is my family," he said. "These are some of my best friends. I've gone through some very hard things that I couldn't have gone through without them. They're my second family. That's what the membership means" (June 25, 2003).

Luanne Helton in Alabama also used the term "family" when describing the emotional and material support she received from her tribal community after her Cherokee conversion. I quote from her at length because she made the connection between tribe and family repeatedly, giving a strong sense of the emotional intensity with which she recounted her experience of community. Helton began by saying, "I am a much more complete person now than I was before I joined the tribe" (May 21, 2003). She went on to describe the various kinds of support she received from her "tribal family" during her recent separation from her husband:

> It's real hard for me right now.... I believe that marriage is sacred. I believe
> that marriage is not something to be taken lightly. It's something that you
> work at, give your all, and it is very difficult for me to face the end of my mar-
> riage. And my tribal family this weekend, I just can't.... I can't put it into
> words. My husband came up there Sunday [to a community-sponsored pow-
> wow], and my initial reaction when I first saw him was to duck and run. He's
> not a bad man or anything. He's not been cruel as far as beating me or any-
> thing like that. That's not part of the picture, but that was my initial response.
>
> But I found myself suddenly surrounded by members of the Warrior
> Society. Members of the Warrior Society are veterans of military service, and
> they stayed between him and me. Well, I had told one man, my tribal brother,
> that he was coming and I just didn't want him to bother me. I was there this
> weekend for my uplifting. I needed that, and this is what happened. That

security, that safety was the most overwhelming thing I have felt in a long time. There was nothing that I wanted, but people brought me food. I've had tribal members give me money since this has come about. It is so overwhelming to me, to experience the love of my tribal family. Like I said, when those warriors surrounded me, it overwhelmed me…it overwhelmed me…. And I mean that's the way the Cherokee have always been. I was just so totally overwhelmed by the outpouring of love and by the safety I felt….

I had a couple come to the house today and brought a big box of frozen foods out of their freezer and gave me a hundred dollars. Now that's just the kind of people they are. It's not just me. Anybody! They would do this for anyone in the tribe. There's just such a tremendous, overwhelming sense of family, and I couldn't live without it. (May 21, 2003)

One of the most obvious aspects of Helton's statement is its passion. Clearly, she was facing a difficult period in her life and was better able to cope because she had the emotional and material support of her new tribal community. Equally important, the tribe provided her with a sense of family connection—something she asserted no less than four times—and it did so at the very moment when kinship ties were breaking apart in another arena of her life.

Not surprisingly, what is happening with these new tribal families is similar to what is taking place all across America in small support groups such as Alcoholics Anonymous meetings, women's book clubs, and Bible study groups. As religious studies scholar Robert Wuthnow chronicles in his thought-provoking book *Sharing the Journey: Support Groups and America's New Quest for Community*, 40 percent of all Americans regularly participate in such groups because they provide individuals with a greater sense of spiritual connection and community (Wuthnow 1994:31–55). They also enable people to build their self-esteem as they come to understand and narrate their lives in new ways (163–186). Although the metaphor of family is regularly used to describe these powerful experiences of belonging, Wuthnow argues that support groups are distinct from actual families that live and interact with one another on a daily basis, because "they do not bind their members to one another legally or financially, nor do they link individuals with the wider legal, governmental or economic structures of our society" (361). He suggests that support groups are "more like informal circles of friends than families or churches" and stresses that their ties are much more transient (361).

Although the parallel between support groups and these new tribal communities is obvious, there is an important distinction. The kinship that race shifters described themselves as experiencing is not just a metaphor but also a literal usage that assumes (or imagines) a biogenetic bond, a common tribal blood. In fact, these new Cherokee tribes are often composed of interrelated families who descended from the same set of hypothetically Cherokee ancestors or even a single Cherokee individual. Certain ancestors function almost like totemic figures, drawing people together into a greater sense of relatedness. It matters little whether people can actually prove their genealogical ties or whether those ties are real or imagined. Theirs is still a kin relationship, as anthropologists have always understood it. If individual tribal members choose to no longer participate in the life of the tribal community, they are still counted as relatives. Even members of self-identified Cherokee tribes who do not trace their genealogical ties to the same set of relatives still view themselves as kin. For every racial shifter I have ever spoken to—and every citizen Cherokee, for that matter—Cherokee blood is a literal, shared substance that binds them to one another and to every other Cherokee on the planet. In discovering and reclaiming these connections, Cherokee converts are extending their kinship ties in new directions that allow for the creation of new tribal communities. Whether or not their families of origin are intact, these new tribal communities still do the work of family, helping to provide emotional and material support to their members. These relationships also help to justify their collective identity and their movement away from what they believe to be normative patterns of self-absorbed existence in contemporary America.

Although some observers might find it hard to imagine that race shifters could feel these communal and familial ties so intensely, given their recent discovery or reclamation of their Cherokeeness, the new communities of converts often function like more established tribes. They become the basis not only for a new sense of identity but also for a new form of civic engagement, in which the local tribe becomes a vibrant site of social support and political action. Whether they organize to host a local pow-wow, to feed and clothe their needy, or to seek state recognition, racial shifters are translating communal ties into social and political action, much in the same way that federally recognized tribes have done. With the utopian zeal and unabashed idealism of the recently converted, race shifters are creating new tribes, new micro-polities—or new forms of civil society, if you will—that find their coherence in ideas about shared blood, religion, race, culture, and kinship.

Cherokee neotribalism is fundamentally about a search for transcendence and a life filled with meaningful social interaction. When race shifters talked about what life was like before their conversion, which they experienced primarily as white people, they described a feeling of emptiness and melancholy, as if they were barren vessels yearning to be filled with meaning and purpose. They eventually found meaning in their family genealogies and often in the one nonwhite lineage that they are willing to acknowledge—their Cherokee ancestry, no matter how ill defined. For them, Cherokeeness has an unusual ability to provide a meaning system that affects every sphere of their lives because it implicitly harkens back to a historical moment when spiritual, familial, political, and other spheres of society were largely inseparable.[10] Whereas whiteness was experienced as disconnected, Indianness provides the solace of the whole. Talking about this newfound sense of holism, some race shifters told southern studies scholar Joshua Haynes (2001:69) that being Cherokee means that they "can embrace a whole culture, and a whole heritage that is unique." More specifically, June Red Wolf Jenks said that it provides "a different way of viewing the world, a comprehensive mindset versus the narrow mindset of Euro-Americans" (March 9, 1996). According to these perceptions, being and becoming Cherokee seems to be a sturdy basis on which to build community and locate a meaningful sense of self.

Given the transformative effect of this new, all-encompassing meaning system, it comes as no surprise that race shifters have become deeply attached to their recovered Cherokee identity and its redemptive powers. Consider, for example, the comprehensive and highly emotional manner in which several race shifters described their experience of tribal membership. Drew Martin in Oklahoma said, "It's the first thing I ever really had in my life, you know. I always knew it, but your enrollment and everything, brotherhood with friends and your people—it just means the world to me. It means more than anything I ever had" (May 24, 2003). Homer Schumacher in Southern California said, "To my sister, myself, and the rest of our family, being Cherokee is a very important spiritual and emotional part of our everyday life" (June 25, 1996). Raven Moon, a sixty-six-year-old sales clerk in Washington, said that her Cherokee tribal membership provided her with crucial moral and emotional support. "It means a lot to me," she said. "I have learned the medicine teachings and teach them to those who truly seek them. It is my life" (March 29, 1996). Darren Bounds in Alabama said that being part of a tribe is "a pride thing." His words showed a hint of defiance about how federally recognized Cherokees might judge him: "It's being a member of a group of people who walk a certain way and have a certain attitude about life, who stand up and make that claim of 'This is my home.' I may not be part of the politically correct Cherokee Nation according to certain politicians in Oklahoma, but I'm part of the greater Cherokee nation. I put my name and my life on the line as being part of that" (May 18, 2003). In each of the previous examples, race shifters in different states and different regions of the country talked about Cherokeeness as a fundamental aspect of their post-conversion existence—it is "my life," "part of our everyday life," "the first thing I ever had in my life," and "I put my life on the line." Their personal transformation is so complete that their everyday lived experiences are now viewed through the lens of Cherokeeness rather than whiteness.

Spreading the Cherokee Gospel: Racial Conversion as a Social Process

Such dramatic personal transformations do not happen in a social vacuum. Racial conversion is fundamentally built on shared ideas about descent, spirituality, and community. As for any convert, individual faith is rarely enough. Instead, racial shifters must come to see themselves and their world differently, in ways that correspond to the perceptions and beliefs of other converts (Greil and Rudy 1983:24). This social dynamic, of "coming to accept the opinions of one's friends," as sociologists John Lofland and Rodney Stark have put it (Greil and Rudy 1983:24), is central to any type of conversion, whether religious or secular. However, for Cherokee descendants to accept these new ideas and opinions from their Cherokee-identified peers, they must first be exposed to them on a regular basis, and social networks are critical to the process. Some race shifters learn of local Cherokee communities from newspaper ads or Web sites and then begin to attend powwows, business meetings, and other social activities on their own, eventually developing a social network. The vast majority describe an experience of having met a racial shifter who persuaded them to start thinking of themselves as Cherokee and who then took the responsibility for introducing them to the local tribal community (which in almost all cases is not a federally recognized tribe).

Consider how this process of socialization worked in the following two stories from Darren Bounds. First, he related what his life was like when he was simply a Cherokee descendant; then, he compared it with life after having met his tribal sister and becoming a Cherokee tribal member:

> We didn't make a big deal about it when I was growing up. It was like a lot of
> Cherokee families. It was one of those...the family just formed the habit of
> saying "Yeah, okay, there's something a little different about Granny," but we
> don't run around saying, you know, "We're Cherokee. We're this. We're that."
> I don't know about anybody else, but in Alabama up until about 1975, it was
> illegal to be a Cherokee, so no wonder people kept their mouth shut about it.
> And it didn't really become significant to me until about mid-life, when I ran
> into my [tribally adopted] sister and a bunch of things conspired to bring me
> into this tribal family. It's the way things happen. Like they say, when the
> Creator is ready for you, you'll be called. (May 18, 2003)

Because his family members were tight-lipped about their Cherokee ancestry, what ultimately brought about Bounds's transformation and allowed him to answer his Cherokee calling was not a family narrative that needed to be investigated but an encounter with a race shifter, a woman who had already gone through the process of self-transformation and was an active member of a local tribe.

Earlier in the same interview, Bounds provided more detail about this important social encounter with his adoptive sister:

> Some time back in the early 1990s, Brave Heart Jumping and I adopted
> each other as brother and sister. At first, we were pretty busy talking about
> other stuff, you know, but I knew she was a member of this tribe and that I
> was Cherokee by blood myself but hadn't really been involved in the culture.
> And gradually, you know, she got me into it. She did, on her own, a little
> ceremony of adoption and gave me a new name, [*says it in Cherokee*] Dancing
> Heart Jumping. Shortly after that, I started coming to powwows, picked up
> my application forms, and got, you know, formally into the tribe. (May 18,
> 2003)

Without Brave Heart Jumping, Bounds might never have come to identify himself as anything more than a Cherokee descendant—much of his current Cherokee identity would have remained dormant. Because she took it upon herself to gradually and repeatedly expose him to Cherokee cultural traditions within the context of her tribal community and to eventually perform the ceremony that would name Bounds as a fellow Cherokee and an adoptive kinsman, he eventually came to see himself as a Cherokee person. Once he realized that he was really no different from her—that they were both equally Cherokees in the eyes of the local community—he took the next step of formally enrolling as a member of one of the largest state-recognized Cherokee tribes in the South.

Bounds's socialization process is typical of Cherokee reclamation. Those who have already experienced racial conversion feel a certain responsibility to bring others into the tribal fold, encouraging other Cherokee descendants to see themselves as tribal people and providing a social context in which they can do so. Whether it takes place between friends, among family members, or in a public setting, the process is a form of religious and racial proselytizing.[11]

Consider the case of Homer Schumacher, a seventy-year-old man living in Southern California who helped start a new Cherokee tribe with his sister. Schumacher regularly gives public lectures to local clubs and school groups about what it means to be Cherokee. "When in public, I talk about and give guidance to other people of Cherokee heritage and encourage them to live our ways," he said. "Even though I do not hold a card from Tahlequah [the Cherokee Nation], I have helped many others to acquire theirs" (June 25, 1996). Schumacher actively encourages people who already identify as Cherokee descendants to live more fully as Cherokees. He helps those who meet the citizenship requirements for the Cherokee Nation, to research their genealogy and fill out the paperwork so that they can formally enroll in a tribe that has the benefit of being federally recognized—something he has been unable to attain for himself. This rhetoric of providing guidance to those in need seems to evoke the stereotype of a wise elder, who in this case points others to a destination he himself cannot reach. For those that do not meet the requirements, he provides a different and much more local tribal context in which they can participate as tribal members alongside his sister and himself. What Schumacher is doing in California is much like what forty-two-year-old Chief Bart Davidson of the Tennessee River Band of Chickamaugan Cherokees is doing in Chattanooga—providing a "sense of tribe for disenfranchised, mixed-blood Cherokees in the area" (April 17, 1996).

Schumacher and Davidson are working to convert people who already identify themselves as Cherokee descendants. Other racial shifters are directing their energies toward people who do not yet identify themselves as Cherokee in any capacity. For example, Chief Seeing Heart Stevens, the founder of the Pan American Indian Association—the same quasi-tribal organization that Lone Warrior joined—described how he and his wife proselytized among her family members. "My wife and I visited her extended family in Alabama and East Tennessee, and not one would admit to having Indian blood," he recalled. "We finally cracked a couple and advised them that it was both legal and proper to be an Indian. Now, they are all Indians" (March 11,

1996). At his and his wife's urging, family members who had stubbornly refused to identify themselves even as Cherokee descendants now see themselves as American Indian people.

Another example of how racial shifters draw in new converts who do not yet identify as Cherokee can be seen in the case of David "Deerwalker" Madison, a forty-year-old man from Alabama. Madison described how he came to be involved in a state-recognized Cherokee tribe, even though he had no prior knowledge of his Cherokee ancestry:

> I had a very close friend. He was an elder in the tribe. His name was Eddie
> Eagle Running, and he was kidding me one day. I would go to powwows with
> him and his son and all, and he said, "Have you ever thought about running
> your genealogy and just checking to see?" And I said, "No," and he said,
> "Your family looks Native American, you know." And I said, "Well, I'm kind
> of light-skinned." And I said, "I got a brother that's really dark, but you know,
> I'm kind of light skinned." And so he got to teasing me, and I thought, well,
> I'm just going to check this. And I got to checking, and I found out that I had
> between one-eighth and three-sixteenths Cherokee [ancestry]. I joined the
> tribe about ten years ago and served four of those years as district board coun-
> cilman.... Now, I'm literally working for the tribe. (May 18, 2003)

Although Madison only discovered his Cherokee connections a little more than a decade ago, he has undergone a radical personal transformation during the past ten years—he now goes by the name of Deerwalker, serves as a tribal councilman, and makes his living working for the tribe and selling Cherokee arts and crafts at local powwows. His transformation is now complete, at least in his self-conception and the view of his local peer group.

Though his experience might seem atypical, several of the people interviewed for this project mentioned that their journey into greater Indian identification began when another racial shifter urged them to investigate their family tree. They required external prompting from someone who could relate to their situation and almost sense their Cherokee potential. The social context is crucial: when and how racial shifters learn of their Cherokee ancestry matters less than the social process by which it is given greater meaning. In other words, most Cherokee descendants do not wake up and suddenly declare themselves Indians. For any number of reasons, including the ambiguity of their personal appearance, lack of cultural knowledge or social connec-tions, or even feelings of ambivalence, most Cherokee descendants are more comfort-able with qualifying their claims to indigeneity: they are part Cherokee, or they have a Cherokee great-grandmother, but they themselves are not Cherokee. Only a smaller (but still significant) number of Cherokee descendants undergo racial conversion and begin fully identifying themselves as Cherokee people.

For those who do make this transition, their new perspective develops during extended social contact with other race shifters. Whether established racial shifters try to convert family members, friends, or strangers, they approach the world as if it is filled with potential Cherokees. Working with an evangelical mindset, these proselytizers often demonstrate a sense of mission as they search out Cherokee descendants who are just waiting to be discovered or those who already know of their ancestry but are waiting for someone to come along and help them to understand what it all means. In either case, the process is about the already converted helping the Cherokee initiate to undertake the equivalent of a faith journey into greater degrees of Cherokeeness. In a manner that might make some federally recognized Cherokees wince, both the proselytizer and the convert regard the church of Cherokeeness as a welcoming place, with open doors and few gatekeepers. In the minds of race shifters, indigeneity is the big tent that is open to anyone with Cherokee ancestry who comes to share their racial, religious, and social vision.

Searching for Transcendence: Racial Conversion and the American Dream

Since the early 1970s, more and more Cherokee descendants have been reclaiming an American Indian identity and forging new tribal ties—they have undergone an experience of racial conversion and are now true believers in the "Cherokee way." If we look at the recent historical context in which race shifting has been proliferating, we can better understand why this large-scale racial and social transformation is happening now. I would like to suggest that for racial converts, the power of Cherokeeness at this moment in American history is three-fold: first, it provides them with a totalizing meaning system; second, this meaning system speaks to a quintessentially Euro-American desire for hope and transcendence; and, third, it does so in a way that is particularly significant at this time in U.S. history.

In the brief but insightful book *The Real American Dream: A Meditation on Hope* (1999), American studies scholar Andrew Delbanco writes that American history has always been colored by a search for meaning, which he breaks into three phases. The first, focused on God, was conveyed through Christian narratives for nearly two hundred years as Puritans, Quakers, and other small religious sects broke off from their neighbors, fled England, and established a new life here, often coming into close contact with local indigenous communities. The second phase, focused on nationhood, came into being as Christianity was being challenged by enlightenment rationality: it started with the American Revolution and lasted through the 1960s. In this phase, self-actualization was no longer about one's individual religious faith or relationship with the divine, but rather a collective vision of "citizenship in a sacred union" (Delbanco 1999:4–5). Finally, in the third phase, focused on the self, the idea of transcendence was disconnected from any coherent system of shared, public meanings and began instead to be "pursued through New Age spirituality, apocalyptic environmentalism, and the 'multicultural' search for ancestral roots," as well as the overall animating principle of consumption (5). Delbanco is careful to acknowledge that, although a different narrative was prominent in each era, all three have always coexisted (111) without a sharp dividing line between them.

I believe that the third and final phase, with its focus on the self, is most relevant to our understanding of Cherokee conversion. Not only does it characterize the present moment in American history, but its onset also coincides with a rise in neoliberalism, a phenomenon it both reflects and generates. Delbanco (1999:96–97) suggests that something died in the period between the 1960s and 1980s—a collective vision of the country. When this happened, he argues, the self replaced the state as the primary source of hope for contemporary Americans, and the stage was set for capitalist fragmentation. Under the neoliberal policies that followed in the 1980s and beyond, focus on civil society gave way to a focus on individual responsibility and choice, the logic of the market, and hyperconsumption. All bets were placed on the individual, and instant gratification—rather than older visions of civic virtue or metaphysical salvation—came to characterize the good life (96–111).

With this shift toward the self, many Americans began to experience an unexpected side effect that was hardly pleasurable—a sense of social decay and isolation. Instead of belonging to traditionally civic-minded voluntary associations, they started "bowling alone," as political scientist Robert Putnam (2000) puts it in his much quoted formulation. With a similar vision of an atomized America, Delbanco (1999: 114–115) argues that contemporary Americans still crave transcendence and still have the same need for hope but what is different about the present moment is that the means to achieve this dream are inadequate. In other words, people now search for meaning in the context of voluntary associations and small support groups that are "clubbish and resolutely local, and unlikely to lead outward toward a sense of connection with an overarching human community" (114)—an unfortunate move that reflects a turn away from public engagement and a loss of any hope attached to a broader public.

If we apply Delbanco's model to race shifters, then their attempt to find fellowship and community in the new, local tribes they have created becomes nothing more than "low forms of tribalism and cliquishness" (Delbanco 1999:91). However, I believe that what Cherokee converts are doing is much more profound. Yes, some elements of Delbanco's description of the contemporary political moment do apply: race shifters are searching for transcendence and often fixate on their individual behaviors and choices as the means to achieve it. They are also oriented toward their local associations and away from the broader public sphere in which they have experienced so much rejection, often from federally recognized tribes and agencies within the federal government. However, Cherokee neotribalism, as well as the holistic conversion at its core, is a much more powerful and all-encompassing social movement than the kinds of voluntary and often temporary associations Delbanco is describing, such as health clubs, quilting circles, or even the Sierra Club.

What I want to suggest here is that racial conversion is more significant and more profound because within it, all three narratives of American hope—God, nation, and self—are powerfully present in a way that resonates deeply with many race shifters. In their interactions with one another, race shifters usually define their Cherokeeness in spiritual terms and learn that, if they attend to these matters of the spirit, self-actualization is possible. But unlike the more eclectic and individual questing of New Agers (Brown 1997:115, 141), "born-again" Cherokees are more dependent on a communal context in which to express themselves. The creation of new Cherokee tribes is therefore a necessary step toward individual salvation. Co-creating a satisfactory spiritual community for themselves and others who have shared their racial journey, they form new Cherokee tribes that provide a context for them to be Cherokee and act Cherokee within a community of like-minded believers. As these new tribes come into being, they do not simply replace earlier models of *civitas* with *communitas* or substitute one form of communitas for another.[12] Rather, they are a contemporary form of politics that offers both civic engagement and communal spirit in a combination that allows racial shifters to find profound remedies for the ills of the modern, neoliberal age.

To put it another way, new Cherokee tribes offer local spiritual community as an antidote to the excesses of American individualism, secularism, and anomie that racial shifters seem to have been experiencing with particular intensity under neoliberalism. Not quite nostalgic, Cherokee converts are antimodern in a way that evokes Jackson Lears's classic study of early twentieth-century American elites, *No Place of Grace: Antimodernism and the Transformation of American Culture, 1880–1920* (1994). In this celebrated work of cultural history, Lears explores how turn-of-the-century upper-class, white Americans were rejecting "the evasive banality of modern culture" and "attempting to rekindle possibilities for authentic experience, physical or spiritual—possibilities they felt had existed once before, long ago" (Lears 1994:57–58).[13] Lears's elites sought their possibilities in faraway places, in terms of both time and geography, turning to the cultural traditions of medieval Europe and "the Orient" for an exotic solution to their problems. One can imagine this as an analogue to racial shifting, but important differences separate contemporary race shifters from Lears's seekers of a century ago—particularly concerning the role of the self in these transformations.

Lears (1994:306) argues that earlier reformers often lacked "any but the vaguest of ethical or religious commitments" and that their obsessive efforts to find a more meaningful existence were almost always self-referential: "In a secularizing culture, where larger frameworks of meaning were fading, the antimodern quest for 'real life' often focused on the self alone" (58). Although this statement might characterize many American reform movements, it does not apply to racial shifters, who have intense spiritual commitments and who forge such meanings and sentiments in the context of community engagement.[14] Though their racial journey is about restoring a fragmented self and uses the self-referential language of individual will and choice, the members of these new communities come to identify with one another on the basis of their shared bonds of spirit, blood, kinship, culture, history, race, and indigeneity. And as we will see later in the book, they also see themselves as tribal members, as part of a polity that interacts with local, state, and federal authorities for the common good of tribal members. Their self-actualization is fundamentally a social process, developed around collective identities, meanings, and experiences. For this reason, it represents a new twist on the phenomenon that both Lears and Delbanco have sketched in earlier contexts.

Of course, cultural historians have not been the only scholars to address these topics. Returning closer to my own disciplinary home, I would suggest that one way to better understand this shift in racial identification as a form of conversion is to consider what anthropologists and sociologists working within the Weberian tradition have argued about religious conversion. Their work tends to examine the imposition of Christianity within contexts of colonial expansion, so religious conversion is almost always viewed as a process that emerges from a search for meaning in the face of rapid social change and modernization: "These scholars have suggested that a rapid explosion of social horizons, such as occurs under colonial and postcolonial conditions, often engenders a felt need for a more coherent doctrine, a more highly rationalized faith than is offered by 'native' religions. However logical in their own right, goes the argument, those religions are ill-equipped to make sense of the forces unleashed by European modernity" (Comaroff and Comaroff 1991:249). The logical conclusion, then, is that conversion tends to take place when there is a lack of fit between belief systems and sociopolitical circumstances. I want to explore this model's utility without embracing its limitations—for instance, it assumes that conversion is brought on by a state of crisis and that individuals cannot live comfortably with incoherent and widely variable systems of meaning.[15] If we avoid such reductivism, the model can help us to understand the powerful role of meaning systems in racial conversion.

In some respects, Cherokee conversion pushes the Weberian model in a new direction, for rather than looking to European and Christian belief systems, racial shifters are turning to indigenous perspectives as a way of better understanding their circumstances. Because racial shifters feel out of place and alienated within modernity, they begin to use what they deem to be Cherokee points of view to make sense of a changing world and to better explain their roles and relationships within it. In interacting with other racial shifters, they come to see themselves as victims of settler colonial intervention, as people whose Cherokee relatives were forced to give up a variety of social and cultural forms, including spiritual beliefs and practices that did not fit with Christianity. Coming to see previous generations of assimilation in terms of loss and erasure helps them to make sense of their current feelings of spiritual and social alienation. They need to reclaim what has been taken from them, to become Cherokee again, to forge new tribal communities as places of social and spiritual homecoming.

Their conversion is certainly racial in part, because they describe themselves as people who were once misidentified as whites and who are now appropriately identified as Indians, but it entails other, equally profound transformations: once settlers, now they are indigenous; once socially alienated, now they are part of a tribal collective; once spiritually unmoored, now they have new moral convictions; and once culturally empty, now they are fulfilled. Cherokeeness is not necessarily a more coherent doctrine than whiteness, but it does offer a new version of the old narrative of hope. As racial converts, they give new meaning to the past and present and discover a new direction for the future—one that is filled with alternative moralities, new forms of community and kinship, and a greater sense of self-worth.[16]

That race shifters should find so much meaning in reclaiming their ties to indigeneity should come as no surprise, given that from the earliest days of the republic, Americans have looked to American Indian tribes for models of community, spirituality, and self-fulfillment.[17] As Philip Deloria argues in his insightful 1998 book *Playing Indian*, whether dressed up like American Indians during the Boston Tea Party or sporting buckskin and beads as part of the hippie counter-culture, Euro-Americans have long used indigenous forms and expressions as a way of redefining themselves—first as something other than European and eventually as something other than what characterized most of modern American society. However, the move was always about claiming to be indigenized, not indigenous. The early American colonists might have claimed to be made over by their relationship with this land and its original people; the Boy Scouts of America, American Indian hobbyists, hippies, and New Agers might have claimed to act like American Indians and even to channel ancient American Indian souls. But none of them claimed to actually be Indian. Racial shifters, in contrast, do make this claim, and this is part of what makes this social movement so radical and new.

If the promise of the American dream once stopped at the color line, now maybe it does so in reverse fashion, at least for those with white privilege. The vast majority of these racial converts describe their experience of contemporary whiteness as being plagued by guilt, loneliness, isolation, and a gnawing sense of racial, spiritual, and cultural emptiness. If that is the case, then no wonder they choose to migrate out of whiteness and look for meaning elsewhere. To repudiate their whiteness does not mean that they have given up their white-skinned privilege or that they could do so even if they wanted to. It simply means that they are able to find meaning, hope, and transcendence in identifying as American Indians in ways that they never could before when they simply identified as whites.

But as always, there is another side to the story. When race shifters reject their whiteness and reclaim their Cherokeeness, it often goes beyond the realm of the spirit and into the street, as it were. Indigenous reclamation is also a political act—one that is backed by American notions of biological race and genealogical belonging. Some race shifters are aware that, once they begin to identify themselves as Cherokees and to create new Cherokee tribes, their actions have profound political implications across the United States, both locally and nationally. Others, however, are much less politically conscious and see what they are doing only in terms of their local community and its individual relationships and needs. Either way, what happens at the local level does not stay there but rather seeps out into the world and begins to shape broader understandings of what it means to be Cherokee, to be indigenous, and to be a citizen of an indigenous nation. The stakes are high in public debates in which existing

Cherokee tribes respond to the newcomers and try to protect their own sociopolitical boundaries and rights of sovereignty. In the next section of the book, I relate what those on the other side of the fence have to say, and I take a closer look at how federally recognized Cherokees in Oklahoma and North Carolina are reacting to the race-shifting phenomenon.

PART TWO
Citizen Cherokees

They are fulfilling a prophecy from an old medicine person, that there will come a day when everyone will be saying that they are Cherokee. They are growing in numbers, yes, and in the end times, only Indian blood is going to be left. A hole will appear in the sky. People will run around confused, and the water will be poisoned. Then, Mother Earth will be ready to give up.

> —*An elderly man living in rural Oklahoma who is a citizen of the Cherokee Nation, January 19, 1996*

Self-identification does not make you a tribe, just like self-canonization does not make you a saint.

> —*Ellis Burt, Texas attorney who specializes in American Indian law* (Dallas Observer, *September 21, 1995*)

five
Shifting Race, Shifting Status
Citizen Cherokees on "Wannabes"

Coated with a week's worth of road grime, the travelers finally arrive at the ᏣᎳᎩ (Cherokee) Cultural Center,[1] the weariness of having traveled more than a thousand miles etched across their faces. Long strawberry-blonde hair hangs in wisps on the middle-aged woman, who sits quietly on the couch twirling a lock between her fingers. I can almost hear her sigh as she retreats into the shadow of her husband's presence. He is nearly seven feet tall, with a round gut that looks as though it could be shot from a cannon. He wears a red baseball cap with ᏣᎳᎩ emblazoned across the front, Minnetonka brand moccasins made of fringed suede that lace up to the knee, a turquoise, black, and red Southwestern print ribbon shirt tucked into hip-hugging Wrangler jeans, a large belt buckle with the *End of the Trail* motif,[2] and a feather dangling from the end of his long, gray-brown ponytail.

He sits across the table from an older Cherokee man whom he mistakenly assumes is the authority in a room full of Cherokee women. He begins talking about how he owns an Indian shop in north Florida and has become the main source of information for the local community on Indian ways. When children have questions about Indians, they come to him. He wants to know how he can set up a Cherokee cultural center like the one here, in Tahlequah, Oklahoma, so that he can help other Indian people who have lost their way and are trying to return to their traditional language and culture. He says that his grandfather was a Cherokee medicine man and a seer and that he has

91

inherited his grandfather's gift, along with his steel-blue eyes, something that sets him apart from other Indians in the family. He wants to know whether there are elders in the Cherokee community who will teach him how to use and control his powers.

"Well, I can't really answer that question. You have to go and ask those people themselves, and if it's meant to be, then they'll teach you," the older Cherokee man manages to say before the visitor resumes talking. The big Florida man seems so eager to share his story and connect with other Cherokees that his excited speech feels like a levee breaking, like something long held back finally giving way.

"Well, I need some advice, then. Maybe you can help me," he says, hardly stopping for a breath. "I have this sweat out in back of my place, a tradition taught to me by some Southwest medicine people. I know I'm supposed to use willow poles, but I can't find any in my area, so I use oak instead."

The elder looks up at the visitor, and the three Cherokee women stop their conversation long enough to listen. One of them gives me a knowing look, as if to say, "Take note, anthropologist." The big man continues.

"Now, the Southwest people, they use sixteen poles, and the Cherokees, well, I think they're supposed to use seven. But I can't handle that. It's too tight on my back, and I get all constricted. So I use ten. Suits me better."

One of the three Cherokee women gets up from her seat and dismissively throws the word *yoneg* (white man) over her shoulder as she leaves the room, and still the visitor continues to talk. The big man is bursting with stories, but as he tries to forge connections—to establish that he is, thinks, and acts Cherokee—he inadvertently signals certain stereotypes that push his audience away.

"I know it's not traditional and all," he says, "but that's not what I'm so worried about. You see, we got this lady who comes to the sweat who keeps trying to pass herself off as a medicine woman. She's a wannabe." The Cherokee elder's expression changes not a wit, but the two remaining women raise their eyebrows, signaling their shared sense of irony. "And that's not the worst of it," the big man continues. "When we get together for our sweats, I swear, every time this lady just ups and takes her clothes off. Now, you tell me, what am I supposed to do with that business? I mean, that's just not right."

The Cherokee elder takes his time before he speaks. He contemplates the big man's words, letting their various meanings wash over him. Finally, he clears his throat and begins, "Well, I don't know much about sweats. That's not our tradition. What I do understand from those who have been willing to teach me is that you go into a sweat as you come into this world. That's why the men sweat first, then the women," he says calmly, matter of fact, as if speaking to a child. "But I don't know…maybe you know better," and with that subtle statement of disapproval, he redirects the river of words back to the man who is left swimming in his own confusion.

After a long silence, the elder gets up from the table, bringing the conversation to an end. Though somewhat stunned at the dismissal, the big Florida man still manages to be courteous and to thank the elder for his time. "*Wado*," he says in Cherokee, and then turning to his wife, who even now sits twirling a lock of her hair, he takes her by the arm and gently adds, "C'mon, Sugar. Let's go."

*　*　*

Federally recognized Cherokees in Oklahoma and North Carolina often find themselves face to face with people like the man from Florida who, in their eagerness to reclaim Cherokee tribal ties, have adopted a stereotypical Native American identity born of the Hollywood western and other popular media. These individuals might don generic Indian-style clothing, assume an Indian-sounding name, sprinkle their speech with newly learned Cherokee words, or speak of the Great Spirit and the evils of the white man, all in an effort to set themselves apart from the non-Indian mainstream and to mark themselves as indigenous people. Such claims and practices are tolerated in many contexts, both Indian and non-Indian, but they can be offensive to life-long Cherokees and to Native American people more broadly.

Consider, for example, the sweat lodge that the man from Florida described running on his property. Because it is not specifically a Cherokee practice, rarely if ever does one find federally recognized Cherokees in Oklahoma and North Carolina using a "sweat," and then, only when they are participating in an intertribal event, such as a program for troubled American Indian youth. When the man from Florida spoke about his sweat lodge, a red light went on for the citizen Cherokees in the room. From later conversations, I suspect that their response was one of quiet caution, a hesitancy to see a ceremony that belongs to a particular group of people fall into the hands of those who, out of ignorance or illegitimacy, might do it (and themselves) harm. Even if the tradition at risk is from another tribe, citizen Cherokees are often sensitive to issues of cultural appropriation and misrepresentation. To many of them, building a sweat lodge in a hodge-podge fashion is akin to building a church and substituting a large plastic X for the crucifix. Most Christians would not tolerate such an insult, much less people frolicking naked on the altar and explaining to a curious public, "Hey, it's the Christian way."

Though the behavior of the man from Florida represents a more assertive reclamation of Cherokeeness than what I have seen in most race shifters, it is not exceptional. For example, in his brief time at the Cherokee Cultural Center, the man exhibited a constellation of familiar behaviors that caused Cherokees in the room to classify him as a "wannabe," the term that is most often used to describe and disparage a non-Indian who wants to be Cherokee.[3] The most obvious of these behaviors included his heavy-handed, pan-Indian style of dress, his open quest for spiritual knowledge and experience, and his self-identification as a Cherokee without specific kin and community references. The scene also captured the misunderstandings, tensions, and even bruised feelings that frequently characterize interactions between citizen Cherokees and race shifters. Not all race shifters dress in a stereotypically American Indian fashion, rename themselves with names styled after the movie *Dances with Wolves*, or boast about a Cherokee princess in the family tree. However, enough do engage in these clichéd behaviors that citizen Cherokees have come to use them to draw distinctions between themselves and community outsiders, especially those race shifters who seem to crowd in upon Cherokee communities in ways that might induce cultural claustrophobia.

As this discussion suggests, when federally recognized Cherokees encounter race shifters, powerful stereotypes come into play. Both citizen Cherokees and race shifters carry a set of assumptions about what is or is not appropriate Cherokee behavior. For citizen Cherokees, who are the focus of the next chapters, these stereotypes help to establish a discursive boundary around an idealized notion of Cherokeeness, as well as a practical standard for deciding who gets in the door. These assumptions frame questions about tribal belonging and about who should or should not be included within the body politic of the tribe. Many citizen Cherokees debate these questions in different ways—different from race shifters, different from one another, and different from how I initially thought about them. In many ways, these conversations are part of a larger discussion about Cherokee immigration. Though my use of the term might strike some readers as odd, Indian tribes are polities with their own governmental bureaucracies, figures of authority, systems of justice, laws, geographic boundaries, cultural contexts, political ideologies, histories, and shared senses of peoplehood. All of these are the classic characteristics of nations, but in indigenous nations, with their diverse constituencies and various resources at stake, debates about the boundaries of citizenship are understandably fierce.

Though there are many interested parties in these debates, I turn now to citizen Cherokees and their perceptions of race shifters for several reasons. First, their opinions of race shifting have very real effects: it is citizen Cherokees who have the power to make tribal law, amend tribal constitutions, and choose to exclude or include race shifters within their national boundaries. Second, because citizen Cherokees associate race shifting with whiteness, their take on the phenomenon provides a window into their construction of whiteness, Cherokeeness, and racial difference more broadly. A sizable amount of scholarship has explored how whites construct American Indian difference (Indianness in the white imagination, or *The White Man's Indian* [Berkhofer 1979]), but only a handful of scholars have tackled the flip side of this relationship, that is, whiteness in the Indian imagination.[4] Exploring citizen Cherokee perceptions of whiteness, including its association with race shifting, will allow us to better understand the flow of power in and around such racial discourses and how that power is enacted.

In light of these concerns, this chapter explores several important labels that citizen Cherokees use when they describe and classify race shifters: the overarching term "wannabe" and two of its subsets, "New Ager" and "Cherokee princess."[5] Although they are not the only labels applied to race shifters, they are the ones that dominate conversations about race shifting among all three federally recognized tribes in Oklahoma and North Carolina. Each of these labels defines race shifters as fundamentally "other," as non-Cherokee and more specifically as white. Other terms, which I take up later, such as "outtaluck," "descendant," and "Thindian," are more ambiguous. These labels also carry a set of related explanations about why the bearer of the term would want to reclaim a Cherokee identity. As I hope to show, citizen Cherokees almost always view racial shifting as a status move, an effort on the part of whites to acquire forms of symbolic and material power that are now attached to indigeneity. Whether or not the details of these arguments are true, they provide a window into the overall production of racial value in Cherokee contexts. Unpacking this discourse helps us to see the different economic, social, cultural, and political values attached to both Cherokeeness and whiteness and how these different values might motivate specific racial desires and a large-scale migration from whiteness to indigeneity. Race shifters might experience a profound conversion to indigeneity, one that remakes their identity and worldview, but not everyone in Indian country, especially citizen Cherokees, has faith in their transformation.

Racing and Classing "Wannabes"

You can be almost anywhere in Cherokee country—at a stomp dance, the diner down the street, or someone's house—and if you bring up people who have consciously chosen to reclaim an indigenous identity, citizen Cherokees almost always label them "wannabes." I never used the term unless someone else did first. During my fieldwork, I tried to avoid it because of its distinctly negative connotations, but I had a hard time communicating the scope of my research without someone else invoking it. During formal interviews and informal conversations, I would describe the phenomenon of race shifting, hoping to avoid leading questions, and people would usually end up saying something like, "Oh, you mean wannabes! Why didn't you just say so?" Or someone would introduce my project on my behalf and say, "She's writing about wannabes." Often, I would avoid any confrontation by allowing this shorthand to stand in for the complexities of what I was really writing about, but I always tried to bring the conversation around to a more neutral place. As much as I sought to use less loaded language myself, I often heard my interviewees moving in the opposite direction, toward the ideologically charged realm of stereotype.

Stereotypes frequently came into play when citizen Cherokees talked about "wannabes" and characterized them in racial and political terms. When citizen Cherokees use the term "wannabe," they are almost always describing a physically white individual who is not a citizen of a federally recognized Cherokee tribe. A "wannabe" might be a member of a state-recognized Cherokee tribe, but typically he or she is someone without any form of official recognition who merely self-identifies as Cherokee. One Oklahoma Cherokee man I interviewed, Thomas Watie, a fifty-four-year-old Cherokee language teacher, said that as far as he was concerned, "wannabes are white until they prove otherwise, but what characterizes this group of people is that they can't prove [their Cherokee ancestry]" (January 12, 1996).[6] Unlike "white Cherokees" or even "white Indians," terms meaning people who are white in physical appearance but who have documented their Cherokee ancestors and met the genealogical standard for tribal enrollment, "wannabes" are understood as noncitizens, non-Indians, and non-Cherokees.[7] They are, as Watie said, "people who are trying to be something they are not," who meet neither the political nor the racial definition of tribal belonging (January 12, 1996).

The racial component of the "wannabe" label does not stand alone but, as is so often the case, blurs into ideas about class. When citizen Cherokees articulate a conception of "wannabes" as whites, they frequently link this whiteness with certain class characteristics, mainly with a gritty, working-class standard of living and at times even with dire poverty.[8] For example, in a joint interview with John Ross, former chief of the United Keetoowah Band and current citizen and employee of the Cherokee Nation, and with Troy Wayne Poteete, former Cherokee Nation tribal council member and current tribal justice, I asked how they would describe the people who were drawn into race shifting, "wannabes" as they termed them. Ross said, "Well, I think to me...it's people who are not well off, but white people mostly." Poteete added, "Generally, I see a less educated, less sophisticated white person" (August 1, 2003). Both Ross and Poteete suggested that "wannabes" are whites with a relatively low class standing. Echoing this characterization, Richard Allen, who also works for the Cherokee Nation, described a conversation about "wannabes" he had with someone from a different tribe in Oklahoma and how that person had said, "In Oklahoma, we'd call these people poor white trash" (July 31, 2003). Though the expression "poor white trash" originated from Allen's companion rather than from Allen himself, he seemed to endorse the phrase as a valid description of at least a good portion of race shifters. The statement is not unlike what Betty Baker, a feisty clan mother from the Eastern Band, told me when she declared that "wannabes want to be Cherokee so they don't have to be white trash anymore" (October 22, 2003).

When citizen Cherokees articulate the complex motivations behind race shifting, the first order of explanation is almost always a material one, the idea that poor whites want to be Cherokee for the presumed financial and material benefits, such as free health care, housing, per capita payments, college scholarships, and hiring preferences. Melissa Hunter, a thirty-nine-year-old citizen of the Eastern Band, explained it as follows: "They think we've got abundant housing, that we're just going to put them in a house. There's this whole idea about our lifestyle out there in the general public—that the federal government hasn't done anything to help—that paints us as a bunch of freeloading Indians that get free hospital care, free education, that we have all this free land we don't have to pay taxes on...and, I mean, that's not true" (October 22, 2003). Hunter's argument that financial gain motivates racial shifting is characteristic of what citizen Cherokees say in both Oklahoma and North Carolina. However, Eastern Band members have traditionally been much more vocal and explicit about this concern than their Oklahoma counterparts, largely because theirs was the first of the three federally recognized Cherokee tribes to experience the added pressures and payoffs of casino money.[9]

Since 1995, Eastern Band citizens have been eligible for per capita payments generated by a successful tribal casino operation, and many fear that tribal newcomers are motivated by this potential source of income. Helena Johnson, a twenty-eight-year-old college student who works in the Eastern Band tribal enrollment office, told me, "Personally, I think they want [tribal citizenship] for the money now. With the casino opening...people know we get benefits from that. I mean, people will call and say, 'How can I sign up to get that casino money?'" (October 22, 2003). Johnson supported her argument by saying, "I've been working here since December of 1998, and I know that I've heard [a fellow employee] say when we started getting per capita payments that [enrollment inquiries] just shot up, just like that," snapping her fingers for emphasis. She continued, "Some days, we may have more people coming in or phone calls than others, but there's not a day that goes by that, I bet, we don't get at least twenty-five to thirty phone calls" (October 22, 2003), implying that these are individuals hoping to cash in on a newfound connection to the tribe.

I heard these arguments from Eastern Band members in fall 2003, when I visited the reservation to do interviews for this project, and in the course of one of our conversations, I was asked whether Cherokees in Oklahoma shared their perceptions. I said that most Oklahoma Cherokees agreed that material benefits motivated race shifting among poor and working-class whites, but I was quick to add that this collective perception had not been borne out in my own research. I described how the race shifters I had interviewed varied greatly in class terms and how many of them had explicitly denied any financial motivations behind their desire to reclaim a Cherokee identity. Eastern Band members were not impressed. They argued that I needed to be careful about accepting such claims at face value.

Robert Thompson, who works at the Eastern Band tribal museum, made such a case when he told me that he had heard numerous people claim that their sole motivation was knowledge, not money: "I'm doing my genealogy...but I don't want anything, you know. I'm just trying to find this person [an ancestor] and just to know that I'm Cherokee. I don't want anything. I don't want any per capita. I don't want any of your benefits, but I do want to know" (October 22, 2003). Thompson stated that he typically responds to these assertions by saying, "Well, if you already know, then why are you wasting your time trying to find out about them? If you already know, then why are you doing this?" Thompson said he believes that the only reason people try to document something about their family history they already believe in their hearts is that, in the end, "they do want the per capita, because they do want this other stuff" (October 22, 2003).

Eastern Band citizen Betty Baker was even more skeptical of these disavowals, saying to me, "Any time they say, 'Oh, it's not about the money!' it usually is. So I don't care what they tell you. It's still about money" (October 22, 2003). She continued, "You know, I mean, how can you be proud of who you are when you don't know who you are or where the hell you come from? God! I don't care what anybody tells me. Their reason for going on and on and on about being Cherokee, it's about the money, and I'll never be convinced otherwise" (October 22, 2003).

In each of the previous examples from Oklahoma and North Carolina, ideas about race and class were articulated together, describing "wannabes" not simply as whites but as poor whites. In its most cynical form, the stereotype suggests that wannabes are whites who have nothing to lose, who have nothing better to do with their racial identity than cash it in like so many casino chips. Because race shifting is conceived of in specific race and class terms, citizen Cherokees rarely see it as something that poor people from other races engage in or as something that middle-class or wealthy whites would likely desire. Rather, citizen Cherokees associate different types of impoverishment, in both material and symbolic terms, with the specific racial and class status of "wannabes," and it is for this complex set of reasons that they believe it is primarily, though not exclusively, poor and working-class whites who want to be Cherokees.

Beyond Materialism: Other Forms of Racial Value

Citizen Cherokees tend to follow the money, at least when they assume that material forces are at work in the mechanics of race shifting. Yet, their skepticism toward race shifting is not based exclusively on the presumption of material greed, which many Indian people associate with whiteness for obvious historical reasons. They also recognize more symbolic values attached to Cherokee identity and how these might motivate working-class whites to shift their racial status. The link between whiteness and "wannabes" plays a critical role in these interpretations because federally recognized Cherokees view whiteness in much the same way that race shifters do—as a state of being that is racially, culturally, and socially unfulfilling. Scholars sometimes talk about the unmarked quality of whiteness, meaning that its actual substance often goes unrecognized. This lack of visibility sets up whiteness as flavorless or even as an imaginary void, one that race shifters might seek to fill and that citizen Cherokees might use to explain the "wannabe" quest. In fact, many Cherokee citizens express such sentiments in plain English: "I can't really name anybody from other racial or ethnic groups that are seeking [to be Cherokee] except for what you would consider white, Anglo-Saxon, Protestant people," Richard Allen of the Cherokee Nation told me. "My experience has been, they are a people who are in essence white and seeking something that they just don't have in their lives and hoping to find it in the Indian world" (July 31, 2003).[10]

Citizen Cherokees are aware that symbolic capital might be at work in the hearts and minds of race shifters and almost always focus on the supposed blandness or emptiness of whiteness as another way of explaining "wannabe" racial desire.[11] But citizen Cherokees give this interpretation several different inflections. The seeking of an American Indian identity, at least as citizen Cherokees articulated it, signals a host of racial, cultural, and social longings, many of them with significant psychological connotations. Some people suggested that "wannabes" are uncomfortable with their identity—with who they are in racial, social, and cultural terms. Others put it more in terms of deracination. "You know, they don't know who they are," Melissa Hunter said: "They have no idea. Everybody's so mixed, or they haven't kept up with it, that they don't know who they are" (October 22, 2003). Others perceived a sense of desperation arising out of deracination. "Desperate for what?" I asked. "Desperate to know who they are! To identify with something," Diana Terrapin told me (July 31, 2003). Still others, like Jean Blackwell, an employee at the Cherokee Nation's cultural resource center, spoke with compassion about how Cherokee identity might be a salve to the wounds inflicted by the tumult of contemporary life: "Wannabes are trying to find an identity because it is such a cruel world. They are trying to come full circle. They want a sense of being, a sense of self" (January 29, 1996). Going beyond more narrowly psychological explanations, many federally recognized Cherokees linked this desire for an identity with a need for social belonging. "They want to be Native American so bad," Megan Cassis, a Cherokee Nation citizen, told me. "They just feel that need to belong. They need a link with something, even if they can't trace it. It still gives them that feeling of belonging" (February 7, 1996).

John Ross, a fluent Cherokee language speaker in Oklahoma, spelled out an additional motivation for race shifting: "The Cherokee people always had a history. They got the culture, the heritage. And the immigrants that came over, generation after generation, they don't have that, and they want that part of our heritage" (August 1, 2003). Here, Ross used "immigrants" as a stand-in for "whites," and even though this usage overgeneralized the immigrant experience as one of cultural assimilation, it served his purpose in setting up a void that might explain racial shifting. However, I do not believe that Ross meant to ignore the social, cultural, and political distinctiveness of many early European immigrants, such as the Irish, Jews, and southern Italians, whose links to whiteness were tenuous at best. Instead, his use of the term "immigrants" had another, more important valence: immigrants cannot have a history or culture that is indigenous. Like other citizen Cherokees, Ross was still suggesting that "wannabes" want to be Cherokee so that they can have a culture and a heritage, something that "immigrants" (whites) lack. The question remains as to whether he meant that they want to have an indigenous culture or to have a culture, period.

Troy Wayne Poteete was even more explicit about the cultural and racial emptiness that he believes fuels the desires of "wannabes":

> I don't classify someone who comes along and says, "I'm of Cherokee ancestry."... I don't classify those as wannabes. I classify all those people as of Cherokee heritage, of Cherokee blood. But when we think about wannabes, we're thinking about those people we can almost always recognize.... They come in with these ridiculous stories about Great-grandma was a Cherokee princess, and on and on. It's people who seek to appropriate an identity, a Cherokee cultural identity, who can't possibly have that, because you can't appropriate that. It's people who want to be Indian, but they're not....
>
> We look on those people as if *they want to fill something up that they don't have.* So you don't want to be hard hearted, because they don't have...they weren't

blessed like we were. And so as aggravating as the wannabes are, Circe, I don't want to personally attack them, because if they knew who they were, then they wouldn't want to be who we are. (August 1, 2003; italics added)

With some sympathy for their plight, Poteete suggested that "wannabes" want to be Cherokee because they are seeking a cultural and racial identity, because they need to fill a void, yet these are things that in his mind they cannot possibly achieve. According to Poteete, racial and cultural identities are essential attributes that cannot be learned, borrowed, or appropriated later in life. According to this logic, one either is Cherokee or is not. One either was raised as a Cherokee in a Cherokee community or was not. One either has Cherokee blood or does not, and no gray area exists in between. This is why Poteete made a firm distinction between "Cherokee descendants," meaning those with Cherokee ancestry, and "wannabes," who are presumed to have no Cherokee ancestry and thus no connection to the tribe. Cultural ties would also make a difference to people like Poteete, who can appreciate the complex fate of someone who was raised in a Cherokee community by a Cherokee family but who was non-Indian, such as an interracial stepchild or adoptee. Growing up Cherokee, even without Cherokee ancestry, is a meaningful attribute to most Cherokee citizens. However, it is something that "wannabes," by definition, almost never possess.

Even as citizen Cherokees draw out these distinctions, their empathy for the rootless can at times be profound. Robert Thompson of the Eastern Band, for example, suggested that the desire for belonging expressed by many race shifters was a fundamental attribute of all human beings: "I have met some tremendous people that are wannabes. They are good people.... We're sheep, anyway, as people. All people, we like to identify with a group.... All human beings, it don't matter. We have a longing to belong somewhere, to be a part of something bigger than ourselves" (October 22, 2003). Citizen Cherokees may express greater empathy for race shifting born of deracination rather than dollars, but in either case the empathy rarely leads to opening the gates to Cherokee country, socially or politically. Many citizen Cherokees seem to shake their heads sadly as they observe the gathering at their door. But such sympathy does not mitigate their discomfort at any cultural encroachment that might be taking place.

My use of spatial metaphors is intentional—citizen Cherokees often see race shifters as people hungry for a sense of place.[12] Federally recognized Cherokees tend to emphasize that being indigenous is about having an original relationship to a specific geographic territory, something that in and of itself has "intrinsic value." Consider, for example, the following exchange that I had with Joe Mouse, who then worked in the Cultural Resources Department of the Eastern Band:

CS: Why do you think they [race shifters] want to be Indian?

JM: The intrinsic value!

CS: What is the intrinsic value, though? I mean, like, what is it about being Indian?

JM: Ties to the land, original people, I don't know.... Maybe it gives them a
       greater sense of belonging, of, you know, those sorts of things, a satisfying
       self-identity. (October 23, 2003)

Like Joe Mouse, Richard Allen of the Cherokee Nation emphasized that, in claiming indigeneity, race shifters are able to access a valuable sense of place that grounds them in both geographic and social belonging. However, he took this argument a step further by suggesting that among "wannabes," there is a "psychological need to identify with something," in this case to "identify with a people who have always been here." Allen argued that in identifying as Indians, "wannabes can say that their ancestry has always been tied to this land and can forgive themselves for having ancestry that wasn't" (July 31, 2003). In other words, he suggested, by emphasizing their indigenous rather than white identity, "wannabes" are able to assuage any sense of white guilt that they may have inherited as descendants of a complex colonial history. In making their metaphoric claim on native land, they have found a place to stand that is free of guilt or shame over settler colonialism.

The Symbolic Capital of Racial and Colonial Suffering

Citizen Cherokees are very aware of the larger context in which racial shifting is occurring; they often note the deep romantic fascination with racial difference that has flourished in the United States since the late 1960s. (This is not to discount earlier, more localized versions of this phenomenon, such as white primitivism during the Harlem Renaissance.) In particular, citizen Cherokees often argue that during this same period, American society came to deeply romanticize American Indian culture and history in a problematic way that has obscured racial and political differences and fueled race shifting. For example, Anna Long, a middle-aged Oklahoma Cherokee woman, told me, "Tribes are in the news, in general, and there's a fascination with Indians. It's just interesting to people. They look at their family tree, and what could be more interesting than an American Indian? Is there anything as exciting and romantic?" (February 13, 1996). Another woman, Melissa Hunter, of the Eastern Band, told me, "The Native American culture has been so romanticized, and for good reason. There was good stuff there. [But non-Indians] didn't understand there were times of starvation, times of disease, and all kinds of stuff that we've had to deal with, you know, and prejudice. They don't know all that's there, and a lot of times what you'll hear is the more flowery interpretation" (October 22, 2003).

Like many Cherokee citizens, Hunter believes that racial shifters have selective memories that emphasize the more romantic aspects of American Indian culture and history while ignoring anything controversial or traumatic. What race shifters actually say on the subject is quite different. As the narratives in chapter 2 make clear, most race shifters are not only willing to acknowledge a history of collective victimization; they actually choose to emphasize this when asserting their own status as Indians. The triumphs and tragedies of Cherokeeness are romanticized in equal measure, in a manner that might seem paradoxical and in a way that would probably surprise most citizen Cherokees.

Indeed, the tragic elements of Cherokee history are as important to race shifters' sense of Cherokeeness as the celebrated ones. In ways that citizen Cherokees rarely seem to articulate, race shifters are quick to acknowledge the collective suffering that binds them to other Cherokees through the pain of history. As if the experience of colonial imposition and racial discrimination was a badge of honor and might offer proof of belonging, many racial shifters offer narratives of racial victimization as evidence of their own indigenous difference. Consider the following account from Missy Black, a race shifter in Alabama:

> My niece started in this [participating in the local state-recognized tribe] as a shawl dancer because she went to Wyoming for the summer to work on a dude ranch and while she was out there, she would go into town and they [the townspeople] would call her a "prairie nigger." And she was, like, she was amazed by it. She loved it. She was, like, "They actually know that I'm an Indian." And that's what they called them, the townspeople there in Wyoming. They thought she was one of the reservation Indians out there, so she loved it. And she came back here, she started searching and all, and she found our grandmother's roots. And we had always been told we had a Cherokee grandmother, but we didn't really pursue it until [my niece] had this experience. (May 18, 2003)

In this particular example, the niece heard a racial slur aimed in her direction and loved it because the label implied the very thing she sought—social recognition as a Native American person. In this case, the need for social recognition seems to eclipse the normal pain and negativity that would be associated with such an experience. Certainly, most citizen Cherokees would tell the story differently, and I doubt that many of them would tolerate, much less appreciate, a crude anti-Indian epithet.

The seemingly glib celebration of painful moments in Cherokee history is one of the characteristics of race shifting that is most perplexing to citizen Cherokees. The presentation of what is seen as ill-placed pride in narratives of victimization is something that often defines a "wannabe." Many citizen Cherokees are aware that racial shifters often reference key moments in Cherokee history, particularly the Trail of Tears. Racial shifters frequently claim the Trail of Tears as part of their own history, but their desire to connect through shared history often has the opposite effect. Federally recognized Cherokees are often confused by such claims and will tend to classify those who romanticize any form of racial suffering, whether in the past or in the present, as "wannabes." For instance, Diana Terrapin, who works at the Cherokee FIRST (Friendly Information Referral Service Team) center of the Cherokee Nation, said to me, "We have people call in say, 'Oh, we want to retrace the Trail of Tears. Is there anybody there that would be willing to go with us, to help walk and retrace the

Trail of Tears?' And it's, like, why? We had a lot of people who died on that, and we don't want to go and ride your cars, or ride on horseback or your bicycles or your motorcycles. If you want to do it the way they did it, then do it in the wintertime. Don't take anything with you. Then, yeah, then I might care about what you're saying. But when you just want to do it in luxury, the way you do it now, no way" (August 31, 2003).

Betty Baker in North Carolina expressed a similar sense of confusion and even resentment: "I guess when you've been discriminated against, not only by the non-Indian society but the Indian society too, that I just don't understand why anybody would want to be Cherokee. And, again, being old as dirt and you've heard these true stories about the Trail of Tears, why would anybody want to be Cherokee? I mean, our people went through hell, and there's times when I go through hell because I'm Cherokee. I mean, just a couple of weeks ago I was refused service at a motel at the edge of the boundary, only ten miles away, because of the color of my skin" (October 22, 2003).

In both of these examples, Cherokee women are confused by what they believe is "wannabe" behavior—the desire to reenact or take pride in moments of Cherokee suffering, usually as a way of buttressing identity claims. For them, the Trail of Tears is something that calls to mind so much visceral pain, maybe even via the story of a great-grandparent's misery along the way, that it is difficult to imagine wanting to directly reenact such an experience. They do not suggest that the Trail of Tears should be forgotten—a memorial marker or public commemoration of some type is seen as appropriate—but they would prefer not to revel in the suffering of the past or to open themselves up to more suffering in the present, especially in a way that strikes them as being superficial or deluded. The distinction can be a subtle one but is nonetheless significant. Citizen Cherokees also do not wish to claim a victim's status in order to reinforce their sense of Indian identity. For them, the only reason they can imagine "wannabes" being comfortable with claiming racial victimization is that they must have experienced those moments of discrimination at some personal, geographic, or historical distance. In other words, citizen Cherokees believe that only a racial tourist could enjoy a stroll through the grim back alley of American racism.

Here is how the subtlety shakes out. Many citizen Cherokees share stories of racial victimization, but it is all about context. Race shifters tend to evoke these as a way of supporting the legitimacy of their identity claims, whereas citizen Cherokees tend to reference them when pointing to various forms of social inequity.[13] For example, Melissa Hunter in North Carolina described the public persona that "wannabes" create when they evoke the Trail of Tears: "The persona that they have, their public image…maybe it makes a more sympathetic audience because most Americans know about the plight of Native Americans. They may not know the depth the way that we know it, because we have family histories, but they kinda know that, yeah, the Native Americans were shafted in general. But it's cool now to belong to that downtrodden group, you know, the underdog group" (October 22, 2003).

North Carolina Cherokees are not the only ones who recognize a certain currency in belonging to the underdog group that might motivate racial shifting. An Oklahoma Cherokee man in his early fifties said to me, "At this point in time in history, it's not such a quote 'bad thing' to be an American Indian" (July 31, 2003). Both of these citizen Cherokees suggested that, in the current racial climate in this country, racial victimization, rather than being tolerated or even excused, is a source of public sympathy. Being Indian—and even the historical or contemporary forms of racial discrimination it entails—is no longer such a "bad thing" but is instead a positive, as if oppression were "cool."

Citizen Cherokees even take these arguments about shifting racial status a step further and suggest not only that it is now good to be Indian but also that for poor and working-class whites, it is better to be Indian than white. As Richard Allen put it, "for wannabes to become Indian now is a step up in society for them" (July 31, 2003). Similarly, Troy Wayne Poteete described a conversation he had with a state representative in Arkansas about self-identified Cherokees and their motivation for reclaiming an indigenous identity. "What makes these people tick?" Poteete asked the politician. He described what he was told:

> Well, just think about it. We've got some of these people out here who are, well, they're just poor, ignorant, white. What a lot of people might call "white trash," some of them are. Some of them are just way down there, where they're just hardly productive. They're ignorant. Their habits are poor. Those folks are nobodies, and nobody pays any attention to them in the community. But when they move over here in the next county, where they're not known, and appropriate the identity of "Oh yeah, I'm a Cherokee," then all at once, out of the abundance of caution to be politically correct and out of the respect that these people have for private people, especially for the tribes that came out of the Southeast, they're automatically extended courtesies.

When I asked Poteete to tell me what the politician meant when he said that they are "extended courtesies," he explained that because their racial status has shifted in the community, they are now interesting and important to people who never cared about them before. "Now, people are going to them because they're Indians," he said, "and the newspaper guy comes and interviews them, and they have an opinion about everything to do with any Native American issues, and they get to voice that and get to pretend to be Indian" (August 1, 2003). Poteete suggested that this movement is facilitated by a new racial climate of political correctness that encourages respect for racial difference, one in which Indians are supposedly extended the courtesy of getting to voice their opinions.[14] His narrative was primarily about racial inversion, as much about Indian empowerment as about the social and political marginalization experienced within white poverty.

The Symbolic Power of American Indian Spiritual Redemption

Many citizen Cherokees see race shifting as functioning as a salve not just for white material poverty but also for white spiritual poverty—good for the pocketbook and good for the soul. In both cases, the operative metaphor is bankruptcy, a symbolic impoverishment from which they believe race shifters are fleeing. In Oklahoma and North Carolina, citizen Cherokees argued that many race shifters are motivated to reclaim their Cherokee heritage and identity because they find themselves living in a state of spiritual bankruptcy—something citizen Cherokees associate with non-Indian society as a whole. For example, one Oklahoma Cherokee man said, "There are two kinds of wannabes. Some want the economics. That's a minority of 'em. The majority want to fill a spiritual void" (January 24, 1996). Another Oklahoma Cherokee man said, "They're looking for some sort of spirituality" (July 31, 2003). These statements might ring true for many race shifters, who set up a similar dichotomy between white spiritual impoverishment and Cherokee spiritual wealth when they describe their motivations for reclaiming their indigenous identities. As they see it, their change of identity brings new value to their lives in the form of spiritual redemption and a community of like-minded practitioners. Citizen Cherokees, however, view these spiritual claims as problematic.

Citizen Cherokees around the country believe that when race shifters begin to look for alternative religious practices outside the more familiar contexts in which they were raised, they tend to find spiritual solace in American Indian–style cultural traditions that have been largely invented and celebrated by New Age practitioners. Indeed, there is widespread concern that a significant number of race shifters are imitating, appropriating, and sometimes even exploiting Cherokee religious traditions— sometimes for profit, sometimes not. For example, when I asked Joe Mouse of the Eastern Band why so many people were now claiming to be Cherokee, he said, "You see the different influences at different times of this New Age phenomenon, you know, self-consciousness and meditation, people patching Indianness to meditation, theology, and religion, and experiences of climbing up on the mountain and seeking a vision—this sort of thing" (October 22, 2003).

A Cherokee Nation citizen made the connection between the New Age phenomenon and race shifting more explicit when he described "wannabes" as follows:

> You know, they read some New Age book about vision quests or sweat lodges, and they make contact with us, and they want to do that.... I tell them that's not the way Cherokees practice it and it's not going to happen. They'll even go so far as to say, "Well, I'll find somebody else to do it," because they're looking for that particular experience. Experience is probably a key word because we're talking about the experiential. There seems to be a certain lack of spirituality in whatever religion that they may have, and they're looking for something

different. Cherokee spirituality has that particular element of experiential activity, and that includes song, dance—things of that nature—and it appeals to a certain element of people who lack something in their lives they're not finding elsewhere. (July 31, 2003)

Troy Wayne Poteete made the same connection: "Most of the wannabes, Circe, that I come into contact with, and heaven knows I've suffered a bunch of 'em and never gladly.... What I see them come in with is a bunch of spiritual, New Age mumbo jumbo, and they want to be real spiritual and follow the old ways, and I'm thinking, "Do you think anybody's going to sell you that whole onion by the pound?" (August 1, 2003). Of course, not all race shifters are "wannabes" and not all are New Agers, though citizen Cherokees do not always makes these distinctions. Yet, without question, New Age practitioners have become significant figures in citizen Cherokee discussions of race shifting.

For most citizen Cherokees, the conversation about New Agers and racial shifting revolves around issues of cultural appropriation. Consider, for example, how these streams of discourse come together in the term "white shamanism," which was first coined in 1979 by literary scholar Geary Hobson (Cherokee/Quapaw/Chickasaw). Hobson (1979:102) describes white shamans as "the growing number of small-press poets of generally white, Euro Christian American background, who in their poems assume the persona of the shaman, usually in the guise of an American Indian medicine man. To be a poet is simply not enough; they must claim power from higher sources." This claiming of power, which Hobson refers to as a form of cultural imperialism, exploded during the 1960s and 1970s as a popular, pseudo-Indian style of writing that has continued in more recent decades within numerous New Age publications.

The story of New Age appropriations of American Indian spirituality is a familiar one that reaches far beyond Cherokee country. Shari Huhndorf, in her book *Going Native: Indians in the American Cultural Imagination*, argues that the New Age movement is yet another version of Euro-American colonization: "Compelled by the conviction that modern western societies confront terrible crises, the movement goes native in its quest for solutions" (Huhndorf 2001:162).[15] Furthermore, she argues that the New Age fascination with all things Native American reveals an ongoing colonial compulsion to own indigenous cultures and even indigenous identities. Because native culture and identities have become objects of desire in recent decades (163–167), New Age beliefs and practices provide a context in which even non-Indians can claim the indigenous as their own.[16]

Whatever the motivations for white shamanism, citizen Cherokees have a complicated response to it, one that is echoed around Indian country. Some American Indian observers see white shamans as fleeing from actual Native American people to a place where they can stake their indigenous claims without being challenged. For example, poet Wendy Rose (Hopi) says that they surface mostly at "bogus 'medicine wheel' gatherings, ersatz sweatlodge ceremonies, and other fad events using vaguely Indian motifs. You will not usually find them around Indians at genuine Indian events" (Rose 1992:414). But in the past decade and a half, I have heard many Oklahoma Cherokee people describe situations in which "wannabes" have tried to participate in legitimate Cherokee ceremonies intended only for community members. Ceremonial stomp grounds seem to draw the most attention because race shifters tend to ignore the fact that an overwhelming majority of the Cherokee Nation is Christian. Sometimes these uninvited guests are asked to leave, sometimes not, but their presence at these religious events can still create some discomfort and confusion among citizen Cherokees, from whom these intrusions provoke wry observations, resentment, and even some sympathy.

Based on numerous conversations with citizen Cherokees, I know that many would suggest that New Agers and "wannabes" are well meaning in their desire to fill their own spiritual voids and to do so in a positive manner that would enhance rather than supplant native people and their societies. Yet, there is also concern about the potential impact of white shamanism.[17] If most race shifters are moving toward Cherokeeness in general, relatively few of them are moving toward spiritual practices that are uniquely Cherokee. Indeed, spirituality may be the most pan-Indian of the various aspects of the race shifter experience. One reason for this lack of tribal specificity is that much of what informs race shifter understandings of Cherokee spirituality comes from New Age sources. When New Agers appropriate Native American spiritual practices, they commonly borrow pan-Indian ceremonies, such as burning sage, using a sweat lodge, carrying a pipe, or seeking a vision. Although these activities are not necessarily the sole province of a specific tribal nation, they are heavily influenced by traditions from indigenous nations originating in the Great Plains. As a result, there has been an outpouring of grief and concern in these communities regarding them. Such concern is evident not just in conversations I have had in Cherokee country but also in the large number of articles on this topic appearing in two leading Native American newspapers. For instance, at the height of the New Age movement in the early 1990s, at least eleven articles on "wannabes," New Agers, and their Plains-style practices appeared in *Indian Country Today*, the most widely read newspaper in Indian country, in a three-month span. And in another leading newspaper, the *Lakota Times*, seventeen articles on the same subject, written largely by Lakota and Dakota authors, surfaced in a thirteen-month period between mid-July 1990 and September 1, 1991.[18]

Citizen Cherokees are clearly reading these articles and watching news coverage of New Age pseudo-Indian practices because what takes place in the public sphere is often what proves most irritating. Such media coverage of white shamanism contributes to the sense among citizen Cherokees that race shifters and New Age practitioners are one and the same thing. Typically, race shifters who fit the profile of New Ager or "wannabe" perform their own version of Plains-style ceremonies and then label those practices as something else, usually as Cherokee, Choctaw, or Creek. For instance, when I was living in Tahlequah, Oklahoma, in the mid to late 1990s, I heard many Oklahoma Cherokees express dismay about the news coverage of the 1995 Olympic torch run through New Echota, Georgia, the original capital of the Cherokee Nation dating to the early nineteenth century. What bothered citizen Cherokees was the sight of apparent New Agers claiming to be Cherokees, dressed in beaded buckskins, feathers, and chest plates, burning sage and waving tobacco ties at the runners. Most of these people were members of state-recognized and self-identified Cherokee tribes in the area; many citizen Cherokees viewed the event as a problematic mix of New Age shamanism and good old "wannabeeism." One Oklahoma Cherokee described his reaction to the *Cherokee Observer*, an independent Cherokee newspaper in Oklahoma: "I've got to tell the truth. When I went to New Echota and saw Chief Dugan Alva Crowe and Jack Cloyne [both state recognized] in traditional Cherokee dress and then saw a group claiming to be Cherokee dressed like the set of *Dances with Wolves*, I couldn't help but let out a chuckle. After thinking about it, that chuckle turned to a groan of disgust" (*Cherokee Observer*, October 1996).

In another example, Cherokee scholar Richard Allen writes about how a 1994 memorial ceremony for American Indian veterans, hosted by the Nez Perce but held in Oklahoma, was infiltrated by a "wannabe charlatan":

> Sitting at the head table was an individual wearing a turban-like headpiece with feathers attached here and there, with a matching ribbon shirt (somewhat similar to 19th century Cherokee dress), a tobacco or medicine pouch hanging from his neck onto his chest, and a Plains-styled peace-pipe in front of him on the table. He introduced himself as "...a Cherokee spiritual leader, pipe-carrier and member of the Bear clan." After the ceremony, when confronted about his claims...he stammered something about being given these rights as a spiritual leader by his great-great-grandmother who was from "Alabama, Tennessee or Kentucky." Upon further inquiry, he stated that he was not "referring to membership in the family clans but the 'medicine clan' of the Cherokees." (Allen 1995:5–6)

The statements of this individual would raise obvious questions for many citizen Cherokees in the know. Not only is there no Cherokee bear clan, but also there are no special Cherokee medicine clans.[19] Both of these examples show how some race shifters can appropriate stereotypical Indian spiritual traditions and then represent them as Cherokee.

As a result of the perceived tendency among race shifters to misappropriate Native American spirituality, many Oklahoma Cherokees (and, presumably, citizens of other Indian nations, given their reactions in the newspapers) have become increasingly protective about traditional spiritual practices and knowledge. When I first arrived in Tahlequah in 1995 and began to make inquiries about religious practices and their connection to tribal identity, many people were cautious about speaking to an outsider—or at least anyone whose work could be seen as a conduit to outsiders seeking traditional Cherokee knowledge. One ceremonial ground leader expressed his concern that if I were to publish anything about the traditional religion, it would surely become fodder for "wannabe" appropriations. He agreed to provide me with introductions to various community members only if I kept my focus on my research and refrained from describing traditional religious practices in anything but the broadest of terms. He also warned that if I wanted to be accepted among Oklahoma Cherokee people, I had better not do anything that would inadvertently cause them to think that I was a New Ager or a "wannabe." In particular, he said, I should refrain from wearing feathers or buckskin and from asking too many probing questions—the latter of which was a tall order for an anthropologist in the field.

This advice served me well because only later did I realize the extent to which the overall New Age phenomenon was affecting Cherokee people and their responses to me as an outsider, particularly one with the power to represent Cherokee culture in a public forum. As I gradually learned, curiosity about Cherokee spiritual practices is not perceived as a harmless matter. Because of the potential for abuse in the form of individuals like the big man from Florida described at the start of this chapter, many Cherokee Nation citizens are deeply skeptical of any outsider, whether New Ager, race shifter, or anthropologist, who seems to be curious about the ceremonial grounds. The implication is that if you do not have the knowledge already, then you should not have it now. With varying degrees of success, citizen Cherokees are setting a boundary around Cherokeeness in an effort to preserve its special qualities and keep out the worst interlopers.

Part of what motivates racial shifters to reclaim Cherokeeness is the belief that being Cherokee gives one a natural right to American Indian spiritual traditions and their power. Thousands of New Agers and race shifters are drawn to the sacred power of Cherokee culture in the face of what they perceive to be their own culture's shortcomings. What race shifters claim to have experienced in their former whiteness is social disconnection and spiritual emptiness, whereas in Cherokeeness, they have found just the opposite—experiential religion, a community of believers, and a tribe of their own. This difference of racial experience is what sets race shifters apart from Cherokee descendants who never make the switch. But sacred power is only one form of symbolic capital that motivates racial shifting. In the final section of this chapter, I explain how race shifters have their cake and eat it too, which is to say that at the same time many of them are embracing powerful forms of racial and cultural alterity as a way to access spiritual power, many are also embracing the royal scepter of aristocracy, especially if it involves a remarkably common ancestral figure—a Cherokee woman who embodies the complex role of the Indian princess.

Cherokee Princesses and Other Gendered Genealogies

Citizen Cherokees in both Oklahoma and North Carolina agree that another way in which race shifters access symbolic capital is by laying claim to high-status Cherokee genealogies that are gendered in powerful ways. For instance, many of the race shifters that citizen Cherokees might classify as "wannabes" trace their lineages to women, in particular to a "fertile but nebulous Cherokee grandmother," with a common refrain being "My great-great-grandmother was a Cherokee princess" (Allen 1995:2). The Cherokee people have never had a royal family with aristocratic titles passed down through the generations, yet many race shifters have enthroned a Cherokee princess in a place of prominence on the family tree and are quick to evoke her when asserting their Cherokee identities. One of the most ubiquitous expressions of race shifting, the Cherokee princess ancestor claim has become a particular source of amusement and sardonic comment among citizen Cherokees and other American Indians. What has become a cliché around Indian country is that when "wannabes" lay claim to a Native American tribal identity, they overwhelmingly identify as being part Cherokee, more often than not "through some distant grandmother who was, as the phrase always goes, a 'Cherokee Princess'" (Green 1988:46). The figure is almost always Cherokee, female, and obscured in the mists of memory and history. Like the early hominid Lucy, the Cherokee princess is the common ancestor of thousands of race shifters.

Whether these genealogical claims are fact or fiction, the question remains, why is the ancestor of choice usually a woman and a princess? Several American Indian scholars have explored some of the racial and gendered meanings behind these Indian princess grandmother claims. Vine Deloria Jr. offers a provocative explanation: "A male ancestor has too much of the aura of the savage warrior, the unknown primitive, the instinctive animal, to make him a respectable member of the family tree. But a young Indian princess? Ah, there was royalty for the taking. Somehow the white was linked with a noble house of gentility and culture if his grandmother was an Indian princess who ran away with an intrepid pioneer" (Deloria 1988[1969]:3). As always, Deloria is funny and insightful, but the force of his satire overwhelms the possibility of a more nuanced explanation for the proliferation of Cherokee princesses. Demographer Russell Thornton, a citizen of the Cherokee Nation, offers another interpretation, suggesting that until the mid-nineteenth century, a skewed demographic ratio led to the common union of Indian women and non-Indian men, so earlier generations of multiracial Cherokees were likely to trace their Cherokee ancestry through their mothers (Thornton 1990:173). This might account for the princess's gender, but not the royalty itself, which seems vulnerable to charges of fabrication or wishful thinking.

Yet another factor leads to a more sympathetic interpretation, and that is the variety of ways in which the term "princess" has been used to describe American Indian women both historically and currently (Green 1988). For example, Cherokee anthropologist Candessa Morgan (2006) describes how early American colonists occasionally used the term "princess" to describe the daughter of a chief and any other American Indian woman with a significant degree of political power and how some tribes followed suit by adopting the same language to refer to high-status Indian women in negotiations with non-Indians. Much more recently, however, she points to the fact that in the early decades of the twentieth century, "princess" became a common term of affection, and the YMCA created the popular Y-Indian Princess program for fathers and daughters (Morgan 2006:4). Of even greater significance in Morgan's opinion is the fact that in the past several decades, many American Indian tribes and organizations have adopted the practice of designating young Indian women as Indian princesses. These titles are often associated with particular powwows, but they can also include tribal, national, state, and local titles, such as the Kiowa Tribal Princess and the Eastern Shoshone Indian Days Queen (Morgan 2006:4).[20] Given the widespread use of these titles and their varied meanings, many people, both Indian and non-Indian, may have an "Indian princess" somewhere in the family tree, though the details of such designations can become blurred with geographic, social, and historical distance.

Although these explanations offer insights as to why the Indian ancestor of choice is usually female and a princess, they say little about why she is Cherokee. Again, I suggest that the Cherokee grandmother proliferates in large part because Cherokeeness connotes civilization, cultural syncretism, and a comfortable degree of whiteness related to relatively open standards for tribal enrollment in two of the three federally recognized Cherokee tribes. Given the large size and diversity of the Cherokee population, both in historic and present times, and the ubiquity of Cherokee imagery, many Americans are familiar with Cherokees in ways they are not with other tribes, such as the Lumbee, Osage, or Tlingit. It makes perfect sense, then, that those who have a vague family history of Indian ancestry would claim what is most familiar and that their American Indian female ancestors would come to be known as Cherokee. The Cherokee princess is a wistful figure that signals what might have been—tribal connections built around a more specific knowledge of kin—if their families had been able to resist the pressures of assimilation.

Before exploring the ways in which citizen Cherokees deal with the Cherokee princess phenomenon—something that signals racial and cultural ambiguity and raises a red flag for many citizen Cherokees—I should note that race shifters wrestle with some of the same issues. Many race shifters, even those who might be classified as "wannabes," discuss and poke fun at those who claim to be Cherokee princess descendants. For instance, Sarah Glory, a former chief of a state-recognized Cherokee tribe in Alabama, described the many people she met who were surprised by her own claims to an indigenous identity, because she looked white. Taking these comments in stride, she said that she would often respond with a sense of irony, saying, "You know, my great-great-grandmother was an Indian princess!" She laughed aloud as she told the story, because she is well aware that "there never were any Indian princesses" and finds it amusing that "there are more Indian princesses out there than you can shake a stick at" (May 18, 2003). David Madison, member of the same state-recognized tribe, shared this sense of irony and enjoyed poking fun at stereotypical expectations. He described how another tribal member and he had set up booths at their local powwow and a visitor had come up to them and said, "Yeah, my grandmother was a full blood. She was in the Pocahontas tribe." Although he was comfortable with letting the comment pass, his friend had a mischievous sense of humor and responded by saying, "Yeah, my grandfather was too. He was a Cherokee princess" (May 18, 2003).

In both of these examples, race shifters played with discourses about Cherokee princess descendants to distinguish between themselves and others who claim Indian descent. They point to the absurdity of external expectations, including that Cherokees should look a particular way or be royal descendants, because in doing so they can establish their own, accurate understandings of Cherokee culture and history as distinct from those of the general non-Indian population. In other words, because they have an ironic appreciation of the princess phenomenon, they are truly Cherokee—because they get the joke, they cannot be the joke.

Whether or not used in a joking manner, the vast majority of genealogical claims made by race shifters revolve around an American Indian woman. On those rare occasions when a male figure does appear in the family tree, he tends to have an unusually high social status, much like his "princess" counterpart. Citizen Cherokees view this as another way in which race shifters try to access forms of social prestige. Robert Thompson, a citizen of the Eastern Band of Cherokee Indians, put it this way: "Everybody that's a Cherokee wannabe, you know, they're actually related to a Cherokee chief or a Cherokee princess or some well-known figure. Those are the only people having sex! None of the Joe Shmoes!" (October 22, 2003). Unlike other stereotypes that federally recognized Cherokees might have about race shifters, this one was borne out by my interviews.

On those rare occasions when race shifters evoked a male relative, he was almost always a well-known chief or warrior. A typical claim was the one made by a member of a self-identified Cherokee tribe in Arkansas, June Davis, a woman who described herself as "the seventh-generation granddaughter of Chief John Watts" (April 26, 2003). Mary Ann Allen, another member of the same self-identified tribe in Arkansas, described how she came to document her lineal connections to a high-status Cherokee man:

> We'd heard stories all of our lives about Cherokee grandparents and Cherokee connections in our families. So we've always had all these names and things, back to Attakullakula. And I started collecting books and anything I could find about him and about the Cherokee Nation as a whole and got to doing more and more arts and crafts.... Well, it wasn't until, I guess, five years ago that my family really tried to get the paperwork together that was necessary to prove our lineage back to that man. We finally got all the birth certificates and the marriage licenses, the death certificates and all the things we had to have to prove it all the way back to him, and we can actually go back two generations past him, to his father and his grandfather. So that makes us about twelve generations that we can go back to Attakullakula. (April 26, 2003)

Sometimes these claims to high-status male relatives are supported by genealogical research, and sometimes they are not—a fact that few shifters are willing to acknowledge.

However, Mary Anne Allen's husband, Bob Allen, was willing to describe the disconnect between his own family narrative and the genealogical facts when he said, "My aunt, she always said that Grandpa Malachai was a chief, but from the work that [my wife] and I have done, he wasn't a chief. But she always has to say, 'Yeah, he was a chief!'" (April 26, 2003). Chief or no chief, citizen Cherokees are often frustrated with what they perceive to be the growing fabrication of high-status Cherokee ancestors. Andrew Ross, a citizen of the United Keetoowah Band of Cherokee Indians in Oklahoma, expressed his anger to me by saying, "You hear the Cherokee princess grandmother syndrome so much that you start to resent it. They should all be shot!" (January 19, 1996).

Another example of an angry response is that of Willie Creekkiller, who wrote in a letter to the editor of the *Cherokee Observer*, "I know that old song and dance by heart. Some white person comes up to you and says, 'My great-great-great grandmother was a famous Indian princess.' I have heard it so many times it makes me want to puke" (*Cherokee Observer*, November 1996). Creekkiller described his encounter with a self-avowed princess. As he told the tale, his friend Don and he were at a company picnic. Being the only Indians in attendance, they felt marginalized and stood in the corner observing the proceedings:

> This white lady came to where we were standing. She was dressed in the latest expensive fashions that money could buy. She stopped in front of us and she looked us over from head to toe like we were some kind of aliens.... Well, she commenced into the old song and dance routine. Somewhere back in the early 1700s, she was related to this very famous Indian princess.
>
> Don spoke and said "Ma'am, I know just who you are talking about. My tribal history is well versed on this Indian princess...although I cannot recall her name right at this moment. Our tribal leaders still speak of her even today." I thought this lady was going to bust at the seams she was so thrilled.... The white lady said, "Please, please tell me more."
>
> Don said, "Ma'am, I'm not sure if you want to hear what I have to say about your ancestor. She was famous all right but in a different way.... I hate to inform you that your ancestor was banished from her tribe because she turned her back on her own people. The only people she would have anything to do with were white men. She became the worst whore our people ever knew. Last count she had born about 25 bastard children. Also, she had several sisters and they were banished from the tribe for the same reason." The white lady turned red in the face and made a hasty retreat.... Don turned and said, "I wonder if she still claims to be Indian?" I thought I was going to laugh myself silly.... just one of the funny things that happened along the trail walked by a Cherokee half breed." (*Cherokee Observer*, November 1996)

I include this text because it provides an excellent example of how dominant ideas about race, class, and gender intersect with and shape Cherokee reactions to the

Cherokee princess phenomenon. As I read it, Creekkiller characterizes the woman making these claims as upper class and materialistic, given the way he describes her dress and mannerisms. Most Oklahoma Cherokees attribute this behavior to whites generally, while defining themselves in opposition as antimaterialistic and down to earth. If a Cherokee community member is perceived as becoming too arrogant or overly concerned with material possessions, he or she can lose status and respect in the eyes of the broader tribal community. The woman indicates whiteness not only with her style of dress but also when she stares at Creekkiller and his friend as if they were aliens, making them feel like racial objects. Only in the context of racial objectification does she then launch into her narrative of having a Cherokee princess ancestor, something that instantly signals social and cultural distance from Cherokee life.

The tale also suggests a desire to control Cherokee women's sexuality as a way of ensuring racial purity. Within the story, a Cherokee woman's behavior is censured because she chooses sexual liaisons with white men over Cherokee men—an act that Creekkiller reads as racial and national betrayal. He critiques this betrayal by using the powerful label of "whore," adding a layer of sexism on top of his already complex racial and cultural attitudes. Thus, the multiracial offspring of an Indian "whore" become "bastards," and she, her sisters, and their children are literally banished from the social body of the tribe. Essentially, this tale is an attempt to alter the meaning of the princess in the family tree, converting her from royalty to whore. The story is a vindictive, nasty tall tale. It represents a disavowal of all Cherokee women who behave like princesses, as well as any of their descendants who would dare to be proud of such origins.

For Creekkiller, the image of the Cherokee princess evokes anger and outrage over interracial sex and multiracial offspring. Even though the children in the narrative have Cherokee mothers—something that is often a critical measure of belonging in matrilineal clan societies like the Cherokee—this fact matters little to Creekkiller in his social classification of these multiracial children and their descendants. For Creekkiller, the children of Cherokee "princesses" who sleep with white men are definitively non-Indian and non-Cherokee, as if their matrilineal bond had become tainted through the act of miscegenation. Not surprisingly, the story reveals a common racial hegemony associated with notions of social and biological purity, but it also provides evidence of a contradictory and ambivalent racial consciousness. Ironically, Creekkiller signs the letter identifying himself as a "half breed." The story then parallels his own family history. Though we cannot be certain whether he has internalized a sense of race betrayal regarding his own non-Indian ancestry or he simply has a well-developed sense of satire, we do know from Creekkiller's self-description that he sees himself as Cherokee but that he also feels the need to qualify (and quantify) his identity in racial terms. As I read this letter, Creekkiller seems oblivious to the contradictions, and despite calling himself a "half breed," he portrays himself as wholly Indian—as one of two Indians at an event full of white people. He has made his choice, a critically different choice from that which was made by some of his own ancestors and by the Cherokee princesses of his imagination.

Although Creekkiller's testimony provides a poignant example of self-abnegation, gendered racial conflict, and anger, most interactions between federally recognized Cherokees and race shifters are not vitriolic. They are, however, rife with misunderstandings and frustrations. As I demonstrate in the preceding pages, citizen Cherokees are convinced, first, that "wannabes" are primarily poor and working-class whites who identify themselves as Indians in the hope of attaining economic benefits and, second, that doing so also provides "wannabes" with symbolic and psychological benefits, especially in the realm of spirituality. These might include a well-defined racial and cultural identity rather than the vagaries of unmarked whiteness, access to newfound spiritual powers or traditions, and a sense of geographic belonging as an indigenous person rather than the sense of dislocation that comes from recognizing one's status as a colonial interloper—not to mention the guilt that can fester under the veil of white privilege when it is acknowledged. Race shifters, however, tend to reject most of the qualities attributed to them by citizen Cherokees. Although most race shifters agree that being Cherokee has intrinsic social and symbolic value, they are less willing to see race shifting as rooted in whiteness or as a quest for social recognition and power (in fact, most seem never to have made this connection). They also differ from citizen Cherokees in believing that the motivations for race shifting are not primarily economic but spiritual and communal.

Despite these differences of opinion, race shifters and citizen Cherokees around the country agree on one fundamental point: there is redemptive power in being Cherokee, and the only way to understand that power is to look beyond strictly material considerations. According to this perspective, being Cherokee goes far beyond whether one can access tribal and federal monies that have been earmarked for tribal citizens; it is also about having a distinct culture, a tribe, and an original relationship to the land. To be Cherokee is to express one's difference from white America and, in the current political climate in the United States, to hope that difference will garner social respect and a chance for greater political autonomy. All of these forms of value—social, political, cultural, spiritual, racial, and economic—are attached to what it now means to be indigenous in the United States, and it is in this context that citizen Cherokees and racial shifters clash over who has the right to be and become Cherokee.

s i x
Documenting Descent and
Other Measures of Tribal Belonging

Troy Wayne Poteete is a good storyteller. With a flair for words that stands out even among Southern men who share his talent, he always spins a good yarn about Cherokee people and their politics—a subject he knows well. When I first met him, in 1996, he was a relatively new tribal council member. These days, he is a sitting justice on the Cherokee Judicial Appeals Tribunal, the supreme court of the Cherokee Nation, a position with political influence. In late summer 2003, his dark brown eyes flashed with anger as he told me about a group of people establishing a new tribe—the Southern Cherokee Nation—in his hometown of Webbers Falls, Oklahoma. Poteete was not the only person in the Cherokee Nation who was angry with the newcomers for seeming to horn in on tribal territory, but because they were based in Webbers Falls, he seemed especially aggrieved, as if he were taking the matter personally.

"This particular group is brassier than any group we've ever seen before," he said, "because you always see these groups in Arkansas or Missouri or Alabama or Kentucky, but this group comes down to Webbers Falls!" Not only was it his hometown, but it was also a place of special significance to Cherokee history. He explained that within the historic Cherokee Nation, Webbers Falls was "the seat of government for this whole district" and many Cherokees with Southern sympathies settled there. These were Cherokees who were pro-slavery before and after tribal removal from their southeastern homelands in 1838 and who sided with the South during the Civil War. "But this group," he continued, "they come and sit themselves right down in the community and claim to be Southern Cherokees. I said, 'People, what are you thinking? If they're the Southern Cherokees, then who the hell are we?'"[1]

Poteete's sense of outrage was compounded by the fact that the new tribe's genealogical claims were unfamiliar and seemed disconnected from well-known southern Cherokee families like his own. "We know who we are," he said. "If you want to know whether or not someone is Cherokee, all you gotta do is go ask your granddad or your grandma or somebody, and they're going to tell you." For Poteete, the newcomers' claims were not persuasive. "First place, their genealogies ain't going to hold water, and their history.... Like they claim, 'Oh, we had this treaty and da, da, da.'" With obvious skepticism, he went on to explain that the Southern Cherokee Nation claims rights under the Treaty of 1866, a Reconstruction-era treaty between the Cherokee Nation and the U.S. government. According to Poteete, their claim completely ignores earlier legal documents, such as the 1839 Cherokee Constitution—the governing document that is still celebrated every Labor Day when Cherokee Nation citizens gather together for the Cherokee National Holiday. Poteete added that even if the newcomers were really Cherokees, as they claimed to be, they still did not have the right to create a separate tribe: "All those people, they came in here and said, "We're descendants of the Southern Cherokee who went underground after the Civil War." Well, that sounds good, but nobody went underground except them that died of old age and is buried out there...and I'll take you to their graves!"

Poteete did not always feel so threatened by new claims to Cherokee identity. "When I was a kid, first starting out, I didn't know what they were doing. I thought they were just harmless, empty people." But now he feels differently: "We've got a problem out here! The wannabes, they're a problem!" Poteete ridiculed the standards of membership for self-identified tribes in Oklahoma, Missouri, and Arkansas—the very ones he felt were pressing in upon the Cherokee Nation. He claimed that anyone could join any of them, even a donkey: "I could join my pet jackass if I wasn't afraid I'd get in some trouble with the post office to go ahead and enroll her," he said, "but I'm afraid that bunch [the Southern Cherokee Nation] will come back and claim I fathered them or something. If I could handle all the papers in it, I do believe I could enroll my red dog-hound and my pet donkey! I could invent 'em a genealogy that would pass their muster!"

* * *

Poteete's mocking tone might seem uncharitable, but he is not alone in expressing a sense of cynicism born of frustration. Most citizen Cherokees look at race shifting with skepticism, if not dismay, because they believe that the kinship claims of race shifters cannot be substantiated. As noted in chapter 5, not everyone can be the great-great-granddaughter or grandson of a Cherokee chief, much less a Cherokee princess, and the ubiquity of such claims calls them into question. Some race shifters also question these types of claims when they poke fun at self-proclaimed Cherokee princesses and call other race shifters "wannabes." But even when race shifters make identity claims that fall more within the realm of possibility, citizen Cherokees often remain skeptical. So when the Southern Cherokee Nation suddenly emerged in Webbers Falls, Oklahoma—claiming an identity, a history, and even a treaty that Cherokee families in the area already recognized as their own—someone like Poteete was not about to start celebrating the arrival of long-lost kin. Rather, he approached those claims with cynicism, questioning who the people were, why he had never heard of them before, and what could possibly motivate their sudden assertion of a tribal identity separate from that of the Cherokee Nation.[1]

Under these circumstances, citizen Cherokees often make the leap to allegations of ethnic fraud—people intentionally misrepresenting themselves or their community—but they also worry about misrepresentations that stem less from opportunism than sheer confusion. Because of these concerns, they tend to use specific measures when evaluating Cherokee kinship claims. Usually, they expect Cherokee people to be able to recite the names of family members who are in some way connected to local Cherokee families and communities. Most carry around an elaborate cognitive map of how these families are tied to one another, and the very first thing they do when they meet is to figure out how they are related, if at all. Essentially, they try to place a new person on the grand familial map, just as anyone would do when attending a large family reunion and meeting distant kin for the first time. When someone claims to be Cherokee without reference to local Cherokee families and places or does it in a way that cannot easily be mapped in terms of the Cherokee Nation's or Eastern Band's sense of kinship and experience, it immediately arouses citizen Cherokees' suspicions. Race shifters, in contrast, are more flexible about what sorts of claims they will accept, and they care less about references that are local and familiar and more about the power of the individual story. They usually are much more familiar with their own family genealogy than with the genealogies of other Cherokee families, something that also sets them apart from citizen Cherokees and their more elaborate knowledge of Cherokee kinship.

Even though both groups evaluate Cherokee kinship claims differently, both are concerned about ethnic fraud. Their shared anxiety about Cherokee imposters has led to an almost obsessive need to substantiate Cherokee kinship claims. Both groups want to distinguish their vision of real Cherokees from the ersatz Cherokees or "wannabes" lurking in their midst, and both believe that documentary evidence offers an important key to making these distinctions. Yet, they tend to raise the issue in different contexts. For instance, citizen Cherokees mention their concerns about documentation mainly in reference to any newcomer whose kinship claims are unfamiliar, whereas race shifters mention it more readily as a way to authenticate their own identity claims, as if their more fragile claims require some sort of documentary anchor. More important than these minor differences is that, for both groups, having proper documentation has come to symbolize the veracity of Cherokee kinship claims in a way that tends to eclipse other ways of knowing.

Although citizen Cherokees often go over race shifter claims with a fine-tooth comb, some are starting to ask themselves hard questions about their emphasis on documentary evidence. For instance, what if the stories of race shifters are inaccurate in the specifics, as many citizen Cherokees suspect, but correct in terms of the broader claim to Cherokee kinship? What if many of these people are actual Cherokee descendants but cannot substantiate their claims with the proper paperwork? Should having the right paper trail be the primary measure of their tribal belonging? Citizens of federally recognized Cherokee tribes have to struggle with these questions on a daily basis. On the one hand, they have all had to document their tribal connections with genealogical precision, something to which non-native families are rarely subjected. Like most Native Americans, citizen Cherokees know the discomfort of being subjected to intense bureaucratic scrutiny in the process of being repeatedly inscribed in the written records of federal, state, and tribal authorities. On the other hand, many of these same Cherokees place great value on oral history and might even privilege oral accounts over written sources. Because of these factors, citizen Cherokees face a conundrum of sorts: they do not want to dismiss family histories based on oral traditions lest this somehow call their own oral histories into question, but they feel uncomfortable accepting at face value the kinship claims of people they do not know, particularly those whose narratives of belonging raise skeptical eyebrows.

This conundrum is one of several that citizen Cherokees face as they evaluate the kinship claims of race shifters using different measures of tribal belonging. Some forms of Cherokee kinship reckoning, such as those based on ideas about blood, matrilineality, and clan, have a deep cultural history reaching as far back as anyone can remember. Other forms of reckoning rely on documentary evidence and derive from a much more recent bureaucratization of indigenous identity, in which tribal citizenship is tied to resources and rights that have to be assigned and managed. Although different forms of kinship reckoning can sometimes be at odds with one another, the documentary ideal has now become one of the most commonly referenced and consistently applied measures of tribal belonging among Cherokees of all stripes.

This chapter explores the tensions and contradictions that emerge as citizen Cherokees negotiate these different forms of kinship reckoning, as well as the way the ideal of documentary evidence is implicated within them. First, I examine how citizen Cherokees debate the consequences of privileging documentary evidence over oral history in evaluating kinship claims and how they use the terms "outtaluck" and "should-be" to critique this practice. Then, I explore how, with the right paper trail, race shifters might be classified as "wannabes," descendants, or even tribal citizens as they pass through various levels of documentary scrutiny. Even after this move takes place, some citizen Cherokees use the idea of blood quantum to further qualify descendants as "Thindians" or "white Indians" rather than simply as fellow Cherokees. These various terms and practices of social classification reveal the overall climate of racial and cultural assessment that now exists among citizen Cherokees—something that has developed over the past forty years as race shifting has flourished and more and more people have reasserted a Cherokee tribal connection.

Reckoning with Oral History and the Limits of Documentation

In late October 2003, I was in Cherokee, North Carolina, sitting across a desk from Joe Mouse, a former graduate student of mine and a citizen of the Eastern Band of Cherokee Indians who was working in the tribal administration. I had come to North Carolina for a weeklong visit because I wanted to have an opportunity to include Eastern Band perspectives in my research. I knew that the Eastern Band was collaborating with the Cherokee Nation, sharing information and ideas and trying to develop a joint response to the race-shifting phenomenon, but I wanted to hear from everyday tribal citizens on the topic as well. Would their perspectives follow the logic of the tribal administration or reflect some other concern entirely? Though Mouse was a tribal employee, I knew that he and I had enough rapport that he would speak his mind, so I was direct when I asked how he reacted to claims of Cherokee kinship that came from people who were new and unfamiliar and whether he accepted these claims at face value. He described his conflicted feelings on the matter:

> I believe there are people who can genuinely lay claim and have documented their descent and there are people who will make claims of descent based on stories handed to them by grandparents or great-great-grandparents or whatever. We can't really discount that. We can't deny the legitimacy of their claims of oral histories and then at the same time try to substantiate our tribal oral history, the oral histories, in the same manner. There's a conflict there. Because if we say, "Well, we can't believe you because it's an oral history," and then try to assert some belief, tribal belief, from a federally recognized tribal member, oral history is in the same sentence. (October 27, 2003)

Mouse identified a double standard, one in which Eastern Band members want their own oral histories to be respected but are sometimes unwilling to respect those of others (or at least not those of "wannabes" or race shifters).

Although Cherokees in Oklahoma sometimes raised the issue with me, it seemed that Eastern Band members had a greater awareness of this contradiction, or at least they were more willing to talk about it. They seemed to struggle with its implications as they tried to make sense of the frequent Cherokee kinship claims they heard on an almost daily basis. For example, Helena Johnson, who also worked for the tribe in the Eastern Band tribal registration office, acknowledged the paradox of oral histories being seen as suspect by people who generally promote the reliability of nonwritten histories: "Yeah, and you know, I guess this is kind of a contradiction. You can't really blame those people, because they've always been told that. You know? They're well meaning. They don't know any different, but like I've always known I've got Laguna Pueblo blood and I can prove it, you know? But if they can't prove it, then how is anybody gonna know?" (October 22, 2003). I asked Johnson whether she thought this was a double standard, to question the oral histories of race shifters but not those of enrolled Cherokees, and whether she believed that making documentation the gold standard of authenticity would eventually pose problems for Indian people. She agreed that there was a contradiction but struggled with its implications:

HJ: I know those people have always been told that [they are Cherokee descendants], so they don't know any different, you know? And there might be some stuff passed down in our oral history that's been changed through the years that's not true either. But I'm not saying they shouldn't be respected, I guess, just…I have to hear them every day, and some of them are so far-fetched, and you know they may be true. I'm not saying that none of them are true, but they still can't prove it.

CS: I think for you maybe it's the sheer volume of the phenomenon?

HJ: Yeah. I think so. I mean, I hear it day in and day out. I get so tired of hearing it sometimes, like, it never stops. (October 22, 2003)

This conversation with Johnson captured a moment of social and political boundary setting. She acknowledged the double standard on her own but, when pressed, insisted that the fundamental issue is proof or substantiation through something more than family recollection. She insisted on this, in part, because she hears a vast number of unsubstantiated Cherokee genealogical claims on a daily basis—and many of them appear far-fetched to her. Still, she is reluctant to close the door completely. After all, how can you really know what is true, half true, or untrue? For Mouse, Johnson, and many other citizen Cherokees, the main issue at stake in these discussions seems to be one of epistemology—how one knows what one knows and on what basis. In this situation, oral and written systems of knowledge transmission are coming into conflict with each other as Cherokee citizens interpret outsider claims to genealogical belonging.

Some citizen Cherokees in both Oklahoma and North Carolina are like Johnson in insisting that race shifters provide proof or substantiation, but others recognize that colonial histories are contested histories and that some legitimate Cherokee descendants will never be able to document their ancestry in order to enroll in a tribe. They point, for example, to the fact that vital records throughout the South were clouded by racial segregation, so much so that anyone who was listed on a birth, death, or marriage certificate as "colored" could have been African American or Native American. When citizen Cherokees recognize the possibility of racial distortion or omission in the documentary record, they seem less sure about how to interpret race shifters' claims. Anne Wallace, an elderly Cherokee woman in Oklahoma, said that she felt confused about people who could not substantiate their tribal ties. "I really don't know how to feel about them," she said. "If they are Cherokee and they can't prove it, I don't have the right to say they are not, but then many claim that the whole world owes them" (January 30, 1996). In this case, the tension is between the rights of the legitimate few, meaning the right of Cherokee descendants to self-identify as Cherokee despite not meeting tribal enrollment standards and the right of Cherokee citizens to reject the illegitimate many, at least after considering what they see as their underlying motivations and other relevant factors.

Race shifters share many of the same concerns about documentation. Like citizen Cherokees, they believe that written records discovered during the process of genealogical research offer the only foolproof method by which they can substantiate their identity claims. Consider, for example, what one woman in her mid-forties had to say about the matter. A member of a state-recognized Cherokee tribe in Alabama, Luanne Helton does genealogical research and spends much of her free time helping others find the documentation they need to formally enroll in her tribe. She said, "If a person can document their lineage, then in my opinion they're Cherokee, if they can document it." Helton also said she believes that all Cherokee tribes, new and old, should have the same basic standard for membership, what she calls "the general standard for genealogical proof,"[2] adding, "Every person who has ever been involved in genealogical research knows that a fact is no better than a fairy tale if you can't document it and documentation is something that is essential. If a person can document their lineage, then they should have the right to claim that ancestry" (May 21, 2003).

Even race shifters who agree with Helton sometimes find that they are not able to meet the standards they themselves have helped set. Vera Sheppard, a founding member of the Cherokee Confederacy of Southern California, a self-identified tribe, acknowledged that "having proof of Cherokee blood is extremely important. It is the only way to document one's heritage." But she added, "It seems to be impossible, however, if the ancestors were not on any rolls. Ours apparently were not. I have traveled to many states and looked at every roll available, all to no avail" (June 16, 1996).

Both Helton and Sheppard place great value on written documentation, seeing it as the only way to substantiate their Cherokee lineages, and both have expended much time and energy searching for genealogical records. Helton has been successful in her search, whereas Sheppard has not. Helton belongs to a state-recognized Cherokee tribe that requires members to document their Cherokee ancestry, and she speaks from the position of having already had her identity validated. Sheppard belongs to a self-identified Cherokee tribe that she helped found with her older brother and has never had any form of external recognition, except that which is provided by her own tribal community. Her tribe lies at the other end of the spectrum from Helton's in that it requires no documentation of Cherokee ancestry to belong, only that tribal members continue to look for records and research their Cherokee heritage. Sheppard's statement captures the sense of conflict around documentation that exists for many race shifters: they have an ideal standard for assessing tribal belonging, that of genealogical proof, but only some of them are able to meet it. Sheppard now finds herself in an uncomfortable position. To maintain her tribal status, she must keep searching for genealogical records, but she no longer believes that she will ever find them. For her, the ongoing effort to validate the stories of her parents and grandparents feels like an exercise in futility, so she must find a way to be comfortable with an identity that is rooted in her personal knowledge of those stories rather than in written records.

Although some race shifters, like Helton, have oral histories of family names and places that easily map onto Cherokee experience (in other words, they make sense and seem plausible to most Cherokee listeners), others, like Sheppard, have stories that reach so far back in time or so far outside known Cherokee customs and landscapes that they seem vague and unreliable. More often than not, the measure of proof in evaluating these racial reclamations is not whether these stories feel right or seem plausible but whether they are supported by written records. As most of the people who participate in these discussions see it, oral histories represent possibility but are open to overly elastic interpretation, retelling, and even outright fabrication, whereas the written record is something less vulnerable to the vagaries of time and imagination. As a result, even for those who would question the emphasis on written records—such as the elderly Cherokee woman in Oklahoma who worries about those who might have been omitted from official tribal rolls, or Sheppard in California, who finds herself on a quest for something that might not even exist—having written proof is still a key factor in their discussions and assessments of tribal belonging. Though citizen Cherokees and race shifters consistently make a link between historical documentation and proof of kinship claims, the connection also troubles some of them, not only because it calls into question the validity of their own oral histories but also because they are keenly aware that written histories offer only partial insights into the grand totality of Cherokee experience.

Many of those who question this linkage would still insist that written documentation is an unfortunate but necessary requirement when trying to assess the validity of race shifters' claims. They argue that these claims need to be carefully evaluated because at different points in history, people have tried to assert a connection to the tribe that either did not exist or was tenuous at best. For example, talking about what motivated race shifters, one Oklahoma Cherokee man said, "The reason why so many of these people pick Cherokee [rather than some other tribe], I think, is because at one time, around 1903 to 1906, almost ninety thousand people applied for membership in the tribe but only twenty thousand actually got title. Many of these people are left over from that period" (January 24, 1996). His statement was ambivalent. On the one hand, "people pick Cherokee" echoed the language of choice that race shifters themselves use, but in this context it suggested an inauthentic claim. On the other hand, part of his speculation indicated that perhaps there had been a historic connection with the tribe that was severed. On the same question, Fergus Beech, a Cherokee Nation Tribal Council member, said, "They want to belong to something, but the tribe has to have regulations. They want to belong, but lots of people couldn't...lots can't" (January 23, 1996).

Both of these statements suggest that the claims of contemporary race shifters take advantage of the situation of those bureaucratically excluded Cherokees from earlier historical periods, primarily during the last half of the nineteenth century and early twentieth century, when vast numbers of claimants were rejected either by the tribe itself or by federal officials.[3] Some of these families were legitimately Cherokee—former citizens and Cherokee descendants who were bureaucratically overlooked. Other claimants were non-Indian opportunists looking for land rights, also known as "intruders," a term that some citizen Cherokees still occasionally use to describe contemporary race shifters.[4] These comments also suggest that, just as with any nation, written documentation is needed to verify rights of citizenship and that formal regulations are the basis of sound political practice, at least from the point of view of individuals sympathetic to federally recognized tribal governments.

"Outtalucks" and "Should-bes"

Despite the conflicts surrounding the role of written records of tribal descent and affiliation, these documents remain a significant part of the realpolitik of Cherokee life. However, the exercise is not without empathy. Citizen Cherokees have a sympathetic moniker for those who could have or should have been citizens, who seem more than "wannabe" but who fail to substantiate their connection to the tribe with written records. These individuals are often referred to as "outtalucks" and are considered to be unlucky in one of two ways—either they have no written proof, that they are Cherokee and must rely solely on oral histories, or they have written proof, but it does not meet tribal citizenship standards.

The documentary paradigm is evident in both instances. In the first, the claims of race shifters without written documentation are questioned. In the second, when someone is listed as Cherokee on another tribal roll, as Indian in the U.S. census, or as Cherokee or Indian in federal or state documents such as probate court and vital records, his or her partial documentation carries some symbolic weight among citizen Cherokees—just not enough to cross the threshold of political inclusion. For instance, Charlie Hanson, an Eastern Band citizen, described what happens when people find their Cherokee ancestors listed on a tribal roll other than the base roll—the historical census roll that is used to establish tribal citizenship in the Eastern Band: "Well, people get mad if they do have an ancestor on another roll, besides the Baker Roll, because they can't be enrolled. It doesn't matter if they have an ancestor on every roll before the Baker Roll. If they don't have one on the Baker roll, they can't be enrolled here. And people get pretty upset about that because then they have proof" (October 22, 2003). Although these documents meet an informal burden of proof at the level of social recognition in that they provide evidence to support oral histories, they still do not allow race shifters to establish a political connection with their tribe of origin.

Even inadequate documentation has significance among citizen Cherokees, who place "outtalucks" in a different category from non-Indians or "wannabes." Partial documentation allows citizen Cherokees to make distinctions between "wannabe" and "outtaluck" claims of belonging, which is the primary reason that "outtalucks" are the most sympathetic class of race shifters from the vantage of citizen Cherokees. Many citizen Cherokees consider "outtalucks" to be Cherokee descendants and thus potential Cherokees. For instance, when I asked James Holder, a forty-two-year-old Oklahoma Cherokee man, about undocumented Cherokees, he told me, "Possibly, some are part-Indian and they just got lost. I suppose these people just went into the mainstream and got lost in the shuffle" (January 23, 1996). Though they may be "lost" at the moment, "outtalucks" are potential Cherokees in that they may be able to substantiate their claims and reconnect with the tribe at a later date. They may not be able to reconnect in the same way as those who were raised within or near Cherokee communities, but if they find proper documentation, they have the chance to become tribal citizens.

Also important to note is the much smaller subset of "outtalucks" known as "should-bes." These are Cherokee descendants who lack the appropriate documentation to become tribal citizens but who are nonetheless widely accepted as Cherokees by the local community. In my experience, "should-bes" are usually physically recognizable as American Indians and either live in a Cherokee community or speak the Cherokee language. They have kinship claims that other tribal members accept as valid, and they regularly participate in Cherokee social and cultural events. In fact, "should-bes" are so fully integrated within Cherokee communities that they are known simply as Cherokees, and the issue of what they "should be" is raised only when talking about their lack of voting rights and citizenship status. One individual who qualifies as a "should-be" in the eyes of many Oklahoma Cherokees is the well-known sculptor Willard Stone, whose work has been exhibited as Cherokee art in numerous venues, from the Cherokee Heritage Center in Park Hill, Oklahoma, to the Smithsonian Institution in Washington, D.C. Although he was not formally enrolled as a citizen of the Cherokee Nation, Stone lived much of his life in Locust Grove, Oklahoma, a small Cherokee community, and many people from that area recognize him as one of their own. "Should-bes" find social acceptance among Cherokee people even when they lack the documentation needed for tribal citizenship, but these circumstances are extremely rare.

As I have already suggested, the vast majority of Cherokee citizens in Oklahoma and North Carolina evaluate race shifter claims based on whether they sound plausible and whether they can be substantiated with written documentation. Though many Cherokees feel conflicted about tribal regulations and the fact that they privilege written histories over oral histories, they believe that the contemporary political moment leaves them with few options. The sheer number of race-shifting claims means that they need to be evaluated by some efficient mechanism, and tribal bureaucracies are able to assess written claims and documentation much more efficiently than oral versions. Thus, practical administrative considerations—which entail a bureaucratization of indigenous identity—play an important role in shaping the overall discourse and practice of Cherokee social classification. Because individual Cherokees, as well as the various tribal administrations, place a great deal of importance on the written record as proof of belonging, these practices have fed a genealogical mania among race shifters to produce written records that legitimate their claims. Some Cherokee citizens go so far as to say that Cherokee identity claims should be asserted only after documentation or proof has been obtained. For example, I asked Helena Johnson in North Carolina whether she thought that people who are descendants have the right to claim that they are Cherokee. She responded, "Well, they can claim that they are. It doesn't mean they're enrolled. I have no problem with that…. I don't have a problem with people claiming it, if they really are. If they have proof that they are, I don't have a problem with that. But now everybody just saying, 'My great-great-grandma told me that her dad was a full-blood,' you know. I don't like that. I don't agree with that" (October 22, 2003). For this young woman, Cherokee descendants who are not eligible for enrollment can legitimately call themselves Cherokee, but only if they have written documentation to substantiate their claims. She seemed to suggest that everyone who bases his or her Cherokee identity solely on oral histories is making an unproven (and probably false) claim.

Other Cherokees insist on the importance of documentation for different reasons. They suggest that efforts made by race shifters to document their genealogical claims go far beyond the desire for social and political recognition and instead are about a powerful relationship to historical memory and ancestry that is fundamental to the self-definition of Cherokee people. Diana Terrapin, a middle-aged Cherokee woman who works at Cherokee FIRST, the Cherokee Nation's information center, expressed her feelings on the subject:

> If they have and they know their ancestors from their family just talking
> about it, saying, you know, "Your great-great-grandma came across the Trail
> of Tears," then when they come here looking for that ancestor on our books,
> they're not going to be on there, because they didn't make it here. And so
> when I talk to them, I tell them…"If you know that your ancestor was one of
> the ones that came on the Trail and was Cherokee, what you are doing on your
> part with doing the research (and they really go out of the way doing all this
> research), what that does for that person that came over on the Trail of Tears,
> you're keeping that person alive." So, you know, I don't have any ill
> feelings toward them, you know, because they are keeping their ancestor alive
> that way. (July 31, 2003)

Even though she has a great deal of interaction with the general public, including race shifters who come to the Cherokee Nation in search of genealogical records, Terrapin approaches their quest with sympathy and compassion. She recognizes the brutal legacy of forced removal and the fact that not all Cherokee descendants will be able to find the names of their ancestors in the tribal archives because some of those ancestors who walked the trail died along the way. Rather than question the motivation behind these efforts, she sees them as evidence of the strength of generational ties among Cherokee descendants. For her, the effort is about honoring and remembering the sacrifices of those Cherokees who came before and about doing it in the face of what would otherwise be colonial erasure.

A race shifter's quest for documentation might not result in social or political inclusion, but it may garner the respect of citizen Cherokees, who admire it for keeping alive ancestral memories and historical experiences. Though sentiments differ—

some focus almost exclusively on the political meanings of documentation, others on the social, moral, and cultural implications—most citizen Cherokees around the country and almost all race shifters agree on one thing: knowing about their origins is also about knowing who they are, and thus any effort to document historical memory and ancestry is as much about the present as about the past.

"Descendants" and "Thindians": Blood Measures and the Negotiation of Racial and Cultural Marginality

Among both race shifters and citizen Cherokees, connections to Cherokee forebears and their experiences are often addressed using the idiom of blood, as I have noted elsewhere (see chapter 1, this volume). Having Cherokee blood links race shifters to Cherokee kinfolk, history, and culture and in the process redefines race shifters as Cherokee descendants rather than non-Indians. The ability to establish blood ties is profound: when race shifters are classified as Cherokee descendants, they escape the whiff of illegitimacy that is associated with "wannabes" and become something entirely different. Yet, "Cherokee descendant" is not a cut-and-dried classification but rather a broad social category that can include everything from a noncitizen "outtaluck" with documentation of tribal descent, to a recently enrolled citizen with a relatively low blood quantum, to a long-term tribal citizen with a white appearance. The common ground is that all of these people have genealogical ties to Cherokee ancestors that are accepted by Cherokee citizens because they have been verified either with documentation or with an oral genealogy that is detailed and recent enough to pass muster.

The flexibility and openness of "blood" as a signifier gives it great power in everyday discourses of tribal belonging; more often than not, it is the language of both inclusion and exclusion. Diana Terrapin described the significance of Cherokee blood while discussing Cherokee people who survived the Trail of Tears:

> By them suffering through all that, well, it's like…they made it, you know? There was that blood. There was something inside of them that made them go on. And so when the ones we talked about earlier [Cherokee descendants], the ones that just have a little bit of that blood, I tell them when they just have a very little bit, I tell them, "One day, that little bit of blood, that Indian blood that is in you, is going to rise up, and it's going to help you through some time, something that you didn't think you were ever going to get through. And then, when it does happen, you are going to recognize it, and it's because somebody endured a hardship for you to be here right now." (July 31, 2003)

Terrapin seemed to suggest that race shifters with verifiable blood ties can receive a symbolic consolation prize. Although their connection to the Cherokee past may be insufficient to make them tribal citizens, it still has value. When needed, this part of their being will allow them to face difficult times and endure. Cherokee blood has this power because it originates in Cherokee people who faced and survived hardships in the past. In other words, Terrapin believes that facing adversity builds strength of character and that this character trait is passed down through the generations. However, whether she meant that it is socially transmitted or something innate is unclear. The difficulty of interpretation lies in the fact that contemporary Cherokee citizens use the essentialist language of blood in both a literal and metaphoric sense, especially when discussing race shifters with Cherokee ancestry.

As individuals with a documented blood connection to the tribe, Cherokee descendants are in an ambiguous category. They have the potential to be accepted as fellow Cherokees but are placed into a questionable category for any number of reasons having to do with their social networks, cultural knowledge, and physical appearance. "Cherokee descendant" is not a political distinction, but a social one, because it includes noncitizen race shifters as well as tribal citizens. Cherokee descendants are considered to be quasi-Cherokees—people with legitimate genealogical or even political connections to the tribe that are insufficient to warrant their full social acceptance. Even descendants who are tribal citizens are sometimes called white Indians, white Cherokees, or Thindians, all of which signal racial, cultural, and social marginality.[5] Cherokee descendants are considered to be somehow betwixt and between, for they are neither fully Cherokee nor "wannabes," a category that is decidedly non-Indian. Their marginal status is not based on the newness of their claims, but on the complex interaction of social, cultural, and genealogical measures. Although the specific criteria vary from person to person, consider the distinction made by Melissa Hunter, an Eastern Band Cherokee citizen in her early forties: "I normally apply 'wannabe' to somebody with no descent.... Those people [with Cherokee ancestry] who don't know their cultures, we call them Thindians...my sister-in-law calls them white Indians" (October 22, 2003). In this case, cultural knowledge is an important measure of Cherokee identity and is something that can be qualified in racial terms.

Although cultural knowledge plays an important role in shaping whether someone with Cherokee ancestry will be accepted as Cherokee, another important measure of tribal belonging is genealogical distance—which is ironic, at least in Oklahoma, given that the Cherokee Nation is the largest federally recognized tribe without a blood quantum standard for tribal citizenship. From what we know of the early eighteenth-century Cherokee kinship system, distance between generations was not a significant factor in determining relatedness. Within the same clan, a Cherokee woman shared clan ties with her great-great-grandchildren to the same extent as she did with her great-grandchildren and grandchildren. Clan membership cut between and across the generations, so the offspring of two Cherokee sisters were considered to be siblings and in turn these children considered both women to be their mothers. Today, however, citizen Cherokees in Oklahoma and North Carolina have adopted many aspects of the Euro-American kinship system, particularly the idea that kin relatedness becomes increasingly distant and more tenuous with each successive generation. For example, Betty Baker in North Carolina had this to say about Cherokee descendants who did not qualify for tribal enrollment: "It comes to a point when you ask yourself, When are you Indian, and when are you not? The blood's so thin that it's not even there. I mean, we're not the only ones facing that. Everybody is. Eventually, we're just gonna be one big race" (October 22, 2003). Her statement is similar to many I have heard in Oklahoma, implying a point of no return when blood connections are stretched so thin across the generations that they no longer matter—hence the term *Thindians*.

A paradox is apparent in citizen Cherokee responses to race shifters when they convey the sense that quantity of blood should not matter and yet it does. In general, Cherokee citizens in Oklahoma believe that all ancestral ties matter—even those that are genealogically distant—but they are still ambivalent about the overall implications of these ties for social classification. For example, Richard Allen, an Oklahoma Cherokee man in his mid-fifties, said:

> There are those who have Cherokee ancestry that I accept with no problem. I know that they have a certain amount of blood.... It may be so minuscule it seems unreal, but it's there. They do have ancestry. For instance, I think there is one family now that has a blood quantum of 1/4096. There's no denying that they had an ancestor somewhere twelve generations back who was a full-blood, and that blood is carried forward. You can't deny that person is related, you know, going back twelve generations to the Cherokee. However, there are others that they're related to as well that maybe have had more influence on the culture than did the Cherokee in their family. (July 31, 2003)

Like other citizen Cherokees in Oklahoma and North Carolina, Allen used the language of blood to describe the nature of these connections. Because certain race shifters have Cherokee blood, they are relatives, and blood is the vehicle that carries their ancestral connections forward. However, this blood tie can be "so miniscule it seems unreal," as Allen said, and its tenuousness is something that can be measured in the language of blood quantum and generational distance. In effect, he honors Cherokee blood connections regardless of generation—a reflection of Cherokee kinship logic that can benefit race shifters. Nevertheless, and somewhat paradoxically, these connections are also quantifiable according to Euro-American kinship beliefs and thus may be said to exert less influence over someone's identity than do ancestral connections that are seemingly less distant. Blood matters—that much is certain—but whether blood quantum matters is more ambiguous and contested.

What citizen Cherokees are expressing is a contradiction born of two rival classificatory schemes: a Cherokee one that reckons kin across the generations (via blood) and a Euro-American one that defines kin according to generational distance (via blood quantum). Oftentimes, when citizen Cherokees in Oklahoma and North Carolina try to assess their relatedness to race shifters and to one another, they slip into the language of blood quantum. The move is not surprising, given that for centuries the federal government has both denied and assigned rights to American Indian people on the basis of blood quantum standards. As a result, most tribal governments have incorporated some version of these standards in their tribal membership rules. For example, the most common blood quantum requirement imposed as a standard of tribal citizenship is one-quarter degree of Indian blood, the same standard that has traditionally been used in much twentieth-century federal legislation.[6] Many Indian and non-Indian people assume that blood quantum provides a measure of racial belonging and cultural distinctiveness, and Cherokees are no different—although the three federally recognized tribes differ on whether blood quantum is codified: the Cherokee Nation imposes no blood quantum standard for citizenship, but the other two federally recognized Cherokee tribes do. These legal and political systems of social classification are often at odds with individual and community standards, yet in general, Cherokee people around the country use blood quantum to assess racial distinctiveness, such as whether someone is sufficiently Indian. At times, they also use it as a predictive measure of cultural difference, the assumption being that someone with more Cherokee blood is likely to have more knowledge of Cherokee culture than someone with less Cherokee blood.

However, debates about blood quantum have a different flavor in different Cherokee contexts. Because Cherokee histories and experiences vary considerably based on time and place, the issues and stakes surrounding blood quantum are very different in the towns of Cherokee, North Carolina, and Tahlequah, Oklahoma. In Cherokee, North Carolina, the prerequisite for tribal enrollment (which entitles a person to per capita payments from tribal gaming enterprises) is set at 1/16 blood quantum or degree of Cherokee blood, excluding tribal descendants with 1/32 degree or less.[7] In a sense, blood quantum rules are seen as a filter that keeps out tribal relations who might (it is assumed) be motivated by greed. Eastern Band citizen and anthropologist Michael Lambert says, "It is possible that some tribes imposed restrictive membership rules because of per capita payments" (personal communication, November 13, 2003). Lambert understands the protective impulse behind blood quantum legislation in an era of per capita payments but worries that it can seriously impact "the responsibility of every tribal member to protect and enhance the political standing of the tribe" (November 13, 2003). He goes on to say that "many tribes could greatly increase their political clout by increasing their membership" but fail to do so because of blood quantum policies (November 13, 2003). He suggests that rather than impose blood quantum standards that limit their membership and their political base, tribes should use more expansive standards of citizenship and thus grow in numbers and political power—an interesting possibility that would surely bring in certain types of racial shifters with verifiable claims.

Race shifters face a very different situation in Oklahoma, where neither federally recognized tribe has per capita payments and the largest tribe has no blood quantum rule whatsoever. In part because the Cherokee Nation sets no blood quantum barrier to citizenship, it has grown into one of the largest and most powerful tribes in the United States, with well over 250,000 members. But this size and power have come at a price. Many Cherokees in Oklahoma, as well as citizens of other American Indian tribes, believe that the Cherokee Nation's enrollment policies have fundamentally changed its cultural and racial character in a way that invites race shifting and other phenomena widely understood as dilutions of Cherokee substance.

Though the stereotype is far from true, the Cherokee Nation has garnered a reputation as a nation of racially and culturally white Indians. For this reason, some Cherokees in Oklahoma have defected from the Cherokee Nation to join the United Keetoowah Band of Cherokee Indians, across town in the little city of Tahlequah. They have done so not because the United Keetoowah Band offers per capita payments—as noted above, neither of the Cherokee tribes in Tahlequah does, though each offers other economic benefits to its citizens—but because the United Keetoowah Band sets its citizenship standards at one-quarter degree of Cherokee blood. Because only a little more than one-fifth of Cherokee Nation citizens and almost no race shifters can meet this standard, the United Keetoowah Band prides itself on being a tribe of "real Indians." Those who have made the switch will laughingly say, "I've gone over to the dark side," an ironic reference to the movie *Star Wars* and the presumed dark skin of tribal members. Thus, the local political struggles between these two Indian nations occupying the same geographic territory, the United Keetoowah Band and the Cherokee Nation, are often couched in racial terms as struggles between real Indians and white Indians, between substantially blooded, culturally authentic Cherokees and inauthentic, culturally assimilated Thindians.[8] It is a nasty stereotype to be sure, but one that has increasingly dogged the Cherokee Nation as its citizenship base and the overall number of race shifters have grown over the past three decades.

On Blood, Kinship, and Paper Trails: Race Shifters Respond

In political conflicts about Cherokee identity, such as this one between the Cherokee Nation and the United Keetoowah Band, as well as those between citizen Cherokees and race shifters, the language of blood always takes center stage. Blood is at the core of these struggles because it has become a powerful measure of social, racial, cultural, and political belonging and is widely perceived to be the very substance that binds Cherokee people together and unites them across their differences. For this reason, race shifters cannot simply assert blood ties without suggesting that they, too, are part of the Cherokee family, with rights to Cherokee culture and political recognition. Yet, the sheer number of these claims means that Cherokee tribal governments must have a practical means for assessing their validity, especially when trying to determine eligibility for tribal citizenship. Although individual tribal citizens exercise their own judgment, using standards that may or may not reflect those of their respective tribal governments, all three federally recognized Cherokee tribes have policies that require claims of Cherokee blood ties to be validated through documentation. Two of the tribes also require these ties to be quantified—the Cherokee Nation accepts those with any amount of ancestry, as long as it is properly documented, whereas the other two tribes accept only those with a specific blood quantum.

Ironically, the Cherokee Nation is the most open of the three tribes in terms of its citizenship requirements, and yet, because of its size and prominence, it has drawn angry criticism from many race shifters for what they view as its exclusionary standards of membership.[9] "The Cherokee Nation is a separatist organization that refuses to recognize their own authentic ancestors," said Chief Seeing Heart Stevens of the Delilah White Cloud Tribe of Cherokees in West Virginia. "It denies membership to ethnic Cherokees, except for those who are descended from a white man's roll" (March 11, 1996).[10] Stevens criticized the Cherokee Nation not only because it excludes him and his relations, "ethnic Cherokees," but also because, he believes, the Cherokee Nation is allowing an artifact of white colonial rule—the Dawes Rolls—to determine who is a Cherokee citizen. The Dawes Rolls were created at the turn of the twentieth century as one of the initial steps in the process of allotment, which dramatically reduced the tribal land base by parceling it to individual citizens and opening up the remainder for non-Indian settlement. Stevens believes that the Cherokee Nation is reproducing white measures of indigeneity in its own citizenship standards, the implication being that the tribe's policies are linked not only to a history of settler colonialism but also to white racism.

Consider also the racial subtext of the very next statement that Stevens made: "There's a persistent rumor that the Dawes Rolls favored those with Confederate ancestors and that the majority of Cherokees were left off for political reasons" (March 11, 1996). He and other race shifters believe that Cherokee citizens in the 1860s who sided with the South were wealthier than Union sympathizers and that decades after Reconstruction, the former Confederates still had enough wealth and political influence to skew the tribal rolls in their favor. Part of what they are alluding to is a widely held but nonetheless erroneous belief that pro-slavery Cherokees were more assimilated in both racial and cultural terms—meaning that they were more likely to have mixed blood, share white attitudes, and a higher economic standing—than those Cherokees who were anti-slavery. Although few historians would support Steven's statement, it reflects a common belief among race shifters that the rift between the Cherokee Nation and them can be traced to racial and political conflicts more than a century old.

The anger that race shifters like Stevens feel toward the Cherokee Nation is often rooted in untenable assumptions about the historical record, as well as misconceptions about present-day policies. Many race shifters are confused about the requirements for tribal citizenship and seem to conflate the practices of the three federally recognized tribes. The most common misperception is that the Cherokee Nation, in addition to imposing a standard of documented lineal descent that can be traced to the Dawes Rolls, has a blood quantum requirement like the other two tribes'. In late May 2003, that argument was made by members of the Southern Cherokee Nation in Webbers Falls, Oklahoma, the same self-identified tribe that Troy Wayne Poteete alludes to at the start of this chapter. My research assistant, Jessica Walker Blanchard, conducted an interview with a tribal officer named Drew Martin and his wife, Kate, who was quick to chime in with her opinion and active in tribal affairs despite being non-Indian.

At the time of the interview, the Southern Cherokee Nation allowed anyone with Cherokee ancestry to join its ranks, but it granted voting rights only to those with Southern Cherokee ancestry. Walker Blanchard wanted to know why someone other than a Southern Cherokee would want to join the organization if his or her rights within the organization would be so limited. This is how the Martins responded to her question:

> DM: I think, because the Cherokee Nation and others are such frauds, they don't want to be a part of it! And he [*points to another tribal member whose ancestors fought against the Confederacy*] is as much a part of [the Southern Cherokee Nation] as I am.
>
> KM: It's blood quantum.
>
> DM: Yeah, they have a blood quantum over there. If you marry a white or if you get down with someone else, they discriminate against their own kids, grandkids....
>
> KM: They have the most rights in their tribe. I don't know what the percentage is, like one-fourth or one-eighth, but if you're any less than that, you're out. Like, as far as money or anything like that, that's people that are so greedy, they're not going to have their own kids and grandkids [included in the tribal rolls]! In this tribe, if you prove one drop of Southern Cherokee blood, you're Southern Cherokee, period.
>
> DM: This is for our kids.
>
> KM: 'Cause it comes back up.... The Indian is in here [points to her heart]. It's not just what's running in your veins.
>
> DM: Kate, you're a German.
>
> KM: Yeah, I know, but I live with the biggest Indian in the county [*laughter*]!
>
> DM: Go get me a cup of coffee. I love you to death, but you're a damn German from Pennsylvania.... I don't want to be any more than I am. I'd just as rather be fishin' as I would be on this council, but we gotta do it.... It's for all of us. If we don't do it and the chief doesn't make laws that are right for the whole tribe, we ain't going to have nothing. (May 24, 2003)

What is surprising about this exchange is how the conversation quickly devolved from a bland discussion about membership requirements in the Southern Cherokee Nation to an angry attack on the Cherokee Nation, as if the two were directly implicated in each other. The Martins' misplaced anger about blood quantum requirements seems to suggest that the Southern Cherokee Nation arose in response to the perceived exclusiveness of the Cherokee Nation, a tribe they paint as being so greedy that it is willing to discriminate against its own, which of course in this context means discriminating against them.

In considering comments like these, I cannot help but wonder whether some of the members of the Southern Cherokee Nation, particularly those who were raised in Oklahoma, are actually eligible for citizenship in the Cherokee Nation but have never pursued the option because they mistakenly believe that the tribe would exclude them based on some arbitrary measure of racial belonging. And I wonder, too, whether there would even be a need for alternatives like the Southern Cherokee Nation if race shifters did not have these misperceptions to begin with. But even if they had a clearer understanding of Cherokee Nation policy and could meet the citizenship requirements, I doubt that many race shifters would leave their communities to join ranks with the Cherokee Nation or any other federally recognized Cherokee tribe. Race shifters have an ongoing antagonism toward the federally recognized Cherokee tribes that is fueled by their exclusion and the misinformation that surrounds it. They also have other motivations for their separatism, including antiauthoritarian attitudes that transcend their relationship with the Cherokee Nation and distinct notions about what constitutes authentic Cherokee practice.

Marge Peterson provided a thought-provoking example of the antagonistic attitudes that race shifters can have toward federally recognized Cherokee tribes that present documentary hurdles to tribal citizenship for what seem to be dubious reasons—at least to those who are excluded. I asked Peterson, the principal chief of the Southeastern Cherokee Confederacy in Georgia, whether there was anything she wanted to say about the topic of nonrecognized Cherokees that had not already been covered. She responded with a pointed critique of recognized Cherokee tribes and their documentary practices:

> Those of us who do not have absolute recorded proof of our lineage endure a tremendous amount of ridicule from the federally recognized tribes. They call us wannabes, apple Indians, and yahoos, and by some we are treated as less than human. Yet, there has never been an accurate accounting of the numbers of Cherokees in all the rolls and censuses that have been recorded.... So who are these federal tribes to say that I am not genuine?
>
> By all accounts, there are few if any full bloods alive today. The only difference between them and us is, they and their ancestors chose to accept the abuse, of the government and allowed themselves to become virtual prisoners on the land. They live in a welfare state and continue to endure the abuse, and for what? MONEY. Thanks, but no thanks. I don't want it. I sincerely grieve for the hardships they have had to endure over the decades, but they could have changed part of their history. I place total blame on their leaders.
>
> Yet at the same time, I have a yearning to be accepted, not for monetary reasons but for the work we are doing to try and make life better for all Native Americans. How much more fruitful our efforts would be if we worked together instead of against each other. (April 23, 1996)

Obviously, Peterson felt bitter, the object of ridicule. She first responded by suggesting that Cherokees who have been made "official" by flawed documents are in no position to judge "unofficial" Cherokees like herself. Immediately following this point, however, Peterson took a much more critical and even judgmental tone when she raised the issue of blood quantum and used it to advance an argument about racial difference. She seemed to imply that if the federally recognized tribes were more racially distinct, meaning more full blood and less mixed blood, then their racial authenticity would entitle them to pass judgment on people like herself. As it is, they are no more genuine than she and her race-shifting peers. Because they are racially mixed, just like her, she challenged their authority on Cherokee matters, including their right to criticize and exclude her.

Like many race shifters, Peterson painted the federally recognized Cherokee tribes not as indigenous people with a unique political status but as sellouts who have chosen to endure the oversight of the federal government out of greed. Ironically, she accused the federally recognized tribes of the very same thing that they accuse race shifters of doing—being Indian for the money. Her reference to welfare might even suggest her own anti-Indian sentiments; she dismissed treaty obligations and political rights as mere government handouts in a way that would sound at home on right-wing talk radio. She placed the blame for American Indian misfortunes on Indians themselves rather than acknowledge the legacy of colonial intervention in their lives.

These biting criticisms are not unique to Peterson; they circulate widely among race shifters who are responding defensively to painful experiences of mockery and exclusion. Their comments show not only what race shifters think about citizen Cherokees but also what they think about themselves. When race shifters argue that the Cherokee Nation is fraudulent—not really Cherokee—because it uses external documents to define its citizenry and this process reproduces racist practices and logics that are unfairly exclusive—by extension they argue that they are less racist, more inclusive, and more legitimately Cherokee because they do not define themselves according to non-Indian standards. In other words, they invert what citizen Cherokees say about race shifters and claim the mantle of authentic Indianness: not only are they *real* Cherokees, but also they are *better* Cherokees than anyone else. This rhetorical strategy might not impress citizen Cherokees, but it is an important part of race shifters' antiauthoritarian culture: it allows them to recast a serious flaw (at least in the minds of citizen Cherokees) as their greatest virtue. In a sense, race shifters are depicting the Cherokee Nation as those "hang around the fort" Indians whose cynical adaptation to colonial norms has left them unable to appreciate their wilder and less documented cousins.

The Cherokee Nation might wince at such accusations, but race shifters hold them as an article of their antidocumentary, antiauthoritarian faith. What makes them better in their own minds is their fierce independence. Race shifters see their independence as evidence that they were better able to fight off the shackles of colonialism. They see themselves as the ones whose ancestors actively resisted removal by hiding out from the Trail of Tears and refused to enroll when it came time for allotment. Theirs is a bold story of autonomous agency—one in which they are not accounted for in federal, state, and tribal records because they bravely refused to be counted. For many race shifters, the term "undocumented" evokes a stereotypical vision of pristine native life, uncorrupted by colonial bureaucracies and their minions. I often heard race shifters say, "We don't need anyone to tell us who we are" when asked to compare themselves with federally recognized Cherokees, as if asserting their independence from the federal government and federally recognized tribes was a badge of honor and mark of their legitimacy.

Radical self-definition is an understandable response to feelings of exclusion, but an undercurrent of wistfulness also often characterizes the way that race shifters talk about themselves and their relationship to citizen Cherokees. Though some race shifters may reject federal recognition as a flawed process, almost all of them still wish to be seen as Cherokee people in the eyes of others, both Indians and non-Indians.[11] As Marge Peterson put it, they have a "yearning to be accepted," and this yearning is more about a desire for social recognition than for the formal political recognition that stems from federal acknowledgment (April 23, 1996). Motivated by a desire to be seen as legitimately Cherokee, race shifters have come up with several strategies for recognizing one another as Cherokee community members, including the formation of tribes in which their claims to indigeneity are more readily accepted.

However, there is an irony in these various approaches to social recognition: nearly all of them reproduce the same documentary paradigm that has been established in federal and federally recognized tribal policy. For instance, the leadership of the Northern Cherokee Nation of Old Louisiana Territory requires tribal members to use genealogical records to trace their lineages back to a specific group of Cherokees—in this case, the Old Settlers, who voluntarily settled in Arkansas prior to removal in 1838. They require this kind of documentation even though they acknowledge, as Arlo Davis did, that "some will be left out that [they] know are Cherokee, but [they] cannot prove it. They cannot prove it" (February 22, 2003). In imitation of the federally recognized Cherokee tribal policies that they often disparage, they sometimes hold to the documentary paradigm because they would rather exclude people who they "know are Cherokee" than risk including someone who is not Cherokee and further jeopardizing their reputation.

Other race-shifting communities also trace themselves back to a particular group of Cherokees in ways that seem designed to persuade citizen Cherokees that their claims to indigeneity should be taken seriously, though the opposite effect is more common. As noted earlier in the chapter, the Southern Cherokee Nation in Webbers Falls requires that its members provide evidence that they descend from Cherokee families who were Southern sympathizers, before receiving full rights within the tribe. The Southern Cherokee Nation not only holds to this documentary ideal in its formal membership requirements but also produces its own documents that further mimic the standards of the federally recognized tribes. For instance, the Southern Cherokee Nation—like the Cherokee Nation, Eastern Band, and United Keetoowah Band—provides its members with tribal enrollment cards that specify a Cherokee blood quantum. Yet, even as the tribe does this, it does so in a way that seems to maximize its members' claims to indigeneity and in a way that many citizen Cherokees find troubling. A Southern Cherokee Nation member named Morris Carter explained how their complex system of documentation works: "My card says I'm just as much Indian as a full-blooded Indian. There's no such thing as a full-blooded Indian on our cards. The card shows I'm one-half—64/128—and that's considered half. I'm not half. I'm a quarter Indian myself by my own figuring out, but everybody has a card showing your blood is one-half. So if you got a little bitty speck of Indian in you and you can prove it, you're a half Indian. You're Indian" (May 24, 2003).

In this case, the specific blood quantum of tribal members is subject to manipulation. Membership is determined solely by whether they can meet the tribe's requirements for proof that they have Cherokee ancestry, and that proof lies in historical documents: the one-half blood quantum is an inaccurate but symbolically powerful measure of genealogical belonging. In a seemingly bizarre racial calculus, any individual who can document a "little bitty speck of Indian" is represented as "half Indian," en route to being wholly Indian.[12] What these tribally produced documents affirm is that the bearer not only is recognized by the tribe but also is Indian enough to meet almost any standard of racial authenticity. Perhaps citizen Cherokees would be more persuaded if the Southern Cherokee Nation did not seem to manipulate the documentation process in ways that seem inaccurate and self-serving.

Ironically, even those self-identified tribes that most challenge the documentary paradigm—such as the Cherokee Confederacy of Southern California, mentioned earlier in the chapter—also produce their own documents that in some way mimic the practices of federally recognized tribes. Recall Vera Sheppard, who said that her tribe in Southern California did not require any documentation of Cherokee blood to belong, only that its members keep researching their Cherokee heritage. Despite what seems like a rejection of the documentary standard, Sheppard's tribe also created laminated tribal enrollment cards with a tribal seal, a photo identification, and an enrollment number, which resemble those produced by federally recognized Cherokee tribes (June 16, 1996). When members of the Cherokee Confederacy of Southern California were questioned about their status, as they often were, they could flash these cards as evidence of their legitimacy, even while arguing that documentation is not essential to tribal identity or membership.

The Cherokee Confederacy of Southern California's paradoxical relationship with the documentary paradigm is a far cry from the Cherokee Nation's insistence upon it. Yet, despite the different standards and practices among various communities of race shifters and the three federally recognized Cherokee nations, documented Cherokee ancestry has become a primary measure of Cherokee belonging as both citizen Cherokees and race shifters confront and evaluate the claims of their potential kinfolk. Though the concept of blood is configured in multiple ways, it bridges geographic and political distance, and it is the idiom that official Cherokees in Oklahoma and North Carolina use as they debate and evaluate the claims of race shifters. But this blood requires verification, so claims to Cherokee ancestry are usually seen as valid and legitimate only when they are documented. Although this outcome may seem like a pragmatic necessity, given the various administrative considerations of tribal, state, and federal governments, the language of blood and documentation can so overwhelm the discourse of Cherokee belonging that it can obscure the nature of race shifters' claims. Maybe the trick is not to let such practical matters of tribal administration and paper trails overly determine our readings of race shifters' stories and their overall situation. If we judge the claims of race shifters as simply right or wrong, true or untrue, based on whether they have written documentation to support them, then surely we will miss something significant about what these stories mean and why there are so many of them at this particular moment in time. In other words, being Cherokee is about blood—at least in the ways this term is broadly understood in Indian country—but it is not about blood only.

Cultural "Doing" as Another Measure of Racial "Being"

The idea that Cherokee blood is a fundamental attribute of tribal kinship is an old one that relates to the matrilineal Cherokee clan system. For this reason, when citizen Cherokees are open to the possibility that some race shifters might have Cherokee ancestry, their discourse softens. Most citizen Cherokees are much more tolerant of race shifters who are able to document their Cherokee ancestry. Most understand why Cherokee descendants would be curious about their ancestral culture and why they would want to reconnect with their tribe of origin. Yet, having Cherokee blood is not the only criterion by which citizen Cherokees judge race shifters' claims. Alongside their ideas about kinship and ancestry, they also reference distinctive ways of thinking, speaking, and behaving that they feel define them as a people. Their discussions about whether race shifters can or should be brought into the tribal fold are revealing because they suggest different ideas about the power and nature of culture and almost always lead to further debates about whether culture should be used as a primary measure of Cherokee belonging.

A key issue in these debates is whether Cherokee culture is something that race shifters can and should learn later in life. As in the arguments about documenting blood ties, the debate hinges on essentialist claims about Cherokee identity. This version of cultural essentialism is not a simplistic notion that culture is innate and exists within a Cherokee child at birth, but rather the idea that enculturation within a given Cherokee family, at a young age, is a foundational experience that establishes a lifelong Cherokee sensibility. For example, some Cherokees believe that race shifters, even those with Cherokee ancestry, can never come back to Cherokee culture later in life. Consider the following exchange I had with Cherokee Nation citizen Richard Allen:

> RA: What they [race shifters] like to say to me is that they're coming back to claim their heritage or reclaim their heritage, and I suggest to them, they've already grown up in one heritage. They can't come back and claim something they didn't have. I don't deny that they have Cherokee blood and that they can become more aware of Cherokee history, culture, and tradition. But I don't think they should become more than who they are if they weren't reared within that, quote, Cherokee spirituality.

CS: So you're really talking about culture. You're saying culture is what you're raised with, that it's not something you can learn, really, as an adult. It's a way of looking at the world?

RA: Yeah, I think it certainly is. It's a worldview that you're reared with, because early on you're exposed to certain behaviors, certain beliefs, certain stories, certain practices that are Cherokee and have been Cherokee for thousands of years. They may have been modified over the years, but they're still Cherokee practices. And for someone to all of a sudden suggest that they're going to, quote, reclaim these things, it's not going to occur. (July 31, 2003)

According to this line of reasoning, race shifters can never reclaim Cherokee culture and become truly Cherokee in a cultural sense, because Cherokee culture is the product of early childhood exposure to Cherokee cultural practices. What a curious adult might learn in a book or even in a Cherokee community is no substitute for childhood enculturation. Adult learning will likely create a heightened awareness and a greater understanding of Cherokee culture—making it explicit and conscious. However, this new perspective is not considered to be commensurable with the unique, foundational worldview that arises out of childhood experience, when Cherokee culture becomes so deeply embedded in daily practice that it is taken for granted.

Whereas some citizen Cherokees hold up childhood enculturation as a formative experience that seems to close the door to race shifters, even those with blood ties, others suggest that culture is something more pliable, a product of human interaction that can be learned later in life. They go so far as to suggest that culture—regardless of when it is acquired—is the medium through which different types of Cherokee descendants can become more fully Cherokee. Robert Thompson, an Eastern Band Cherokee man in his early forties, explained it to me this way: "We get so many people calling for genealogy. They want to do this, and I tell them, I say, 'You can spend ten years trying to track down your ancestry to prove that you're a Cherokee. Now why don't you do this: Why don't you spend that ten years and learn to be a good Cherokee? Why don't you learn the language? Why don't you learn the history? Why don't you do the culture? Why don't you really become Cherokee?'" (October 22, 2003). In other words, blood ties and their documentation have their place, but real Cherokeeness comes from walking the walk and talking the talk, both of which can be learned at almost any stage of life by almost any Cherokee descendant who is serious about becoming more fully Cherokee. Thompson believes that people with Cherokee ancestry who are interested in reconnecting with their Cherokee heritage can actually "become Cherokee" if they are willing to put in the hard work of learning about Cherokee history and culture. He went on to state that "in reality, [being] Cherokee's not really about blood. Cherokee's not about, you know, having long hair. Cherokee's about a culture, you know, the clan, the language. I mean, I'm just a human being, just like everybody else. What makes me different is that culture" (October 22, 2003). In other words, Cherokee "being" is directly related to cultural "doing."

Race shifters might be encouraged by such a sentiment among citizen Cherokees, because it seems to leave open the door to cultural belonging even to those who cannot document their claims or whose blood quantum is insufficient for United Keetoowah Band or Eastern Band membership. It seems to suggest that people of goodwill, convinced of their ancestral connections even without definitive proof, could work hard to learn Cherokee culture and in so doing become a part of that community. But the legacy of essentialism lingers, even in seemingly antiessentialist contexts. Thompson's statements seem to privilege cultural behavior over other attributes in determining who is Cherokee and who could become Cherokee. However, in these existential debates, the distinction between nature and culture, being and doing, is not as straightforward as it might seem. For example, only moments later, Thompson told me this: "You know John Ross?[13] He was one-eighth. His momma was a Cherokee. Our mom was a Cherokee. Her mom was a Cherokee. He was Cherokee. That was old clan law. The way that I see it, I'm long hair [a Cherokee clan] here, I'm a long hair in the Cherokee Nation, I'm a long hair with the United Band of Keetoowahs" (October 22, 2003). In this instance, having Cherokee blood does matter—not the fact of ancestry itself or the amount of blood degree, but whether one is the descendant of a Cherokee mother and thus belongs to a matrilineal Cherokee clan. As Thompson suggested, Cherokee citizens in all three federally recognized tribes are connected to one another via ancestry and kinship, a tie that, as I have already demonstrated, is often expressed in the idiom of blood, and many of them recognize the importance of clan belonging. Thus, cultural knowledge (familiarity with the Cherokee matrilineal clan system) allows them to make sense of being, to know when the facts of descent matter and when they do not.

Most citizen Cherokees talk about racial identity using concepts that seem contradictory—ideas about "being" versus "doing," nature versus culture, and what is learned versus what is innate. When considered at a deeper level, these ideas are embedded in one another. Race signals all of these things, bridging their various divides. However, a small minority argues that culture shapes racial identity to such an extent that the facts of descent are almost irrelevant when determining whether someone is Cherokee. When citizen Cherokees do make this argument, culture takes on essentialist connotations yet again. Consider, for example, what Thompson said about interracial adoption: "Let's just say I found this little white baby, and I fell in love with this little white baby and raised him as my child, and I spoke to him in Indian, and I told him the stories, and he knew my whole family history. He played with his so-called pseudo-cousins. When he's all grown up, don't tell me he's not a Cherokee" (October 22, 2003).[14] In this instance, culture has transformative power and can make a white baby boy into a Cherokee man. Understanding the Cherokee language, hearing the stories and the history—at least in the case of a child—gives rise to a Cherokee person with a Cherokee worldview. What makes this example not so straightforward (meaning that it is an anti-antiessentialist or even quasi-essentialist argument) is that it is linked to early childhood enculturation, being raised by Cherokees within a Cherokee family.

Like the earlier statement from Richard Allen, who suggested that Cherokee descendants could not become Cherokee because they had not been raised as Cherokees, this man suggested that non-Indians can become Cherokee only if they are raised as Cherokees. In both cases, "doing" trumps "being," and culture is what gives rise to a Cherokee sensibility and identity. But culture also seems to have taken on some of the mantle of essentialism when it is linked to early childhood experience rather than more self-conscious forms of adult acquisition.

Because citizen Cherokees believe that Cherokee culture is an essential property of Cherokee people, it has great power in shaping their social boundaries. It also shapes a moral sensibility—the idea that when Cherokee people practice Cherokee culture, something is right in the world. When non-Cherokees practice Cherokee culture, including New Age "wannabes" and race shifters without Cherokee ancestry, something is wrong. Citizen Cherokees believe that people who engage in these behaviors are guilty of naive misrepresentation at best or cynical appropriation at worst. Depending on where citizen Cherokees are situated with respect to Cherokee culture, particularly in terms of language, religious affiliation, and residential community, they can have very different ideas about how these activities might affect their local contexts, their sociopolitical rights, and the world at large.

The idea that culture is an essential property belonging to a certain group of people may seem straightforward, but it gets more complicated when citizen Cherokees consider race shifters with Cherokee ancestry who wish to learn and practice Cherokee culture later in life. If culture is something that can be learned in adulthood, then it has the power to make Cherokee descendants into "real" Cherokees, or into better Cherokees at the very least. If, however, it can be learned only in the process of first enculturation, then race shifters with Cherokee ancestry can never attain cultural authenticity in the eyes of citizen Cherokees. Despite their blood, they even run the risk of cultural appropriation and misrepresentation, as in the case of non-Indian "wannabes." In the first instance, for Cherokee descendants to learn about Cherokee culture and specifically about Cherokee religion is morally just and is good for them and Cherokee society as a whole. In the second instance, the move to reclaim Cherokee culture is seen as morally problematic.

When citizen Cherokees debate these issues, which bear heavily on the morality of race shifting and their political reactions to it, context is everything. Though they dismiss non-Indian appropriations of Cherokee culture, often with anger, they are much more tolerant of efforts made by plausibly Cherokee descendants to reconnect with Cherokee culture and Cherokee people. However, even in the case of Cherokee descendants, citizen Cherokees are deeply concerned that these efforts take place within and under the supervision of what they believe to be legitimate Cherokee communities. For most citizen Cherokees, this means within the context of their own or other federally recognized Cherokee tribes, not under the aegis of state-recognized or self-identified tribes, something I describe in the next chapter. The hope is that these interactions will allow them to exercise some control over how Cherokee culture is transmitted and represented in the broader U.S. society.

In this sense, citizen Cherokees believe that place matters in their assessment of race shifters' attempts to learn Cherokee culture. For example, I asked Helena Johnson, an Eastern Band citizen in her twenties, how she felt about Cherokee descendants creating their own tribal organizations and about their collective efforts to learn Cherokee culture. She said, "I think I would rather them be here [Cherokee, North Carolina]. As long as they had the right information, they know the things, they're not giving people the wrong information and misrepresenting us, I would rather them be here" (October 22, 2003). When I asked her to clarify whether she meant that Cherokee descendants could learn appropriate behavior only from the Eastern Band tribe itself, she continued, "Yes, that, and plus if they are descended from here, then they are, they are a part of us, you know. They may not be on the roll, but they are part of us, and I feel that's where they belong. This is home to them" (October 22, 2003). Two concerns about place are being raised here. One is that unless Cherokee descendants reside within Cherokee country proper, they will have no social context for learning and will run the risk of misrepresenting Cherokee culture and Cherokee people to the world at large. The other concern is that Cherokee descendants should have a home with Cherokee people. This home is not about tribal citizenship or a political identity, but about a cultural identity tied to a particular place and context. Accordingly, Cherokee culture practiced in its appropriate social, political, and geographic context has the potential to reconnect long-lost Cherokee kin with one another.

In many ways, when citizen Cherokees are open to the possibility of Cherokee descendants learning appropriate cultural behavior and reconnecting with their communities of origin, the discussion shifts from being about "wannabes" to being about "could-bes"—about who might be able to be brought back into the tribal fold and how. The possibility seems to hinge on whether race shifters can enter into relationships of mutual respect and reciprocity with Cherokee people rather than misrepresent or appropriate Cherokee culture and whether recognized tribes can assert control over noncitizens and their behaviors. Anne Wallace, a middle-aged Oklahoma Cherokee woman, said to me, "The bottom line is that I don't mind people saying that they're Cherokee, as long as they're not trying to get something out of it. I don't like it when they steal from Cherokees and give nothing back" (January 30, 1996).

The question of how race shifters who are Cherokee descendants can be regulated and encouraged to give back to their communities of origin is open to debate. Many citizen Cherokees believe that the answer fundamentally lies in tribal politics, in the ability of Cherokee leaders to reach out to noncitizen communities and build some sort of bridge. One vision of how this might be accomplished comes from Eastern Band citizen Robert Thompson:

> If I were a chief, I would probably contact all of these different Cherokee tribes, and I'd say, "If you really, really want to be some type of political organization, you need to come and be here and meet with us and meet with the Cherokee Nation, the UKB [United Keetoowah Band]," and I'd say, "Hey, enough of this crap. You guys say that you're Cherokee, but you're not doing Cherokee stuff."...

I'd bring these people up to speed on where we are and where we need to go. I'd say, "You guys are doing all this stuff. You're trying to hold these pow-wows. You're trying to do all this crazy stuff. You do not get our endorse-ment.... You start doing good things, you know, you start supporting the tribe as a whole, then we can start talking about you being a part of who we are." Because, I mean, rather than try to cut them out, try to bring them in and say, "Hey, we've got resources here and here and here and here, you know, and these people, there's a lot of them down there, you know."... I don't know what to say. Some of them know lots about genealogy, history, whatever. They can come and help teach. They've got all this stuff. There are some really smart people in those groups. You don't organize and create this whole politi-cal tribe by being really stupid, you know? (October 22, 2003)

I include this quote because it provides an excellent example of how concerns about culture and politics intersect in discourses of race shifting. The crux of the mat-ter, as Thompson sees it, is whether race shifters can be redirected toward culturally appropriate behavior. If their talents, abilities, and resources could be channeled in another direction, one that contributes meaningfully to Cherokee people as a whole, they might be able to be brought in to the tribal fold in some capacity. If nothing else, they might enjoy new forms of social recognition and respect from other Cherokee leaders and communities. Though this more inclusive response to race shifting might seem like one man's unique vision of Cherokee politics, it actually represents a sizeable minority opinion that is articulated in both Oklahoma and North Carolina in contrast to those who would prefer to keep tribal boundaries more rigid. Yet, this vision may prove difficult to implement given the various factors—from references to Cherokee princesses to suspicions about financial motivations—that color citizen Cherokee per-ception of race shifters, and it is reasonable to wonder whether these new alliances would ever materialize and allow race shifters to feel like anything more than second-class community members.

Whether citizen Cherokees believe that race shifters should be included or excluded, culture plays a key role in their debates about tribal belonging. Part of its power rests in the easy way the concept of culture slips into essentialism. Culture—whether it is perceived as something appropriated or rightfully reclaimed—is also used as a measure of racial difference, so much so that cultural knowledge and behav-iors can facilitate racial transformations. The relationship between racial being and cultural doing is believed by many Cherokees to have moral force, so only certain kinds of people have rightful access to certain cultures. They believe that culture is not up for grabs to anyone who can take it. Cherokee people are supposed to practice Cherokee culture, just as Japanese people are supposed to practice Japanese culture. When "wannabes," New Agers, and race shifters without verifiable Cherokee ancestry prac-tice Cherokee culture, their actions are suspect and even subject to moral condemna-tion—they are guilty of appropriating culture without the racial right to do so. But race shifters with Cherokee ancestry, in some contexts, just might have that right. If more citizen Cherokees adopt the minority position that cultural knowledge is transformative of racial being and can be acquired later in life, racial shifters with Cherokee ancestry might eventually be able to reconnect to their tribe of origin in ways more meaningful and long-lasting than anything we have seen thus far. If not, the "entities using the Cherokee name" and the three federally recognized Cherokee tribes will continue to regard one another with suspicion.

seven
States of Sovereignty
Tribal Recognition and the Quest for Political Rights

I have a postcard of Diego Rivera and Frida Kahlo on my refrigerator at home. They are standing beside an enormous papier-mâché devil, a puppet of sorts, which leers and towers over them. Every time I notice the *gigante*, as the puppet is known in Mexico, it reminds me of the last time I saw such a beast in action. It was not in Mexico but in Tahlequah, Oklahoma, during the 1998 Cherokee National Holidays. Each year on Labor Day weekend, the Cherokee Nation hosts a celebration that draws nearly seventy thousand people—locals and tourists alike—which has quite an impact on the small town of Tahlequah, a place that usually counts its population at a little more than ten thousand souls.

During the National Holidays, one of the most eagerly anticipated and well-attended events is the State of the Nation address by the principal chief. Not unlike a State of the Union address by a U.S. president, the speech provides the chief with an opportunity to summarize the recent affairs in the nation and to outline his or her political vision for the coming year. In 1998, however, for the first and only time in Cherokee history—at least as far as anyone could recall—the principal chief did not bother to show. The crowd waited and waited for Joe Byrd (principal chief from 1995 to 1999), but the only likeness of Byrd that could be found anywhere in the vicinity was a giant papier-mâché puppet, some twelve to fifteen feet in height, that had been created by an irreverent bunch of Cherokee art students from the local college. Though the puppet's distorted and somewhat demonic-looking visage made it difficult to tell who it was supposed to represent and why, a hand-lettered sign hanging around its neck quickly revealed "Chief Byrd, Puppet Dictator." The students were protesting the chief and a series of highly controversial events he had recently set in motion.

The turmoil started in February 1997, when Cherokee Nation marshals, acting under the orders of a Cherokee Supreme Court justice, raided the offices of the chief, expecting that they would find evidence he had been misappropriating tribal funds (Sturm 2002:103). Byrd was not about to take such accusations lying down. He fired the marshals and encouraged the Tribal Council to impeach the Cherokee Supreme Court. Much to his chagrin, the court continued to function and ordered him to reinstate the marshals. He responded by hiring a new set of marshals, who were eager to do his bidding and who came to be known locally as "the goons." At that moment, the executive, judicial, and legislative branches of the Cherokee government were torn asunder. Old political and family allegiances—which in Cherokee country are often one and the same thing—weighed heavily upon the new circumstances, with nearly everyone having to pick sides. The pressure mounted in June, when Byrd's administration closed the doors of the Cherokee courthouse, locking out the justices and marshals whose services he had abruptly terminated. A month later, the growing tensions erupted in a brawling fight between Chief Byrd's "goons" and the fired marshals, who punched it out on the steps of the Cherokee courthouse, the historical and symbolic center of the Cherokee Nation government—the same place where the gathered crowd now waited for the controversial chief to appear (Sturm 2002:103).[1]

These events were recent memory for many in the crowd. Given the knock-down, drag-out confrontation that had taken place nearby a little more than a year ago, people did not know what to expect, and the air was rife with apprehension. The local Cherokee students were not the only ones engaged in political protest. Many people wore T-shirts emblazoned with a large yellow banana to suggest that the chief's actions had undermined the Cherokees' own constitution, even their very sovereignty, and that the Cherokee Nation was now nothing more than a banana republic. Adding to the contentious atmosphere was a real threat of violence: at that very moment, across the street from the courthouse, on the roof of a local bank, a SWAT team waited with rifles drawn, ready to put down any insurrection that might threaten the tourists. Rumor had it that this show of force had been requested by the Bureau of Indian Affairs in Muskogee, Oklahoma, though no one was sure whether the team had the right to be there.

After an hour or so, when it became clear that neither the chief nor his deputy was going to make an appearance—and given the circumstances, who could blame them?—other well-known Cherokees began to take to the stage in an effort to calm and reassure the crowd. Former principal chief Wilma Mankiller was one of the first to speak. She urged the people to take back their government and to have faith in their ability to weather this particular political storm. She reminded them of their tribal history and how Cherokee people had survived the fires of controversy and internal division on more than one occasion. Shortly after Mankiller spoke, actor Wes Studi took to the microphone. Having acted in movies such as *Powwow Highway* and *Geronimo*, Studi is an icon of Native American cinema and probably the best-known Cherokee outside Oklahoma, though few outsiders would recognize him as anything but an Indian actor. Born in Nofire Hollow, Oklahoma, a traditional Cherokee community, to a traditional Cherokee family, Studi spoke movingly to the people as one of their own, urging them to find their way out of the troubled situation. After a short while, community elders also began to make their voices heard. The crowd opened to let them pass and listened to their words of encouragement with eager attention.

When a well-known elder by the name of Dan Rogers, from Pryor, Oklahoma, took to the stage, a hush fell over the crowd. The silence was generated, in part, by what Rogers had to say but mostly by the company he kept. Joining Rogers on the stage were three men, each appearing, at least on the surface, to be white, with non-Indian features including freckled, pale skin and long, reddish-brown hair. Certainly some citizen Cherokees fit such a description, including Rogers himself. It seemed that the crowd cared less about the men's appearance than about their dress. Each man in this unfamiliar trio was wearing a quasi-traditional Plains Indian–style outfit, replete with buckskin leggings, breastplates, medicine pouches, and eagle, hawk, and turkey feathers woven through their long, braided hair. More dramatic still, two of the men were carrying six-foot-tall lances, the other a large bow and quiver of arrows, and the crowd joked that maybe, like the SWAT team across the street, they were needed to put down the rabble-rousers.

Of course, their getups surprised many in attendance. Most Cherokees in rural Oklahoma have an air of informality about them. The standard uniform consists of jeans or shorts, T-shirts, and baseball caps, with maybe a pair of boots, a long-sleeved shirt and bolo tie, or a simple blouse added for dressier occasions. Even when they dress in traditional regalia, Cherokee women tend to wear calico tear dresses, and men wear woven jackets, medallions, and turbans in the style of Sequoyah. They do not wear skins and feathers, like traditional powwow dancers—unless, of course, they are at a powwow.

Seeing the strange clothing and unfamiliar faces, the crowd murmured, wondering who these people were and what in the world Dan Rogers had gotten himself into. Then Rogers spoke: "These are our long-lost brothers from back East—the Georgia Tribe of Eastern Cherokee."

Some in the crowd were surprised to learn that there were Cherokees still living in Georgia: "I thought they only lived in Oklahoma."

"No, no. There's some in North Carolina too."

"And Georgia too, I guess."

Many in the crowd were skeptical, even infuriated, that "some bunch of wannabes would take advantage of our elders!"

"Can you believe the gall of them showing up at our National Holiday, dressed in a bunch of dead animals?"

Still others expressed empathy, saying, "Well, if you've got the blood, then it'll call you home."

Whereas local Cherokee people from Tahlequah and nearby counties expressed all kinds of opinions about the newcomers, the tourists had a much more consistent response: almost without exception, they flocked to the side of the Georgia Cherokees, begging for a photo of the men, asking to hold their lances and bows, and happily chatting away about what a good picture this would make for the album back at home—as if to say, "Finally, some real Indians"—all the while seeming oblivious to the hundreds of Cherokee citizens in their midst, dressed in a style virtually indistinguishable from their own.

* * *

The dramatic showing of the Georgia Cherokees sparked heated debates among those in attendance, with people questioning their dress, bloodlines, origins, and intent. Why would members of the Georgia Tribe of Eastern Cherokees come to the Cherokee National Holidays in Oklahoma when, clearly, they had decided to create a tribe of their own? State-recognized tribes such as this one have emerged as race shifters start to collectivize their identities and to seek new forms of social and political recognition. State-recognized tribes are controversial for a variety of reasons, but largely because they challenge the standard practice of federal recognition. They also create considerable confusion over what it means to assert a collective Cherokee tribal identity and then have it formally recognized by an external power. For example, is being a member of a recently created, state-recognized Cherokee tribe like the Georgia Tribe of Eastern Cherokees somehow on a par with having citizenship in a larger, older, federally recognized Cherokee tribe like the Cherokee Nation? Or, as some have suggested, is it something altogether different? In this chapter, I explore the social and political impact of these new players on the field, who are sometimes embraced as long-lost kin, sometimes rejected as illegitimate, and sometimes, as in the case of the Georgia Cherokee, both at the same time.

Achieving the legal status of Cherokee tribe has never been the clear-cut proposition that outsiders might expect, and in recent decades, the process has become even more fraught with confusion. Traditionally, Native Americans have been legally acknowledged as such by the federal government, specifically by the Office of Federal Acknowledgment in the Bureau of Indian Affairs, a federal agency housed in the Department of the Interior. Yet, in everyday administration, federal standards for official recognition are immensely variable. For example, legal scholar Sharon O'Brien notes that in federal legislation alone, thirty-three definitions of the term "American Indian" are in use, based on blood quantum, tribal citizenship, residency, or a combination—any of which may or may not correspond to the standards and definitions used by tribal governments (Garroutte 2003:16).[2] Negotiating the meanings these different sets of rules and laws hold for Indian lives is challenging enough, but in the past three decades, being indigenous in this country—at least in a legal sense—has become infinitely more complex as state governments take an increasingly active role in defining communities as Indian tribes, something that was not in their purview for most of the twentieth century.

What states are doing, in many ways, revives colonial-era practices and reflects the ongoing tension over states' rights that has long characterized U.S. federalism. Though some state governments and their colonial predecessors recognized the political rights of Native American nations in government-to-government treaties, proclamations, and laws as early as the mid-seventeenth century, most deferred to the federal government on such matters for much of U.S. history.[3] Only in the past three decades have states become more involved in the process again, recognizing tribes on an ever more frequent basis. In doing so, states have added a competing element—a sort of wild card, if you will—to the already chaotic process of tribal recognition, sparking bitter debates between federally recognized, state-recognized, and self-identified Indian communities.

At the root of this controversy is the demographic explosion in newly identified Indian people and tribes—what I have characterized as racial shifting. This has fueled a need for alternative forms of tribal community and tribal recognition, and the possibility of these alternatives has in turn encouraged more racial shifting. Nowhere is this more apparent than in Cherokee country, where literally hundreds of unacknowledged and state-recognized communities—like the Georgia Tribe of Eastern Cherokee—assert a Cherokee identity and vie for different forms of political recognition that would affirm their status as sovereign peoples. Some of the most intense fighting has been over access to state economic resources, because state governments now have to decide whether to privilege federally recognized tribes or their own state-acknowledged tribes for funding. Other conflicts have emerged over rights of representation. People argue about who should talk to the local Lion's Club, who should have access to local sacred sites, who should repatriate and conduct ceremonies for dead ancestors, and who should sit on the State Commission for Indian Affairs.

In all the acrimonious debate about who is really Cherokee, who is not, and on what basis, one term keeps popping up again and again, and that is "sovereignty." Its ubiquity stems not from the fact that sovereignty is a complex idiom that can be read in many ways. Even if sovereignty is used in a variety of contexts to mean different things, it has a common semantic core that refers to political autonomy—the ability to exercise a certain amount of control over one's social, political, and economic life and one's geographic territory. Yet, many Native Americans articulate a contradictory stance. They claim, on one hand, an inherent sovereignty as an autonomous, self-governing people (a nation) and, on the other, a type of sovereignty that stems specifically from their government-to-government relationship with the United States or at times even with its states (Biolsi 2005; Wilkins and Lomawaima 2001). The first type of sovereignty derives from the people and is therefore closely linked with understandings of both peoplehood and nationalism, but the second type is less autonomous. In fact, it relies upon negotiation, reciprocity, and relations of interdependence with outside powers (Cattelino 2008:162–165).[4]

One of the most critical examples of this interdependence is that tribal sovereignty—not as an ideal but as a legal right and an actual practice—is often tied to various forms of external recognition, so much so that the nature and exercise of sovereignty depend on who is recognizing whom in which context (Cattelino 2007).[5] Tribal sovereignty, then, is a form of power that is both independent of and dependent on broader social and political forces. Because of this social and political interdependence, Cherokee people are invoking sovereignty in the great debates over tribal recognition at the very moment they feel that they are losing control. What we are hearing are the tracings of power being etched into this debate, because contested Cherokee identities are tied to contested understandings of sovereignty and practices of tribal acknowledgment and sovereignty that have emerged in the wake of colonialism, nation-building, and U.S. federalism. In this chapter, I use examples from Cherokee country to illustrate how the recent resurgence in state recognition of Indian tribes has complicated the nature and meanings of contemporary tribal sovereignty and to explore such conflicts and their broader implications.

The Varieties of State Recognition

What is happening in Cherokee country is a microcosm of what is happening throughout the United States as states respond in fifty ways to these tribal newcomers. Traditionally, two main parties have been involved in negotiations over tribal sovereignty—the federal government and federally recognized tribes. Historical interactions between these parties set legal precedent, established lines of communication, and put in place the fundamentals of the political process. Now, states are blurring these lines. From New England to Montana, state-recognized tribes have become significant players, growing in size and number and becoming more outspoken about securing their own rights, whatever these may be. Given the increasingly visible role that state-recognized tribes are playing on the national scene, it surprises me how little is known about them—there are few reliable sources of information on state recognition.[6] Though I had come to expect something akin to the neat lists of federally recognized tribes available in numerous government documents, scholarly publications, and Web sites, it took me considerable research to compile my own list of state-recognized tribes. What I have been able to gather (table 7.1; see appendix 2)[7] is that at least sixty-two different tribes are now recognized by eighteen different states. This includes fifteen state-recognized Cherokee tribes—24 percent of the total. None of the sixty-two is currently federally recognized, but several have petitions pending.

Though state recognition has deep roots in U.S. history, particularly along the eastern seaboard, the majority of state-recognized tribes achieved this status only in the past thirty years. In the wake of the Red Power movement, nonrecognized Indians began making stronger demands for official political recognition at both federal and state levels. These demands gathered steam over the past three decades, fueled at times by the lucrative potential of Indian gaming. The upshot has been a rash of newly

Table 7.1 Number of State-Recognized American Indian Tribes by State

Alabama	8	New Jersey	3
Arkansas	1	New York	1
Connecticut	3	North Carolina	6
Delaware	1	Ohio	3
Georgia	3	South Carolina	6
Kansas	2	Tennessee	1
Louisiana	6	Virginia	9
Massachusetts	2		
Michigan	3	Total tribes:	62
Missouri	3	Cherokee tribes:	15
Montana	1		

state-recognized tribes; they now outnumber those with longer standing. Two of Virginia's tribes, for example, were recognized in colonial-era treaties, whereas the other seven were recognized after 1980 in resolutions before the Virginia General Assembly (H.R. 1294 [2007]; Sheffield 1997:72). State recognition has much looser standards than does the federal process.[8] In the case of Virginia, the seven new tribes needed only to be organized as corporate entities, to have a tribal roll, and, more important, to be able to lobby effectively for recognition. Virginia is not unusual in the apparent casualness of its recognition process—the same minimal standards and dependence on legislative maneuvering also exist in other states. Louisiana, for instance, requires no documentation whatsoever, only that a petitioning tribe submit concurrent resolutions to the state senate and house of representatives. If the tribe seeking recognition is politically astute and can convince politicians of its legitimacy, then the resolution is likely to pass. In many cases, states might say yes because they have little to lose in recognizing a group of native people with a resolution that often rests more on symbolism than anything else, whereas saying no might risk bad publicity and expensive legal battles.

State recognition, then, is often an exercise in pure politics, relying on external measures of authenticity less than the federal recognition process does.[9] Because state recognition flows more out of the pragmatism of contemporary politics than the ostensibly detached empiricism of the social sciences (that is, the historical, anthropological, and genealogical impetus behind the federal acknowledgment procedure), the practice varies widely from state to state.[10] A few states imitate the rigorous posture of the federal government to greater or lesser degrees. For example, the Tennessee Commission for Indian Affairs, in its 1990 "Recognition Criteria for Native American Indian Nations, Tribes or Bands," reproduced federal standards almost verbatim (T.C.I.A. § 4-34-103 [1990]). In 1976, the North Carolina Commission on Indian

Affairs established procedures for state recognition that were slightly less rigid. Both sets of criteria, much like the federal standards, rely heavily on evidence of external recognition by non-Indians—an obvious bias. Some states have no guidelines or procedures whatsoever. Georgia, for instance, recognized three groups as Indian tribes in 1993 but set up no standards for the process. Other groups seeking recognition from the Georgia state legislature have been defeated, largely because of the efforts of federally recognized tribes, such as the Cherokee Nation and the Eastern Band of Cherokee Indians in North Carolina, who have a historic—albeit unpleasant—connection to the State of Georgia and have lobbied hard that only the federal government should have the right to recognize Indian tribes.

Although federally recognized tribes have urged states to get out of the tribal recognition business, states continue it for many reasons. Sometimes, as in Georgia, the state is seeking to clean up its reputation in regards to indigenous people. From a cynical point of view, a state that forcibly removed its indigenous population in the past may try to make amends by finding and recognizing some remnant Native American communities in the present. Indeed, two of the three tribes currently recognized by the State of Georgia identify themselves as Cherokee. To promote state recognition, local politicians and tribal activists argue that Native American tribes within state borders help to generate tourism. Even Cherokees outside the Southeast, such as John Ross, say this about state recognition: "It helps the state. It helps the counties. It helps the cities. So it's popular to say, 'Hey let's have more Indians. Let's build more houses.' All the money's coming in. It's benefiting the non-Indians. So it's got to be popular" (August 1, 2003). Also, state legislators with ties to tribal communities seeking state recognition have used their political influence to sway the legislative process. Examples include Georgia state representatives Bill Dover (Georgia Tribe of Eastern Cherokees) and June Hegstrom (Cherokee of Georgia Tribal Council), who sponsored bills for state recognition and other Indian-related legislation in the mid-1990s (*Atlanta Journal-Constitution*, April 29, 1993, and February 20, 1995).

When Georgia began to recognize tribes in 1993, many federally recognized Cherokees were outraged. Shortly thereafter, Jonathon Taylor, principal chief of the Eastern Band of Cherokee Indians, wrote a letter to Joy Berry, the executive director of the Georgia Human Relations Commission: "In the eyes of the Cherokee tribes in North Carolina and Oklahoma, the Legislature of Georgia has degraded the culture and heritage of Cherokee people by 'recognizing' these 'wannabe' Indians who are trying to cash in on the popularity and political correctness of Indian people.... Now, legal rights and privileges formerly available to federally recognized Native Americans, who are also citizens of the State of Georgia, are replaced with rights extended only to those new groups created by the Georgia Legislature" (Taylor 1994). Both Chief Taylor and Chief Wilma Mankiller, in separate and numerous letters to the Georgia state legislature, expressed their concerns that the rights and sovereign entitlements of their own tribal communities would be undermined by state recognition, which would result in what was rightfully theirs going to non-Indians. Their concern was not simply that state recognition meant more people having to share the same resources, rights, and privileges but that the claim on those resources was illegitimate in the first place. In their eyes, it was "wannabes" or possibly even Cherokee descendants making these claims, not fellow Cherokee tribal citizens.

Underlying many, if not most, critiques of state recognition of tribes is a concern about race shifting—that somehow white race shifters, eager for a piece of what they may see as the Indian pie, for either material or symbolic reasons, are circumventing the rigors of the federal recognition process. Race shifting and the ever-present epithet of "wannabe" are usually in the background of any discussion of state-recognized tribes because, fairly or not, federally recognized tribes tend to view these groups not just as collective Johnny-come-latelies asking for tribal status but as composed, to a considerable extent, of individual Johnny-come-latelies. This perception is the reason that state recognition is tied in so many citizen Cherokee minds to the presumption of race shifting in a manner that can exaggerate the sociological reality. Whatever the reality, state recognition—like race shifting—has the odor of illegitimacy about it.

In the face of such stinging accusations of illegitimacy, some self-identified Cherokee groups have responded that they are more authentic than either federally recognized or state-recognized Cherokees because they do not require outside validation. For example, at the height of the controversy in Georgia, Marge Peterson, a member of a self-identified Cherokee tribe located in the state, wrote a letter to Zell Miller, the governor of Georgia: "Our group has not petitioned for [state] recognition because we know who we are and do not need Ms. Mankiller or Jonathon Taylor to judge whether we are legitimate or not.... 'Grandfather' did not appoint Ms. Mankiller or Jonathon Taylor to judge who is or is not one of his children. And regardless, if Ms. Mankiller or Jonathon Taylor never recognize us, WE WILL NOT GO AWAY! We are here forever, because we will see to it that our children and grandchildren will know and will teach their children the same" (Peterson 1993).

Agreeing with Peterson, Arlo Davis and Robby Giles, members of a self-identified Cherokee tribe in Arkansas, said that no outside government, whether federal, state, or tribal, has the right to define who is and is not Indian. "They have no right, and neither does another tribe.... You see the groups that split off from our group, we don't say they're not Indian. We say they're not the original group. But we don't deny they're Indian, because it's not for us to say," Davis explained. "That would be like taking a dog out here and turning him loose and calling him a rabbit," Giles quickly added (February 22, 2003). Although such responses are not uncommon among self-identified Cherokees, many others in these groups long for any form of recognition, not only because they seek external validation but also because they are well aware that relationships built on mutual recognition provide for certain political rights and benefits.

Because many self-identified Cherokee tribes will never meet the requirements for federal recognition, their only hope for achieving such external validation lies with the states. Yet, because of the inconsistencies and variations in the state recognition process, no one is certain what state recognition means. Is it inexpensive symbolism for state legislators or something more legally substantial? With so much procedural variation, does state recognition mean one thing in Louisiana and something else in North Carolina? Bestowing state recognition without any standards and procedures or any efforts to verify the claims of petitioners seems as politically meaningful as naming a street Elvis Presley Boulevard in Memphis, Tennessee—a token affirmation of presence that has no teeth. Historical context is equally important. Surely, when Virginia signed a government-to-government treaty with the Pamunkey in 1658, it had different intentions than did Arkansas in 1997 when it recognized the contributions of descendants of the Northern Cherokee Nation of Old Louisiana Territory to the state, proclaiming April 8 as Northern Cherokee Day (Arkansas H.C.R. 1003 [1997]). Both groups claim state-recognized status, yet only one has received any direct benefits. This is not to suggest that contemporary state recognition is little more than symbolism: material resources are also at stake. At times, state recognition may provide nothing more than a mention in a legislative memorial, but at other times, it can mean funding, benefits, even a reservation. It may also eventually prove to be a step on the way to federal recognition, which may explain why the state recognition controversy matters so little to non-Indians but a great deal to Cherokee people of all sorts (Garroutte 2003:173n40).[11]

Among federally recognized, state-recognized, and self-identified Cherokee communities, the political and legal contests between state-recognized and federally recognized tribes produce the most overt tensions. In direct competition with each other, they fight for local political influence and for federal and state funding. Though most federal funding is earmarked for federally recognized tribes, state-recognized tribes are sometimes able to access federal funds. In 2002, the Administration for Native Americans, an agency within the U.S. Department of Health and Human Services, granted $282,020 to four state-recognized Cherokee tribes in Georgia, Missouri, and Virginia (Administration for Native Americans 2003). Not surprisingly, certain federally recognized Cherokees view this as siphoning off funds intended for them and for other federally recognized Indian tribes. Wilma Mankiller, principal chief of the Cherokee Nation at the time, wrote in a letter to members of the Georgia State Assembly: "The Cherokee Nation and Eastern band will not tolerate any groups purporting to be a Cherokee Nation.... Steps must and will be taken to investigate how these groups were able to secure state recognition, how these groups are securing federal funds, and how to correct these injustices" (Mankiller 1995). State-recognized Cherokees view this in an altogether different light. Georgia state representative Bill Dover, a member of the Georgia Tribe of Eastern Cherokees, said, "The issue is not federal programs or a land grab. It's the opportunity to preserve our heritage proudly" (*Atlanta Journal-Constitution*, April 29, 1993). To Dover and others, gaining federal funding is not a matter of being lucky or being able to work the system—it demonstrates that state recognition signifies political legitimacy as a sovereign Indian tribe. In debates about Cherokee recognition, resources, and rights, all roads lead back to sovereignty.

Competing Sovereignties and U.S. Federalism

Today, many Cherokee-identified populations claim sovereignty, but those claims are not uniform in either their articulation or their practice. In considering the gradations of sovereignty that are at stake, how do the claims of state-recognized Cherokee tribes stack up against those of federally recognized Cherokee tribes and of states themselves? These are questions that have not been addressed on a consistent basis, within either the academy or the law.[12] One important exception is the work of attorney Christopher Reinhart, who has described the effects of state recognition of Indian tribes on recent legal decisions in Connecticut (Reinhart 2002).[13] With two federally recognized tribes and three state-recognized tribes, Connecticut provides an interesting case study because its courts are already familiar with some of the intricacies of federal Indian law. Yet, as Reinhart demonstrates, recent cases involving state-recognized tribes make the ambiguities of federalism and its relationship to different practices of sovereignty readily apparent.

For example, in 1997 the Connecticut Supreme Court ruled, in a case involving a member of the state-recognized Paucatuck Eastern Pequot Tribe, that state criminal law applies to members of state-recognized tribes even if the crime occurred on a reservation. The defendant had argued that Connecticut could not assume criminal jurisdiction over his case because it had not followed the procedures set forth by the federal Indian Civil Rights Act of 1968. The court ruled, however, that because the defendant was not a member of a federally recognized tribe, he did not qualify as an Indian under federal Indian law (Reinhart 2002:2–3; *State v. Sebastian*, 243 Conn. 115 [1997]).

To reach this decision, the court considered whether the constitutional power of Congress to regulate Indian affairs preempted state law and whether the tribe had any "residual and demonstrable tribal sovereignty under federal case law." The court reasoned that federal recognition was "the very essence of the government to government relationship underlying federal criminal jurisdiction" and that, because the tribe's state recognition had no bearing on federal recognition, it was irrelevant to the case at hand. If the individual had been a member of a federally recognized Indian tribe, federal law would have applied and the outcome might have been very different. Even though the individual was an Indian in the eyes of the state, he was not an Indian for the purpose of determining state criminal jurisdiction. Federal recognition trumped state recognition in this regard. Tribal sovereignty was a concern of the court. It wanted to be sure that its decisions did not infringe upon the tribe's ability to exercise its sovereignty, at least in a way that was inconsistent with federal law. In the end, the court decided that sovereignty could not be invoked, because it is a collective rather than an individual right and the state-recognized tribe itself was not a party to the suit (Reinhart 2002:2–3; *State v. Sebastian*, 243 Conn. 115 [1997]).

State-recognized tribes have an ambiguous and evolving status. The *Sebastian* case seems to imply that, without federal recognition, state-recognized tribes in Connecticut cannot exercise tribal sovereignty in the judicial arena. In several cases, state courts have determined that, for most purposes, the state has criminal and civil jurisdiction over state-recognized tribes and individuals (Reinhart 2002:1–6; *Golden Hill Paugessett Tribe of Indians v. Southbury*, 231 Conn. 563 [1995]; *Schaghticoke Tribe of Kent, Connecticut, Inc. v. Potter*, 217 Conn. 612 [1991]; *State v. Sebastian*, 243 Conn. 115 [1997]). Yet, in all of these cases, the question of whether a state-recognized tribe enjoys sovereignty and, if so, to what extent has never been directly decided. The closest approximation took place in 2001 when, contrary to earlier decisions, the Connecticut Superior Court ruled that a corporation could not sue a state-recognized tribe, because it had been recognized as a "domestic dependent nation" and self-governing entity in a state statute (*First American Casino v. Eastern Pequot Nation*, CGS § 47–59a [2001]; Reinhart 2002:5).

In all the cases preceding this one, the state courts linked sovereignty with federal recognition, for they allowed federal recognition to supercede state recognition when determining who had criminal or civil jurisdiction. In this most recent ruling, no such association was made. By virtue of their state recognition, these tribes, at least in Connecticut, enjoy an aspect of sovereignty—sovereign immunity—and are as free from suit as are federally recognized tribes. As state courts struggle to interpret the meanings of tribal sovereignty invoked in various contexts across the United States, state recognition of tribes adds another element to the already baroque complexity of Indian law.

Representing Cherokee Culture in the Public Sphere: Another View of Sovereignty

The law is not the only place where debates about sovereignty are heard. Time and again, the issue of the public representation of culture—who has the right to represent what in which context—has been a matter of serious debate among Native American people. Though federally recognized and state-recognized tribes tend to lead the discussions, self-identified tribes also voice their opinions and claim the right to represent, display, and perform what they see as their culture. Nowhere are these debates about cultural representation, tribal status, and sovereignty more hotly contested than among Cherokees. For instance, during Halloween 2000, the Echota Cherokee Nation, a state-recognized tribe in Alabama, staged a large protest against a local haunted house known as the Trail of Fears. They argued that it was morally inappropriate to evoke images of Cherokee suffering in a commercial context. In making these public assertions, the Echota Cherokees laid claim to the Trail of Tears as a part of their own history, suggesting that the event belonged to them as a people and not to some commercial property (Haynes 2001:93–94). Of course, this claim is ironic: the Echota Cherokees would not exist in Alabama if they had not somehow managed to escape the forced removal to the West, a fact not lost on many Oklahoma Cherokees, whose ancestors suffered and died along the trail. Then again, citizens of the federally recognized Eastern Band of Cherokee Indians in North Carolina also claim the Trail of Tears as a part of their collective history, and most of their ancestors were spared the direct trauma of removal.

Other examples of contests surrounding cultural representation involve less notable—even less plausible—moments in Cherokee history and once again reveal the discursive links between questions of official recognition, individual race shifting, and legitimacy. The words and actions of one woman in particular have generated a substantial amount of tribal scrutiny and media attention. For more than thirty years, Dr. Leslie Panchula Uhlan—also known as Princess Che'Kee'—staged public "Cherokee" events that received press coverage in sources ranging from the *New York Times* to the *Miami Herald*, as well as numerous smaller publications. Most of this coverage centered on her performances of what she called Chakabesh, a winter ceremony to "welcome the Celestial Bear to the earth during the season of the cold moon" (*Smithtown Messenger*, March 12, 1981). Year after year, beginning in the late 1970s, Uhlan erected a full-size teepee for three months on the front lawn of her ranch-style family home in Smithtown, Long Island.[14] Although teepees are usually constructed with animal hides, Princess Che'Kee' employed something akin to a tarp that had been customized by sailmakers in Port Jefferson, New York. As she explained to a *New York Times* reporter in 1980, the synthetic tarp was not her first choice. During a recent move from Connecticut to Long Island, her "time-honored teepee [had been] lost and there was not enough time to follow the old procedures for constructing a new one for the beginning of the Season of the Cold Moon" (*New York Times*, January 13, 1980).

The teepee was the centerpiece of Princess Che'Kee's public display of Cherokee culture—in a sense, it was her own Cherokee Cultural Center. After the teepee was placed in the yard, Princess Che'Kee' invited schoolchildren, news reporters, and neighbors to attend ceremonies that coincided with the winter solstice and Christmas season. She stood before her teepee in Plains-style regalia and lit a sacred fire at the center of the lodge—in later years, she plugged in blinking Christmas lights to avoid hazards associated with a fire untended during the night (*Newsday*, February 11, 1980). Then she would smudge herself, her visitors, and their surroundings with the smoke of burning juniper and cedar in order to sanctify the events that were about to take place.

With the help of her children, Little Deer and Dancing Leaf, she set out plates of food, laid out tiny moccasins, and marked the teepee for ceremonial painting—all in the name of welcoming earthbound travelers, both animal and human, who might be seeking shelter and sustenance (*New York Times*, January 13, 1980). As she explained to reporters, the ceremony was meant to lure "a Cherokee Indian God, the Great Celestial Bear," to Earth: "Food is left in the teepee for the bear to eat. When the bear is content, it goes into the family's home to find a smaller teepee, a lodge filled with Indian artifacts. The bear rewards family members who think kind thoughts by placing gifts in their moccasins, which line the entrance to the lodge. But those who harbor selfish or evil thoughts find their moccasins upside down and empty" (*Newsday*, February 11, 1980). By early the next morning, visitors would find that the lodge had been painted with several vaguely Indian symbols, including a cactus, the sun, the moon, and some stars, a horse, an eagle feather, and a stone (*New York Times*, January 13, 1980). Most people who passed the eye-catching teepee during its three-month appearance might have assumed that an American Indian lived at the Long Island residence. Most people who listened to her talk would assume that she was passing on traditional Cherokee practices.

The real story is more complicated. Princess Che'Kee' did these things as a self-identified Cherokee woman, in the name of Cherokees, despite the fact that Cherokees never lived in teepees and there is no record of a Cherokee ceremony such as the one she performed. In fact, her ceremony is primarily a blending of New Age and pan-tribal elements; the name Chakabesh is likely borrowed from the Anashinaabe or Cree peoples, and although there are many stories of a celestial bear and his adventures among American Indians, including Cherokees, her version seems to pull mostly from Micmac and Iroquois traditions (Hagar 1900). Furthermore, many Cherokees, both Christian and non-Christian, would be offended by the reference to Bear as a Cherokee god. Considering that the ceremony is mostly a hodgepodge of New Age fantasy, racial stereotype, and actual American Indian traditions divorced from their specific tribal contexts, no wonder one paper reported, "Area experts in Indian lore believe that [Princess Che'Kee' and her family] are one of the few families on Long Island who observe the seasonal rite" (*Newsday*, February 11, 1980).

Princess Che'Kee' is a colorful, if extreme, example of how self-identified Cherokees assert themselves within what I have called a presumed void of Indianness. With the help of the local and national news media, she proclaimed her Cherokee identity for the world to see and became a Cherokee in the eyes of the broader public, at least in a part of the United States where there is relatively little mainstream knowledge about American Indians. During her regular public appearances, she became seen as an authority on Cherokee culture, Indian ways, and all manner of things having do with ecology and the natural world. She taught the local Boy Scouts what they needed to know to earn their Indian lore merit badges. Jim, a twelve-year-old Scout who helped her to carry on the annual Chakabesh ceremony, said that it was fun to do, adding, "I'm also learning to do beadwork, and as a reward for doing all this, I'll get my Indian Lore Merit Badge" (*Smithtown Messenger*, March 12, 1981).

As Princess Che'Kee' told one reporter, educating children about "the reality of American Indian traditions" was a central focus of her activities (*Newsday*, February 11, 1980). She often visited area schools, as well as Boy Scout and Girl Scout troops, giving lectures and leading field trips in an effort to dispel stereotypes. She noted, "They see Indians on T.V., and that's great, but that's not the way we are" (*Newsday*, February 11, 1980). To this day, she presents herself as an authority on Indian topics, and in May 2008 she spoke before a group of fifth-graders in Palm Beach, Florida, her new hometown, about the history and culture of Native Americans (School District of Palm Beach County 2008). Much of her staying power has to do with the fact that Princess Che'Kee' fulfills non-Indian expectations about how Cherokees should dress and behave. In most accounts in mainstream newspapers, she is presented as a benevolent figure who has dedicated her life to sharing native ways of knowing with a wider public.

Among citizen Cherokees, the reactions to Princess Che'Kee' have been altogether different. Her main detractors are found among federally recognized Cherokees on the eastern seaboard, where her performances are viewed as inauthentic, her claims to Cherokee identity disputed, and her motivations questioned. For example, in 1993, Gerald Parker, the vice chief of the Eastern Band of Cherokee Indians, called her a fake and accused her of using an Indian name for business purposes. "We object to it," he said, "but we cannot stop it" (*Miami Herald*, June 26, 1993). Princess Che'Kee' responded to these accusations by claiming that she was one of the last descendants of the Croatan Clan of the Cherokees of North Carolina. Parker challenged her again, saying that there were seven known Cherokee clans and the Croatan was not one of them (June 26, 1993).[15]

Vice Chief Parker and other citizen Cherokees have voiced several concerns about the various claims and performances of Princess Che'Kee'. To them, she is not just someone who occasionally "plays Indian" with other hobbyists to fulfill some deep-seated social desire (Deloria 1998; Green 1988; Huhndorf 2001). Rather, she made a more dramatic assertion. She claimed not only to be Cherokee but also to be one of the few survivors of a remnant clan, the only one who still knows and practices a unique form of Cherokee culture. More than just a sole survivor, she assumed the mantle of political leadership. Claiming that she was protecting her people from extinction, Princess Che'Kee' cast herself as a brave voice for a mysterious eighth clan, whose preservation required that she adopt non-Indians as clan members—though they had to pay for the honor and for the classes on Croatan culture that she offered (*Miami Herald*, June 26, 1993). Though claiming a clan identity and esoteric religious knowledge may seem less overtly political than claiming a tribal identity, Princess Che'Kee made no such distinction. Instead, she hoped to boost membership in her clan so that she and other members could qualify for federal recognition as a Cherokee Indian tribe and then apply for state or federal Indian benefits and services (*Miami Herald*, June 26, 1993). What began as a series of public performances, along with professions of a social identity and cultural knowledge that set her apart from the mainstream, morphed into an explicit desire for political recognition and all the rights and benefits this brings.

Public representations of Cherokee culture, such as those of the New Echota Cherokee Nation and Princess Che'Kee', have a powerful effect on discourses and practices of tribal sovereignty. Such representations shape what the public knows, or thinks it knows, about Indians as a whole and about specific tribal groups—and whether a group of people deserves recognition as a Native American tribe. Chief Wilma Mankiller made these connections explicit in 1995 when she provided written testimony regarding the federal acknowledgment process before the U.S. Senate Committee on Indian Affairs. "The Cherokee Nation and other tribes have been embarrassed by groups such as 'The [state recognized] Echota Cherokee Nation' showing up at the National Congress of the American Indian dressed in stereotypical Hollywood garb," she complained. "A tribe's sovereignty, reputation and identity are at stake" (U.S. Senate Committee on Indian Affairs 1995).

For the Cherokee Nation, such public invocations of their name, national seal, and culture are not matters of libel, intellectual property, or copyright, though citizen Cherokees have used this language on occasion. Rather, the sentiment is more akin to what U.S. citizens and leaders might feel if a growing number of small countries started to publicly proclaim that they, in fact, were the United States of America, that they, too, had claims to the United States' cultural identity, its political rights, and even parts of its geographic territory. Such claims would seem ludicrous, especially at first, but would probably become more disturbing if other governments in the international community began to recognize them as legitimate. From the Cherokee Nation's point of view, if almost anyone can claim a tribal identity and achieve alternative forms of recognition and the sense of sovereignty that goes with it, what happens to the hard-fought gains of the Cherokee Nation? Does it risk becoming just another "entity using the Cherokee name"? Federally recognized Cherokee tribes worry that the answer, at least in some arenas, may be yes. They argue that state recognition of new Cherokee tribes creates public and legal confusion, undermines perceptions of Cherokee historical and cultural authenticity, and defies the principle that sovereignty is fundamentally based on nation-to-nation relationships.[16]

Given these concerns, both the Cherokee Nation and the Eastern Band of Cherokee Indians have urged state governments, time and again, to get out of the business of recognizing Indian tribes and to leave matters of recognition to the federal government. The Tribal Council of the Cherokee Nation has gone so far as to pass a resolution stating that, as a policy, the Cherokee Nation "shall not endorse, acquiesce, or support for federal or state recognition any other group, association or club which identify themselves as a separate tribal entity for purposes of having a government to government relationship because of Cherokee Ancestry" (Cherokee Nation Resolution No. 14-00 [2000]). On May 11, 2005, the principal chief of the Cherokee Nation, Chadwick Smith, also asked the federal government to consider a moratorium on the recognition of any additional Cherokee groups, stating flatly that the Cherokee Nation opposed such recognition (U.S. Senate Committee on Indian Affairs 2005). The United Keetoowah Band of Cherokee Indians, also federally recognized, has been less consistent in its stance toward state-recognized and self-identified Cherokee tribes but lately has taken a more hard-line approach in keeping with the two other federally recognized Cherokee nations. For all three, a clear political hierarchy seems to be at work: Cherokee newcomers should be recognized by legitimate Cherokee governments first, by the federal government next, and by their respective state governments last, if at all. Of course, as self-identified Cherokees might point out in frustration, the only Cherokee governments recognized as legitimate are those that are federally recognized in the first place.

Some federally recognized Cherokees have taken an even more combative stance against state recognition, fearing that presumed "wannabes" might use it to game the system. They argue—much as self-identified Cherokees do about federal recognition—that state recognition is a form of administrative "extermination." For example,

Isabel Catolster of the Eastern Band of Cherokee Indians provided the following written testimony in 1994 to the Council of Churches meeting in Tulsa, Oklahoma, on racism as a human rights violation in the United States:

> I am here also as a representative of a handful of federally recognized Indians, from several tribes who, for different reasons, currently reside in the Southeast, and who have come together to fight the latest, and perhaps most vicious assault on our sovereignty: the legal recognition by state governments of European-American groups as Indian tribes. If allowed to continue, *this will be the final chapter in our extermination*. The process of non-Indians recognizing each other as indigenous people is complex and subtle, and we do not pretend to fully understand its origins. Yet, it is clear the European American people have few options for dealing with the reality of the destruction they have brought to this world. Perhaps by reinventing themselves as Indians, therefore denying that they are unwelcome guests in our lands, they can continue the destruction without feeling guilty. (Catolster 1994; emphasis added)

According to Catolster, not only is state recognition a "vicious assault" on tribal sovereignty, but it is also a process whereby non-Indians—in this case, specifically whites—recognize one another as Indians to alleviate any sense of guilt associated with their white privilege. According to her, the "extermination" of tribal sovereignty, and figuratively of Native American people themselves, will happen not because state recognition excludes those who should be included but because it includes under the mantle of Indian those who should not be included and puts race shifters on the same level as federally recognized Indians. In other words, it not only allows racial, cultural, and political appropriation to go unchecked but also rewards such posturing with the lofty mantle of sovereignty, erasing the historical, legal, and political differences between, say, Princess Che'Kee' and Chief Wilma Mankiller.

In debates such as these, what matters is not whether we think of Cherokee identity as a social and political construct, an essential property, or something in between, but how these different understandings determine social classification and are used to measure and assign political legitimacy and legal rights. These issues affect Native North America much more broadly, as can be seen in the numerous newspaper articles, tribal publications, and scholarly articles written by Indian people expressing concerns over federal recognition, state recognition, "wannabes," "outtalucks," and other variations on the theme. Most Indian people care deeply about how tribal identity is measured and understood and how these understandings shape practices of social and political recognition. Many also care about how this impacts tribal sovereignty, even if some regard it as an alien and even irrelevant concept (Alfred 1999). The Cherokee case provides an opportunity to see how these debates have crystallized within a specific context. As more and more people reclaim an indigenous identity in the process of race shifting, adding fuel to the state recognition process, issues that now seem Cherokee-specific will soon affect other tribal communities as well.

The complexities of the political situation in Cherokee country beg us to reconsider these different processes of recognition and their implications for Native American tribal sovereignty. The discourses and practices of indigenous recognition are quite complex within the U.S. context, but we need to keep in mind that the United States is not alone in this regard. Nation-states often bear the legacies of empire and colonialism, in that the creation of a national body gives rise to different populations that access sovereignty in different ways. In the United States, these inequalities surface in the varying ability of Native Americans to forge relations of autonomy and interdependence, including those of being recognized or acknowledged by other tribal, state, and federal governments.

As sovereign powers engage in competing practices of official recognition, we hear increasingly bitter debates about political, racial, and cultural authenticity among different Cherokee people, many of whom are concerned that state recognition will dilute whatever political power tribes have in the United States, because it seemingly invites new claims of tribal identity and sovereignty. Instead of Indian removal or the Oklahoma land run, which undermined Cherokee territorial claims in the nineteenth century, many federally recognized Cherokees fear an assault on political and symbolic ground that they have staked out for generations. State-recognized Cherokees reject such sentiments, arguing instead that they are more than just descendants and that they deserve something they have long been denied. They turn to the states, they suggest, only because the federal government is too obtuse, and federally recognized tribes are too rigid and defensive, to see the legitimacy of their claims. The great irony lying at the center of these debates is that as different types of Native American communities assert their indigeneity, they complicate, vie for, and even challenge the relationships of mutual recognition and interdependence upon which sovereignty rests.

e i g h t
Closing

Labor Day weekend is a time when nearly everyone connected to the Cherokee Nation, from citizen to social scientist, returns to Tahlequah to see family and friends. So it was that on a sweltering Friday afternoon in late August 2008, I found myself sitting at a table in the Northeastern State University ballroom, having lunch with a graduate student and her new baby boy and younger sister.[1] We were waiting for the next round of presentations to begin, part of a large academic conference sponsored by the Cherokee Nation and its Great State of Sequoyah Commission. Formed four years before the 2007 Oklahoma Statehood centennial, the commission was originally designed to monitor and challenge any political insensitivities in the Sooner celebrations, with the expectation that many official commemorations would ignore the devastating consequences of statehood for Indian nations. The Cherokee commissioners did not want to see the same old symbolic reenactment of Oklahoma statehood taking place on the front steps of the state capitol. After all, the mock wedding of a Cherokee maiden dressed in buckskins to a young white cowboy wearing a Stetson may sound like an event from a century ago, but it was a state-sanctioned public ceremony that had been a regular part of Oklahoma statehood celebrations since 1907.[2]

When they began their work, the commissioners wanted Oklahomans to understand that the Cherokees had never agreed to any "marriage," but they soon realized that the troubling ceremonies of Oklahoma statehood were not the only topic that needed to be addressed. To explore other issues that were equally pressing in the view of the Cherokee Nation, a full-scale public conference was established in 2005. For the next several years, the invited speakers at the State of Sequoyah Conference, mostly Cherokee and other American Indian intellectuals, covered a wide array of topics, from language preservation and tribal sovereignty to media representations and ethnobotany. These presentations piqued the mostly Cherokee audiences' interest, generating a good deal of conversation without much controversy. However, something changed in 2008, when the conference took on a more contentious tone.

I felt it that day in late August when I was waiting for the last presentation of the afternoon session to begin on a topic that seemed relevant to my research on racial shifting. Glancing at the program, I realized that I was already familiar with the presenters, who were all members of the Cherokee Nation Task Force, or as it is more commonly known, the "Wannabe Task Force." A group of Cherokee Nation employees, including a tribal council member, a tribal judge, a Web designer, and an administrator, the Task Force was formed in 2007 with the goal of rooting out fraudulent Cherokee identity claims, especially those that might pose a threat to Cherokee Nation sovereignty.[3]

Given this emphasis, it was no surprise that the Task Force had scheduled a presentation titled "Stealing Sovereignty: Fraudulent 'Tribes' and Individuals," which I expected would cover much of the same ground I had seen them tread on other occasions.[4] As they had done previously, the Task Force members began their presentation in high humor by introducing themselves using their new "Indian names"—Chief Flies High and Eats Pie, Princess Buffalo Wings, Chief Talks Trash, Princess Prairie Dolphin and her sister Princess Dream Catcher, and last but not least, Chief Clan Mother of Balance and All Things Spiritual. These names were meant to poke fun at race shifters, and judging by the raucous laughter, nearly everyone in the room understood the joke.

When the laughter subsided, the Task Force got serious about the threat of race shifters from the Cherokee Nation point of view. One speaker began with an overview of the federal recognition process and noted that the average number of petitions for tribal recognition had doubled in the wake of the 1988 National Indian Gaming Act, and that, currently, thirty of those petitions came from self-identified Cherokee tribes. The next speaker continued with a critique of the growing number of new Cherokee tribes, which she saw as inherently dubious undertakings: "You can't just create one. You can't just make up an Indian tribe, culture or people. You can't split off from another tribe" (*Tahlequah Daily Press*, September 1, 2008). Members of the Task Force took turns making the same point—that these allegedly fraudulent groups were laying the groundwork for federal recognition through suspicious means. For example, members argued that these new tribes were creating an Internet presence using various trademarks including the Cherokee Nation Seal, incorporating themselves as nonprofit organizations, and accessing federal funding with a surprising degree of success (Allen et al. 2007).[5] One member of the Task Force pointed to the economic impact of the new tribes on the federally recognized ones: "We fear that millions of dollars are leaking out to these groups. People want to be politically correct and want to be inclusive of Indians. They don't want other people squalling that they're discriminating, but we just don't know how many millions of dollars have been lost." All of the presenters expressed concern not only that these groups were siphoning off federal resources but also that their individual members, the "box checkers" as they put it,[6] were getting hold of American Indian scholarships that rightfully belonged to Cherokee citizens.

Their greatest concern, however, was the fact that several self-identified Cherokee tribes had already been granted state recognition in places like Alabama, Georgia, and Missouri. Not only did state recognition afford a certain degree of political legitimacy in the eyes of the larger public, but it also had real consequences in terms of federal and state Indian law. For instance, the Task Force noted with dismay that state-recognized Indians could legally sell their wares under the 1990 U.S. Indian Arts and Crafts Act and were welcomed as artists and community consultants at the National Museum of the American Indian.

To some members of the audience, these developments were outrageous and disturbing. Many Cherokee citizens in the room seemed shocked by what was presented as a dangerous combination of ethnic fraud and political chicanery. Their emotions seemed to peak as the presenters ticked off the various illegal activities that a few self-identified and state-recognized Cherokee tribes had been involved in and said how shameful it was that these things were being done in the name of Cherokee people. As an example of the crimes, one member of the Task Force described a group in Arkansas that had defrauded the Department of Education for funding under the Title VII American Indian Education Act program. Task Force research showed not only that the group had enrolled new members in an effort to increase the overall numbers of people registered as American Indians in the Arkansas public schools but also that auditors at the Department of Education's Office of the Inspector General were investigating whether the group had skimmed 5 percent of the federal money slated for the education of their tribal members (*Native Journal*, January 22, 2006). Another case involved a man in Kansas who was convicted in federal court of selling tribal memberships to illegal Mexican immigrants for up to $1,400, with the promise that they would automatically be granted U.S. citizenship (Hegeman 2008).[7]

Finally, the Task Force described a case that infuriated at least one of the presenters to the brink of tears. She explained that a self-identified Cherokee group in Alabama had been charged with kidnapping a little girl who had been enrolled as a member of the organization, taking her from her mother. According to the local news coverage and records filed in the Superior Court of Arizona, Maricopa County, several members of the group, including the child's former foster parents, had an official they described as their tribal judge draft a letter assigning custody of the child to the former foster parents. The group justified their actions under the Indian Child Welfare Act. Two women who were tribal representatives then traveled to Arizona, where they presented the letter to a sheriff's deputy as if it were a legitimate court order. Because the Arizona deputy was familiar with the Indian Child Welfare Act, he accompanied the women as they forcefully took the child away from her mother and older sister. The women then traveled with her across state lines to Alabama (*East Valley Tribune*, January 24, 2007). In all of these examples, tradition, decency, and the fear of financial loss by the Cherokee Nation are being juxtaposed against the supposed criminality, underserved gains, and unregulated border crossings of racial shifters.

Task Force members were quick to condemn what they called the race shifters' illegal activities, but they also said that these were only a small part of a much larger problem presented by "wannabes" and their new tribal organizations. Although tribal sovereignty had long been under assault by federal and state courts, Congress, and private interest groups, they said, what these new "false tribes" were doing was much more insidious. In conclusion, Task Force members echoed the words of a recent report they had submitted to the Cherokee Nation: "More and more federal programs are treating false tribes the same as true tribes. More and more of the general public are losing the distinction between false and true tribes. The international community learns about Indians largely from the Internet, where false tribes look just like true tribes. The confusion is diluting what it means to be a sovereign Indian nation, and this will affect Congress and the courts when we are fighting for justly deserved rights against imposters" (Allen et al. 2007:17).

Because of these concerns, the Task Force urged Cherokee citizens to take action, to watch out for "imposters" and challenge them directly, even if some were their friends. In terms of policy changes, the Task Force wanted a ban on both federal and state recognition of any group claiming to be Cherokee, an end to federal funding for any Cherokee group that was not federally recognized, and amendments to both the federal Indian Arts and Crafts Act and the National Congress of American Indians' membership policy to exclude all state-recognized Indians. Finally, one Task Force member called for making impersonation of a tribe or tribal citizen a felony. These and other suggestions let everyone know that the Task Force meant business when it came to "entities using the Cherokee name."

After a dramatic half hour, the members of the Task Force took their seats on the stage and looked to the audience for a response. Comments from the audience made it clear that the Task Force had made an impression. Although some people seemed to think that the speakers' suggestions were a bit draconian, most thought that they were warranted, given the extent of the problem being presented. One thing appeared certain—nearly everyone agreed that something needed to be done. The Task Force was quick to reassure the audience that its members had already begun to take action. They had been able to get the Cherokee Nation and the Eastern Band of Cherokee Indians to endorse many of their suggestions. Only a little more than four months earlier, on April 9, 2008, the leadership of the two tribes had passed a joint resolution opposing state-recognized and self-identified Cherokee tribes and following the Task Force's recommendations almost to a tee.

Even earlier in the year, one of the members, tribal councilwoman Cara Cowan Watts, had sponsored an act before the Cherokee Tribal Council that was unanimously approved and signed into law on January 21, 2008. Known as the Legislative Act Requiring Truth in Advertising for Native Art, it established strict new guidelines for the purchase, sale, and promotion of American Indian arts and crafts within the Cherokee Nation and by its businesses. Reaching beyond the requirements of the 1990 American Indian Arts and Crafts Act, the Cherokee Nation defined an Indian as a citizen or member of a federally recognized American Indian tribe and forbade the Cherokee Nation from knowingly offering for sale or promoting any art that was produced by people who did not meet this strict definition.

Of the two actions taken at the prompting of the Task Force, the new legislation had the most direct, local impact and generated the most controversy. It meant that the Cherokee Nation had to inventory its own artistic holdings and ensure the legitimacy of what was being offered as Cherokee art in the Cherokee Nation Gift Shop and at the Cherokee Nation Heritage Center. Not one racial shifter would be allowed to sell his or her work on the property of the Cherokee Nation. The act was an aggressive measure intended to police the encroachment of race shifters upon citizen Cherokees and their nations.

One of the people most affected by this legislation was Murv Jacob, one of Tahlequah's best-known residents, a successful artist who has been painting Cherokee-inspired subjects for nearly forty years. Perhaps it was no surprise that Jacob would challenge the Task Force that afternoon. Even before the Task Force presentation had started, Jacob—who identifies himself as a Cherokee descendant—had made a dramatic appearance. He showed up at the conference and started handing out copies of a letter to the editor that he had written that appeared in that morning's edition of the *Tahlequah Daily Press*. This strongly worded letter was directed at the Task Force, in particular its most prominent member, Cara Cowan Watts, the tribal councilwoman who sponsored the legislation restricting the sale of Cherokee art. The audience members who paused to read the flyer being placed in their hands got another point of view on these matters. Jacob wrote that he did not understand why Councilwoman Cowan Watts spent so much time and energy attacking him as a "fake Indian" and "wannabe" when there were more pressing issues affecting the Cherokee Nation. He then went on to defend his own Indian identity:

> I've got a good bit of Kentucky Cherokee blood, also some German and Hillbilly.
> I never refer to myself as an Indian. I have never said I was a member of any
> tribe. But I will never, no matter how vicious their attacks, deny my ancestry.
> I've met very few folks who are actually "Indians." A card doesn't make you
> Indian. "Kowan's Kulture Kommittee" removed all my artwork and books from
> both the Cherokee Nation Heritage Center and the little Cherokee Nation Gift
> Shop because I do not have a tribal membership card. In her little world, I have
> become a persona non grata. (*Tahlequah Daily Press*, August 29, 2008)

If the KKK reference was too subtle for some readers, Jacob continued with a more direct assault on those who dared to police Cherokee identity with such zeal. Calling into question the Indianness of Councilwoman Cowan Watts and, by extension, the entire Cherokee Nation, from Principal Chief Chad Smith to its most distant citizens living outside tribal jurisdiction, Jacob wrote sarcastically:

> Cowan, the keeper of Chad's most recent sacred fire of racial purity, is a scant 1/256ths Cherokee on her CDIB card. Only in the wacky world of Cherokee Nation does she receive all those tribal benefits, plus a $50,000-per-year salary, plus mileage and expenses, and Cowan, 1/256 Cherokee, attacks me from the impenetrable position of tribal sovereignty. There are thousands of Cherokee Nation tribal members with such laughable, minimal blood quanta, some as low as 1/2048. "White" Indians is what they are most often referred to throughout Cherokee history. You'd never guess they were Indians if they didn't have that card.... I believe they will be decertified as the blatant frauds they are. (*Tahlequah Daily Press*, August 29, 2008)

Obviously, Jacob's message was controversial, even inflammatory in the context of the Task Force's presentation. Several people at the conference had already seen his letter in print and tried to stop him from circulating the flyer, but when he refused to leave quietly, they forcibly removed him from the room. Jacob yelled, "I'm being dragged out of here," as one man grabbed him by the arm, pushed him toward the door, and about five other men joined him in the hall. With raised voices and thrusting fingers, they circled Jacob, called campus security, and made it clear that he was not welcome. As Jacob was escorted out of the building, one member of the Task Force commented to the startled audience, "That's a local artist without any Cherokee ancestry." Jacob returned to his studio only a few blocks away, and there were no further incidents that day, but his letter to the editor and his behavior at the conference sparked debate for several months to come.[8]

One person who seemed to sympathize with Jacob was James Murray, a Tahlequah resident but not a Cherokee, who also attended the conference. Five days later, in a letter to the editor of the *Tahlequah Daily Press*, he acknowledged that Jacob's behavior had been disruptive but wondered whether it was not a reasonable response to "racism, slander and ignorance" (September 3, 2008). Echoing some of Jacob's sentiments, Murray characterized the Task Force presentation as "part Klan rally and part self-congratulation." He said that if the Task Force were really concerned with fraudulent identity claims and saving federal money, then it would "go a step further and say the feds could save hundreds of millions by instituting a blood quantum, releasing from membership hundreds of thousands of 'white' Cherokees." He also said that it required an "astounding delusional and racial world view for a 1/256th Cherokee to accuse anyone of 'cultural appropriation.'" Murray simultaneously critiqued and perpetuated blood ideologies:

There is some appropriating going on, and it's more perverse than "New-Agey" white people taking on Indian names and wearing feathers. It is the Cherokee Nation appropriating discredited 18th and 19th century ideologies of "citizenship by blood." These concepts, retrieved from the ash heap of history, were learned from the white man. Nowhere do they exist in the traditional Cherokee worldview. Now, they have returned under the guise of "sovereignty." These ideologies were learned from white colonists, but the "white" Cherokee "elite" have learned these lessons well. White Indians, like Cowan and Poteete, mistake race for culture, blood for community, and exclusion for strength. (*Tahlequah Daily Press*, September 3, 2008)

Murray was right that certain ideologies are at play in the Cherokee Nation's discourse of exclusion, but they are not the ones he identified. Instead, he made the same mistake as Jacob in conflating his own discourse about blood quantum with that of the Cherokee Nation about citizenship based on blood descent. The Cherokee Nation and the Task Force are not rejecting race shifters because they fail to measure up in terms of blood quantum. Rather, they are rejecting them because they have no proof of Cherokee descent or, if they do, it does not meet the standards for tribal citizenship.[9] In addition to defending tribal citizenship and sovereignty, Task Force members take a hard line against race shifting and "wannabes" because, as the name suggests, they simply do not believe that race shifters are their relatives. They are convinced of this, just as surely as race shifters are convinced otherwise.

This fundamental difference of opinion is a major source of contention between race shifters and citizen Cherokee hardliners, and yet both groups base their claims on similar cultural logics—that at some minimal level, what defines their Cherokeeness is descent from Cherokee forebears and this fact of kinship is what entitles them to define themselves as a tribal people. In this regard, both groups make constant reference to Cherokee blood, emphasize blood belonging as the basis of shared kinship, and fixate on the need to document blood ties. Just as Murv Jacob asserted that he would never deny his Cherokee ancestry and insisted on his right to make a living painting Cherokee subjects, so, too, Task Force members question his Cherokee ancestry and defend their right to police tribal boundaries and protect their citizens from ethnic fraud. Although social scientists are quick to reduce essentialist claims like these to strategic interests, something more nuanced is happening here for both race shifters and citizen Cherokee hardliners, something that stubbornly refuses that sort of interpretation.

* * *

As the conflict at the State of Sequoyah Conference suggests, when citizen Cherokees take an aggressive stance against race shifting, accusing race shifters of ethnic fraud and cultural theft, race shifters respond by accusing these same citizen Cherokees of narrow-minded racism and needless exclusivity. Yet, in each case, the argument about the legitimacy of race shifting is built largely around assumptions about indigenous ancestry. On one side, racial shifters believe that they are Cherokee descendants (even if at times the evidence is slim) and that, as such, they have a right to learn about Cherokee culture so that they can more fully identify themselves as indigenous people. Many also believe that their racial journey from Indian to white and back again is one of racial reclamation and self-actualization, a journey whose destination is the necessary revelation of an essential self that has long been forced into hiding. With this goal of indigenous self-expression in mind, race shifters reckon that if their tribes of origin will not have them, then they are entitled to create new Cherokee tribes. On the other side, many citizen Cherokees view this same racial movement in an altogether different light, as a simple move from authentic whiteness to ersatz indigeneity and therefore as a form of white appropriation that threatens Cherokee cultural and social integrity, as well as political sovereignty. Because many assume that the vast majority of race shifters have no actual Cherokee ancestry, they do not see race shifters as long-lost Cherokee kinfolk trying to find their way home, but merely as white people bent on stealing Cherokee culture and identity just as they once took possession of Cherokee land.

These opposing interpretations of racial shifting—as reclamation or appropriation—were at the heart of the conflict that afternoon in Tahlequah. Yet, as I have demonstrated, each side also represents just one extreme in a much more complicated debate. Most citizen Cherokees, and indeed most race shifters, have a more nuanced interpretation that positions much of what is happening in this movement somewhere between reclamation and appropriation. In making their assessments, these more moderate voices take into account a combination of factors that usually include formal political affiliation, cultural behavior, physical appearance, overall social acceptance, self-perception, and documentary evidence of tribal ties, all of which fall along a continuum from authentic to fake and which they privilege to varying degrees in different contexts (figure 8.1).

These are not the only factors that citizen Cherokees and race shifters consider, but they are most frequently the subject of debate. Even if a certain citizen Cherokee takes the position that race shifting is mainly a form of appropriation, she might make allowances for individual cases of racial shifting that make sense to her, such as people who look and act Cherokee and have firm documentary evidence of their tribal ties but fail to meet the criteria for citizenship. Similarly, a race shifter might argue that his own racial reclamation is totally justified but still question the claim of someone who fails to meet his standards of racial authenticity, such as having some sort of community affiliation, acting appropriately Cherokee, and possessing genealogical evidence of Cherokee ancestry. He might even use the language of citizen Cherokees in dismissing this other racial shifter as a "wannabe." But whether they are lenient, charitable, empathetic, ambivalent, mistrustful, or downright intolerant of one another, race shifters and citizen Cherokees are not likely to stop arguing about how to define Cherokeeness anytime soon. Race shifting was a subject of debate in Cherokee country long before I first started thinking about this topic in the early 1990s, and in recent years, the

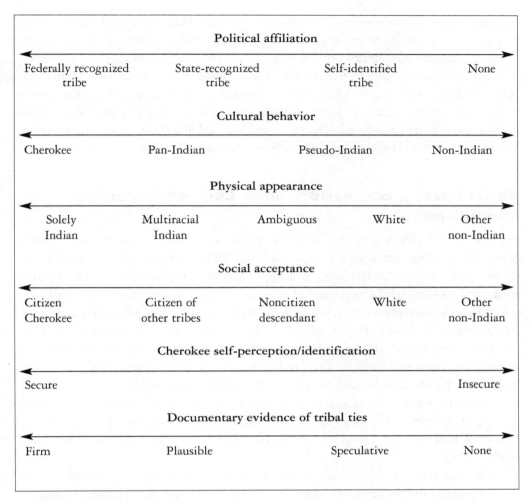

Political affiliation

Federally recognized tribe	State-recognized tribe	Self-identified tribe	None

Cultural behavior

Cherokee	Pan-Indian	Pseudo-Indian	Non-Indian

Physical appearance

Solely Indian	Multiracial Indian	Ambiguous	White	Other non-Indian

Social acceptance

Citizen Cherokee	Citizen of other tribes	Noncitizen descendant	White	Other non-Indian

Cherokee self-perception/identification

Secure	Insecure

Documentary evidence of tribal ties

Firm	Plausible	Speculative	None

Figure 8.1 Cherokee identity matrix

tensions surrounding this debate seem only to have grown as the Cherokee Nation and Eastern Band of Cherokee Indians move to protect their resources and reputations from what they perceive to be an insidious threat.

During my decade and a half of study and reflection on the topic, I have come to realize that the only way to understand this conflict and the debates surrounding it is to consider not only the painful differences in sociopolitical position and cultural interpretation that drive a wedge between these communities but also the common ground that unites them. Although race shifters and citizen Cherokees often arrive at different conclusions about the nature and meaning of race shifting, both groups use similar racial and cultural logics to interpret these claims as part of a much broader discourse about what it means to be Cherokee and to be American Indian in this country. These different logics have long been at work in the United States and have been internalized by almost everyone, not just citizen Cherokees and race shifters. What I want to draw attention to in the case of race shifting is how shared logics that assume the possibility of movement from one racial category to another often clash with those that uphold a rigid racial essentialism. These clashing interpretations of the very nature of race, culture, and indigeneity are a significant part of what fuels the controversy surrounding Cherokee identity claims. So, in the last pages of this book, let me explore the different racial and cultural logics that underlie these claims, the way they are working in the Cherokee world, and what they say about race in America today.

Racial Passing and Performance: Contested Readings, Shared Logics

To better frame this controversy, let me begin by considering how the idea of racial passing shapes interpretations of racial shifting. More than any other concept in our shared vocabularies of difference, "passing" suggests the possibility of racial movement.[10] Because racial shifting implies a status change—a move from one racial category to another—it often evokes the idea of passing for most Cherokees and most other Americans, even though the concept has rarely been applied to Native American identity shifts. The historical roots of passing in the United States lie in African American experiences, so most literary and scholarly work on the subject has tended to focus on black movements into whiteness, rather than other forms, including white movements into Indianness (Ginsberg 1996:2–3). Only in the past decade or so have scholars begun to examine other kinds of racial, gendered, and cultural passings—those that are temporary, move back and forth, and defy all expectations about social hierarchy (3–16).

The legacy of the African American experience is that for most Americans, the idea of passing hinges on an essentialist understanding of racial identity. It assumes that one can pass only as a member of a race that is different from one's actual race, which implies that race is an essence rather than a social construct (Ginsberg 1996:4). Subjects who are passing know that they are something other than what they pretend to be, so their internal sense of racial subjectivity is different from that of the racial category they inhabit and perform. This understanding of passing implies that there is a split between racial identification (how one sees oneself—the authentic, essential self) and racial desire (how one wishes to be seen—the inauthentic, constructed self) (Rottenberg 2003:441–444).[11]

Other scholars have already acknowledged the link between racial passing and racial essentialism (Ginsberg 1996; Mallon 2004; Michaels 1995; Rottenberg 2003). What I want to emphasize here, to set the stage for better understanding different interpretations of racial shifting, is how the essentialist connotations of the term "passing" reflect the legacy and logic of hypodescent, or the "one drop rule,"[12] in ways that color the entire race-shifting phenomenon. Hypodescent was an ideological and legal response to the history of sexual exploitation of enslaved African American women at the hands of white men. Because sexual violence under these conditions produced multiracial bodies from black female bodies, hypodescent ensured the ongoing functioning of the racial and sexual hierarchy that kept black and brown people, including those with white ancestry, in a structurally inferior position (Ginsberg 1996:5). The rigid racial essentialism of hypodescent meant that the multiracial offspring of a black and white couple would always be black and could never be white.

However, the same racial ideology was not at work in American Indian communities. As Native Hawaiian scholar J. Kehaulani Kauanui argues in her recent book *Hawaiian Blood: Colonialism and the Politics of Sovereignty and Indigeneity*, the federal government compelled American Indians to socially, politically, and culturally assimilate to the standards of white society, the presumption being that they could actually cross over and become white (Kauanui 2008:17–18). Rather than a rigid racial essentialism, the age-old, vanishing Indian paradigm assumed the possibility of racial transformation—the idea that Indians could eventually be incorporated within the white national body (Kauanui 2008:18). In fact, measures of blood quantum and even ideas of hypodescent were rarely used to include multiracial Indians within the category of indigeneity but rather were more often used to exclude them from accessing resources as Indians (Gonzales, Kertesz, and Tayac 2007; Kauanui 2008:21–25). Whereas multiracial blacks, no matter how varied their ancestry and behavior, were always black, multiracial Indians had a difficult time being Indian enough to meet the standards of bio-racial and cultural authenticity to which they were subjected.

Recognizing these different histories of racial formation and selective assimilation helps us to better understand how certain racial logics came to be, how they worked in the past, and how they work to explain racial shifting in the present in ways that are often contradictory. Consider, for example, how common ideas about racial passing, assimilation, hypodescent, and essentialism are all being used to describe what is happening in Cherokee country, yet people are reaching radically different conclusions about the overall meaning of this racial movement. As I argue in the first half of the book, race shifters are fairly consistent in asserting that they and their Cherokee families were forced by historical circumstances to pass as white. They argue that the colonial pressures of assimilation left their families with little choice, so rather than a betrayal of their tribe of origin, detribalization was a strategy of survival. Although generations of cultural and biological assimilation may have resulted from this choice, they now believe, in retrospect, that their families never really crossed over and became white. Rather, they could never truly assimilate to whiteness because they have nonwhite ancestry and that is what defines them. Against the narrative of assimilation, contemporary race shifters evoke the logic of hypodescent (and lineal descent) to reassert their claims to indigeneity. According to this logic, all it takes is one drop of Cherokee blood, one Cherokee ancestor in the family tree to make them Cherokee.

Ironically, the same logic that allows them to reclaim their Cherokeeness also denies their whiteness, for it reproduces the idea that whiteness is the one racial category that is pure and unadulterated.[13] Hypodescent and passing work together in the race shifter imagination: as long as they know of a single Cherokee ancestor, then they can maintain that their individual families were only feigning whiteness, passing into the dominant culture while their Cherokeeness lay dormant waiting to reemerge. This passing could even have been unconscious because their Cherokeeness was suppressed from memory, yet its essence remained. Because race shifters believe that their families were never really white—and actively disavow this possibility—reclaiming their status as Cherokee is not about racial passing in the present, but racial passing in the past.

Federally recognized Cherokees also utilize the logics of passing and assimilation, albeit in different ways. As I suggested earlier, citizen Cherokees usually argue, in two distinct ways, that race shifting is a form of racial passing in which whites pretend to be Indian. These are not the only arguments they make, but these are the most common. The first argument is that even if some race shifters have Cherokee ancestry, at the point in time that their families failed to resist the pressure to assimilate and left the tribal fold to cross over into white society, they ceased to be Cherokees. The resentment is palpable—the suggestion being that race shifters are Johnny-come-latelies whose families were not willing to stay Cherokee when the going was tough and now want to be Cherokee only when they have nothing to lose and something to gain. The second argument is that race shifters have no Cherokee ancestry and have either deceived the general public or deluded themselves that they do. In both cases, race shifters are classed as non-Indians who wrongly identify themselves as Indians. Whether for lack of blood or lack of culture, they are whites who "wannabe" socially recognized as something other than what they actually are.

Whiteness plays a crucial role in both of these citizen Cherokee interpretations. According to the first line of thinking, racial shifters are the descendants of Cherokees who cut their tribal ties to assimilate into white society, whereas in the second case, they are whites trying to pass themselves off as Cherokees. Both interpretations involve movements between Indianness and whiteness that in either direction are deemed problematic in the minds of most citizen Cherokees. For citizen Cherokees, detribalizing and conforming to dominant standards of social, cultural, and political belonging is almost as problematic as trying to appropriate an identity that does not belong to one. In the assimilation model, Cherokee logics of lineal descent are undermined as Cherokees are absorbed away from the tribe and into the dominant society. In the appropriation model, white racial shifters are stealing tribal substances to make them their own. In both cases, white society is stealing indigeneity—erasing it where it existed or fabricating it where it does not—in a way that disrespects the nature and meaning of Cherokeeness.

Whiteness works in these interpretations in another way that also generates resentment and skepticism about race shifting among citizen Cherokees. The ready ability of phenotypically white racial shifters to make themselves over as Cherokee Indians may be linked to what anthropologists Jane Hill (1994) and Mary Weismantel (2001) have described in different contexts as the incorporative power of whiteness. What they highlight with this concept is a process that is the near opposite of selective assimilation. As I have already noted, in the case of selective assimilation, dominant society rejects nonwhite cultural difference and demands that everyone conform to white standards. But once this superficial conformity takes place, some racial others (Native Americans) will be assimilated into the larger society, and others (African Americans) will not. In contrast, Hill (1994) and Weismantel (2001:212–215) argue that white society has a tendency to commodify and then absorb the symbolic and material aspects of nonwhite society that it finds most desirable. Yet, at the end of this process, race is a barrier that is actively maintained by those with white privilege. Although compelling, this line of thinking implies that racial shifting, rather than a reaction to the painful legacy of assimilation, is merely a form of cultural cross-dressing in which whites selectively try on a nonwhite cultural identity without compromising their white identities or white racial privilege. Obviously, it is more than that.

Although I acknowledge that many aspects of white privilege are maintained in racial shifting, I believe that what we are witnessing in Cherokee country is much more dynamic and nuanced in ways that are both promising and problematic. For instance, it seems that at certain times and in certain places, racial shifters are able to re-create themselves as American Indians, irrespective of their racial origins. Most of the time, their ability to create an impression of cultural difference is the key to their racial claims being accepted in the eyes of the larger public. For example, in the vignette at the start of chapter 7, when a group of white tourists came to the Cherokee National Holidays in search of American Indians and saw cultural difference inscribed in the regalia of the Echota Cherokee of Georgia, they readily accepted the assertion that these were legitimate Cherokee people. They ignored the Cherokee citizens gathered all around them in blue jeans, ball caps, and T-shirts and started taking pictures of the people who fulfilled their stereotypical expectations of how Cherokees are supposed to dress and behave. For them, red hair and freckles made little difference in the face of feathers and animal skins, and the possibility of racial passing or appropriation was probably never even raised.

As this example demonstrates, most non-Indians are so unfamiliar with American Indian realities that they will accept the visible inscription of stereotypical cultural difference as evidence of indigeneity, whereas the exact same behavior often raises suspicions among American Indians. The point is not that one group of people is informed about Cherokee life and the other ignorant but that these racial claims and performances are read in radically different ways. Whether racial shifting is seen as a legitimate form of racial reclamation or an illegitimate form of racial appropriation, or something more complex, it is an ongoing process that is always contingent, variable, contradictory, and incomplete, and this messiness is what leaves room for different interpretations.

Attending to this messiness is an exhausting business. As literary scholar Catherine Rottenberg has suggested, to claim a new racial subjectivity, or reclaim an old one, requires constant maintenance and reiteration (Rottenberg 2003:436–437). The people making the claim must continue to name themselves as Cherokees and inhabit that identity on an ongoing basis. In this regard, race shifters must repeatedly perform their racial difference using social and cultural markers if they are ever to gain social recognition as Cherokee people. However, because their performances are always read in terms of the specific context in which they take place, their social recognition is never uniformly accepted (Rottenberg 2003:447). Although race shifters might face some skepticism, even outright rejection, their performances can still have power beyond opening the door to social or political recognition. At stake is also the question of self-recognition, because the race shifter performance can allow more internal changes in racial identification. These enable race shifters to bring their racial *desire*— to be accepted as Cherokee—in line with their racial *identification*—either as whites, as former Cherokees assimilated to whiteness, or as misrecognized Cherokee descendants. The sheer repetition of things Cherokee that takes place in these performances eventually enables race shifters to internalize a sense of indigenous identity as fundamental to their very being, and these new, internalized identities are accepted and encouraged nowhere more than in the social networks that racial shifters are building.

Part of the power and challenge of racial shifting is that self-identified Cherokees are building forms of community that are based largely on ideas of racial, cultural, and spiritual kinship linked to various essentialisms. These groups, tribes, and bands—and their meeting places, council houses, and parcels of land—replicate and replace what many race shifters believe has been eroded by the heavy hand of modernity and powerful discourses and policies of assimilation. These new "structures of feeling," to borrow a phrase from cultural theorist Raymond Williams (1977), provide racial shifters with a sense and an actual place of belonging—a tribal home, if you will. However, given their newness, it would also be logical to ask about the stability of these communities, as citizen Cherokees often do. What I can ascertain from my many years of following these communities is that most of them are not very stable and tend to fissure and fall apart, only to be re-formed at some later date with new members and new leaders.

Not all groups do this. Some have been around for three or four decades, some even longer. My point is not that these communities are inherently unstable but that they do not need to be stable. Because certain essentialist logics allow for the fungibility of tribal membership, tribal members can easily be replaced by almost anyone with a claim to American Indian descent.[14] If anyone with a Cherokee ancestor is a Cherokee, this logic allows for a fluidity of tribal association that works well in the contemporary moment because populations are increasingly mobile. Even as specific tribal structures come and go, these ideas help to ensure the longevity of the overall movement, for as long as there are people who have or believe they have Cherokee blood and who are not recognized as Cherokees in other contexts, race shifting is likely to continue.

Racial Being, Cultural Doing, and the Space in Between

Although racial essentialism can give freedom to the race-shifter narrative, as we have just seen, it can also limit racial mobility by suggesting that something about racial identity is so fundamental and immutable that any kind of racial movement is troubling. According to this more restrictive way of thinking, people are not supposed to shift race, with the exception of discovering some fact of birth later in life, and even this kind of reconnection is often called into question. When these sorts of assessments are being made, context is everything: the essential facts of racial being have to fit with expected cultural norms and behavior, or else a boundary crisis takes place, as is now happening in Cherokee country. As I discussed earlier, when citizen Cherokees dismiss the claims of race shifters, it is almost always because they see them as white "wannabes" rather than as actual Cherokee descendants. They are far more tolerant of and even empathetic toward race shifters who seem to have plausible genealogical connections.

Citizen Cherokees react like this because of their own ideas about kinship and belonging and also because, like most Americans, they believe that whites are not supposed to do Cherokee things and are certainly not supposed to identify as something other than what they are. Although it disregards the complex nature of many racial identity formations, the underlying logic of this position is that each race—and each tribe—has unique cultural properties that should not be accessed by outsiders. Such essentialist logic is often used to limit rights of cultural access, to say that someone is inauthentic because he or she lacks Cherokee ancestry (usually expressed through the idiom of blood). However, it can also be used in a more inclusive sense to open up the possibility of racial belonging, as race shifters do when they claim indigeneity on the basis of these same blood connections. When citizen Cherokees and race shifters imply that whites are empty vessels with no culture of their own—unlike all other racial groups—they contradict the typical essentialism of equating a race with a culture. Such is not the case, however, when they construct white cultural identity in negative terms such as greedy, materialistic, selfish, or even bland.

As I have demonstrated using examples from both sides of this debate, race shifting can be cast as neocolonial appropriation, rightful reclamation, or something in between. What I have not explicitly said until now is that each of these interpretations highlights the power of culture and its relationship to racial formation. What I am arguing is that race and culture slide along a single continuum in the social construction of difference, so beliefs about cultural "doing" are fundamentally linked to beliefs about racial "being," and vice versa (Sturm 2002:123). This book provides numerous examples of the ways in which race shifters and citizen Cherokees use race and culture as interchangeable qualities and how this use of the terms corresponds to the way most of us actually experience them. Moreover, this same conflation of race and culture is what both sides reference when they try to, respectively, empower or disempower race shifter claims. Because racial being and cultural doing mutually reinforce and contradict each other, indigenous identity can never simply be about one or the other. For both race shifters and citizen Cherokees, being a Cherokee descendant is not enough to justify a race shifter's claim to indigeneity if that claim is not accompanied by appropriate social and cultural behavior. Conversely, citizen Cherokees generally believe that it is inappropriate for race shifters to act and identify themselves as Cherokees if they are not verifiable descendants. Although the variations on this theme can be far more complex than the examples I have just given, the upshot remains that being Cherokee, or in this case, becoming more fully Cherokee, is about the proper intersection of racial being and cultural doing.

Maybe now that we have seen the character of these existential debates that are fundamental to Cherokee life in many respects, we can ask ourselves whether race and culture should play such a critical role in defining Cherokee identity. Although many people, Cherokees and non-Cherokees included, evoke culture as a measure of indigenous difference, some scholars have cautioned against this tendency, suggesting that cultural definitions of identity pose particular problems for indigenous people. For example, sociologist Eva Garroutte, a citizen of the Cherokee Nation, writes:

> In reviewing cultural definitions of identity, it sometimes appears that they present an insoluble dilemma. On the one hand, many Indian people agree that their identities are closely bound up with distinctive ways of being in the world. Yet this is a position that easily edges over into an unrealistic demand that "authentic" Indian lifeways must embody the farthest, most exotic extreme of otherness (such that no Indian person could ever satisfy the requirements). And there are good reasons why Indian communities might want to forgive themselves, and others, for the cultural losses they have suffered. (Garroutte 2003:81)

At the end of the paragraph, Garroutte alludes not only to the experience of settler colonialism but also to the pressures of assimilation that specifically targeted American Indians. Her point about the pitfalls of cultural authenticity is similar to the one made by Kauanui (2008:11), who argues that settler colonialism depends not just upon the subordination of indigenous people but also on their disappearance and that anytime native people are defined as inauthentic, this status is both "a desired outcome of assimilation and a condition for dispossession." In other words, when Indians are deemed to be losing their social and cultural distinctiveness, their political rights to separate nationhood are more easily challenged.

Although non-Indian people and their identities are also scrutinized and judged according to standards of cultural and racial authenticity, one of the key differences between non-Indian and Indian experiences is how these definitions can reverberate in the political arena. For example, the conflation of race and culture poses certain political dangers for American Indians that non-Indians will never have to face. Unlike other racial groups in the United States, American Indian people have a unique political status as citizens of sovereign nations. The status of indigenous sovereignty, although supported by a significant body of federal and tribal law, is always under threat. Part of its vulnerability lies in that cultural and racial definitions of Indian identity take on political significance in a manner that many native scholars believe fundamentally obscures and undermines the exercise of tribal sovereignty.

Anthropologist Michael Lambert, a citizen of the Eastern Band of Cherokee Indians, described Cherokee identity politics as "a battle over sovereignty":

> One of the terrains on which this is being fought is that of how we define "Indian." The current effort to define Indian as a racial/cultural group is an effort to extinguish Indian sovereignty. The only way for Indian nations to defend and expand their sovereignty is to make exclusive claim to defining who is Indian and what it means to be Indian. If Indians have sovereignty, then culture, behavior, and belief should have nothing to do with who is or is not Indian. After all, we wouldn't deny someone's Germanness because they hate sauerkraut, nor would we have the audacity to recognize someone as German simply because they love it. German is what German does. Indian is what Indian does....
>
> What does this have to do with non-enrolled Cherokees identifying as such? I see the basis of claims to Indian identity to be political acts. This is, and has been, a battle over sovereignty. One who bases their claim to Indian identity on any basis other than sovereignty is not taking a pro-Indian position. Those who base their claim on culture are following a very problematic path, for reasons outlined above. Also, we should remember that culture was one of the original reasons given for dissolving tribal sovereignty. It also bolsters the position of those who believe that Indians and "Indian ways" are fundamentally incompatible with modernity and destined to disappear. This also raises very problematic issues surrounding the definition of "authentic" Indian culture. A sovereign people [does] not have to meet any cultural expectations. (Personal communication, November 13, 2003)

According to this line of thought, if Indian people have meaningful sovereign rights, including that of self-definition, then those rights should not be limited by external standards of cultural authenticity. Furthermore, if a tribe wishes to impose standards of culture on its own citizens, then that is its prerogative as a sovereign people. However, this is not the right of outsiders, nor is it the right of people like race shifters, who may have had ancestors that at one time were included under the tribal mantle. Ultimately, Lambert suggests that race shifters who identify as Cherokee on the basis of culture, race, or anything other than political sovereignty are fundamentally undermining tribal rights of self-definition and self-determination.

Although Lambert's arguments might seem cerebral and abstract, they are in fact representative of the kinds of debates that Cherokee people are having about racial shifting. Cherokee people are deeply concerned about tribal sovereignty and debate these issues as a part of daily life, even if at times they might use slightly different language to do so. Many would agree with Lambert that if indigeneity is defined primarily in political terms—as a unique status with an accompanying bundle of rights that are tied to specific lands, historical experiences, and laws—then it should not matter whether American Indians look, sound, and act like non-Indians.[15] But reality is infused with all sorts of unruly passions and inconvenient ideas, and the fact of the matter is that in the United States, indigenous identity, property, and rights of sovereignty are regularly linked to external perceptions of racial and cultural difference.

Take, for example, the way the term "tribe" is often conflated with "nation" in contemporary political discourse by and about indigenous people. Despite the conflation, "tribe" has different connotations—evoking collectivity, homogeneity, and primitiveness—and is more explicitly and overtly racialized than is "nation." By this, I do not mean to suggest that the idea of nation is not intimately linked with concepts like blood, race, and culture; there is a whole body of scholarly literature, including my own, that makes that connection (Smith 1995; Sturm 2002; Williams 1989, 1993). Rather, I am arguing that—legal standards aside—in constructing everyday understandings of indigenous nationhood and in looking at how these different understandings play out in political negotiations, Native American tribes are more overtly racialized than are non-Indian nations.

These common-sense understandings imply that non-Indian nations have greater racial, cultural, and social diversity than do Native American tribes. Non-Indian nations can naturalize citizens. Tribes do not (or at least if they do, the process is referred to as adoption rather than naturalization). Non-Indian nations also are seen as having a greater degree of sovereignty than do American Indian tribes. Furthermore, when Native American polities express racial and cultural diversity—as many of them do and have, some even for centuries—they are less likely to meet outside standards of Indianness, meaning that they are less likely to look or act Indian and thus to be treated and recorded as such. A lack of documents, in this regard, can greatly undermine a tribe's ability to qualify for federal recognition. Moreover, because tribal sovereignty relies less on autonomy and independence than it does on mutual recognition and interdependence, this situation poses a unique problem for native people and places limits on their ability to define themselves as they see fit (Cattelino 2007, 2008; Sturm 2007). Tribes who fail to meet federal standards may never be formally recognized (and thus will have a difficult time exercising any form of sovereignty), whereas those who do meet these must manage their public impression and maintain their sense of distinctiveness or run the risk that their status as sovereign peoples might somehow be challenged.

What I am arguing is that the conflation of race and culture places American Indians on dangerous ground. Both concepts are regularly used as measures of indigenous difference that serve to delimit the American Indian population and deny their continued existence and ongoing political rights. We may see the justice in self-determination and wish that these measures were not applied in such a way, but because race and culture form the bedrock on which we construct our understandings of difference, they are likely to continue to confound strictly political definitions of indigenous identity and sovereignty for some time to come.

More than a century ago, in the opening sentences of *The Souls of Black Folks*,

W. E. B. Du Bois (2005[1903]:3) wrote, "the problem of the Twentieth Century is the problem of the color-line." Though his words were meant to describe the challenges facing African Americans at the time, they hold true for Native Americans, as well as other racial minorities living in the United States. Despite what some pundits might say in the wake of President Barack Obama's historic election, race continues to divide our communities. Given the unique set of circumstances facing Native Americans, specifically that their individual and collective political rights are tied to external forms of social and political recognition, it just may be that the problem of the twenty-first century in Indian country is not just the color-line but also the culture-line and the painful way in which these boundaries are regulated, not just by the federal government but also by citizen Cherokees and race shifters alike.

Racial Alchemy in the Twenty-first Century

A new racial alchemy is at work in this country. The centuries-long process of indigenous assimilation—a process encouraged by ideology, informal social practice, state-sanctioned policy, and law—now seems to be reversing. In this book, I have traced the fates of people who were born and raised in families that have long identified themselves as non-Indian, who are now reclaiming their identities as Cherokee people. Some of these people have good evidence that they have Cherokee ancestry; others do not. But almost all of them operate from the position of believing their own claims. Only a tiny (but still troubling) number make these assertions knowing that they are untrue. Although these various expressions of racial shifting are distinct in many respects, they have a significant collective effect. Together, they are redefining what it means to be indigenous in the United States.

At the same time, these new forms of Cherokee identification and tribalism are not without challengers, among doubtful non-Indians and citizens of federally recognized tribes. As the scene at the 2008 State of Sequoyah Conference makes clear, citizens of the three historic Cherokee tribes—the Cherokee Nation, Eastern Band of Cherokee Indians, and United Keetoowah Band—are deeply skeptical of these new claims to Cherokee identity and are asking some hard questions about this racial movement. They want to know why this reversal is happening now and what it means for their own communities and nations. No doubt, particular social and political trends in the second half of the twentieth century set the stage for racial shifting. Although I have already outlined the different racial logics that underpin this movement, as well as the objections to it, I want to answer the question of "Why now?" more directly in these concluding pages.

The search for meaning and belonging that characterizes racial shifting is part of an old American story, but as American studies scholar Philip Deloria argues in his book *Playing Indian*, something happened in American society in the decade between the mid-1950s and the mid-1960s that allowed whites greater freedom to appropriate nonwhite racial and cultural identities (Deloria 1998:164). Racial appropriations that a decade earlier had been considered transgressive and outrageous—such as Norman Mailer's usage of the term "white Negro" to describe the Beats—had by the mid 1960s become so commonplace, they hardly bore mentioning. Deloria describes this moment as one in which "symbolic border crossings of culture and race had become so painless, that the meanings defined by those boundaries began to disintegrate" (164).

In this new context, white Americans, often with the encouragement of the counterculture and later New Age movements, began to seek new meanings for their lives in the power of indigenous cultures and identities (Deloria 1998:164–180). The move was nothing new for Euro-Americans, who had long defined themselves as distinct from Europeans by evoking American Indian imagery and experiences as their own in some limited sense (185). As I have shown in this book, what distinguishes racial shifting from these earlier forms of appropriation is that the vast majority of race shifters see themselves not as whites who "play Indian" but as long-unrecognized Indians who have been forced by historical circumstances to "play white." This fundamental difference of self-perception has gradually come into being over the past forty years and suggests some seismic upheaval in the American racial landscape.

Sociologists Joane Nagel (1996) and Stephen Cornell (1988) agree with Deloria that the 1950s were the turning point in U.S. racial politics when the seeds of ethnic renewal began to take root among American Indians. However, they offer another explanation for this process. Nagel and Cornell each contend that federal Indian policies of the mid-twentieth century that were meant to assimilate Native Americans, in particular, relocation and termination, actually had the opposite effect. Relocating American Indians to large urban areas brought them together in new ways, allowing them to see their commonalities. More specifically, Nagel (1996) argues that this new urban Indian population was primed for "ethnic renewal" when the civil rights movement erupted in the early 1960s. American Indians responded to the new political atmosphere with increased racial pride and demands for their collective political rights. In response, the federal government offered new programs that were meant to overcome some of the discrepancies in education, employment, and health care that American Indians were facing (Thornton 1990). These new economic opportunities coincided with a new social climate in which overt forms of racial discrimination were no longer socially acceptable. As a result, during the 1970s, Native American identity took on greater social, political, and economic value, a fact that goes a long way toward explaining the surge in American Indian self-identification (a 72 percent increase) recorded in the 1980 U.S. census (Thornton 1990).

These sociological explanations do an excellent job of helping us understand why ethnic renewal and political resurgence took place among urban Indians during this period, but they are less satisfying when applied to racial shifters. Certainly, many Cherokees relocated to urban areas in the 1950s and 1960s, particularly Los Angeles, San Francisco, and Denver, and their children and grandchildren were among those who participated in the high-profile political activism of the early 1970s.[16] However, unlike racial shifters, most of these urban Cherokees and their families were only a generation or two removed from tribal life, and many of them traveled back and forth between their urban residences and Oklahoma or North Carolina for family events and ceremonial occasions or simply because they were homesick. Most maintained their tribal ties in one form or another and never stopped identifying themselves as Cherokee people, whereas racial shifters followed a very different path. By the late twentieth century, there was no question that they understood themselves to be white, a perception that was shared by the people around them. Race shifters might have continued to view themselves as Cherokee descendants, but their families had not identified as Native American for four or five generations, if not longer. However, as they looked at the pride and meaning American Indians were expressing in the era of ethnic renewal, race shifters began to feel a sense of loss for the Cherokee branch of their family tree or perhaps for a phantom limb that never existed but whose presence was nonetheless vividly imagined and felt.

Given this context, it just may be that the efforts of racial shifters to reject their whiteness and reclaim their Cherokeeness speak less to the failures of assimilation than to its success, as well as the painful sense of loss that accompanies the process. As I demonstrate in the first half of this book, many racial shifters express a sense of loss when they describe their former white lives and how they felt empty and incomplete, as if something was missing that they could not readily identify. They often say that they were confused by their own sadness and describe a period of searching for explanations and meaning in different social and religious contexts. During this period, many of them also began to look to their own family histories and became interested in the now widespread genealogical "roots" movements that have flourished in the United States since the late 1970s. Only when they discovered new information about their Cherokee origins and to reinterpret their existing family histories did they come to see their melancholy in racial terms.

Racial shifters soon realized that what was missing from their lives was all that had been lost when their families assimilated into whiteness. The genealogical details might not always be verifiable, but the emotions are real enough. These feelings of sadness and loss over assimilation are quite common, as David L. Eng and Shinhee Han write in "A Dialogue on Racial Melancholia" (2003:344–349). They note that in the context of racial passing, whiteness is often described as a kind of contagion, as a "vexing condition" (343) that can infect the psyche of nonwhites who try to live as whites. They also say that assimilation typically brings on feelings of "racial melancholia" because people experience it as a form of cultural, historical, and political erasure (347–348). Thus, it makes perfect sense that, when race shifters begin to see themselves as former Indians and to link their melancholy to assimilation, they would try to mitigate their sadness by reclaiming what has been lost to them and shifting their racial self-identification from white back to Cherokee. If whiteness is the disease for these individuals, then at this particular moment in our national history, indigeneity is the cure.

Still, why now? Why have racial shifters come to fully experience and articulate these feelings of loss and racial melancholia only in the past several decades? What partially account for these new sentiments among race shifters are two fundamental changes in our public discourses about race. First, in the wake of civil rights activism, ethnic renewal, and debates about multiculturalism, nonwhite identities have been afforded greater value in many contexts in the United States. At the same time, whiteness has taken on increasingly negative connotations. In my interviews with race shifters, they associated whiteness with racial and cultural emptiness, social isolation, and even guilt over colonialism, slavery, racism, and ongoing forms of white privilege. For most race shifters, "becoming white" and even just "being white" are now increasingly viewed as disappointing, unfulfilling, and lacking in pizzazz—as if sometime during the Nixon administration, whiteness ran out of gas after four hundred years of aggressive movement across North America. The disappointments and failures of whiteness are reason enough for some Cherokee descendants to reject the forces of assimilation that once made them white, and these may be reason enough also for some white people without Cherokee ancestry to reject their own whiteness and claim an alternative identity.

What I am suggesting in pointing to the negative associations of whiteness is that there is growing insecurity about what it means to be white in American society. Obviously, whiteness is an unwieldy category that can obscure immense social, cultural, economic, political, and even racial diversity. But white privilege is still an ongoing reality of American life and is something that most whites (and phenotypically white racial shifters) take for granted. They do so because the distinct character of whiteness is often rendered invisible. Whiteness is racially normative, just as heterosexuality is sexually normative, and only when someone departs from these norms is his or her difference recognized. The very invisibility of whiteness is what allows it to be taken for granted as a social, cultural, and racial norm and ensures its ongoing power as a form of material and symbolic property (Harris 1993; Kauanui 2008). The flip side of this normativity is that whiteness is also made to appear empty and meaningless at a time when racial and cultural difference is increasingly valued. This "plain vanilla" idea of whiteness as some sort of racial, cultural, and social void now coexists with the more explicitly negative connotations of whiteness that elicit feelings of guilt. These emerging perceptions of whiteness as being empty and guilty circulate widely among race shifters, citizen Cherokees, and other sectors of our society and provide an opening for some of these individuals to challenge what dominant white standards have come to mean for their own lives. In this context, racial shifting seems quite appealing.

What makes race shifting not just desirable but possible is how race has been refigured in public discourses that have dominated the American political scene over the past three decades. For example, beginning in the late 1970s and continuing to the present, many politicians and public intellectuals have promoted a discourse of difference in which "culture" substitutes for race and works much like ethnicity in its evasions (Omi and Winant 1994; Winant 1997). Within these debates, differences of history, experience, and identity are often recognized as having social significance, but because they are rooted in culture rather than biology and are envisioned as mere constructs, they appear to have no weight. A prime example can be seen in the neoliberal rhetoric, supporting free-market economics, corporate growth, and anti–"big government" agendas, that has shaped U.S. domestic and foreign policy since the early 1980s (Duggan 2003:ix–xii). Neoliberalism has had broad bipartisan appeal, including everyone from conservative Republicans like George W. Bush to centrist Democrats like Bill Clinton (Duggan 2003:xiv–xv). In the recent book *The Twilight of Equality: Neoliberalism, Cultural Politics, and the Attack on Democracy*, American studies scholar Lisa Duggan (2003:xii, xiv) examines some of the hidden social agendas of neoliberalism, arguing that one of its most dangerous characteristics is its claim to universalism and multicultural neutrality. Because neoliberalism tends to isolate economic issues from those of race and presents itself as something that promotes greater wealth and democracy for everyone regardless of race, it is often perceived as being politically neutral (Duggan 2003:xiv; Winant 1997:80–82).

Herein lies a problem that obscures the real workings of race in the United States. Because of its pretense to universalism and neutrality, neoliberalism's racial politics are debated relatively rarely, yet neoliberal policies have had far-reaching effects on minorities, who are disproportionately poor (Duggan 2003:11–12). As deregulation and privatization bring severe cuts in social services, particularly in welfare and affirmative action programs, the poor are encouraged to take individual responsibility for finding solutions to their own problems, rather than look to the federal government for assistance (Duggan 2003:12). Although some neoliberal thinkers and policy makers recognize that there are structural limitations imposed on minorities, particularly on African Americans, they offer redress only in the form of class-based initiatives that cut across racial lines and make no special allowances for special circumstances.[17] The problem with such an approach is that it implies that no one has life experiences that are better or worse than anyone else's in any substantive way. In other words, the neoliberal emphasis on class and culture as substitutes for race has a tendency to purge discussions of difference and identity from all politics. Neoliberalism allows us to skirt issues of race, power, and privilege by creating the illusion of a level playing field. In fact, by de-emphasizing "the 'dirty little secret' of continued racial hostility, segregation and discrimination of all sorts," neoliberalism implicitly denies the continued existence of racism, white racial privilege, and their social effects (Winant 2004:9).

The nature of whiteness is a critical factor in these racial evasions, according to sociologist Howard Winant (1997). Not only does neoliberalism appeal to the specific economic and political interests of poor, working-class, and middle-class whites, but it also fails to hold them accountable for the "cultural and moral dimensions of white supremacy," including their willingness to receive either "psychological wages" or material benefits at the expense of nonwhites (Winant 2004:10). In this sense, neoliberalism provides an essential backdrop for understanding the persistence and proliferation of race shifting in the more conservative climate of the 1980s and 1990s. The policies of Ronald Reagan and George H. W. Bush marked not simply a retreat to an earlier form of political conservatism characterized by overt expressions of white supremacy, but a more veiled form of racism in which culture replaced race as a measure of essential difference (Gerstle 2001:347–374). Scholars have shown that the use of political code words for race increased during these years, including references to welfare mothers, the inner city, student athletes, and the threat of escaped prisoners to law-abiding communities, all part of a language that has continued to be used by neoconservatives and neoliberals alike (Takagi 1992:172–275).[18]

The coded language of race under neoliberalism includes Native Americans as well. Consider, for example, what took place on July 9, 1998, during the third episode of Bill Clinton's nationally televised (PBS) *Dialogue on Race*, when poet, novelist, and filmmaker Sherman Alexie (Spokane) confronted the president with the fact that many American Indians are living in what amounts to third world conditions on reservations (Hitchens 1999:48). Clinton responded by saying, "When I was running for president in 1992, I didn't know much about the American Indian condition except that we had a small but significant population of Indians in my home state and that *my grandmother was one-quarter Cherokee*. That's all I knew" (Lehrer 1998; italics added). Of course, as journalist Christopher Hitchens points out, this assertion, if true, "would have made [Clinton] the first Native American President" (Hitchens 1999:48). But why did Clinton choose to make such a claim at that particular point in time? What did it mean for him to claim indigeneity while denying his knowledge of that indigeneity in the face of Alexie's assertions? Clinton is basically saying, "I feel your pain... because it is my pain too, at least now, when it is politically useful." Beyond such classic Clinton rhetoric, I think we are witnessing a prime example of clever, neoliberal dissimulation in which power claims ignorance of racial oppression while simultaneously implying a common ground, a racial background that may or may not be true.[19] Either way, it is certainly irrelevant to Alexie's question.

In a neoliberal environment in which race has little weight (and indigeneity is continuously denied), even the most powerful white man in the United States can gesture toward alterity in order to deflate Alexie's oppositional stance and suggest, in effect, that we are all just the boy from Hope, Arkansas, lighting out for the American dream with nothing but a failure of nerve and ambition to stop us. It goes beyond the old white liberal cliché of "Some of my best friends are *X*" to suggest, "Some of my best ancestors are *X*." Obviously, shifting into Indianness when it is politically convenient is intellectually bankrupt, and Alexie called him on it. In response to Clinton, he said, "I think people are always talking about race. It's coded language.... Usually, what they will do is come up to me and say they're Cherokee. But that's usually what it amounts to. Nobody talks about Indians" (Lehrer 1998). What Alexie is saying is that people are comfortable asserting claims to Indianness when it suits them personally and politically but nobody is talking about race per se. What I am arguing is that neoliberalism offers a thinly veiled racism of a new variety, one in which such claims can be made without being questioned, one whose very emphasis on culture, class, individualism, and choice paves the way for race shifting by denying not only the persistence of racism but also the meaningfulness of race. This denial of the substance of race, meaning its correlation with social status and political power, encourages people to elide racial differences (à la Clinton) and to freely seek what they see as fuller, more culturally meaningful identities elsewhere.[20]

In these times, the growing emphasis on race as a matter of culture, personal recognizance, and individual choice, instead of being something more substantial, long-term, and inherent, has been a significant factor in the growth in race shifting. If people are now exercising their "ethnic options," as Mary Waters (1990) puts it, then racial shifting represents a retreat from whiteness for those who have a choice—meaning those fourth- and fifth-generation descendants of European immigrants who look white and thus are racially unmarked or those who are phenotypically ambiguous and thus open to interpretation and even racial reinvention. Of course, one of the painful ironies of the neoliberal regime is that not everyone has the luxury of choice. Most African Americans, for instance, have much more difficulty choosing indigeneity, even if they might be closer to the American Indian stereotype than a blue-eyed, blonde-haired Euro-American.

Beyond considering what choices are possible, we also have to consider what it is that racial shifters are trying to achieve. As I see it, these shifts in racial self-identification are fundamentally about a desire to leave behind the negative connotations of whiteness and move toward the various forms of value that are now attached to indigeneity. For race shifters, the material value of Indianness can include everything from funding for education, health care, and housing to preference in hiring and a right to sell their artistic handiwork as American Indian made. Its symbolic value can include greater access to sacred power, a vibrant sense of community, a totalizing meaning system that can be adjusted to suit individual needs, and the moral superiority of being recognized as indigenous in a settler colonial context. All of these forms of value attract racial shifters to Cherokeeness, but not all of them are equally accessible. In fact, racial shifters are less likely to take advantage of the material resources attached to Indianness, because such access is usually limited to citizens of federally recognized tribes and in some cases state-recognized tribes. However, all racial shifters, regardless of the nature of their tribal affiliations, benefit from the symbolic values of Indianness.

Given that the symbolic values of Indianness are more readily accessible to race shifters, it might be helpful to start thinking about how racial shifters are trying to reject (though often unsuccessfully) the "wages of whiteness" of earlier generations. I borrow this concept from David Roediger's path-breaking book *The Wages of Whiteness: Race and the Making of the American Working Class* (1991). In this book, Roediger explains how working-class Euro-Americans, specifically Irish Americans, often came to these shores as indentured servants and in social positions that were similar to those of African Americans in northeastern cities. Although they did not initially identify themselves as white, they slowly began to do so as a way to distance themselves from African Americans and their status as slaves. Roediger builds on the insights of W. E. B. Du Bois (2005[1903]) to argue that in becoming white, working-class Euro-Americans received certain psychological benefits from their new racial status that compensated for their ongoing class oppression. Although Roediger's work overlooks the racial and gender diversity of the American working class and tends to emphasize psychological explanations at the expense of historical and material ones, his ideas have much to offer our understanding of racial shifting. As in the case of Roediger's working-class Irish immigrants, contemporary racial shifters who become Indian are able to distance themselves from their former racial status and to obtain new symbolic and psychological benefits.

Although the wages of whiteness are still in evidence, they are in decline. For many race shifters, the more appealing prospect is what we might call the "wages of Indianness." In emphasizing the symbolic capital that has been increasingly attached to Indianness, I am trying to offer a corrective to explanations of racial shifting that have overemphasized material interests to the point of obscuring what are in fact much more complicated social processes. Rather than continue to reduce racial shifting to some sort of strategic interest based on the hope of accessing Indian resources or rights, we need to look beyond the material to the symbolic and see how these work together to engender movements into Indianness.

For example, if we consider the growing number of white writers, artists, and other public figures who choose to represent themselves as American Indians—the most notorious being Asa (aka Forrest) Carter, a former white supremacist and Ku Klux Klan leader, who claimed to be Cherokee when he published his best-selling autobiography, *The Education of Little Tree* (1976)—we can understand why they believed that their creative work would garner more attention as something that was Indian made rather than white made. As Ojibwe novelist David Treuer explains in an insightful article on the topic, these individuals did not suddenly become better writers when they claimed to be Indian, but their ersatz Indian personae seem to have paid off in more ways than one. What they could not publish as whites, they were able to publish as Indians, which garnered them greater publicity and higher sales figures (*Slate Magazine*, March 7, 2008).[21] The symbolic and material value of Indianness worked in tandem for people like Carter. If a self-avowed racist was willing to make such a claim as a way to access values attached to indigeneity, then why would someone with fewer biases not do the same?

As in the case of Carter, racial shifting highlights the complexities and contradictions of race in the twenty-first century and shows that some very old ideas are coming together with new ones in ways that allow for new forms of indigenous identification. Racial shifting is fueled by the same old essentialist logics of race as something inherently based in blood, kinship, biology, nature, and genes, as well as new understandings of race as something that is fluid, contextual, largely cultural, and a matter of individual choice. These different, even contradictory, understandings of race are coming together in a new social, political, and economic context, one in which indigenous identity is increasingly valued at the same time that whiteness is being challenged. Because this discourse is so variable and can have radically different implications and applications, it is not always clear when citizen Cherokees or racial shifters are utilizing one rationale or another. Usually, their arguments are quite complex and draw on a variety of ideas, as discussed with the Cherokee identity matrix earlier in this chapter.

In many respects, what matters is not which racial logics people are using, but to what end they are being used. As anthropologist Ella Shohat (1992:110) asks, "who is mobilizing what in the articulation of the past, deploying what identities, identifications and representations, and in the name of what political visions and goals?" We might ask ourselves the same thing about the competing discourses surrounding racial shifting. Whether they are claiming, reclaiming, or disclaiming indigeneity, different people have different relationships to one another, different political ambitions, and different historical positions vis-à-vis settler colonialism. Recognizing these differences helps us to make sense of the implications of these claims. Some of them are about hierarchy and survival, whereas some are about pushing back against oppression. But whatever is being said, we need to have more conversations, and we need to ask different questions than we have asked before.

One of the final things to consider is whether racial shifting is a progressive move that challenges the legacy of a racist system or whether it is something that undermines the various forms of symbolic and material property that now belong to indigeneity. Another way of thinking about this is to ask, if so many people are identifying in these new and more challenging ways, does it matter any more what we consider to be normatively Indian? Even if such a category does exist, do we want to name it? The flip side of this question is, if people are feeling and experiencing these new forms of indigenous identification, should these identities be mirrored in governmental structures at the tribal, federal, or state level? At stake is the cultural and political survival of indigenous people in the face of threats to their tribal sovereignty and resources. Ultimately, these questions are not for outsiders to decide but rather are the responsibility of tribal people (a category whose membership is not always agreed upon). At the same time, the U.S. government has had a historic role in these matters and should be held accountable to American Indian people and their governments.

As tribal people and their governments begin to answer these questions and to confront the thousands of race shifters seeking to join their ranks, the real nature of the race shifter journey—the depth of its meaning—cannot be understood quickly or easily as authentic or inauthentic, power-evasive or not, a blessing or a curse to federally recognized tribes or indigenous people generally. Rather, these stories of racial reclamation have to be weighed in more metaphoric ways that account for the permutations of the psyche and the soul, especially in a complex, shifting country like the United States, where the possibilities of self-transformation and reinvention are so highly prized. Only in doing so might we understand what lies under the surface of these stories, something that many citizen Cherokees realize as they meet a race shifter and listen to his or her story. The details of some claims to indigeneity may be literally true; others are surely the products of invention and wishful thinking. Yet, all of these stories of genealogical belonging spiral backward to reveal older histories of racial erasure, the suppression of indigeneity, and the legacy of assimilation, just as surely as they also reflect a long and continuous history of white power, appropriation, and cultural longing. These stories are always greater than what we can first fathom, and only in acknowledging their larger historical and political contexts can we begin to recognize and make sense of their differences.

appendix one
Self-Identified Cherokee Organizations

Total Number = 238[1]

Alabama

Cherokee Nation of Alabama, Birmingham
Cherokee River Indian Community, Moulton
Cherokee Trust, Alexander City
Cherokees of Jackson County, Higdon
Cherokees of Northeast Alabama, Collinsville
Cherokees of Southeast Alabama, Hoover
Echota Cherokee of Alabama, Sylacauga
Echota Cherokee Tribe of Alabama, Maylene
Echota Cherokee Tribe, Birmingham
Free Cherokees, Eagle Bear Clan, Hamilton
Langley Band of Cherokee Indians in the Southeastern United States, Birmingham
North Alabama Cherokees, Creek Path/Willtown District, Scottsboro
Southeastern Cherokee Confederacy, Fox Clan, Huntsville
United Cherokee Intertribal, Guntersville
United Cherokee Tribe of Alabama, Daleville
United Cherokee Tribe of Alabama, Midland City

Alaska

Southeastern Cherokee Confederacy, Big Lake
Southeastern Cherokee Confederacy, Kenai

Arizona

Cherokee Family Ties, Mesa

Arkansas

Arkansas Band of Western Cherokees, Mountain Home
Arkansas River Band of the Southern Cherokee Nation
Buffalo River Band of the Southern Cherokee Nation, Green Forest
Chickamauga Cherokee Nation, Green Forest
Free Cherokees, Arkansas Bear Tribe Band, Mountain Home
Free Cherokees, Dung Beetle Society, Portland
Free Cherokees, Good Medicine Band, Hot Springs
Free Cherokees, Helena
Lost Cherokee of Arkansas and Missouri, Jonesboro
Neches Tribe–Cherokee Nation, Hot Springs
Northern Cherokee Nation, Fayetteville
Old Settler Cherokee Nation of Arkansas, Timbo
Ozark Mountain Cherokee Tribe of Arkansas and Missouri, Melbourne
Western Arkansas Cherokee Tribe, Midway
Western Cherokee Nation of Arkansas and Missouri, Paragould
White River Band of Northern Cherokee Indians, Fayetteville
White River Band of the Chickamauga Cherokee Nation, Waldzon

California

Ani-Yun-Wiya Society, Bakersfield
Cherokee Seven Clans Council, Bakersfield
Cherokees of California, Marysville
Free Cherokees, Sutter Creek
Running Water Cherokee Indians, Bakersfield
Southeastern Cherokee Confederacy, Buffalo Clan, Ontario
Southeastern Cherokee Confederacy, Manzanita Band, Redding

Colorado

Echota Cherokee, Denver

Connecticut

Free Cherokees, Madison
Free Cherokees, Moon Band, Groton
Free Cherokees, Snake Band, Oakville

Florida

Amonsquath Tribe of Cherokees, Bear Clan, DeFuniak Springs
E-Chota Cherokee Indian Tribe of Florida, DeFuniak Springs
E-Chota Cherokee Tribe of Florida, Sneads
Free Cherokees, National Veterans Band, DeLand
South Florida Cherokee Band, Bowling Green
Southeastern Cherokee and Creek Tribe, Orange Springs
Southeastern Cherokee Confederacy, Bear Clan, Orlando
Southeastern Cherokee Confederacy, Beaver Clan, Fort Walton Beach
Southeastern Cherokee Confederacy, Blue Clan, Sebring
Southeastern Cherokee Confederacy, Crow Band, Ocala
Southeastern Cherokee Confederacy, Jacksonville
Southeastern Cherokee Confederacy, Long Hair Band, Tallahassee
Southeastern Cherokee Confederacy, Many Lakes Band, Wachula
Southeastern Cherokee Confederacy, Orlando
Southeastern Cherokee Confederacy, Pine Knot Clan, Tarpon
Southeastern Cherokee Confederacy, Rattlesnake Band, Bradenton
Southeastern Cherokee Confederacy, Sebring
Southeastern Cherokee Confederacy, Turtle Clan, Jacksonville
Southeastern Cherokee Confederacy, Wild Potato Clan, Gainesville
Southeastern Cherokee Confederacy, Sarasota
Southern Band of Cherokees, Deland
Tchlaki Croatan Nation, Pompano
Tuscola United Cherokee Tribe of Florida and Alabama, Geneva

Georgia

American Cherokee Confederacy, Leesburg
American Cherokee Council, Ochloknee
Bird Clan of the Northwest Cherokee Wolf Band, Albany
Cane Break Band of Eastern Cherokees, Dahlonega
Chattahoochee Valley Band of the Southern Cherokee Nation
Cherokee Indians of Georgia, Albany
Cherokee Indians of Georgia, Columbus
Cherokees of Georgia, Hilliard
Chickamauga Cherokee Band of Northwest Georgia, Rossville
Dahlonega Band of the Southern Cherokee Nation, Dahlonega
Etowah Cherokee Nation, Quitman
Free Cherokees of Northwest Georgia, Rossville
Free Cherokees, Ball Ground
Free Cherokees, Good Medicine Band, Cummings
Free Cherokees, Good Medicine Society, Mableton
Free Cherokees, Marietta
Free Cherokees, Turtle Clan, Atlanta

Georgia Tribe of Eastern Cherokee, Dawsonville
Ossahatchee Creek Band, Etowah District, Southern Cherokee Nation, Hamilton
Pearl River Band, Etowah District, Southern Cherokee Nation
Southeast Kituwah Nation, Wayatali Uku, Warner Robins
Southeastern Cherokee Confederacy, Adel
Southeastern Cherokee Confederacy, Bird Clan, Waycross
Southeastern Cherokee Confederacy, Deer Clan, Quitman
Southeastern Cherokee Confederacy, Donaldson
Southeastern Cherokee Confederacy, Eagle Clan, Albany
Southeastern Cherokee Confederacy, Fire Clan, Macon
Southeastern Cherokee Confederacy, Holly Clan, Dearing
Southeastern Cherokee Confederacy, Leesburg
Southeastern Cherokee Confederacy, Lake Park
Southeastern Cherokee Confederacy, Lower Etowah Clan, Rossville
Southeastern Cherokee Confederacy, Ocklocknee
Southeastern Cherokee Confederacy, Panther Clan, Bainbridge
Southeastern Cherokee Confederacy, Sylvester
Southeastern Cherokee Confederacy, Thomasville
Southeastern Cherokee Confederacy, Valdosta
Southeastern Cherokee Council, Ochloknee
Southern Band of Cherokees and Creeks, Ellijay
Tugalo Cherokee Tribe, Canton
Uganawvkalvgv Kituwah Ayeli, Warner Robins
United Cherokee Nation, Zirkel and Patterson

Idaho
Wild Potato Clan of the Northwest Cherokee Wolf Band, Nampa

Indiana
Lone Wolf Band of Cherokee Indians, South Bend
Midwest Cherokee Alliance, Frankton
Southeastern Cherokee Confederacy, Paint Clan, Rochester

Kansas
Neosho River Band of the Southern Cherokee Nation

Kentucky
Delilah Whitecloud United Cherokee Indian Tribe of Kentucky, Tremont
Rainbow Cherokees, Frankfort
Southeastern Cherokee Confederacy, Black Wolf and Warrior Society, Wallins Creek
Southeastern Cherokee Confederacy, Evarts

Louisiana

Amonsquath Tribe of Cherokee, Deer Clan, Farmersville

Maryland

Free Cherokee, Bird Clan, Chapitco
Free Cherokees, Mechanicsville
Free Cherokees, Wild Potato Band, Hollywood

Massachusetts

Free Cherokees, Eagle Council, Reading
Free Cherokees, Wild Potato Band, Feeding Hill

Michigan

Free Cherokees, National Veterans Band, Holt

Mississippi

Free Cherokees, Star Hawk Band, Jackson

Missouri

Amonsquath Tribe of Cherokee, Deering
Amonsquath Tribe of Cherokee, Hannibal
Amonsquath Tribe of Cherokee, Powhatan Clan, Sparta
Central Missouri Cherokee Tribe, Centralia
Cherokee Nation West, Southern Band of the Eastern Cherokee Indians of Missouri
    and Arkansas, Seneca
Chickamauga Cherokee Nation, Rockport
Elk River Band of the Southern Cherokee Nation
Free Cherokees, Dogwood Band, Ashland
Free Cherokees, Hummingbird Clan, Columbia
Missouri River Band of the Southern Cherokee Nation
Northern Cherokee Nation of Old Louisiana Territory, Columbia
Northern Cherokee Tribe of Indians of Missouri and Arkansas, Clinton
Northern Cherokee Tribe of Indians, Columbia
Northern Cherokee Tribe of Missouri, Columbia
Ozark Mountain Cherokee Tribe of Arkansas and Missouri, Alton
Sac River and White River Bands of the Chickamauga Indian Nation of Arkansas and
    Missouri, Fair Play
St. Francis River Band of Cherokee Indians, Fisk
Wilderness Tribe of Missouri, Alton

Nebraska

Southeastern Cherokee Confederacy, Coyote Band, Barnston

New Jersey

Echota Chickamauga Cherokee Tribe of New Jersey, Irvington
Free Cherokees, Osprey Band, Mays Landing
Sand Hill Band of Cherokee and Lenape Indians, Paterson

New York

Free Cherokees, Deer Council, Brooklyn
Free Cherokees, Many Walks Council, Stony Creek
Free Cherokees, North Hudson
Free Cherokees, Wolf Council, Scottsville
Mary Trail of Tears Long House, Brooklyn
Nuyagi Keetoowah, New York
Southeastern Cherokee Confederacy, Mastic

North Carolina

Cherokee Indian Tribe of Robeson and Adjoining Counties, Red Springs
Cherokee Indians of Hoke City, Lumber Bridge
Cherokee-Powhatan Indian Association, Roxboro
Creek-Cherokee Indians, Pine Tree Clan, Cherokee
Free Cherokees, Chapel Hill
Ridge Band of Cherokees, Ridgecrest
Southeastern Cherokee Confederacy, Cedar Grove
Southeastern Cherokee Confederacy, Haw River
Southeastern Cherokee Confederacy, Silver Cloud Clan, Cedar Grove

Ohio

Cherokee Delaware Indian Center, Coshocton
Cherokee United Intertribal Council, Columbus
Eastern Cherokee Nation, Overhill Band, Columbus
Etowah Cherokee Nation, Portsmouth
Free Cherokees, Hokshichanklya Band, Creola
Ohio Cherokees, West Portsmouth

Oklahoma

American Cherokee Confederacy, Horse Clan, Francis
Canadian River Band of the Southern Cherokee Nation
Northern Cherokee Tribe of Indians, Weatherford
Northern Chickamauga Cherokee Nation of Arkansas and Missouri, Miami
Southern Cherokee Nation, Webbers Falls

Oregon

Northwest Cherokee Wolf Band of the Southeastern Cherokee Confederacy, Talent

Northwest Cherokee Wolf Band, Deer Clan, Bend
Northwest Cherokee Wolf Band, Paint Clan, Salem
Southeastern Cherokee Confederacy, Badger Band, Golden Hill
Southeastern Cherokee Confederacy, Medford
Southeastern Cherokee Confederacy, Paint Band, Salem
Southeastern Cherokee Confederacy, Wolf Band, Phoenix

Pennsylvania
Inagei Tsalagi, Cherokees of Virginia, Allison Park
Southeastern Cherokee Confederacy, Philadelphia
Tsalagi Elohi Cherokee Earth, Chesne
United Cherokee Tribe of West Virginia, Sewickly

South Carolina
Cherokees of South Carolina, Columbia
Free Cherokee–Chickamauga, Chesne

Tennessee
Cherokees of Lawrence County, Leoma
Chikamaka-Cherokee of the Southern Cumberland Plateau, Tracy City
Chickamauga Circle of Free Cherokee, Chattanooga
Elk Valley Band–Council of Chickamauga Cherokee, Estill
Elk Valley Council Band of Free Cherokees, Pigeon Forge
Etowah Cherokee Nation, Cleveland
Etowah Cherokee Nation, Pigeon Forge
Faraway Cherokee Association, Memphis
Free Cherokees, Chickamaugan Circle, Ooltewah
Free Cherokees, Good Medicine Society, Grandview
Free Cherokees, Grandview
Original Cherokee Nation, Chattanooga
Southeastern Cherokee Confederacy, Red Clay Inter-Tribal Indian Band, Ooltewah
Tennessee Band of the Cherokee, Strawberry Plains
Tennessee River Band of Chickamauga Cherokee, Chickamauga Station
Turkeytown Association of the Cherokee, Nashville

Texas
American Cherokee Tribe of Texas, Lumberton
Cherokee Nation of Texas Reservation Limited, Corpus Christi
Cherokee Nation of Texas, Tsalagi Nvdagi, Troup
Court of the Golden Eagle, The Cherokee Nations, Dallas
Free Cherokee Tennessee River Band of Chickamauga, Jasper
Free Cherokees, Hummingbird Clan, Dallas

Southeastern Cherokee Confederacy, Hawk Clan, Mineral Wells
Southeastern Cherokee Confederacy, Sequoyah Clan, El Paso
Southeastern Cherokee Tribe and Associated Bands, Porter
Sovereign Cherokee Nation–Tejas, Mesquite, Dallas
Texas Band of Cherokee Indians of the Mount Tabor Indian Community, Converse
Texas Buffalo Bayou Band of Chickamaugan Cherokee, Southern Cherokee Nation, Houston
Texas Gulf Coast Cherokee and Associated Bands, New Caney

Utah

Cherokee Indian Descendents Organization of the Ani-Yun-Wiya, Logan
Colorado River Band of the Southern Cherokee Nation, Millville
Rocky Mountain Band of Cherokee Descendents, Magna

Vermont

Free Cherokees, Tribal Council, Springfield
Green Mountain Band of Eastern Cherokee, Bristol
Odali Utugi (Hope Mountain) Peace Village, Lincoln

Virginia

Buffalo Ridge Cherokees, Amherst County
Cherokees of Virginia, Birdtown
Free Cherokees, Spider Clan, Richmond
Inagei Tsalagi, Cherokees of Virginia, Rapidan
Southeastern Cherokee Confederacy, Crimora
Southeastern Cherokee Confederacy, Pine Log Clan, Fairfax
Turtle Band of Cherokee, Evington
United Cherokee Tribe of Virginia, Madison Heights

Washington

Anisahani Blue Clan, Woodland
Free Cherokees, Four Directions Council, Toledo
Southeastern Cherokee Confederacy, Haddock/Compton Clan, Vancouver

West Virginia

United Cherokee Nation of West Virginia, Glen Morgan

Wisconsin

Southeastern Cherokee Confederacy, Milwaukee

appendix two
State-Recognized American Indian Tribes

Number of states: 18
Number of tribes: 62
Number of Cherokee tribes: 15[1]

Alabama
Cherokees of Northeast Alabama
Cherokees of Southeast Alabama
Echota Cherokee Nation
Machis Lower Alabama Creek Tribe
Mowa Band of Choctaws
Piqua Sect of Ohio Shawnee
Star Clan–Muscogee Creek Tribe
United Cherokee Inter-Tribal Council

Arkansas
Northern Cherokee Nation of Old Louisiana Territory

Connecticut
Golden Hill Paugussett Tribe
Paucatuck Eastern Pequot Tribe

Schaghticoke Tribal Nation

Delaware
Nanticoke Indians

Georgia
Cherokee of Georgia Tribal Council
Georgia Tribe of Eastern Cherokee
Lower Muscogee Creek Tribe

Kansas
Delaware Muncie
Wyandot Nation of Kansas

Louisiana
Caddo Adais Indian Tribe
Choctaw-Apache of Ebarb
Clifton Choctaw
Four Winds Band of Cherokee
Louisiana Band of Choctaw
United Houma Nation

Massachusetts
Heron Pond Wampanoag Tribe
Nipmuc Tribal Council of Massachusetts

Michigan
Burt Lake Band of Ottawa and Chippewa Indians
Grand River Band of Ottawa Indians
Swan Creek Black River Confederated Ojibwa Tribes

Missouri
Chickamauga Cherokee Nation of Arkansas and Missouri
Northern Cherokee Nation
Northern Cherokee Nation of Old Louisiana Territory

Montana
Little Shell Tribe of Chippewas of Montana

New Jersey
Nanticoke Lenni-Lenapes of New Jersey

Powhatan Renape Nation
Ramapough Mountain Tribe

New York
Ynkechauge Indian Nation of Poospatuck Indians

North Carolina
Coharie Intra-Tribal Council
Haliwa-Saponi Tribe
Lumbee Tribe of North Carolina
Meherrin Indian Tribe
Persons County Indians
Waccamaw-Siouan

Ohio
Allegheny Lenape Nation
Tallige Fire Cherokee Nation
United Remnant Band Shawnee Nation

South Carolina
Eastern Cherokee
Pee Dee Tribe of Upper South Carolina
Southern Iroquois
United Tribes of South Carolina
Waccamaw Indian People
Wassamasaw Tribe of Varnertown Indians

Tennessee
Etowah Cherokee Nation

Virginia
Chickahominy Indian Tribe
Eastern Chickahominy Indian Tribe
Mattaponi Tribe
Monacan Indian Tribe
Nansemond Indian Tribal Association
Pamunkey Nation
United Cherokee Tribe of Virginia
United Rappahannock Tribe
Upper Mattaponi Indian Tribal Association

a p p e n d i x   t h r e e
1828 Excerpts from the *Cherokee Phoenix*

The following excerpts are taken from the *Cherokee Phoenix*, the first American Indian newspaper. Elias Boudinot, a prominent Cherokee citizen, served as the paper's first editor and began printing a bilingual English-Cherokee edition in 1828. Today, the paper continues to be printed by the Cherokee Nation. The *Bunker Hill Aurora* was another nineteenth-century newspaper, published in Charlestown, Massachusetts. The *Cherokee Phoenix* had a wide circulation and often reproduced articles on Cherokee and other American Indian–related topics from other newspapers. These two excerpts provide additional historical context for understanding Cherokee responses to race shifters, at least in those instances in which Cherokees believe that their claims are fraudulent.

AN IMITATION INDIAN—A person made his appearance in the city on Thursday last, dressed in the costume of an Indian, and calling himself "Gen. William Ross," which is engraved upon an apparently silver breast plate. He says his father is Daniel Ross, who is the Chief of the Cherokee Indians, and that he is an authorized agent of the nation. He states a number of particulars, concerning the Cherokees, and says he was educated at Wilmington, N.C. He speaks the English language fluently, especially when he forgets himself—says he knows a little French, is perfectly familiar with Cherokee, & can converse some in Choctaw. His dress is, red inexpressibles of some thin materials, with shoes, a gown of wide-striped calico, a red-ribbon and a considerable quantity of wax beads round his neck-handkerchief, a kind of open worked Vandyke, a wig of black, coarse hair, an ordinary hat trimmed fantastically, and tin bracelets around his wrists. He is rather a small man, but with nothing of the true Indian in his form or gait.

—*Bunker Hill Aurora* (*Cherokee Phoenix*, July 2, 1828)

Mr. Boudinot: In the last number of the *Phoenix* I noticed an extract, taken from Bunker Hill Aurora, describing a fellow, who pretends to be a son of mine. The same vagrant has had the impudence to address me two or three letters, at different times, signed, "Gen. Wm. Ross, his mark," one, postmarked Chillicothe, stated "he wanted money to enable him to carry on a suit at law," and another letter dated in Cincinnati, stated, "he was released by the act of insolvency," one other from Wheeling, which I have not opened. The fellow's design in getting these letters written for him, must have been with the view of covering his knavery. I have lately learned, the same person has been seen in New York, and while there was committed to jail. Should this imposter gain credence with the credulous, so that they become loseres [*sic*] by his acquaintance, I can have no sort of objection (by way of atonement) to the hanging of this "Gen. Wm. Ross," if merited. I have no knowledge who this vile wretch can be, and I believe he has no connexion (sic) whatever with the Cherokees, and certainly not with me, or family.

I am respectfully your ob't serv't.

—Daniel Ross (*Cherokee Phoenix*, July 21, 1828)

appendix four
Mail Survey of Self-Identified Cherokees

No.	Name*	Date	Age	Gender	Occupation	Place Raised	Current Residence	Tribal Role
1	Marge Peterson	April 23, 1996	56	Female	Accountant	Tennessee	Georgia	Member
2	Seeing Heart Stevens	March 11, 1996	65	Male	Retired	New York	Florida	Chief
3	Cara Wesley	March 29, 1996	73	Female	Homemaker	Kansas, Washington	Washington	Member of elder council
4	Alice Wolfhawk	March 26, 1996	50	Female	Homemaker	North Carolina, Tennessee	Tennessee	Member
5	Billy Blackbear	March 20, 1996	72	Male	Engineer	Oklahoma	Florida	Assistant chief
6	David Walks Alone	March 11, 1996	61	Male	Writer	Kentucky, Florida	Maryland	Grandfather chief
7	Jimmy Big Man Snead	April 6, 1996	57	Male	Retired military	—	Washington	Sub-chief
8	Lisa Warrior Heart	March 18, 1996	32	Female	Nurse	Georgia	Georgia	Member
9	Mark Ryan	March 13, 1996	77	Male	Farmer	North Carolina	North Carolina	Chief
10	Rich Tsalagi Patton	April 23, 1996	63	Male	Retired military	Texas	Texas	Chief
11	Vera Sheppard	June 16, 1996	73	Female	Retired	California	Arizona	Founding member
12	Homer Schumacher	June 25, 1996	70	Male	Retired	California	California	Chief
13	Raven Moon	March 29, 1996	66	Female	Sales clerk	Washington	Washington	Member
14	Bart Davidson	March 15, 1996	42	Male	Social security disability recipient	Tennessee	Tennessee	Chief
15	June Red Wolf Jenks	March 9, 1996	39	Female	College professor	Kentucky	Georgia	Member

* All names are pseudonyms.

appendix five
Formal Interview Data, Self-Identified and State-Recognized Cherokees

No.	Name*	Date	Age	Gender	Residence	State-Recognized?	Tribal Position	Interviewer†
1	Drew Martin	May 24, 2003	40s	Male	Oklahoma	No	Tribal council member	JW
2	Brent Stephens	June 25, 2003	40s	Male	Oklahoma	No	Tribal council member	JW
3	George Richey	July 22, 2003	50s	Male	Oklahoma	No	Chief	JW‡
4	Luanne Helton	May 21, 2003	50s	Female	Alabama	Yes	Genealogist	JW
5	Benny Jones	March 8, 1996	40s	Male	Pennsylvania	Yes	Member	CS
6	Jessica Gates	March 29, 2003	40s	Female	Alabama	Yes	Member	JW
7	Will Kinsey	April 26, 2003	60s	Male	Arkansas	No	Member	JW
8	Bob Allen	April 26, 2003	70s	Male	Arkansas	No	District council member	JW
9	Mary Anne Allen	April 26, 2003	60s	Female	Arkansas	No	District council member	JW
10	June Davis	April 26, 2003	30s	Female	Arkansas	No	Member	JW
11	Lois Camp	October 27, 1995	20s	Female	New Hampshire	No	Independent	CS
12	Darren Nixon	May 24, 2003	60s	Male	Oklahoma	No	Marshall	JW
13a	Heart of the Wolf	February 22, 2003	70s	Female	Arkansas	No	Member	JW
13b	Heart of the Wolf	February 23, 2003	70s	Female	Arkansas	No	Member	JW§
14	Missy Black	May 18, 2003	40s	Female	Alabama	Yes	Member	JW

#	Name	Date	Age	Sex	State		Position	Interviewer[†]
15a	Joe Perry	July 8, 2003	60s	Male	Texas	No	Chief	JW
15b	Joe Perry	March 18, 1996	50s	Male	Texas	No	Chief	CS ‡
16	David Hooper	July 8, 2003	40s	Male	Texas	No	Deputy chief	JW
17	David Madison	May 18, 2003	40s	Male	Alabama	Yes	Member	JW
18	Kristin Wilson	July 17, 2003	40s	Female	Alabama	Yes	District council member	JW
19	Joan Barrett	May 18, 2003	60s	Female	Alabama	Yes	Member	JW
20	Running Wolf	March 29, 2003	50s	Male	Arkansas	No	Independent	JW
21	Charlene Hamilton	May 18, 2003	40s	Female	Alabama	Yes	Second vice chief	JW
22	Sarah Glory	May 18, 2003	60s	Female	Alabama	Yes	Chief	JW
23	Morris Carter	May 24, 2003	70s	Male	Oklahoma	No	Member	JW
24	Darren Bounds	May 18, 2003	40s	Male	Alabama	Yes	Member	JW
25	Kate Wallace	April 26, 2003	40s	Female	Arkansas	No	Member	JW
26	Arlo Davis	February 22, 2003	64	Male	Arkansas	No	Deputy chief	JW
27	Robby Giles	February 22, 2003	40s	Male	Arkansas	No	District council member	JW
28	May Bellflower	May 17, 2003	40s	Female	Alabama	Yes	Member	JW
29	Sheryl Jones	May 17, 2003	50s	Female	Alabama	Yes	Member	JW
30	Lindsey McGee	November 9, 1995	30s	Female	Oklahoma	No	Independent	CS

* All names are pseudonyms.

† JW = Jessica Walker Blanchard; CS = Circe Sturm

‡ Phone interview

§ E-mail interview

a p p e n d i x s i x
Formal Interview Data, Federally Recognized Cherokees

No.	Name	Date	Age	Gender	Occupation	Residence	Citizenship
1	Joe Mouse	October 23, 2003	50s	Male	Historic preservation officer	North Carolina	Eastern Band
2a	Troy Poteete*	August 1, 2003	48	Male	Lawyer/tribal judge	Oklahoma	Cherokee Nation
2b	Troy Poteete*	January 24, 1996	41	Male	Tribal council member	Oklahoma	Cherokee Nation
3	John Ross*	August 1, 2003	48	Male	Tribal community services liaison	Oklahoma	Cherokee Nation
4a	Richard Allen*	July 31, 2003	56	Male	Tribal policy analyst	Oklahoma	Cherokee Nation
4b	Richard Allen*	January 11, 1996	49	Male	Tribal policy analyst	Oklahoma	Cherokee Nation
4c	Richard Allen*	November 8, 1995	48	Male	Tribal policy analyst	Oklahoma	Cherokee Nation
5	Michael Lambert*‡	November 13, 2003	30s	Male	University professor	North Carolina	Eastern Band
6	Helena Johnson	October 23, 2003	28	Female	College student	North Carolina	Eastern Band
7	Melissa Hunter	October 22, 2003	39	Female	Tribal cultural resources center employee	North Carolina	Eastern Band
8	Charlie Hanson	October 22, 2003	40s	Male	Tribal cultural resources center employee	North Carolina	Eastern Band
9	Betty Baker	October 22, 2003	60s	Female	Tribal cultural resources center employee	North Carolina	Eastern Band
10	Diana Terrapin	July 31, 2003	46	Female	Tribal information center employee	Oklahoma	Cherokee Nation
11	Robert Thompson	October 22, 2003	40s	Male	Tribal museum administrator	North Carolina	Eastern Band
12	Will Taylor	February 12, 1996	44	Male	Tribal council member	Oklahoma	Cherokee Nation
13	Mark Anders	March 8, 1996	66	Male	Genealogist/writer	Texas	Cherokee Nation
14	Sequoyah Little	March 29, 2003	60s	Male	Crafts vendor	Arkansas	Eastern Band
15a	David Cornsilk*	July 1, 1998	40s	Male	News reporter	Oklahoma	Cherokee Nation
15b	David Cornsilk*	October 28, 1995	40s	Male	Salesperson	Oklahoma	Cherokee Nation
16	Tom Wycliffe	July 2, 1998	40s	Male	Lawyer	Oklahoma	Cherokee Nation
17	Charlie Scott	June 19, 1998	40s	Male	Nonprofit manager	Oklahoma	Cherokee Nation
18	Tricia Longhorn	June 23, 1998	30s	Female	Secretary	Oklahoma	Cherokee Nation
19	Jim Mooney	June 33, 1998	76	Male	Retired tribal politician	Oklahoma	Cherokee Nation
20	Sam Holder	June 17, 1998	53	Male	Nurse	Oklahoma	Cherokee Nation
21	Betty Six	July 8, 1998	67	Female	Cherokee language teacher	Oklahoma	Cherokee Nation
22	Dora Smith	June 30, 1998	71	Female	Domestic worker	Oklahoma	Cherokee Nation

23	Velma Swimmer	July 3, 1998	50s	Female	Lecturer/writer	Oklahoma	Cherokee Nation
24	Dean Swimmer	July 17, 1998	40s	Male	Construction worker	Oklahoma	Cherokee Nation
25	Phil Guess	July 20, 1998	50s	Male	Tribal politician	Oklahoma	United Keetoowah Band
26	Barbara Smith	July 19, 1998	60s	Female	Homemaker	Oklahoma	Cherokee Nation
27	Anne Wallace	January 30, 1996	48	Female	Tribal council member	Oklahoma	Cherokee Nation
28	James Holder	January 23, 1996	42	Male	Photographer	Oklahoma	United Keetoowah Band
29	Hazel Smith	January 23, 1996	49	Female	Tribal council member	Oklahoma	Cherokee Nation
30	Fergus Beech	January 23, 1996	69	Male	Tribal council member	Oklahoma	Cherokee Nation
31	Alice Moss	January 30, 1996	45	Female	Tribal employee trainer	Oklahoma	Cherokee Nation
32	Thomas Watie	January 12, 1996	54	Male	Cherokee language teacher	Oklahoma	United Keetoowah Band
33	T. Dreadfulwater	January 29, 1996	49	Male	Linguist/scholar	Oklahoma	Cherokee Nation
34	Tom Goings	January 24, 1996	44	Male	Farmer	Oklahoma	Cherokee Nation
35	Lisa Mooney	February 13, 1996	35	Female	Executive secretary	Oklahoma	United Keetoowah Band
36	Andrew Ross	January 19, 1996	39	Male	Media specialist	Oklahoma	Cherokee Nation
37	Jean Blackwell	January 29, 1996	36	Female	Tribal cultural resources center employee	Oklahoma	Cherokee Nation
38	Barbara Stevens	January 29, 1996	34	Female	Tribal council member	Oklahoma	Cherokee Nation
39	Megan Cassis	February 7, 1996	33	Female	Social worker	Oklahoma	Cherokee Nation
40	Bill Lotawatah	February 5, 1996	64	Male	Health administrator	Oklahoma	Cherokee Nation
41	Josh Duncan	November 10, 1996	40s	Male	Tribal museum administrator	Oklahoma	Cherokee Nation
42a	Mitch Adair	February 16, 1996	60s	Male	Traditional healer	Oklahoma	Cherokee Nation
42b	Mitch Adair	March 7, 1996	60s	Male	Traditional healer	Oklahoma	Cherokee Nation
43	Anna Long	February 13, 1996	37	Female	Tribal community services liaison	Oklahoma	Cherokee Nation
44	Lois Hanson	March 6, 1996	70s	Female	Retired craft specialist and basket-maker	Oklahoma	Cherokee Nation
45	Lee Fields	November 30, 1995	30s	Male	Unemployed	Oklahoma	Cherokee Nation
46	Julie Teehee	November 13, 1995	30s	Female	Tribal enrollment employee	Oklahoma	Cherokee Nation
47	Robert Guess	November 8, 1995	31	Male	Tribal education employee	Oklahoma	Cherokee Nation
48	Laura Woodall	November 6, 1995	40s	Female	Head Start teacher	Oklahoma	Cherokee Nation
49	Missy Shade	October 26, 1995	30s	Female	Tribal cultural resources center employee	Oklahoma	Cherokee Nation
50	Dan Nochee	October 27, 1995	50s	Male	Tribal cultural resources center employee	Oklahoma	Cherokee Nation

Note: All participants were interviewed by the author.

* Actual names (all others are pseudonyms).

† Interview took place by e-mail.

Notes

Chapter 1: Opening

1. Since the time of my fieldwork, the Cherokee Nation's official tribal newspaper has reverted to its original name, the *Cherokee Phoenix and Indian Advocate*. This well-known example of Native American journalism was first published in New Echota, Georgia, which was then the capital of the Cherokee Nation, in 1829. For years, the *Phoenix* was printed in both the Cherokee syllabary and the Roman alphabet. For more on Cherokee literacy practices, including their social and political significance, see Margaret Bender's excellent book *Signs of Cherokee Culture: Sequoyah's Syllabary in Eastern Cherokee Life* (2002).

2. My earlier field research on Cherokee identity politics resulted in my first book, *Blood Politics: Race, Culture, and Identity in the Cherokee Nation of Oklahoma* (Sturm 2002).

3. The Native American Graves Repatriation Act has redefined relationships between museums, archaeologists, and native peoples in the United States. It requires all museums receiving federal funding to inventory Native American and Native Hawaiian human remains, funerary objects, sacred objects, and items of cultural patrimony. Once the inventory is completed, a copy is provided to the appropriate tribes and communities, who then have the option to have any of the human remains or sacred materials repatriated at their request. This consultation requirement is a key reason for the shift toward more respectful and tolerant working relationships, though this is an ideal not always realized in practice. For a useful discussion of these issues, see Fine-Dare 2002, especially pp. 139–171.

4. For more on this story, see *Dayton Daily News*, July 20, 1987.

5. With one exception, for which a different source is noted, all quotations from Oliver Collins are taken from the amateur video described above, which is in the author's possession.

6. In the influential 1998 book *Playing Indian*, Philip J. Deloria Jr. chronicles ways in which many white Americans have appropriated certain aspects of Native American culture in an effort to remake and reaffirm their own sense of national identity. However, in this context, "playing Indian" has somewhat different connotations. Given that the Tallige Fire people believe and assert that they have Native American ancestry, their performance is less about appropriation than about reclamation of an indigenous status for themselves and their community.

7. When Collins said that his group was "in association with the Cherokee Nation," it is not clear whether he meant the Tallige Fire Cherokee Nation in Ohio or the Cherokee Nation in Oklahoma. The former has been recognized by the Ohio Senate; the latter is federally recognized.

8. For more on Cherokee death customs, see Withoft 1983.

9. The original quotation appeared in the *Tallige Fire Cherokee Nation Newsletter* around 1988 and is cited in Allen 1995:8. This borrowing from the gay, lesbian, and bisexual community of the metaphor of the closet as a way to describe a hidden aspect of one's racialized self is something that has appeared repeatedly in my interviews with newly self-identified Cherokees and that I explore at greater length in chapter 2. For more on the meanings inherent in the metaphor of the closet, see Eve Kosofsky Sedgwick's 1992 book *The Epistemology of the Closet*.

10. The category of Indian descendant is somewhat ambiguous and is addressed in greater detail in chapter 6. A person can be a lineal descendant of American Indians but not identify him- or herself as an American Indian. This often occurs when the individual has both Indian and non-Indian ancestry and chooses to identify primarily as non-Indian. Usually, the category is employed when the individual believes that he or she does not meet certain racial and cultural criteria associated with having an American Indian identity. At the same time, many descendants with multiracial ancestry do identify as American Indian; various social, cultural, geographic, political, and racial criteria—particularly tribal citizenship status and physical appearance—play into this decision. The category of descendant is also often used in tribal contexts to describe someone with American Indian ancestry who does not meet tribal citizenship requirements. In this case, the term is used as a social qualifier that modifies a specific political status. Although an individual must descend from American Indians to qualify for tribal citizenship in the vast majority of cases, there are often additional criteria for citizenship, such as blood quantum, specific type of lineal descent, or geographic residence.

11. The Stonewall riots occurred in New York City on June 28, 1969, in spontaneous, violent resistance to persecution and police brutality and are frequently cited as the event that launched the gay rights movement. Some readers might be troubled by Collins's use of the term "coming out" in a racial context. However, race shifters also view Native American identities as highly stigmatized and use that interpretation to justify the earlier suppression of their Cherokee identities.

12. Demographer and sociologist Matthew Snipp (Cherokee) notes a vast number of Americans of Indian descent on the U.S. census, 93 percent of whom racially self-identified as white (Gonzales 1998:202). Demographer Jeffrey Passel's earlier research (1976:407) also suggests that most racial shifters previously identified themselves as white. Interestingly enough, scholars have traditionally assumed that only African Americans would be interested in claiming indigeneity. The idea is that racial movement has a particular directionality in that people are always trying to pass into a higher status or to move up the race/class hierarchy. For this reason, much of the literature on the black Indian experience has portrayed this type of movement, or any claim to multiracial identity for that matter, as either instrumental or inauthentic. Important exceptions include Blu 1980, Miles 2005, Naylor 2008, Saunt 1999, and Sider 1993. That most racial shifters previously identified themselves as white raises some interesting theoretical questions about racial value and hierarchy, which are explored in much greater detail in chapter 3.

13. For more on this topic, see the Association of American Indian and Alaska Native Professors (n.d.) statement on ethnic fraud.

14. Russell Thornton, a Cherokee sociologist and demographer, explains that the American Indian population numbers have grown, in part, because the methods for tabulating these census data have improved. He acknowledges that methodological changes alone cannot account for the large increases seen in these demographic statistics. Instead, he suggests that the trend is more likely a result of the Native American activism of the 1970s,

which led to an increase in ethnic pride and cultural awareness, a decrease in the social acceptability (and the practice) of overt racial discrimination, and an increase in "career opportunities made available through affirmative action and related government policies and legal rulings" (Thornton 1990:197).

15. "Indian country" is a political and legal term for the indigenous land base in all its forms, whether that territory is held collectively, as in the case of a reservation, or individually, as in the case of an allotment. Legally, the term denotes lands where tribal and federal laws apply but state law does not (18 U.S. Code §1151; Utter 1993:168–170).

16. When I refer to racial shifters as white, I am referring specifically to the racial dimensions that structure their everyday lives. Race shifters can self-identify as Native American, or more specifically as Cherokee, and still be classified as belonging to a race other than Native American. This is true not only for race shifters but also for many American Indians with multiracial ancestry. When racial shifters are socially classified as white, they benefit from race privilege, even if they face disadvantages in realms such as class, gender, ethnicity, religion, or sexuality. Despite the diversity contained within whiteness, some of its varieties go unmarked and are taken for granted according to racial systems of thought and practice that are currently dominant in the United States.

17. According to the *Oxford English Dictionary* (2009), a "wannabe" is "an admirer or fan who seeks to emulate a particular celebrity or type, esp. in matters of appearance or dress." A contraction of "want to be," the term became popular in the mid-1980s, most notably to describe young female fans who tried to mimic the pop singer Madonna's style (*Sunday Times Magazine*, August 16, 1987). With time, "wannabe" has taken on a more pejorative connotation, signaling a lack of authenticity.

18. All parenthetical dates refer to ethnographic interviews conducted by the author, with a few exceptions. For more detailed information on the nature of these interviews, please see the methodology section later in this chapter.

19. In the past decade, a burgeoning literature in critical white studies has emerged, and several scholars explore how whites maintain race privilege despite their class differences. For more on this topic and the intersection of race and class, see Matt Wray and Annalee Newitz's 1996 edited volume *White Trash: Race and Class in America* and Mike Hill's 1997 edited volume *Whiteness: A Critical Reader*.

20. For more on this topic and the Cherokee Tribe of Northeast Alabama, see Haynes 2001. In his graduate research, Haynes (2001:13) also found that members of this tribe occupied "a wide range of social classes." Haynes's thesis provides an in-depth examination of identity construction among a particular state-recognized Cherokee tribe. Because he approaches the topic from a Southern studies perspective, his work also offers unique and valuable insights about the relationship between Southern regional identity, whiteness, and reclamations of indigeneity.

21. I do not mean to imply that all of these people are race shifters. Many may have identified as Cherokee or part Cherokee all of their lives, as seems to be the case with Johnny Depp, Willie Nelson, and Tommy Lee Jones. Others are non-Indians (for example, Cher, who is Armenian American) who took on the mantle of Indian chic in the early 1970s. For still others, I do not have reliable information. However, it is clear that extremely wealthy individuals also find value in identifying themselves as Cherokee and that the phenomenon of choosing to identify as Indian rather than white is not limited to the poor and working class.

22. Not only has Bill Clinton claimed redness but he has also been claimed by blackness. For a variety of reasons, having largely to do with Clinton's class, regional, and hipster status, prominent African Americans have claimed him as one of their own, waggishly suggesting that he was the first black president (Lott 2003:101). In the excellent article "The

First Boomer: Bill Clinton, George W., and Fictions of State," Eric Lott (2003) describes the ways in which images of the president, particularly his body, racial identity, and culture, reveal and at times obscure the workings of the state apparatus under neoliberalism. The people who have commented on Clinton's blackness run the gamut of political persuasions, including comedian Chris Rock, novelist Toni Morrison, and the rap group Outkast in their song "Ms. Jackson"—all mentioned by Lott—as well as conservative journalist Christopher Hitchens (Hitchens 1999; Lott 2003:101–102). Few people have continued to refer to Clinton's putative blackness since the election of an actual African American, Barack Obama, to the presidency. I discuss the context surrounding Bill Clinton's claim to have a Cherokee grandmother in chapter 8.

23. Racial shifters express ideas about racial authenticity and essentialism quite frequently, as in this speaker's use of the term "real Indians." At times, these ideas provide an important part of the rationale for race shifting—viewing race not as primarily about how one has been socialized but as an innate and essential aspect of self that can be discovered and reclaimed.

24. A case in point is that during fiscal year 2002 the Administration for Native Americans, an agency under the U.S. Department of Health and Human Services, granted $282,020 to four state-recognized Cherokee tribes in Georgia, Missouri, and Virginia (Administration for Native Americans 2003).

25. The vast majority of the scholarly literature on racial passing discusses African Americans passing as white and ignores Indians who are engaged in a similar process. The reason for this gap can be traced to the different histories of assimilation that African Americans and Indians have experienced vis-à-vis whiteness, which I explore in chapter 8. In general, when Native Americans have shifted into whiteness, this has not been understood as passing but as assimilation, whereas the opposite is true for African Americans (Kauanui 2008:17–21). Thus, when phenotypically multiracial individuals claim Indianness, it is understood as a point of pride, a process of reclamation, but when they claim blackness, it is often viewed as an acknowledgment of a more scandalous racial history.

26. Throughout the 1950s, much anthropological research focused on "assimilation studies" in American Indian communities, the idea being that "real" Indians had been lost to intermarriage and cultural exchange and that remnant Indian communities were well on their way to becoming part of mainstream white society. These studies of racial and cultural assimilation were used to support federal policies of relocation and termination that characterized much of the mid-twentieth century.

27. My thanks to anthropologist and friend Wyman Kirk (Cherokee) for his thoughtful and hilarious paper on Cherokee identity and humor, "Cherokees, Barbies, and Blood" (2003).

28. For the Cherokees, there was a greater discrepancy between those with Cherokee-only ancestry (281,069) and those with other tribal or racial ancestry (729,533) than was the case for the Navajos, for whom the respective figures were 269,202 and 291,197.

29. According to the Oklahoma Indian Affairs Commission, in late July 2003, tribal enrollment was 232,928 for the Cherokee Nation and 8,513 for the United Keetoowah Band of Cherokee Indians (Oklahoma Indian Affairs Commission 2003). The official Web site of the Eastern Band of Cherokee Indians in North Carolina listed their enrollment as 12,500 (Eastern Band of Cherokee Indians 2003). Thus, the combined total for the three federally recognized Cherokee tribes at the time was 253,941, whereas the number of Cherokees who self-identified on the 2000 census was 729,533 (U.S. Bureau of the Census 2000).

30. The United Keetoowah Band has a standard of one-quarter Cherokee blood for tribal citizenship. Even with this more restrictive standard, United Keetoowah Band citizens vary

in physical appearance. All it takes is one generation of intermarriage for the children of Indian people to potentially look non-Indian.

31. Analogous to the Dawes Roll for the Cherokee Nation, the Baker Rolls serve as the base rolls for the Eastern Band of Cherokee Indians. Citizenship in the Eastern Band is determined by reference to the Baker Rolls. The first roll was originally compiled in 1924, when the federal government assumed a "trust responsibility" over the Eastern Band. It was amended in 1931 to add a few dozen people who had been overlooked in 1924. The initial roll specified a blood quantum requirement of 1/32 Cherokee blood, though this requirement was later amended so that new applicants for citizenship would have to meet a 1/16 standard (Thornton 1990:141).

32. For more on this topic, particularly the historical emergence of these policies in the Cherokee Nation and their contemporary effects on tribal politics, see Sturm 2002, chapters 3 and 4.

33. Cherokees in Oklahoma actually make a categorical distinction between Indians and Cherokees, a difference that it is also noted in the Cherokee language. "Indian" is an explicitly racial category that is almost always applied to someone with a relatively indigenous physical appearance (dark brown or black hair, dark brown eyes, and brown skin). "Cherokee" is a much broader political category that includes all tribal citizens, regardless of physical appearance (Sturm 2002:108–109).

34. I first encountered this phrase in late fall 1995 in a document titled "Entities Using the Cherokee Name," originally compiled by Isabel Catolster, a citizen and employee of the Eastern Band of Cherokee Indians. Dated March 3, 1995, the list attempted to identify all state-recognized and self-identified Cherokee groups and organizations—all those who asserted a Cherokee tribal identity but were not formally recognized by the federal government. The list was updated over the years and was frequently shared between the administrations of the Eastern Band of Cherokee Indians and the Cherokee Nation. In the mid-1990s, controversy erupted when the United Keetoowah Band of Cherokee Indians, which is a federally recognized Cherokee tribe, found itself temporarily on the list.

The United Keetoowah Band—which is located in Tahlequah, Oklahoma, along with the Cherokee Nation—has had a slightly different and less consistent history in terms of its responses to race shifting. Part of this divergence reflects the troubled history the United Keetoowah Band has had in its political dealings with the Cherokee Nation. Because both are federally recognized tribes with claims to the same people and land, the situation is ripe for conflict. For more on this topic see Leeds 1997.

35. The Cherokee Nation tribal registrar who collected this information is R. Lee Fleming, the current director of the Office of Federal Acknowledgment at the Bureau of Indian Affairs in Washington, D.C., formerly known as the Branch of Acknowledgment and Research. This is the federal agency within the Bureau of Indian Affairs that is responsible for overseeing the federal acknowledgment process, a mechanism by which nonrecognized groups can obtain formal recognition and legal status as American Indian tribes.

36. For a comprehensive list of self-identified Cherokee organizations by state, see appendix 1.

37. Before the arrival of Europeans, about twenty thousand Cherokee people occupied almost 40,000 square miles of territory in parts of what are now Virginia, Tennessee, North Carolina, South Carolina, Georgia, and Alabama (Mooney 1995:14).

38. The Cherokee Nation and Tribe of Mexico is a self-identified group of Cherokees living in northern Mexico in the state of Coahuila. They claim to be descendants of traditional Cherokees who fled Indian Territory and Texas to seek independence and political amnesty in the mid-nineteenth century. Although this group is not recognized by the U.S.

federal government, it was formally acknowledged by the governor of Coahuila, Enrique Martínez y Martínez, on August 22, 2001. There has also been a long tradition of hobbyism in Germany, in part due to the influential writings of novelist Karl May, who deeply romanticized Native American life. However, European hobbyists, like those in the United States, do not claim to be Cherokee descendants or to have any special political rights.

39. Because both my assistant and I had prior relationships with some of the individuals we interviewed, the quality of those interviews tends to be slightly better, in that these individuals were more forthcoming and willing to spend time seriously engaging our questions. The fact of qualitative differences in interviews is something that any field-worker encounters; however, I tend to quote more heavily from those higher-quality interviews that I believe are fully fleshed out yet still representative. This accounts for the fact that certain voices appear repeatedly whereas others appear only once or twice at most.

40. Because of its implications for tribal sovereignty, citizenship status is now regularly acknowledged in public when Cherokee people introduce themselves, particularly in academic contexts. Whereas even a decade ago it might have been sufficient to identify oneself as Cherokee or Oklahoma Cherokee, now the expectation is that one will include a statement regarding enrollment status, such as "I'm an enrolled citizen of the Cherokee Nation."

However, the distinction between citizen Cherokees and race shifters is in some sense overdrawn: there are also tribal citizens who, like race shifters, come to identify more fully as Cherokee at some later point in their life. For instance, they choose to embrace certain aspects of Cherokee social and cultural life beyond the narrower confines of their previous political and legal experience as Cherokee citizens. Thus, there are some parallels here between race shifters and Cherokee citizens about what it means to become more fully Cherokee and indigenous that are worth exploring but are not the principle subject of this book.

Chapter 2: What Lies Beneath

1. The title of this chapter is an allusion to the 2000 Robert Zemeckis film *What Lies Beneath*, a supernatural thriller starring Michelle Pfieffer and Harrison Ford. Like the movie, this chapter is about "ghosts"—of action and inaction, of racial oppression and reclamation—and the way they haunt personal narratives. In particular, I am interested in the way in which people take ancestral histories and reinscribe them in the present to make new meanings out of their lives.

2. For more on genealogical interpretations of Black Dutch ancestry, see Hornbeck n.d.

3. Other multiracial communities of combined Native American, African American, and European ancestry, such as Melungeons and mustees, have also used the term Black Dutch as a strategy of racial reclassification (Nassau 2004).

4. Whether such state laws existed in the late twentieth century is unclear. The state archives, state commissions on Indian affairs, local scholars, and tribes I have contacted during my research have provided conflicting evidence. I am not providing the details of my findings here because I do not want to be in the position of authenticating such claims. Certainly, the nature and variety of local and state anti-Indian legislation is a topic that merits extensive research and further discussion in another context.

5. Congress passed the American Indian Removal Act in 1830, under the leadership of President Andrew Jackson. Removal policy encouraged Native American tribes residing within the boundaries of the United States to exchange their original homelands for territories west of the Mississippi River, with the idea that once they relocated in the West, they could better maintain their political and social autonomy. The fundamental motivation behind the policy was to open up additional American Indian land for white expansion.

Most citizens of tribes living in the Southeast resisted removal, though in the end the policy proved quite effective. Although some Cherokees voluntarily migrated to the West, most were forcibly removed to Indian Territory in 1838 on the infamous Trail of Tears. To get a better sense of the numbers involved, consider that in 1835, only three years before removal, about 16,500 Cherokees lived in their eastern homelands, a large area encompassing parts of present-day North Carolina, Georgia, Alabama, and Tennessee (Thornton 1990:51). Of this original population, only about 1,100 individuals avoided removal by hiding out in the mountains or by taking advantage of a clause in an 1819 treaty that allowed some Cherokees to remain in their homelands if they were willing to become U.S. citizens (Finger 1980:17, 1993:97). The vast majority of those who avoided removal lived in North Carolina; about 300 lived in Georgia, Tennessee, or Alabama (Finger 1980:17).

6. Race shifters counter such claims not only with narratives of victimhood at the hands of whites but also by suggesting that they are somehow better Indians because they managed to come up with an effective (though socially costly) way of outsmarting federal and state agents—unlike the many thousands of Cherokees who were forcibly removed.

7. Some Cherokees who managed to avoid the forced removal of 1838 chose to join their brethren in the West at a later date. Thus, westward migrations happened both before and after removal. Although federal and state governments continued to pressure American Indians remaining in the East to move west, with the exception of the events of 1838, there is little historical evidence to support the idea of ongoing deportations, as suggested here by race shifters. Nonetheless, race shifters' perception that forced removal was a threat into the early twentieth century helps to frame their status as victims and provides an explanation for why their families chose to obscure their racial and political ties to the Cherokee Nation.

8. Attakullakulla (c. 1700–1780) was a renowned Cherokee leader throughout much of the eighteenth century. Born in what is now Tennessee, he had a great deal of political influence and spent much of his life defending the interests of Cherokee communities. He and several other Cherokee leaders traveled to London for a diplomatic visit in 1730, and he remained loyal to the British in his later years. For additional information, see Mooney 1995:40–44 and Schroedl 2002.

9. By noting that the logic of hypodescent is present in the discourse surrounding racial shifting, I do not mean to draw an analogue between African American and Native American experiences of racialization. In *Hawaiian Blood: Colonialism and the Politics of Sovereignty and Indigeneity*, J. Kehaulani Kauanui (2008:16–21) makes a persuasive argument that the racial ideologies surrounding blood and assimilation were distinct for both groups, an issue that I discuss in greater detail in chapter 8.

10. Thanks to Cherokee sociologist Eva Garroutte for her feedback on an early draft of the introductory chapter, which helped me to clarify and reframe my ideas in this paragraph.

11. The narratives of racial shifters also parallel those of the lesbian, gay, bisexual, and transgender community in additional ways. For instance, advocates for both groups tend to evoke histories of legal discrimination and victimization, as well as the painful experience of an essential selfhood denied by the larger society. Although these parallels may be coincidental, there may also be a common discourse and strategy for empowerment that disenfranchised groups in the United States are utilizing, a topic that is beyond the scope of this book but merits further exploration.

Chapter 3: Racial Choices and the Spectre of Whiteness

1. This vignette is based on the field notes of Jessica Walker Blanchard, my research assistant on this project in spring and summer 2003.

2. In 1940, the U.S. Congress passed the Bald Eagles Protection Act, making it illegal for anyone to take, transport, sell, trade, import, export, or possess eagles, their feathers, or their parts. Because of the significance of eagle feathers to Native Americans, the U.S. Fish and Wildlife Service has made the remains of bald and golden eagles available to citizens of federally recognized tribes since the early 1970s. The assumption is that these feathers will be used for strictly ceremonial purposes and that they will not be sold or traded to other Indians or given away to non-Indians. However, they can be given to family members. For more details, see U.S. Fish and Wildlife Service 2009.

3. I use the terms "power-evasive" and "race cognizance" after anthropologist Ruth Frankenberg. In her path-breaking book *White Women, Race Matters: The Social Construction of Whiteness* (1993), Frankenberg notes a critical distinction between whites who are color and power evasive—two attributes that go hand in hand—and those who are race cognizant. She reports that during her interviews, white women who were power evasive tended to utilize a discursive repertoire that emphasized the essential sameness of all people (1993:14–16). Because these individuals failed to recognize significant social, material, and political differences that attach themselves to race, they tended to blame racial minorities for any failings that they may have. In contrast, those women who were race cognizant "insisted on the importance of recognizing difference" (157). Although race-cognizant individuals differed significantly from one another, they shared two important beliefs: "first, that race makes a difference in people's lives and, second, that race is a significant factor in contemporary U.S. society" (157). These individuals were much more willing to acknowledge how race affected differential access to social power.

4. Physical appearance is highly variable among both citizen Cherokees and racial shifters, and both communities have flexible standards about what constitutes an Indian appearance. However, for citizen Cherokees to consider someone to be recognizably Indian, that person must at a minimum have dark brown hair, skin tone in the range from dark olive to a reddish-brown tan, and slightly fuller facial features than those of most Euro-American descendants. The assumption is that these people would physically appear Indian, or possibly even Latino, in the eyes of most Americans. When I characterize someone as having a white appearance, I am generally referring to people with lighter skin and hair, as well as Euro-American facial features. Some might have darker hair and eyes but no other classically Native American physical features.

I characterize people's racial appearances based on my assumptions about how they would be racially classified by any American on the street, meaning by individuals who base their assessments strictly on physical differences rather than personal information. Because I am using broad societal standards that do not always reflect what is happening in particular communities, this means that, at times, I categorize people as having a white appearance when racial shifters might perceive them as having an Indian appearance.

5. During the thirty interviews and fifteen surveys conducted with race shifters, only on one occasion did someone fully acknowledge the complexities of her own racial ancestry. When asked whether she would ever consider marking more than one box on the U.S. Census form, Luanne Helton replied, "Well, I'm white too. I can't be true to myself if I don't acknowledge the fact that I have white ancestors. I have six German lines. I have two Dutch lines. I have four English lines. I am all of those people. But what I feel most nearly and dearly to my heart is my Cherokee" (May 21, 2003). The complexity of Helton's response may, in part, be due to the fact that she is the tribal genealogist and places a great value on accurate genealogical research and records.

6. For other examples and further discussion of color and power evasiveness, see Frankenberg 1993:142–157.

7. In the broader U.S. society, one of the last acceptable bastions of overt prejudice is the demonization of southern white culture. Many race shifters with southern white roots express a desire to distance themselves from the associations of redneck bigotry and southern racism. Haynes's (2001:92) ethnographic research among race shifters in Alabama offers additional insights on this topic.

8. At the same time, Gayle Wald (1996:162) observes that individuals with a white appearance, particularly men, have had greater freedom to manipulate and shift their identities with no social costs to themselves. For more on the topic of racial passing, see Wald's *Crossing the Line: Racial Passing in Twentieth Century U.S. Literature and Culture* (2000), Elaine K. Ginsberg's edited volume *Passing and the Fictions of Identity* (1996), and Susan Gubar's innovative book *Racechanges: White Skin, Black Face in American Culture* (1997).

9. Exceptions to this tendency to remove racial and cultural content from whiteness include the social marking of Jews, Italian Americans, Spaniards, and Arabs, many of whom are still considered by many Americans to be less than completely white, or even nonwhite.

10. My inspiration for the culinary metaphors comes from the work of bell hooks (1992:21–40), who has written extensively about white appropriations of the primitive "other." In a powerful chapter titled "Eating the Other," hooks describes the process by which whites first desire, then commodify, and eventually appropriate certain aspects of African American culture as "cannibalization."

11. "Re-enchantment" is the reversal of the Weberian concept of "disenchantment," by which the compelling aura of mystery is drained from an increasingly bureaucratized world. Weber said, "The fate of our times is characterized by rationalization and intellectualization and, above all, by the disenchantment of the world" (Gerth and Mills 1946:155). The term "re-enchantment" has a more uncertain provenance; one early treatise on the subject is Morris Berman's classic text *The Reenchantment of the World* (1981), in which he rails against a Cartesian worldview, arguing that "scientific consciousness is alienated consciousness; there is no ecstatic merger with nature, but rather total separation from it" (Berman 1981:17). These ideas have also been discussed in several recent volumes, including George Ritzer's *Enchanting a Disenchanted World: Revolutionizing the Means of Consumption* (2005) and Nicholas Gane's *Max Weber and Postmodern Theory: Rationalization versus Re-enchantment* (2002); the latter describes the ways in which recent thinkers such as Lyotard, Foucault, and Baudrillard can aid in "resisting the rationalization and disenchantment of life" (Gane 2002:9).

12. Again, my thanks go to Eva Garroutte for her insights on this topic. In an e-mail exchange dating to 2003, she gave me several pages of thought-provoking feedback on an earlier chapter, and some of her ideas have significantly impacted my writing in this paragraph.

Chapter 4: Racial Conversion and Cherokee Neotribalism

1. Traditionally, anthropologists have used the term "tribe" to denote a community of American Indians, linked by bonds of kinship, culture, language, and polity, who have historically lived together within a distinct territory. This ethnological usage should not be confused with its usage in U.S. federal Indian law (Utter 1993:29). Although there is no single legal definition of "tribe" that fits all cases at all times, typically the political and legal usage of the term refers to a group of American Indians that has been officially recognized by external powers as having a distinct government. Though states and foreign nations recognized tribes during the colonial period, the most historically and legally significant form of recognition has been that of the U.S. federal government (30). Ethnological and political definitions do not always correspond to each other, since tribal political units can comprise

of a number of culturally distinct American Indian peoples. For example, the Cherokee Nation also includes Loyal Shawnees and Delawares within its citizenry.

With this background in mind, I view the Pan American Indian Association as a quasi-tribal entity. On the one hand, the organization explicitly states on its Web site that it is not a tribe in the political sense, has no association with the Bureau of Indian Affairs, and is merely an association of disenfranchised American Indian descendants from different tribal backgrounds (Loving Hands Institute 2008). On the other hand, the association does provide tribal roll numbers, membership identity cards, and certificates to its members. It also asks them to participate in various community ceremonies and public outreach activities. Because most of the association's members are Cherokee-identified, both the Eastern Band of Cherokee Indians and the Cherokee Nation have been concerned about its public activities, fearing that they might create additional confusion over the official political status of these various Cherokee groups.

2. In the context of literary criticism, the term "racial conversion" has been used to describe literature from the second half of the twentieth century in which white southerners describe their experiences of "coming up from racism and embracing racial brotherhood and sisterhood" (Hobson 1999:205). The authors of these works reject the legacy of white racism and white racial privilege but continue to identify themselves as whites. Their conversion involves a fundamental change in their discriminatory attitudes towards racial difference, particularly concerning African Americans. This transformation bears some resemblance to the phenomenon I am describing here. However, when I use the term "racial conversion," I am primarily referring to a change in racial identification and only secondarily to a change in racial attitude and ideology. For more on southern racial conversion narratives, see Hobson's useful article "The Southern Racial Conversion Narrative: Larry L. King and Pat Watters" in the *Virginia Quarterly Review* (1999).

3. In Peter Cahn's (n.d.) thought-provoking book manuscript *The Great Commission: Direct Sales and Direct Faith in Mexico*, the anthropologist discusses religious conversion in a secular context. Cahn examines how direct sellers of Omnilife products in Mexico are influenced by their exposure to new religious ideologies that run counter to their Catholic faith. He argues that they adopt these principles as a way of ensuring their personal success without officially converting. Theirs is an "invisible conversion," but a conversion nonetheless (Cahn n.d.).

4. For me, the best way to understand these transformations is to listen to the rhetoric of Cherokee converts. As Snow and Malachek (1984:171–174) have rightfully pointed out, the only reliable indicators of religious conversion are rhetorical ones, and scholars should focus their attention here rather than on more traditional concerns such as membership and ritual participation, although all of these aspects warrant attention. Membership in Cherokee tribal organizations and communities would not be a reliable indicator of racial conversion, because there is too much variety in membership: people come and go, and their affiliations can be short-lived (171). Public displays that confirm one's status as a Cherokee convert, like a renaming ceremony—what Snow and Malachek call "demonstration events"—are not always reliable for similar reasons (173). These events can simply be ritualized performances with no enduring significance for the participants involved (173). (This is why I wondered whether Lone Warrior's renaming ceremony still held meaning for him.) Another argument in favor of this approach is that discursive practices themselves are constitutive experiences, a point that anthropologist Susan Harding makes convincingly in her article "Convicted by the Holy Spirit: The Rhetoric of Fundamentalist Baptist Conversion" (1987).

5. The land that Cara Wesley referred to is not a reservation in a technical, legal sense, in part, because title to the land is not held in trust by the United States government.

Rather, it consists of several acres of communally owned property, though it remains unclear if tribal members purchased the land together or if it was donated to them by an individual or organization.

6. Among self-identified Cherokee tribes, as well as many federally recognized and state-recognized tribes, there is a large discrepancy between the number of formally enrolled members and those who regularly participate in the social and political life of the tribe. For example, in the case of one large, new state-recognized Cherokee tribe in Alabama, of 34,000 formally enrolled members, only 180 voted in a recent tribal election (Crutchfield and Belanger 2006). However, a much larger number regularly participated in other community events, such as dances, potlucks, and meetings.

7. The dances that take place within communities of race shifters are usually powwows. Like American Indian powwows across the country, these community dances are social gatherings that have a strong spiritual component, where dancing, drumming, and singing are considered forms of communication with the divine. For more on American Indian powwows, see the edited volume *Powwow* by Clyde Ellis, Luke Eric Lassiter, and Gary H. Dunham (2005).

8. This individual evoked the metaphor of the closet, as discussed in chapter 2, by using the term "coming out" rather than the more traditional anthropological term "coming of age." Regardless of terminology, she was describing a rite of passage in which a young teenager was formally recognized as an adult in the eyes of his community.

9. It was unclear whether this little boy was born into a family that had long identified itself as Cherokee or the family had only recently begun to identify itself as Cherokee. I still refer to him as a convert, because in my experience most young children who participate in demonstration events such as these are taking steps alongside other family members to formally affirm their identities as American Indians and to mark a transformation in their social and spiritual status.

10. My deep appreciation extends to Eva Marie Garroutte for making this point about holism and indigeneity in her comments on a much earlier draft of this manuscript.

11. Native American religions are, for the most part, community based and nonproselytizing. There is no single Indian religion; rather, each religious tradition is tribally specific and fits the needs of a particular people.

12. *Civitas* implies rights of citizenship and the more formal, structural relationships that link members of a given political community to one another, whereas *communitas* (Turner 1969) describes a sense of intense social belonging generally brought about by ritual experience, which is less formal and lends itself to a greater feeling of social integration than is often provided by more formal political structures.

13. Lears (1994:4) describes the chief characteristics of modern culture in terms of "its ethic of self-control and autonomous achievement, its cult of science and technical rationality, its worship of material progress."

14. In charting the shift from an industrial society to one characterized by leisure and consumption, Lears (1994:304–305) describes the erosion of a stable and singular sense of self. Like Lears' elites, racial shifters also feel out of place and unreal, as if their core identity has been somehow called into question; but rather than turning to "therapeutic self-absorption," such as might be available to individual seekers via psychotherapy or self-help groups (304), race shifters are turning to moral and ethical frameworks that transcend the self, that find their meaning and coherence in relation to others—in this case in belonging to their tribal communities and the broader collective of American Indian people.

15. For alternative and much more positive models of conversion as something beyond a response to crisis, see Cucchiari 1988 and Harding 1987.

16. My thanks to an anonymous reader for his or her wonderful insights and comments on an earlier draft of this manuscript, some of which I incorporated in this paragraph.

17. For more on indigenous spirituality, specifically concerning nature, and its influence on broader expressions of U.S. nationalism and religious life, see Catherine Albanese's classic work *Nature Religion in America: From the Algonkian Indians to the New Age* (1990).

Chapter 5: Shifting Race, Shifting Status

1. In this sentence, the word *tsalagi*, meaning Cherokee, is written in the Cherokee syllabary. In 1821–1822, the great Cherokee intellectual Sequoyah, also known as George Guess, created the syllabary. A syllabary differs from an alphabetic writing system in that each written character represents an entire syllable rather than an individual phonetic sound. Ꮯ corresponds with "tsa," Ꮃ with "la," and Ꭹ with "gi." Syllabaries tend to be efficient writing systems and relatively easy to learn. After Sequoyah's invention, literacy became much more widespread among monolingual and multilingual Cherokees. Cherokees quickly created new forms of print media in their own language and writing system that buttressed their distinct sense of national identity. For more on the syllabary, its history, and its contemporary use to symbolize Cherokee identity and culture, see Bender 2002.

2. A large sculpture created by James Earle Fraser in 1894, *The End of the Trail* is one of the most widely recognized symbols of the American West. The figure of a solitary Indian man slumped over his weary horse embodies for many Americans a sense of nostalgia, sympathy, and respect for Native American resistance. For others, it reflects the pain of their own colonial subjugation and a disrespectful statement of American Indian defeat and disappearance.

3. Citizen Cherokees in Oklahoma often pronounce the term "wannabe" with the accent falling on the penultimate syllable (wha-NA-bay) to make it sound more pseudo-Indian.

4. For an important exception, see Keith Basso's excellent book *Portraits of the "Whiteman": Linguistic Play and Cultural Symbols among the Western Apache* (1979).

5. Another label that bears mentioning is "Indian hobbyist." Hobbyists are typically white and occasionally African American individuals who play Indian in their spare time but who do not necessarily believe that they themselves are Indians. They are known for their passion for what they consider authentic tribal dance and regalia. They usually seek to project a specific tribal persona, often a character or an identity that they adopt temporarily. Some hobbyists project a Cherokee identity by donning the turban and hunting jacket or calico "tear dresses" fashionable among Cherokees in the early nineteenth century. Others dress in a quasi–Plains style popular on the contemporary powwow circuit.

Hobbyists might attend an intertribal powwow, where Native American participants collaborate with, tolerate, or simply ignore non-Indian dancers. Or they might attend a special hobbyist powwow, filled with non-Indian "weekend warriors" like themselves (Allen 1995:3). They occasionally attend one of the many "all Indian" powwows, meaning those powwows where only American Indians are allowed to participate, that were developed in the mid-twentieth century in response to the hobbyist movement and to what Native Americans felt were increasing incursions on their social and cultural territory (Green 1988:41). The phenomenon also exists in Germany, where Karl May's books have spawned a large hobbyist following. Although race shifters and hobbyists share many similarities, they differ in one significant way: hobbyists do not claim to be Indian, only to have a profound respect and longing for traditional Native American cultures. Consequently, most citizen Cherokees do not see race shifters as Indian hobbyists. For more on Indian hobbyism, see Deloria 1998, Green 1988, Powers 1988, and Taylor 1988.

6. Although there are race shifters living in Oklahoma and North Carolina, I use the

term Oklahoma Cherokee or North Carolina Cherokee to describe citizen Cherokees—individuals who are enrolled members of the Cherokee Nation, the United Keetoowah Band of Cherokee Indians, or the Eastern Band of Cherokee Indians, the three federally recognized Cherokee tribes.

7. The category "wannabe" does not usually include unenrolled Cherokee descendants. These people are usually referred to with much more ambiguous terms such as "outtalucks," "should-bes," and "Thindians." For a more detailed explanation, see chapter 6.

8. Cherokees in Oklahoma frequently conflate whiteness with wealth and materialism, suggesting that whites care more about material possessions than do Cherokees and are more likely to have the wealth to accumulate them. In the case of "wannabes," however, the associations are different. For Oklahoma Cherokees, "wannabes" are a subset of whites who are working class or poor and who claim Indianness in an effort to raise their overall social status.

9. Both the Cherokee Nation and the United Keetoowah Band own and operate casinos in Oklahoma, which provide a significant and growing source of revenue. Both tribes have chosen to reinvest that money in tribal programs rather than offer per capita payments to individual tribal citizens.

10. Cherokee Freedmen, the Black-Cherokee descendants of Cherokees and their former African and African American slaves, do not fall within the category of "wannabe" for several reasons. First, their blackness precludes them from the category because "wannabe" is almost always defined in terms of whiteness; second, they have well-documented historical connections to the Cherokee Nation. The racial ideologies surrounding the contest over Freedmen rights to tribal citizenship are distinct from those concerning "wannabes" and race shifters. One of the distinctions is that the racial identity of Freedmen is often viewed as being over determined by their black ancestry, so much so that their genealogical connections to Cherokee forebears are often eclipsed in the historical record.

11. French sociologist Pierre Bourdieu (1987) developed the term "symbolic capital" to refer to different types of assets, both actual and virtual, that individuals access on the basis of social prestige, honor, and recognition. I use the term in a much more general sense to refer to forms of capital that are distinct from material capital and that are achieved as a direct result of social and cultural valuation—which means that symbolic capital varies across cultures and societies. In making this distinction, however, I do not mean to imply that these different forms of capital are unrelated. Symbolic capital often gives one greater access to material capital, and vice versa.

12. Worthy of consideration in this context are Joshua Meyrowitz's arguments about social belonging and place in the age of television. In *No Sense of Place*, Meyrowitz (1984) points to the ways in which new electronic media and communicative technologies have lessened the significance of geographic and social locations and argues that these technological changes have undermined social distinctions based on age and gender, as well as certain forms of authority. The expansion of the Internet has intensified these trends. Extending Meyrowitz's arguments to other forms of social distinction, such as race, might explain why so many race shifters have used the Internet to create online tribes and communities.

13. Ironically, the two modes of discussing a traumatic past have something in common. Racial victimization was once primarily a shameful and even terrifying experience of social disempowerment, but now it has become a way of marking racial difference and of accessing new forms of social power that are attached to difference itself. This is true for citizen Cherokees and race shifters alike, despite the different subtexts in the narratives they tell.

14. As a counter to Poteete's argument, race shifters rarely acknowledge any need for public recognition or social prestige. Instead, they talk about their racial transformation in much more personal and local terms, as is evident in the narratives presented in the first half of the book.

15. Hunhndorf (2001:163) also argues that the New Age cultural appropriation ulti-mately "distorts Native traditions and turns them into consumer goods" that are heavily influenced by a Western European ethos, including consumer capitalism and bourgeois individualism.

16. The New Age movement does not discriminate in borrowing from non-Western spiritual traditions. Though Native American traditions are a significant influence, so are a variety of Eastern religions, including aspects of Buddhism and Hinduism. For a broader overview and analysis of the New Age movement, see Michael F. Brown's *The Channeling Zone: American Spirituality in an Anxious Age*, which specifically addresses concerns about New Age appropriation of Native American religious practices (Brown 1997:142–173).

17. Some citizen Cherokees would echo the sentiments of Oneida scholar Pam Colorado: "In the end, non-Indians will have complete power to define what is and is not Indian, even for Indians. We are talking here about an absolute ideological/conceptual subordination.... When this happens, the last vestiges of real Indian society and Indian rights will disappear. Non-Indians will then own our heritage and ideas as thoroughly as they now claim to own our land and resources" (Rose 1992:405). The idea here is that whatever the intention of New Age practitioners, there are dangerous, unintentional consequences to their ongoing interest in traditional Native spiritual practices.

18. The following articles appeared in *Indian Country Today* in 1993: "Indian Writers: Real or Imagined?" (September 8); "New Agers' Takeover of Native Ways Already Being Realized" (September 8); "Indian Writers: The Good, the Bad, and the Could Be" (September 15 and October 6); "A Proposed Plan for What Makes an 'Indian'" (September 15); "The Misuse of Religion" (September 22); "Wooden Wannabe Drives Wedges among People" (October 6); "Can 'Indianness' Be Defined?" (October 20); "Highwater's Voice Not Real" (October 27); "Waltzing with Generic Wannabes" (October 27); and "Disputes Dorris's 'Wannabe' Label," (October 27). The following articles appeared in the *Lakota Times* in 1990 and 1991: "Spirituality: Can It Be Shared?" (July 17, 1990); "Spirituality: Will It Be Shared?" (August 7, 1990); "Lakota Rituals Being Sold" (July 2, 1991); "Medicine Men for Rent" (July 10, 1991); "Sacred Pipe Keeper Fears Feds Will Step In" (July 17, 1991); "After the Sweat: Caviar, Wine and Cheese" (July 24, 1991); "Medicine Man Scams Are Far Too Many" (July 31, 1991); "Sharing Spirituality for More Than Necessities Is Not the Indian Way" (July 31, 1991); "Looking Horse, We Need to Protect Our Sacred Lakota Ways" (July 31, 1991); "False Prophets Will Suffer" (July 31, 1991); "Spirituality Comes from the Heart, Not from a Book" (August 7, 1991); "Oh Shinnah: Prophet for Profit" (August 7, 1991); "Paid Ads Call Her 'Medicine Woman'" (August 14, 1991); "Sun Dances Take Place on Artificial Turf" (August 21, 1991); "New Age Fad Will Fall to Traditionalists" (August 28, 1991); "Bad Vibes Rock New Age Mecca" (August 28, 1991); "Is Lame Deer Society of Europe Real?" (August 28, 1991). Many thanks go to historian Steven Crum (Western Shoshone) of the Native American Studies Department at the University of California, Davis, for sharing his research files with me.

19. Typically, a Cherokee healer would descend from one of seven matrilineal family clans. For more on the Cherokee clan system, see Gilbert 1943 and Hudson 1976.

20. These titles are often gained by means of competition, not unlike a beauty pageant, though physical beauty is not the primary standard by which American Indian women are judged. Rather, they are expected to live an Indian life and to demonstrate their cultural and historical knowledge and their sense of social responsibility. The titles have nothing to do with inherited royalty in the European sense. For more on powwow princesses in particular, see Roberts 2005.

Chapter 6: Documenting Descent and Other Measures of Tribal Belonging

1. The Southern Cherokee Nation defines Southern Cherokees as anyone listed on the 1867 Tompkins Roll, as well as anyone who served in Stand Watie's regiments. Stand Watie was a full-blooded Cherokee, infamous for being the last Confederate general to surrender, well after the Civil War ended. Descendants of these individuals who are interested in joining the tribe must prove their lineage using documentary evidence, which can include vital records, U.S. census records, family records, bibles, and newspaper articles (Southern Cherokee Nation 2008).

2. In general, genealogists favor written records that are closely associated with actual historical events. For example, the facts recorded on a birth certificate signed by a physician who witnessed the birth would be considered much more reliable than a sworn affidavit provided by a relative several decades later. Genealogists tend to rely on state-certified vital records, federal census records, court documents, and military records as their primary resources.

3. During this time, federal officials compiled numerous tribal membership rolls for Cherokees living in the eastern and western United States. Their purpose was to identify legitimate tribal members in order to determine their eligibility for land claims, annuity payments, and other rights as tribal citizens. Well-known rolls include the Old Settlers, Drennan, and Dawes rolls for Cherokees living in the West and the Henderson, Siler, Guion Miller, and Baker rolls for those remaining in the East. All of these rolls have been a boon to genealogists searching for family history information. However, each used a slightly different enrollment process to determine eligibility. Some are considered more reliable than others. Some also have large numbers of applicants, many of whom were rejected. The roll that is considered least reliable is the Guion Miller Roll, dating to 1909, with more than forty-six thousand applicants. Not surprisingly, the rolls that are considered most reliable are the ones that are used today by the Cherokee Nation and the Eastern Band as their base rolls, which include the Dawes Rolls and the Baker Roll, respectively.

4. Between 1834 and 1909, Cherokees applied the term "intruder" equally to whites and blacks. The latter category included former slaves, Cherokee Freedmen and their descendants, who had left the territory and then returned, and "state blacks," meaning those African Americans who entered Indian Territory without having any affiliation with the tribe. For more on the topic of Cherokee intruders, see Barnes 1933, McCombs 1973, and Sober 1991.

5. "White Cherokee" usually refers only to tribal citizens, whereas "white Indian" is used to classify both Cherokee descendants and tribal citizens. In either case, the Cherokeeness of an individual is qualified in terms of his or her racial, cultural, or social connections to the tribe. (For more on the usage of "white Cherokee" and "white Indian" in the Cherokee Nation, see Sturm 2002:95–106 and 222n8.) "Thindian" refers to a weakness of genealogical connection, the idea being that blood ties can be stretched thin with greater genealogical distance from Cherokee forebears.

6. For more on blood quantum standards for tribal citizenship set by various tribal governments, see appendix 4 in Snipp 1989. For federal standards regarding blood quantum, see Spruhan 2006.

7. Unlike the other two Cherokee tribes, the Eastern Band of Cherokee Indians also recognizes first-generation descendants of tribal citizens. Thus, if someone does not meet the 1/16 blood quantum standard imposed by the tribe for citizenship but has a parent who is enrolled, he or she is classified as a first-generation descendant and is eligible for free medical care at the local Indian Health Service facilities. Many first-generation descendants have

1/32 degree of blood, but others have anywhere from 1/64 to 1/256 degree of Cherokee ancestry. The latter are first-generation descendants of people listed on the Baker Roll, which is the base roll for the Eastern Band and enumerates Eastern Cherokees with everything from full Cherokee ancestry to 1/128 degree of ancestry. A similarly wide range is found on the Cherokee Nation's base rolls, the Dawes Rolls.

8. Although I note that political differences between the Cherokee Nation and United Keetoowah Band are seen in terms of race, I wish to distance myself from this interpretation. The Cherokee Nation is a multicultural and multiracial polity and has been since the late eighteenth century. Although many of its citizens seem white in physical appearance and behavior, these individuals also often have uniquely Cherokee perspectives and experiences that are not readily accessible to a casual observer. Many other Cherokee Nation citizens would meet any essentialist standard of identity imposed by outsiders, including ones based on race or culture. Many Cherokee Nation citizens look Indian, and several thousand speak the Cherokee language. Although this number may seem a small percentage of the whole, the Cherokee Nation's citizenry is too diverse to reduce it to such simplistic interpretations. Though ideas about "white Indians" versus "real Indians" shed light on local politics and racial meanings, they are not academic interpretations, but political ones. The United Keetoowah Band is also a diverse tribal polity in many respects, and despite its imposition of a one-quarter blood quantum requirement, not everyone who meets this requirement has an Indian physical appearance.

9. Among federally recognized tribes, the Cherokee nation has a reputation for inclusivity. Sometimes its open citizenship standards are used as a point of criticism to suggest that the Cherokee Nation is no longer a nation of Indians. Obviously, this criticism is problematic because it privileges race over polity in defining indigenous nationhood.

10. Though I have rarely encountered the term "ethnic Cherokee," I believe that Stevens is referring to people who are culturally but not racially Cherokee.

11. Most race shifters are quick to reject federal recognition in principle, despite the fact that several of them are members of communities that have attempted the process without success. It is unclear whether their criticisms stem from this experience of rejection or predate it. Today, a handful of communities are open about their desire for federal recognition, but most reject this possibility out of hand, viewing it as something that cannot be attained and might not be advantageous anyway. Despite their rejection of the federal recognition process, many have sought state recognition, with varying degrees of success. For more on the topic of external recognition, see chapter 8.

12. Interestingly, the tribe chooses to certify that its members are "half bloods" rather than "full bloods" because in the case of such variable phenotypes, multiracial ancestry has to be acknowledged, lest the assertion of a uniform racial identity be called into question.

13. A well-known and highly respected principal chief of the Cherokee Nation for much of the nineteenth century, John Ross saw his people through many of the most turbulent times in Cherokee history, including forced removal from their southeastern homelands, the reconstitution of the tribal government in Indian Territory, and the U.S. Civil War.

14. In this hypothetical example of interracial adoption, the baby who becomes Cherokee through a family's love and devotion begins life as white, not black or some other explicitly marked identity, such as Hispanic or Asian. Not surprisingly, even among Cherokees, white seems to operate as the default normative category, second only to Cherokee.

Chapter 7: States of Sovereignty

1. For more details and the political context surrounding these events, see Sturm 2002:101–1033.

2. The source for the thirty-three current definitions is a 1978 Congressional survey (O'Brien 1991). Although I know of no additional surveys that have been conducted, surely this figure underestimates the full complexity of current legal standards of American Indian identity. In the past thirty years, many more laws have been passed that also define who American Indians are for legal purposes, and some of these may include still different definitions. The standards of citizenship for tribal governments are equally variable and complex. For a useful comparative overview of tribal standards, see Snipp 1989.

3. One of the earliest examples of state recognition is that of the Mattaponi and Pamunkey. As legal scholars Kirke Kickingbird (Kiowa) and Karen Ducheneaux note, the Commonwealth of Virginia recognized both tribes in a 1658 treaty (Sheffield 1997:72). Other examples include the Shinnecock Indian Nation, originally recognized by the state of New York in 1792, and the Lumbee, whose recognition in North Carolina dates to 1885.

4. For particularly insightful discussions of sovereignty, see Biolsi 2005 and Willard 2002. In pointing to these distinctions between autonomous and interdependent sovereignty, I am not rejecting the idea of inherent sovereignty, but trying to highlight an understanding of sovereignty in which power, rather than being granted or delegated by an external source, is negotiated within the context of mutual political recognition. Sovereignty, in this instance and in many practical matters, derives from political dialogue and mutual engagement (Cattelino 2007, 2008). Because the practice of sovereignty is tied up with such negotiations, some scholars have argued that it is too dependent on external validation and too derivative of Western thought and practices. For more on this critique of sovereignty, see Alfred 1999.

5. My heartfelt thanks go to Jessica Cattelino for her comments on an earlier draft of this chapter that appeared in an edited volume to which we both contributed (Cobb and Fowler 2007). She helped me to clarify my arguments and to pinpoint the ways in which our ideas about sovereignty, recognition, and interdependence dovetail with one another.

6. This lack of reliable information can pose a problem for those trying to uphold federal law. For instance, what are gallery owners, museum curators, and other consumers of American Indian art supposed to do when trying to comply with the American Indian Arts and Crafts Act of 1990? If the act states that only those who are citizens of federally recognized or state-recognized tribes—or who have been certified by these tribes as Indian artisans—are entitled to label their wares as Indian made, then how are we to know whether someone is a member of a state-recognized tribe? This problem can be easily addressed by someone with the time and energy to contact the various state legislatures and Indian commissions and who is willing to make that information available to the broader public, but the fact that the problem exists highlights some of the political and legal difficulties of the current situation.

7. Data were compiled from several sources, including Access Genealogy 2003; Catolster 1995; DeMarce 2001:5–63; Johnson and Giese 1997; Kauffman 2001; Mankiller 1993; National Conference of State Legislatures 2003; Native Data 2003; Sheffield 1997:63–73; Spike n.d.; U.S. Senate Committee on Indian Affairs 1995:219–241.

8. According to the *Code of Federal Regulations* (25 CFR § 83 [1993]), a tribe seeking federal acknowledgment must meet the following criteria: outsiders have identified it on an ongoing basis as an American Indian tribe; members live in an area or a community that is viewed as distinctly Indian and are descendants of a known Indian tribe; and the group has continuously maintained some form of tribal political organization or influence over its members. The burden of proof rests on petitioners, who have to rely on the work of anthropologists, historians, colonial officers, and government agents to substantiate their claims. It is not sufficient that a tribe has been organized as such for a century or longer. Rather, it

must be perceived as an Indian entity, by non-Indians, according to what are largely non-Indian standards (Greenbaum 1991:107).

However, federally recognized tribes had a hand in determining the original 1978 criteria for federal acknowledgment, so recognition standards are not strictly non-Indian. Also, no petitioner has ever been denied recognition solely on the basis of the criterion requiring evidence that outsiders have long viewed it as an Indian community. Those who fail to meet this criterion always fail to meet additional criteria as well (Valerie Lambert, Choctaw Nation citizen and former Office of Federal Acknowledgment employee, personal communication, April 8, 2010).

9. I do not mean to suggest that only the states have variations in their recognition processes. Scholars who are critical of the federal acknowledgment process have argued that it is much too rigorous and "woefully inconsistent" in that smaller, less aggressive groups and those that suffered colonialism at an earlier date—particularly those on the eastern seaboard—often fail to meet the criteria for recognition because of characteristics or conditions that the federal government created in the first place (Garroutte 2003:27–29). Federal recognition can also be achieved via executive order, as well as congressional fiat, and the U.S. Congress recognized fourteen tribes between 1978 and 2000 without any reference to the Office of Federal Acknowledgment guidelines. For more on federal recognition via acts of Congress, see Cramer 2005:39–56. For other forms of administrative recognition, see Roth 2008:114–115, 125–126. For a useful overview of the federal acknowledgment process from an anthropologist who is less critical and who was a long-time employee of the Office of Federal Acknowledgment, see Roth 2001. For a more critical evaluation of the process, see Blu 2001, as well as Miller 2003 and Miller 2004 on nonrecognized American Indians.

10. Many state-recognized Cherokees argue that even though the process is somewhat arbitrary and the overall effects unclear, state recognition is a useful alternative to federal recognition, given the rigors and inconsistencies of the federal recognition process as they see it.

11. In recent years, a slew of state-recognized tribes have managed to petition successfully for federal acknowledgment—most notably, the Mashpee Wampanoag Tribe of Massachusetts, the Passamaquoddy Tribe and Penobscot Nation, both of Maine, and the Poarch Band of Creek Indians in Alabama. State-recognized tribes are also covered under the Indian Arts and Crafts Act of 1990 and the Native American Free Exercise of Religion Act of 1993.

12. The standard legal interpretation is that states may assert jurisdiction over Native American nations only with congressional approval. However, various laws and acts have challenged this hierarchy, including Public Law 280 of 1953 and the Indian Gaming Regulatory Act of 1988. For a useful article on the topic, see Resnick 1995.

13. The examples in this section are taken from Reinhart's (2002) legislative report, which sorts through and makes sense of recent legal cases involving state-recognized tribes in Connecticut.

14. In the media coverage of her life, Princess Che'Kee' underwent several transformations. She first appeared in the press in the late 1960s as Leslie Panchula, a special education teacher with innovative techniques for teaching mathematics (*Morning Record*, July 1, 1969). The earliest mention of her publicly identifying herself as a Cherokee descendant and becoming involved in local American Indian affairs dates to the mid-1970s, when she was described as "researching American Indian history in Connecticut for the state Department of Environmental Protection" (*Tri-Town Reporter*, April 25, 1976). By 1977, she was no longer described as a Cherokee descendant but rather as a Cherokee who was actively

involved with both federally recognized and self-identified tribes. During this period, she went by the name of Leslie Che'Kee' Panchula Uhlan—Uhlan being her new husband's surname (*Trumbull Times*, June 30, 1977). However, only four years later, she had taken on a royal title and appeared as Princess Che'Kee' in at least four newspaper articles (*Smithtown Messenger*, January 15, 1981; *Smithtown Messenger*, March 26, 1981; *Middletown Press*, October 10, 1981; *Miami Herald*, December 26, 1981).

15. Princess Che'Kee's claim to be a descendant of the Croatan Cherokees raises some interesting questions about her origins. In several newspaper articles, she stated that she was born and raised on the "Cherokee reservation" in Pembroke, North Carolina. However, the only Cherokee reservation that exists in North Carolina is that of the Eastern Band of Cherokee Indians. Pembroke is actually the home of the Lumbee Tribe of North Carolina, a community that has long fought for federal recognition. Although the Lumbees' origins are disputed, they were officially recognized as Croatan Indians by the State of North Carolina in 1855, and in the early twentieth century, they were also known as the Cherokees of Robeson County. Both references to being Croatan and to Pembroke signal a possible Lumbee connection rather than a specifically Cherokee one. However, Princess Che'Kee' also claimed that she was adopted by German-Jewish foster parents, which might open the door to a more direct Cherokee lineage (one that has never been made public). Though it is difficult to discern the facts in her ever-evolving biographical narrative, her adoption—if it occurred—could account for some of her muddled explanations of her own origins.

16. For examples of these arguments, see the Web site of the Cherokee Nation Task Force at http://taskforce.cherokee.org.

Chapter 8: Closing

1. The Cherokee Nation and Northeastern State University (NSU) are both located in Tahlequah, Oklahoma. Though formally separate institutions, they have a shared history. On March 6, 1909, the State of Oklahoma purchased the stunning Cherokee Female Seminary building and grounds from the Cherokee Nation and used them to establish the Northeastern State Normal School, which became NSU in 1985 after a series of name changes. The Cherokee Female Seminary was founded in 1846, so because of the two institutions' entwined histories, NSU can claim to be "the oldest institution of higher learning in the state of Oklahoma" (Northeastern State University n.d.). Other than its convenient location, the specifically Cherokee flavor of NSU makes it appealing to many Cherokee students in the area. The Cherokee Nation and NSU also work cooperatively to design and fund an extensive array of classes and programs on the Cherokee language and culture. For more on the history of the Cherokee Female Seminary, see Devon Mihesuah's 1997 book *Cultivating the Rosebuds: The Education of Women at the Cherokee Female Seminary, 1851–1909.*

2. Oklahoma is known as the Sooner State after the individuals who illegally staked land claims before the passage of the 1889 Indian Appropriations Act, which allowed for the Oklahoma Land Run shortly thereafter. This pioneer audacity is still considered a point of pride. The mock wedding ceremony between the cowboy and the Cherokee maiden was reenacted in 2007 for the Oklahoma statehood centennial on the steps of the courthouse in Guthrie.

3. Task Force documents include the important caveat that they represent the opinions of the authors and not necessarily the official position of the Cherokee Nation. Although the Task Force was originally founded in 2007 by a group of concerned citizens and tribal employees and had a somewhat more informal role within the Cherokee Nation, since fall 2009 it has advised an employee appointed by the tribal administration to monitor

self-identified and state-recognized Cherokee activities. The Task Force's Web site can be viewed at http://taskforce.cherokee.org.

4. Much of what the Task Force presented at the State of Sequoyah conference sounded like what I had heard in Oklahoma City three months earlier at the June 2008 Sovereignty Symposium, sponsored by the Oklahoma State Department of Justice, when Task Force members spoke before a standing-room-only crowd.

5. The full-text version of "Stealing Sovereignty: Identity Theft, the Creation of False Tribes," coauthored by Task Force members Richard Allen, Cara Cowan Watts, John Parris, Troy Wayne Poteete, Teri Rhoades, and Tonia Williams with Kathleen Wesho-Bauer (2007), can be viewed at http://tribalrecognition.cherokee.org/LinkClick.aspx?fileticket=RRHyHM9 gfNA%3d&tabid=106&mid=2118. Exhibit 5 is of particular relevance to their claims regarding federal and state funding streams being channeled to state-recognized and self-identified Cherokee groups.

6. The term "box checker" refers to individuals who identify themselves as American Indian—by checking the appropriate box on a form—in order to gain economic advantages such as scholarships and job opportunities. Task Force members are concerned about non-Indians taking advantage of opportunities that are solely intended for tribal citizens.

7. Although this particular individual is now the self-declared chief of the Kaweah Indian Nation and performed these actions as a Kaweah rather than a Cherokee, the Task Force noted that since 1975 he had been listed as the principal chief of a self-identified Cherokee tribe in Georgia and is the publisher of two Cherokee newsletters with a wide circulation (Allen et al. 2007). So, despite the change in tribal identification, he was still widely recognized as a self-identified Cherokee at the time he was charged and later indicted.

8. Responses to Murv Jacob's original letter continued through 2008 and included the following: in the *Tahlequah Daily Press*, "Cowans' Indian Wars" (August 29); James Murray, "Who's Appropriating?" (September 3); and Sara Hoklotubbe, "'Native Artist' Defined" (September 8) and in the *Cherokee Phoenix*, "Jacob Needs to Face Facts" (October 27) and Joe Scraper Jr., "In Reply to Murv Jacob" (December 3).

9. Sara Hoklotubbe made this point clear when she wrote only a few days later to the *Tahlequah Daily Press* (September 8, 2008) and several weeks later to the *Cherokee Phoenix*, the Cherokee Nation's official tribal newspaper (October 27, 2008), suggesting that Murv Jacob's anger was "misdirected" and that personal attacks were not going to change the situation. She spelled out the problem as follows: "Lots of people say they have American Indian blood. Not all can prove it. The fact that he can't meet the citizenship requirement is not Cowan Watts' fault" (*Cherokee Phoenix*, October 27, 2008). She then went on to state that anyone can write books about or paint American Indian subjects but only federally recognized American Indians have the right to sell their creations in the Cherokee Nation under tribal law (*Cherokee Phoenix*, October 27, 2008). Hoklotubbe's emphasis on standards of citizenship and law in defining American Indian artists was even more apparent when she made the point that their rights are not linked to their blood quanta: "The Cherokee Nation constitution stipulates the guidelines to be a Cherokee citizen. All it takes is one American Indian ancestor listed on the Dawes Roll. The fraction of blood is irrelevant" (*Cherokee Phoenix*, October 27, 2008).

10. Besides "passing," scholars have used other terms to refer to crossing racial identity boundaries, including David Roediger's (2002) "crossing over" and "racechange," the latter of which was inspired by Susan Gubar's (1997) work on blackface. However, most of these usages tend to focus on cultural and performative aspects of race.

11. In a particularly insightful article, "Passing: Race, Identification, and Desire," literary scholar Catherine Rottenberg (2003) draws from Judith Butler's (1993) theoretical

insights about gender identity as "performative reiteration" to examine how racial identity operates in a similar fashion. She tackles this subject by exploring nineteenth-century literature about the experience of black women passing as white. To look at racial passing, Rottenberg uses Butler's distinction between identity and desire. But she explains that, although in hetero-normative contexts there are two ideal genders, in racist regimes of white normativity only one racial option is possible (Rottenberg 2003:436, 441–444). Her work has influenced my own thinking about racial shifting, particularly in the next several pages; however, she does not apply these insights to cases of racial identification in which white normativity is being challenged.

12. The word "hypodescent" describes a particular rule of racial ascription in the United States whereby a child resulting from the union of racially distinct parents is assigned the same race as *t*hat of the lower-status parent. Similarly, the "one drop rule" assigns multiracial children to the same race as their lowest-status ancestor or lower-status parent, regardless of degree of ancestry. For example, if a child were 15/16 white and 1/16 African American, she would be racially classified as African American.

13. Pamela Perry makes a similar argument about how whiteness can be reproduced at the very moment that white privilege is denied, in *Shades of White: White Kids and Racial Identities in High School* (2002:197–198).

14. I want to give credit to Eva Garroutte for this insight, which she offered when she read an earlier draft of the introduction to this book.

15. Within the context of federal Indian law, indigenous status is normally framed in political and not racial terms. Yet, certain practices defy these legal definitions. For more on the conflicting intersections of race, sovereignty, and indigenous status, see Kauanui 2008:9–35 and Wilkins 2007:45–65.

16. Wilma Mankiller is but one example of a prominent Cherokee who came to have a greater sense of political consciousness at this time and who helped occupy Alcatraz Island in San Francisco Bay as part of a large-scale protest over land loss and broken treaties. Later, Mankiller was one of the first American Indian women elected to the office of principal chief. For more about her life and personal transformation during the Red Power movement, see her autobiography, *Mankiller: A Chief and Her People* (Mankiller and Wallis 1993).

17. A classic example of a neoliberal approach to race can be found in the work of William Julius Wilson, who also served as an advisor to President Clinton. In his 1987 book *The Truly Disadvantaged: The Inner City, the Underclass and Public Policy*, Wilson argues that since the late 1960s, capital has been "color blind" and that the largely minority, inner-city underclass was not a product of racial discrimination but of broader social and historical forces. Rather than politically divisive, "group-based" programs like affirmative action, he calls for universal, class-based initiatives.

18. Few politicians, except those on the far right, could get away with saying "welfare mothers" now, in part because this racist term has been decoded. Other terms of race, however, have not received as much scrutiny, particularly codes for whiteness such as "law-abiding communities," "ordinary Americans," "soccer moms," and "NASCAR dads." These continue to be used with abandon.

19. After Clinton's public announcement that he had a Cherokee grandmother, there was a small flurry of media activity. According to these reports, neither the White House nor the Cherokee Nation could find his grandmother's name on the official Cherokee rolls. Some tribal members in Tahlequah questioned his claim on the basis of an Arkansas connection rather than one based in Oklahoma, Texas, or North Carolina. For more on this issue, see the *Washington Times* coverage of November 23, 1998.

20. My heartfelt appreciation to Catherine Cocks, historian, editor, and friend, whose

comments on an earlier draft of this chapter helped to shape my arguments on the implications of neoliberalism for race shifters in this section.

21. In the article "Going Native," Treuer, an Ojibwe from the Leech Lake reservation in northern Minnesota, argues that consumers want tragic Indian stories rather than happy ones and that white impersonation hurts Indian authors, who are often displaced from getting their own, much more variable and nuanced work published (*Slate Magazine*, March 7, 2008).

Appendix 1

1. Data were compiled from the following sources: Access Genealogy 2003; Catolster 1995; DeMarce 2001:5–63; Johnson and Giese 1997; Mankiller 1993; National Conference of State Legislatures 2003; U.S. Senate Committee on Indian Affairs 1995:219–241. Organizations for which locations have not been noted are smaller bands of the Southern Cherokee Nation, which is headquartered in Webbers Falls, Oklahoma, but maintains numerous bands around the country. More specific information about the smaller bands was not available, in part because their leadership and locations have been highly unstable.

Appendix 2

1. As of 2010, tribes listed here have been recognized by their respective state governments but not by the U.S. federal government. Data have been compiled from the following sources: Access Genealogy 2003; Catolster 1995; DeMarce 2001:5–63; Johnson and Giese 1997; Mankiller 1993; National Conference of State Legislatures 2003; Native Data 2003; Sheffield 1997:63–73; Spike n.d.; U.S. Senate Committee on Indian Affairs 1995:219–241.

References

Access Genealogy
2003   State-Recognized Tribes. http://www.accessgenealogy.com/native/staterectribes.htm, accessed June 26, 2003.

Administration for Native Americans
2003   Summary of Expenditures, FY 2002. http://www.acf.dhhs.gov/programs/ana/ programs/grants2002.html, accessed June 26, 2003.

Albanese, Catherine L.
1990   Nature Religion in America: From the Algonkian Indians to the New Age. Chicago: University of Chicago Press.

Alfred, Gerald Taiaiake
1999   Power, Rights, Righteousness: An Indigenous Manifesto. Toronto: Oxford University Press.

Allen, Richard L.
1995   "My Great-Grandmother Was a Cherokee Princess and My Great-Grandfather Was Chief John Ross or Sequoyah or Somebody like That, I Can't Remember": The Second Coming of the Snake Oil Vendors and the Indian Medicine Show, or Lessons on Creating an American Indian Identity. Paper presented to the Five Civilized Tribes Inter-tribal Repatriation Committee, Sulphur, Oklahoma, November 16.

Allen, Richard L., Cara Cowan Watts, John Parris, Troy Wayne Poteete, Teri Rhoades, and Tonia Williams with Kathleen Wesho-Bauer
2007   Stealing Sovereignty: Identity Theft, the Creation of False Tribes. Paper presented at Sovereignty Symposium XX, Oklahoma City, Oklahoma, May 30–31.

Association of American Indian and Alaska Native Professors
N.d.   "We the Association of American Indian and Alaska Native Professors." Untitled statement on ethnic fraud. https://pantherfile.uwm.edu/michael/www/nativeprofs/ fraud.htm, accessed July 26, 2010.

Barnes, Margaret Louise

1933   Intruders in the Cherokee Nation, 1834–1907. MA thesis, Department of History, University of Oklahoma.

Basso, Keith H.

1979   Portraits of the "Whiteman": Linguistic Play and Cultural Symbols among the Western Apache. Cambridge: Cambridge University Press.

Bender, Margaret

2002   Signs of Cherokee Culture: Sequoyah's Syllabary in Eastern Cherokee Life. Chapel Hill: University of North Carolina Press.

Berkhofer, Robert F., Jr.

1979   The White Man's Indian: Images of the American Indian from Columbus to the Present. New York: Vintage Books.

Berman, Morris

1981   The Reenchantment of the World. Ithaca, NY: Cornell University Press.

Biolsi, Thomas

2005   Imagined Geographies: Sovereignty, Indigenous Space, and American Indian Struggle. American Ethnologist 32(2):239–259.

Blu, Karen I.

1980   The Lumbee Problem: The Making of an American Indian People. New York: Cambridge University Press.

2001   Region and Recognition: Southern Indians, Anthropologists, and Presumed Biology. *In* Anthropologists and Indians in the New South. Rachel A. Bonney and J. Anthony Paredes, eds. Pp. 71–88. Tuscaloosa: University of Alabama Press.

Bourdieu, Pierre

1977   Outline of a Theory of Practice. Cambridge: Cambridge University Press.

1987   Distinction: A Social Critique of the Judgement of Taste. Cambridge, MA: Harvard University Press.

Brewton, Barry

1963   Almost White: A Study of Certain Racial Hybrids in the Eastern United States. New York: Macmillan.

Brown, Michael F.

1997   The Channeling Zone: American Spirituality in an Anxious Age. Cambridge, MA: Harvard University Press.

Butler, Judith

1993   Bodies That Matter: On the Discursive Limits of "Sex." New York: Routledge.

Cahn, Peter

N.d.   The Great Commission: Direct Sales and Direct Faith in Mexico. Unpublished MS in the author's possession.

Carter, Forrest
1976   The Education of Little Tree. Albuquerque: University of New Mexico Press.

Catolster, Isabel
1994   Racism as a Human Rights Violation. Written testimony given before the Council
        of Churches meeting, Tulsa, Oklahoma, October 15. Oklahoma Folder, Archive of
        the Tribal Registrar, Cherokee Nation, Tahlequah, Oklahoma.
1995   Entities Using the Cherokee Name, Eastern Band of Cherokee Indians. Archive of
        the Tribal Registrar, Cherokee Nation, Tahlequah, Oklahoma.

Cattelino, Jessica
2007   Florida Seminole Gaming and Local Sovereign Interdependency. *In* Beyond Red
        Power: American Indian Politics and Activism since 1900. Daniel M. Cobb and
        Loretta Fowler, eds. Pp. 262–279. Santa Fe, NM: School for Advanced Research
        Press.
2008   High Stakes: Florida Seminole Gaming and Sovereignty. Durham, NC: Duke
        University Press.

Cobb, Daniel M., and Loretta Fowler, eds.
2007   Beyond Red Power: American Indian Politics and Activism since 1900. Santa Fe,
        NM: School for Advanced Research Press.

Comaroff, Jean, and John L. Comaroff
1991   Of Revelation and Revolution, 1: Christianity, Colonialism, and Consciousness in
        South Africa. Chicago: University of Chicago Press.

Cook-Lynn, Elizabeth
1993   Meeting of Indian Professors Takes Up Issues of "Ethnic Fraud," Sovereignty, and
        Research Needs. Wicazo Sa Review 9(1):57–59.
2001   Anti-Indianism in Modern America: A Voice from Tatekeya's Earth. Urbana:
        University of Illinois Press.

Cornell, Stephen
1988   The Return of the Native: American Indian Political Resurgence. New York: Oxford
        University Press.

Cramer, Renée A.
2005   Cash, Color, and Colonialism: The Politics of Tribal Acknowledgment. Norman:
        University of Oklahoma Press.

Crutchfield, Gail, and Evan Belanger
2006   Tribal Discord Leads to Election. Cullman Times, July 31. http://www.cullmantimes
        .com/local/x1116124724/Tribal-discord-leads-to-election, accessed July 29, 2010.

Cucchiari, Salvatore
1988   "Adapted for Heaven": Conversion and Culture in Western Sicily. American
        Ethnologist 15(3):417–441.

Delbanco, Andrew
1999   The Real American Dream: A Meditation on Hope. Cambridge, MA: Harvard
        University Press.

Delgado, Richard, and Jean Stefancic, eds.
1997   Critical White Studies: Looking behind the Mirror. Philadelphia: Temple University
        Press.

Deloria, Philip J.
1998   Playing Indian. New Haven, CT: Yale University Press.

Deloria, Vine, Jr.
1988[1969] Custer Died for Your Sins: An Indian Manifesto. Norman: University of
        Oklahoma Press.

DeMarce, Virginia
2001   Overview of Cherokee Groups and Federal Acknowledgment process. Unpublished
        MS, Office of Federal Acknowledgment, Bureau of Indian Affairs, Department of
        Interior, Washington, DC.

Du Bois, W. E. B.
2005[1903] The Souls of Black Folks. New York: Simon and Schuster.
1977[1935] Black Reconstruction in America: An Essay toward a History of the Part Which
        Black Folk Played in the Attempt to Reconstruct Democracy in America. New
        York: Atheneum.

Duggan, Lisa
2003   The Twilight of Equality: Neoliberalism, Cultural Politics and the Attack on
        Democracy. New York: Beacon Press.

Durkheim, Emile
1933   The Division of Labor in Society. New York: The Free Press.

Eastern Band of Cherokee Indians
2003   Tribal Enrollment Statistics. http://www.cherokee-nc.com, accessed July 28, 2003.

Ellis, Clyde, Luke Eric Lassiter, and Gary H. Dunham, eds.
2005   Powwow. Lincoln: University of Nebraska Press.

Eng, David L., and Shinhee Han
2003   A Dialogue on Racial Melancholia. In Loss: The Politics of Mourning. David L. Eng
        and David Kanzanjian, eds. Pp. 343–371. Berkeley: University of California Press.

Fine-Dare, Kathleen S.
2002   Grave Injustice: The American Indian Repatriation Movement and NAGPRA.
        Lincoln: University of Nebraska Press.

Finger, John R.
1980   The North Carolina Cherokees, 1830–1866: Traditionalism, Progressivism, and the
        Affirmation of State Citizenship. Journal of Cherokee Studies 5(Spring):17–29.

1993   The Impact of Removal on the North Carolina Cherokees. *In* Cherokee Removal: Before and After. William L. Anderson, ed. Pp. 96–111. Athens: University of Georgia Press.

Frankenberg, Ruth
1993   White Women, Race Matters: The Social Construction of Whiteness. Minneapolis: University of Minnesota Press.

Gabbert, Wolfgang
2001   Social and Cultural Conditions of Religious Conversion in Colonial Southwest Tanzania, 1891–1939. Ethnology 40(4):291–308.

Gane, Nicholas
2002   Max Weber and Postmodern Theory: Rationalization versus Re-enchantment. New York: Macmillan.

Garroutte, Eva Marie
2003   Real Indians: Identity and the Survival of Native America. Berkeley: University of California Press.

Geertz, Clifford
2000   Local Knowledge: Further Essays in Interpretive Anthropology. New York: Basic Books.

Gerstle, Gary
2001   American Crucible: Race and Nation in the Twentieth Century. Princeton, NJ: Princeton University Press.

Gerth, Hans H., and C. Wright Mills, eds.
1946   From Max Weber: Essays in Sociology. New York: Oxford University Press.

Gilbert, William H.
1943   The Eastern Cherokees. Smithsonian Institution, Bureau of American Ethnology, Bulletin 133(23):169–413.

Ginsberg, Elaine K., ed.
1996   Passing and the Fictions of Identity. Durham, NC: Duke University Press.

Gonzales, Angela A.
1998   The (Re)articulation of American Indian Identity: Maintaining Boundaries and Regulating Access to Ethnically Tied Resources. American Indian Culture and Research Journal 22(4):199–225.
2002   American Indian Identity Matters: The Political Economy of Ethnic Group Boundaries. PhD dissertation, Department of Sociology, Harvard University.

Gonzales, Angela, Judy Kertesz, and Gabrielle Tayac
2007   Eugenics as Indian Removal: Sociohistorical Processes and De(con)struction of American Indians in the Southeast. The Public Historian 29(3):53–67.

Green, Rayna
1988   The Tribe Called Wannabee: Playing Indian in America and Europe. Folklore 99(1):30–55.

Greenbaum, Susan
1991   What Is a Label? Identity Problems of Southern Indian Tribes. The Journal of Ethnic Studies 19(Summer):107–126.

Greil, Arthur L., and David R. Rudy
1983   Conversion to the World of Alcoholics Anonymous: A Refinement of Conversion Theory. Qualitative Sociology 6(1):5–28.

Gubar, Susan
1997   Racechanges: White Skin, Black Face in American Culture. Oxford: Oxford University Press.

Hagar, Stansbury
1900   The Celestial Bear. Journal of American Folklore 13(48):92–103.

Hale, Grace Elizabeth
1999   Making Whiteness: The Culture of Segregation in the South, 1890–1940. New York: Vintage Books.

Hanks, William F.
2010   Converting Words: Maya in the Age of the Cross. Berkeley: University of California Press.

Harding, Susan
1987   Convicted by the Holy Spirit: The Rhetoric of Fundamentalist Baptist Conversion. American Ethnologist 14(1):167–181.

Harris, Cheryl I.
1993   Whiteness as Property. Harvard Law Review 106(8):1706–1791.

Haynes, Joshua S.
2001   Power in the Blood: Identity Construction and the Cherokee Tribe of Northeast Alabama. MA thesis, Southern Studies Department, University of Mississippi.

Hegeman, Roxana
2008   Kaweah "grand chief" faces fraud sentencing for defrauding immigrants. Associated Press, published in News from Indian Country, December. http://indiancountrynews.net/index.php?option=com_content&task=view&id=5268, accessed August 3, 2010.

Heirich, Max
1977   Change of Heart: A Test of Some Widely Held Theories about Religious Conversion. The American Journal of Sociology 83(3):653–680.

Hill, Jane H.
1994   The Incorporative Power of Whiteness. Paper presented at the annual meeting of the American Ethnological Society, Santa Monica, California.

Hill, Mike, ed.
1997   Whiteness: A Critical Reader. New York: New York University.

Hitchens, Christopher
1999   No One Left to Lie To: The Values of the Worst Family. New York: Verso.

Hobson, Fred

1999   The Southern Racial Conversion Narrative: Larry L. King and Pat Watters. Virginia Quarterly Review 75(2):205–225.

Hobson, Geary, ed.

1979   The Remembered Earth: An Anthology of Contemporary Native American Literature. Albuquerque, NM: Red Earth Press.

Hollinger, David A.

2003   Amalgamation and Hypodescent: The Question of Ethnoracial Mixture in the History of the United States. The American Historical Review 108(5):1363–1390.

hooks, bell

1992   Black Looks: Race and Representation. Cambridge, MA: South End Press.

Hornbeck, Shirley

N.d.   This and That Genealogy Tips on Black Dutch and Black Irish, Melungeons, Moravians, Pennsylvania Dutch. http://homepages.rootsweb.com/~hornbeck/ blkdutch.htm, accessed July 29, 2010.

Hudson, Charles

1976   The Southeastern Indians. Knoxville: University of Tennessee Press.

Huhndorf, Shari

2001   Going Native: Indians in the American Cultural Imagination. Ithaca, NY: Cornell University Press.

Johnson, Troy, and Paula Giese

1997   U.S. Federally Non-recognized Indian Tribes—Index by State. http://www.kstrom.net/isk/maps/tribesnonrec.html, accessed June 26, 2003.

Kauanui, J. Kehaulani

2008   Hawaiian Blood: Colonialism and the Politics of Sovereignty and Indigeneity. Durham, NC: Duke University Press.

Kauffman, L. Jeanne

2001   State Recognition of American Indian Tribes. Denver: National Conference of State Legislatures.

Kirk, Wyman

2003   Cherokees, Barbies, and Blood. Paper presented at the annual meetings of the American Anthropological Association, Chicago.

Lears, Jackson T. J.

1994   No Place of Grace: Antimodernism and the Transformation of American Culture, 1880–1920. Chicago: University of Chicago Press.

Leeds, Georgia Rae

1997   American University Studies, series IX, History, vol. 184: The United Keetoowah Band of Cherokee Indians in Oklahoma. New York: Peter Lang Publishing.

Lehrer, Jim

1998   A Dialogue on Race with President Clinton. Interview, PBS, July 9. http://www.pbs.org/newshour/bb/race_relations/OneAmerica/transcript.html, accessed July 29, 2010.

Lott, Eric

2003   The First Boomer: Bill Clinton, George W., and Fictions of State. Representations 84:100–122.

Loving Hands Institute

2008   Loving Hands Institute of Healing Arts. Fortuna, CA: Loving Hands Institute. http://www.lovinghandsinstitute.com/htm/paia.htm, accessed July 5, 2008.

Mallon, Ron

2004   Passing, Traveling, and Reality: Social Construction and the Metaphysics of Race. Noûs 38(4):644–673.

Mankiller, Wilma

1993   Letter to the governors of 21 states regarding federal and state recognition of "other purported 'Cherokee' tribes," January 4. Archive of the Tribal Registrar, Cherokee Nation, Tahlequah, Oklahoma.

1995   Letter from principal chief of the Cherokee Nation to members of the Georgia State Assembly regarding state recognition of American Indian tribes, February 15. Georgia Folder, Archive of the Tribal Registrar, Cherokee Nation, Tahlequah, Oklahoma.

Mankiller, Wilma, and Michael Wallis

1993   Mankiller: A Chief and Her People. New York: St. Martin's Press.

Maugham, W. Somerset

1944[1919] The Moon and Sixpence. New York: Penguin Books.

McCombs, Virginia Lee

1973   Intruders in the Cherokee Nation, 1865–1907. MA thesis, Department of History, University of Oklahoma.

Meyrowitz, Joshua

1984   No Sense of Place: The Impact of Media on Social Behavior. Oxford: Oxford University Press.

Michaels, Walter Benn

1995   Our America: Nativism, Modernism, and Pluralism. Durham, NC: Duke University Press.

Mihesuah, Devon A.

1997   Cultivating the Rosebuds: The Education of Women at the Cherokee Female Seminary, 1851–1909. Urbana: University of Illinois Press.

Miles, Tiya A.

2005   Ties That Bind: The Story of an Afro-Cherokee Family in Slavery and in Freedom. Berkeley: University of California Press.

Miller, Bruce G.
2003   Invisible Indigenes: The Politics of Nonrecognition. Lincoln: University of Nebraska Press.

Miller, Mark E.
2004   Forgotten Tribes: Unrecognized Indians and the Federal Acknowledgment Process. Lincoln: University of Nebraska Press.

Mooney, James
1995[1900] Myths of the Cherokee. New York: Dover Publications.

Morgan, Candessa
2006   The Indian Princess: An Intersection of Race, Gender, and Culture. Unpublished MS in the author's possession.

Nagel, Joane
1995   American Indian Ethnic Renewal: Politics and the Resurgence of Identity. American Sociological Review 60:947–965.
1996   American Indian Ethnic Renewal: Red Power and the Resurgence of Identity and Culture. New York: Oxford University Press.

Nassau, Mike
2004   Black Dutch. http://www.geocites.com/mikenassau/BlackDutch.htm, accessed February 16, 2004.

National Conference of State Legislatures
2003   State–Tribal Relations, Indian Tribes in the States. http://www.ncsl.org/programs/esnr/tribes.html, accessed June 9, 2005.

Native Data
2003   State-Recognized Tribes. http://www.nativedata.com/statetribes.htm, accessed June 26, 2003.

Naylor, Celia E.
2008   African Cherokees in Indian Territory: From Chattel to Citizens. Chapel Hill: University of North Carolina Press.

Northeastern State University
N.d.   NSU's Heritage. Tahlequah, OK: Northeastern State University. http://www.nsuok.edu/GettingStarted/NSUsHeritage.aspx, accessed March 28, 2010.

O'Brien, Sharon
1991   Tribes and Indians: With Whom Does the United States Maintain a Relationship? Notre Dame Law Review 66:1481.

Oklahoma Indian Affairs Commission
2003   Overview. http://www.ok.gov/oiac/documents/FY2003.PP.WEB.pdf, accessed July 28, 2003.

Omi, Michael, and Howard Winant
1994   Racial Formation in the United States: From the 1960s to the 1990s. 2nd edition. New York: Routledge.

Owen, Louis
1994   Other Destinies: Understanding the American Indian Novel. Norman: University of Oklahoma Press.

Oxford English Dictionary
2009   OED Online. http://dictionary.oed.com/cgi/entry/00296287?single=1&query_type=word&queryword=wannabe&first=1&max_to_show=10, accessed March 12, 2009.

Pan American Indian Association
1987   Tribal Membership Certificate, August 4. Florida Folder, Archive of the Tribal Registrar, Cherokee Nation, Tahlequah, Oklahoma.

Passel, Jeffrey S.
1976   Provisional Evaluation of the 1970 Census Count of American Indians. Demography 13(3):397–409.
1997   The Growing American Indian Population, 1960–1990: Beyond Demography. Population Research and Policy Review 16(1/2):11–31.

Perry, Pamela
2002   Shades of White: White Kids and Racial Identities in High School. Durham, NC: Duke University Press.

Peterson, Marge
1993   Letter to Zell Miller, governor of Georgia, regarding state recognition of American Indian tribes, November 30. Georgia Folder, Archive of the Tribal Registrar, Cherokee Nation, Tahlequah, Oklahoma.

Pewewardy, Cornel
2004   So You Think You Hired an "Indian" Faculty Member? The Ethnic Fraud Paradox in Higher Education. In Indigenizing the Academy. Angela Cavendar Wilson and Devon Abbott Mihesuah, eds. Pp. 200–217. Lincoln: University of Nebraska Press.

Powers, William K.
1988   The Indian Hobbyist Movement in North America. In Handbook of North American Indians, vol. 5: History of Indian–White Relations. Wilcomb Washburn, ed. Pp. 557–561. Washington, DC: Smithsonian Institution Press.

Putnam, Robert
2000   Bowling Alone: The Collapse and Revival of American Community. New York: Simon and Schuster.

Quinn, William W.
1990   The Southeast Syndrome: Notes on Indian Descent Recruitment Organizations and Their Perceptions of Native American Culture. American Indian Quarterly 14:147–154.

Reinhart, Christopher
2002   Effect of State Recognition of an Indian Tribe. Office of Legislative Research Report No. 2002-R-0118, Connecticut General Assembly.

Resnick, Judith
1995   Multiple Sovereignties: Indian Tribes, States, and the Federal Government.
        Judicature 79(3):118–125.

Ritzer, George
2005   Enchanting a Disenchanted World: Revolutionizing the Means of Consumption. 2nd
        edition. Thousand Oaks, CA: Sage Publications.

Roberts, Kathleen Glenister
2005   Beauty Is Youth: The Powwow Princess. *In* Powwow. Clyde Ellis, Luke Eric Lassiter,
        and Gary H. Dunham, eds. Pp. 152–171. Lincoln: University of Nebraska Press.

Roediger, David
1991   The Wages of Whiteness: Race and the Making of the American Working Class.
        London: Verso.
2002   Colored White: Transcending the Racial Past. Berkeley: University of California
        Press.

Rose, Wendy
1992   The Great Pretenders: Further Reflections on White Shamanism. *In* The State of
        Native America: Genocide, Colonization, and Resistance. M. Annette Jaimes, ed.
        Pp. 403–422. Cambridge, MA: South End Press.

Roth, George
2001   Federal Tribal Recognition in the South. *In* Anthropologists and Indians in the New
        South. Rachel A. Bonney and J. Anthony Paredes, eds. Pp. 49–70. Tuscaloosa:
        University of Alabama Press.
2008   Recognition. *In* Handbook of North American Indians, vol. 2: Indians in
        Contemporary Society. Garrick A. Bailey, ed. Pp. 113–128. Washington, DC:
        Smithsonian Institution Press.

Rottenberg, Catherine
2003   Passing: Race, Identification, and Desire. Criticism 45(4):435–452.

Saunt, Claudio
1999   A New Order of Things: Property, Power, and the Transformation of the Creek
        Indians, 1733–1816. Cambridge: Cambridge University Press.

Schneider, David M.
1980   American Kinship: A Cultural Account. 2nd edition. Chicago: University of
        Chicago Press.

School District of Palm Beach County
2008   Diamond View Elementary to Present a Cherokee Princess. West Palm Beach,
        FL: School District of Palm Beach County. http://www.americantowns.com/fl/
        westpalmbeach/news/diamond-view-elementary-to-present-a-cherokee-princess-
        101996, accessed August 3, 2010.

Schroedl, Gerald F.
2002   Attakullakulla, ca. 1700–1780. *In* The Tennessee Encyclopedia of History and Culture. Caroll Van West, ed. Knoxville: University of Tennessee Press. http://tennesseeencyclopedia.net/imagegallery.php?EntryID=A045, accessed March 9, 2010.

Sedgwick, Eve Kosofsky
1992   The Epistemology of the Closet. Berkeley: University of California Press.
1993   Tendencies. Durham, NC: Duke University Press.

Sheffield, Gail K.
1997   The Arbitrary Indian: The Indian Arts and Crafts Act of 1990. Norman: University of Oklahoma Press.

Shohat, Ella
1992   Notes on the "Post-Colonial." Social Text 10(2/3):99–113.

Sider, Gerald M.
1993   Lumbee Indian Histories: Race, Ethnicity, and Indian Identity in the Southern United States. New York: Cambridge University Press.

Smith, Carol A.
1995   Race/Class/Gender Ideologies in Guatemala: Modern and Anti-modern Forms. Comparative Studies in Society and History 37(4):723–749.

Snipp, C. Matthew
1989   American Indians: First of This Land. New York: Russell Sage Foundation.

Snow, David A., and Richard Malachek
1983   The Convert as a Social Type. Sociological Theory 1:259–289.
1984   The Sociology of Conversion. Annual Review of Sociology 10:167–190.

Sober, Nancy Hope
1991   The Intruders: The Illegal Residents of the Cherokee Nation, 1866–1907. Ponca City, OK: Cherokee Books.

Southern Cherokee Nation
2008   Enrollment Criteria and Instructions. http://southerncherokeeok.com/enrollment.html, accessed September 9, 2008.

Spike
N.d.   Alphabetical Index of State-Recognized Tribes. http://www.thespike.com/tablest.htm, accessed June 9, 2005.

Spruhan, Paul
2006   A Legal History of Blood Quantum in Federal Indian Law to 1935. South Dakota Law Review 51(1):1–50.

Stromberg, Peter G.
1990   Ideological Language in the Transformation of Identity. American Anthropologist 92(1):42–56.

Sturm, Circe
2002   Blood Politics: Race, Culture and Identity in the Cherokee Nation of Oklahoma. Berkeley: University of California Press.
2007   States of Sovereignty: Race Shifting, Recognition, and Rights in Cherokee Country. *In* Beyond Red Power: American Indian Politics and Activism since 1900. Daniel M. Cobb and Loretta Fowler, eds. Pp. 228–242. Santa Fe, NM: School for Advanced Research Press.

Takagi, Dana Y.
1992   The Retreat from Race. New Brunswick, NJ: Rutgers University Press.

Taylor, Colin
1988   The Indian Hobbyist Movement in Europe. *In* Handbook of North American Indians, vol. 4: History of Indian–White Relations. Wilcomb E. Washburn, ed. Pp. 562–569. Washington, DC: Smithsonian Institution Press.

Taylor, Jonathon
1994   Letter from principal chief of the Eastern Band of Cherokee Indians to Joy Berry, executive director of the Georgia Human Relations Commission, August 30. Georgia Folder, Archive of the Tribal Registrar, Cherokee Nation, Tahlequah, Oklahoma.

Thornton, Russell
1990   The Cherokees: A Population History. Lincoln: University of Nebraska Press.

Turner, Victor
1969   The Ritual Process: Structure and Anti-structure. Chicago: Aldine Publishing.

U.S. Bureau of the Census
2000   Summary File 1, Figure 5. Washington, DC: U.S. Bureau of the Census.

U.S. Fish and Wildlife Service
2009   How Can I Obtain Eagle Feathers or Parts? Washington, DC: U.S. Fish and Wildlife Service. http://www.fws.gov/faq/featherfaq.html, accessed July 29, 2010.

U.S. Senate Committee on Indian Affairs
1995   Hearing on S. 479, Federal Recognition Administrative Procedures Act, 104th Congress, 1st Session, July 13, 1995.
2005   Oversight Hearing on Federal Recognition of Indian Tribes, 109th Congress, 1st Session, May 11, 2005.

Utter, Jack
1993   American Indians: Answers to Today's Questions. Lake Ann, MI: National Woodlands Publishing Company.

Wald, Gayle
1996   "A Most Disagreeable Mirror": Reflections on White Identity in *Black Like Me*. *In* Passing and the Fictions of Identity. Elaine K. Ginsberg, ed. Pp. 151–177. Durham, NC: Duke University Press.

2000   Crossing the Line: Racial Passing in Twentieth Century U.S. Literature and Culture. Durham, NC: Duke University Press.

Ware, Vron
1992   Beyond the Pale: White Women, Racism, and History. London: Verso.

Waters, Mary C.
1990   Ethnic Options: Choosing Identities in America. Berkeley: University of California Press.

Weismantel, Mary
2001   Cholas and Pishtacos: Stories of Race and Sex in the Andes. Chicago: University of Chicago Press.

Wilkins, David E.
2007   American Indian Politics and the American Political System. 2nd edition. Lanham, MD: Rowman and Littlefield.

Wilkins, David E., and K. Tsianina Lomawaima
2001   Uneven Grounds: American Indian Sovereignty and Federal Law. Norman: University of Oklahoma Press.

Willard, William, ed.
2002   Sovereignty and Governance. Special issue, Wicazo Sa Review 17(1/2).

Williams, Brackette
1989   A Class Act: Anthropology and the Race to Nation across the Ethnic Terrain. Annual Review of Anthropology 18:401–444.
1993   The Impact of Precepts of Nationalism on the Concept of Culture: Making Grasshoppers out of Naked Apes. Cultural Critique 24(2):143–192.

Williams, Raymond
1977   Marxism and Literature. London: Oxford University Press.

Williamson, Joel
1995   New People: Miscegenation and Mulattoes in the United States. Baton Rouge: Louisiana State University Press.

Wilson, William J.
1987   The Truly Disadvantaged: The Inner City, the Underclass, and Public Policy. Chicago: University of Chicago Press.

Winant, Howard
1997   Behind Blue Eyes: Whiteness and Contemporary U.S. Racial Politics. New Left Review 225:73–89.
2004   Behind Blue Eyes: Whiteness in Contemporary U.S. Racial Politics (expanded version). *In* Off White: Readings on Power, Privilege, and Resistance. Michael Fine, Lois Weis, Linda Powell Pruitt, and April Burns, eds. Pp. 3–16. New York: Routledge.

Withoft, John

1983   Cherokee Beliefs Concerning Death. Journal of Cherokee Studies 8(2):68–72.

Wray, Matt, and Annalee Newitz, eds.

1996   White Trash: Race and Class in America. New York: Routledge.

Wuthnow, Robert

1994   Sharing the Journey: Support Groups and America's New Quest for Community. New York: The Free Press.

Index

Page numbers in italics refer to figures and tables.

Association of American Indian and Alaska Native Professors, 214n13

Attakullakula (c. 1700–1780), 112, 219n8

authenticity: and concept of Indianness in race shifting, 9–14, 216n23; race shifters and question of Cherokee identity, 60

autobiographical reconstruction, racial conversion and new narrative of self, 74

Baker, Betty, 96, 97, 103, 129–130

Baker Roll (1924), 16, 125, 217n31, 227n3, 228n7

Bald Eagles Protection Act (1940), 220n2

Barnes, Margaret Louise, 227n4

Basso, Keith H., 224n4

Bender, Margaret, 213n1, 224n1

Berkhofer, Robert F., Jr., 94

Berman, Morris, 221n11

Biolsi, Thomas, 229n4

Black Dutch, use of term in narratives of race shifters, 35–36, 37, 39, 218n3

blood: and idioms of racial and cultural difference, 7; measures of descent and negotiation of racial and cultural marginality, 128–132; race shifting and metaphor of, 42, 72–73; and response of race shifters to documentation requirements, 132–139. *See also* ancestry; kinship

Blood Politics: Race, Culture, and Identity in the Cherokee Nation of Oklahoma (Sturm 2002), 213n2

Blu, Karen I., 230n9

Boudinot, Elias, 205

Bourdieu, Pierre, 225n11

Brown, Michael F., 226n16

Bunker Hill Aurora (newspaper), 205–206

Bureau of Indian Affairs, 148, 150, 217n35

Bush, George H. W., 188

Bush, George W., 187

Butler, Judith, 232–233n11

Byrd, Joe, 147–148

Cahn, Peter, 222n3

California, and self-identified Cherokee organizations, 194

Carter, Asa, 190

casinos, tribal, 96–97, 225n9

Catolster, Isabel, 163, 217n34

Cattelino, Jessica, 229n5

census: and growth in Native American population between 1960 and 2000, 5, 10, 184; and multiracial designation, 53, 214n12; and self-identification of individuals as Cherokee, 15, 51

ceremonial events: and Cherokee neotribalism, 69–70; and wannabes, 107, 108. *See also* demonstration events; powwow(s)

Channeling Zone: American Spirituality in an Anxious Age, The (Brown 1997), 226n16

Cherokee(s): choice of as identity by race shifters, 58–61; definition of Cherokeeness in terms of whiteness by race shifters, 50–51; distinction between other Indians in Oklahoma and, 217n33; historical territory of, 217n37; neotribalism and narratives of racial conversion, 63–88; and perception of race shifters by citizen Cherokees, 94–115; research collaborations and questions about neotribalism, 15–20; self-identified organizations of, 193–200; sovereignty and public representation of culture, 158–164; and syllabaries, 224n1; and use of term "Black Dutch" in family histories, 35–36; and variability of physical appearance, 220n4. *See also* Cherokee Nation; Eastern Band of Cherokee Indians; United Keetoowah Band of Cherokee Indians

Cherokee Advocate (newspaper), 1

Cherokee Confederacy of Southern California, 123, 138

Cherokee Constitution (1839), 118

Cherokee Cultural Center, 91–93

Cherokee Female Seminary, 231n1

Cherokee FIRST, 127

Cherokee Freedmen, 225n10, 227n4

Cherokee Heritage Center (Oklahoma), 126

Cherokee Judicial Appeals Tribunal, 117

Cherokee Nation (Oklahoma): and casinos, 225n9; and Cherokee National Holidays, 147; ethnographic fieldwork and research collaboration with, 1, 15, 20–21, 22, 25; and neotribalism, 17–18, 136; and Northeastern State University, 231n1; and political controversy on Byrd as principal chief, 147–150; population of, 216n29; and public representations of Cherokee culture, 162; and State of Sequoyah Conference, 165–166, 171, 183, 232n4; Task Force on race shifting, 166–171, 231–232n3–4, 232n6–7; tribal enrollment policy and citizenship requirements of, 16–17, 81, 131–133, 228n8–9. *See also* Cherokee(s)

Cherokee National Holidays, 118, 147, 177

Cherokee Nation and Tribe of Mexico, 217–218n38

Cherokee Observer, 108, 113

Cherokee Phoenix, (newspaper) 205–206, 213n1, 232n8–9

"Cherokee Princess," in conversations about race shifting among citizen Cherokees, 94–95, 109–115

Cherokee Tribe of Northeast Alabama, 37, 47–50, 215n20

chiefs: and claims to Cherokee ancestry, 112–113; and State of the Nation address by principal chief of Cherokee Nation, 147

children: and citizen Cherokees on enculturation, 140, 141–142; and demonstration events by race shifters, 70, 223n9; and kidnapping case involving self-identified Cherokee group, 167–168

Choctaw, 25, 53

Circle of Friends Powwow (Arkansas), 52

"citizen Cherokee," use of term, 26

civil rights movement, 7, 184

Civil War, American, 133, 227n1

clan membership, and Cherokee kinship system, 129, 141

class: and conception of "wannabes" by citizen Cherokees, 95–98, 104, 114, 215n20; and experience of white identity by race shifters, 11; and racial politics of neoliberals, 187

Clinton, Bill, 11, 187, 188, 215–216n22, 233n19

closet, as metaphor in race shifting, 44, 45, 214n9, 223n8

code words, for race in neoliberalism, 188, 233n18

cognitive map, of Cherokee families, 119

Collins, Oliver, 2, 3, 4, 17, 44, 213n5, 213n7, 214n11

colonialism: and race shifting as form of neocolonial appropriation, 179; and symbolic capital of racial difference, 101–104

Colorado, Pam, 226n16

Colorado, and self-identified Cherokee organizations, 194

Comaroff, Jean and John L., 67, 86

"coming out," as metaphor in race shifting, 44–46, 214n11, 223n8

community: and cultural fulfillment through race shifting, 56; and narratives of racial conversion and Cherokee neotribalism, 67–73, 85

Connecticut: and state recognition of tribes, 157, 158, 201–202, 230n13; and self-identified Cherokee organizations, 194

constructivism, and reinvention of Indianness by race shifters, 57

contest dancing, 48, 49

conversion: Cherokee neotribalism and process of, 65–88, 222n4; definition of in scholarly literature, 65, 222n2

Cornell, Stephen, 7, 184

Council of Churches, 163

Cowan Watts, Cara, 169, 170, 232n5

Creek Tribe (Muskogee), 58

criminal activity, as motivation for race shifting, 6, 167–168. *See also* ethnic fraud

Crossing the Line: Racial Passing in Twentieth Century U.S. Literature and Culture (Wald 2000), 221n8

Cucchiari, Salvatore, 66, 223n15

Cultivating the Rosebuds: The Education of Women at the Cherokee Female Seminary, 1851–1909 (Mihesuah 1997), 231n1

culture: association of whiteness with emptiness of, 54–55, 75; blood measures of descent and negotiation of marginality,

128–132; and Cherokee history of adaptation, 59; and "doing" as measure of racial "being," 139–145, 179–183; and fulfillment of racial belonging through race shifting, 56–57; New Agers and appropriation of, 6, 105–109, 160, 226n15–16; and racial politics of neoliberalism, 187; romanticization of Indian in American society, 101–104; sovereignty and public representation of Cherokee, 158–164; and stereotypes of Cherokee, 16–17; white appropriation of African-American, 221n10. *See also* popular culture

Dawes Roll, 16, 133, 217n31, 227n3, 228n7

Dayton Daily News, 2, 213n4

"descendants," and negotiation of racial and cultural marginality, 128–132. *See also* ancestry; hypodescent

Delaware, and state-recognized tribes, 202

Delbanco, Andrew, 83–84

Delilah White Cloud Tribe of Cherokees (West Virginia), 133

Deloria, Philip J., 87, 183–184, 213n6, 224n5

Deloria, Vine, Jr., 110

DeMarce, Virginia, 18

demonstration events, 70, 222n4, 223n9

documentation, of ancestry for tribal enrollment, 117–145, 173, 227n2

double standard, on oral histories, 121–122

Dover, Bill, 154, 156

drum groups, 48

DuBois, W. E. B., 182–183, 190

Ducheneaux, Karen, 229n3

Duggan, Lisa, 187

Dunham, Gary H., 223n7

Durkheim, Emile, 75

Eastern Band of Cherokee Indians (North Carolina): and Cherokee culture, 143; comments of tribal employees on race shifting, 10–11, 121–122; and concept of "wannabes," 96–97; and neotribalism, 17; oral histories and documenta-

tion of descent, 121–122; population of, 216n29; research collaboration with, 1, 15, 22, 23, 25; and state recognition of tribes, 162; Trail of Tears and collective history of, 158; and tribal enrollment policy, 16, 217n31, 227–228n7

Eastern Shoshone (Wyoming), 111

Echota Cherokee of Georgia, 177

Echota Cherokee Nation (Alabama), 158

economics: Cherokee Nation Task Force on impact of race shifting on, 166–167; as motivation for race shifting, 10–12, 131; and perception of "wannabes" by citizen Cherokees, 96–97

Education of Little Tree, The (Carter 1976), 190

Ellis, Clyde, 223n7

Enchanting a Disenchanted World: Revolutionizing the Means of Consumption (Ritzer 2005), 221n11

End of the Trail, The (sculpture 1894), 224n2

Eng, David L., 185

enrollment policies, of Cherokee tribes, 16–17, 59, 81, 111, 131–133, 138, 217n31, 227–228n7–9

epistemology, and oral versus written systems of knowledge, 122

Epistemology of the Closet, The (Sedgwick 1992), 214n9

essentialism: and challenges to material and epistemological bases of Cherokeeness by race shifters, 40–44; Cherokee identity and cultural, 139, 141, 144; and racial passing, 174–175; and reinvention of Indianness by race shifters, 57, 216n23

ethnic fraud, 6, 119, 167

ethnic renewal, 7

Evers, Larry, 43

exogamy rates, and Cherokee history, 16–17, 59

family: and concept of cognitive map, 119; and tribal community in narrative of racial conversion, 76–77. *See also* ancestry; kinship

federal recognition: and Bureau of Indian

Affairs, 217n35; and Cherokee neotribalism, 18; criteria for, 229–230n8; by executive or congressional order, 230n9; failure of tribes to meet standards for, 182, 228n11; and use of term "citizen Cherokee," 26. *See also* Office of Federal Acknowledgment; state-recognized tribes; tribe(s)

Fine-Dare, Kathleen S., 213n3

First American Casino v. Eastern Pequot Nation (2001), 158

Fleming, R. Lee, 217n35

Florida: and Cherokee neotribalism, 18; and self-identified Cherokee organizations, 195

folk theories, on ancestral connections, 41

Frankenberg, Ruth, 50, 52, 220n3, 220n6

Fraser, James Earle, 224n2

Gabbert, Wolfgang, 65

gaming. See casinos

Gane, Nicholas, 221n11

Garroutte, Eva Marie, 180

Geertz, Clifford, 14

gender, and claims to high-status Cherokee genealogies by race shifters, 109–115

genealogical distance, and measures of tribal belonging, 129–130

genetic memory, 41

Georgia: and self-identified Cherokee groups, 18, 195–196; and state recognition of tribes, 154–155, 202

Georgia Tribe of Eastern Cherokee, 149–150, 156

Gerth, Hans H., 221n11

Gilbert, William H., 226n19

Ginsberg, Elaine K., 221n8

Going Native: Indians in the American Cultural Imagination (Huhndorf 2001), 106

Golden Hill Paugessett Tribe of Indians v. Southbury (1995), 158

Great Commission: Direct Sales and Direct Faith in Mexico, The (Cahn n.d.), 222n3

Great Plains, and traditions of indigenous nations, 107

Great State of Sequoyah Commission (2008), 165–166, 171, 183, 232n4

Green, Rayna, 110, 224n5

Gubar, Susan, 221n8, 232n10

Guion Miller Roll (1909), 227n3

Hale, Grace Elizabeth, 50

Han, Shinhee, 185

Harding, Susan, 222n4, 223n15

Hawaiian Blood: Colonialism and the Politics of Sovereignty and Indigeneity (Kauanui 2008), 175, 219n9

Haynes, Joshua S., 78, 215n20, 221n7

Hefner, Robert, 66

Hegstrom, June, 154

Hill, Jane H., 177

Hill, Mike, 215n19

Hitchens, Christopher, 188, 216n22

Hobson, Geary, 106, 222n2

hooks, bell, 221n10

Hornbeck, Shirley, 218n3

Hudson, Charles, 226n19

Huhndorf, Shari, 106, 226n15

hypodescent: and multiracial status, 233n12; and racial passing, 174–175, 176, 219n9

Idaho, and self-identified Cherokee organizations, 196

identity: choice of Cherokee by race shifters, 58–61; conflicts over competing definitions of indigenous, 9; and cultural essentialism, 139; indigenous ancestry and revaluing of Native American, 8; matrix of Cherokee, 173; New Agers and appropriation of Native American, 6; performative aspect of in race shifting, 45–46; redemptive power of Cherokee, 115

immigrants: use of term by citizen Cherokees, 99; and racial status of working-class Irish, 189–190

Indiana: and Cherokee identity in family history, 31–33; and self-identified Cherokee organizations, 196

Indian Appropriations Act (1889), 231n2

Indian Arts and Crafts Act of 1990, 12, 167, 168, 169, 229n6, 230n11

Indian Child Welfare Act, 167–168

Indian Civil Rights Act of 1968, 157

"Indian country," use of term, 215n15

Indian Country Today (newspaper), 107, 226n18

Indian Gaming Regulatory Act of 1988, 230n12

Indianness: Black Dutch as code word for in family histories, 35–36, 37, 39, 218n3; and cultural fulfillment of racial belonging through race shifting, 56–57; forms of value attached to, 189, 190; interpretive leap to by race shifters, 42–43; whiteness and authenticity of as issues in racial shifting, 9–14, 216n23

Internet: new tribes and use of Cherokee Nation trademarks on, 166; and sources of information on federally recognized tribes, 168

interviews, and research methodology, 22–23, 25, 26, *208–209, 210–211,* 215n18, 218n39

"intruders," use of term, 125, 227n4

isolation. *See* alienation

Jacob, Murv, 169–170, 171, 232n8–9

Kansas: and ethnic fraud cases, 167; and self-identified Cherokee organizations, 196; and state-recognized tribes, 202

Kauanui, J. Kehaulani, 175, 180, 219n9, 233n15

Kaweah Indian Nation (Kansas), 232n7

Kentucky, and self-identified Cherokee organizations, 196

Kickingbird, Kirke, 229n3

kinship: blood as metaphor for, 72–73; Cherokee forms of and documentation of descent claims, 119, 120, 129–130, 132–139; and members of self-identified Cherokee tribes, 78; verification of statements about, 14. *See also* ancestry; clan membership; family

Kiowa, 111

Kirk, Wyman, 216n27

Kuhn, David, 2

Lakota Times, 107

Lambert, Michael, 181

land rights, and descent claims by race shifters, 124–125

Lassiter, Luke Eric, 223n7

Lears, Jackson T. J., 85, 223n13–14

Legislative Act Requiring Truth in Advertising for Native Art (2008), 169

Lehrer, Jim, 188

Lofland, John, 79

Lott, Eric, 215–216n22

Louisiana: and self-identified Cherokee organizations, 197; and state recognition of tribes, 153, 202

Lumbee Tribe (North Carolina), 229n3, 231n15

Mailer, Norman, 184

Malachek, Richard, 65, 74, 222n4

Mankiller, Wilma, 148–149, 154, 156, 161, 233n16

Mankiller: A Chief and Her People (Mankiller and Wallis 1993), 233n16

Maryland, and self-identified Cherokee organizations, 197

Massachusetts: and self-identified Cherokee organizations, 197; and state-recognized tribes, 202

Mattaponi (Virginia), 229n3

Max Weber and Postmodern Theory: Rationalization versus Reenchantment (Gane 2002), 221n11

May, Karl, 218n38, 224n5

McCombs, Virginia Lee, 227n4

meaning, racial conversion as search for or resolution of, 73–79, 83–88, 87

media, and coverage of white shamanism, 107–108

memory, in discourse of race shifting, 58

Mexico, and self-identified Cherokee groups, 217–218n38

Meyrowitz, Joshua, 225n12

Miami Herald, 159

Michigan: and self-identified Cherokee organizations, 197; and state-recognized tribes, 202

Mihesuah, Devon A., 231n1

Miller, Bruce G., 230n9

Miller, Mark E., 230n9

203; Tallige Fire Cherokee Nation and repatriation/reburial controversy in, 2–5, 213n7

Oklahoma: categorical distinction between Cherokees and other Indians in, 217n33; and self-identified Cherokee organizations, 198; and statehood celebrations, 165–166, 231n2; and state-recognized tribes, 24

Oklahoma Indian Affairs Commission, 216n29

Old Settlers (Arkansas), 23, 137, 227n3

oral histories: family histories and use of term "Black Dutch," 35–36; and limits of documentation of descent, 121–125, 127; of public disavowal and private preservation of Cherokee identity, 34

Oregon, and self-identified Cherokee organizations, 198–199

"outalucks": and documentation of descent claims, 125–128; use of term, 120

Pamunkey (Virginia), 156, 229n3

Pan American Indian Association, 63–64, 81–82, 222n1

Parker, Gerald, 161

Parris, John, 232n5

Passel, Jeffrey S., 214n12

passing, and interpretations of race shifting, 174–178, 216n25, 232n10

Passing and the Fictions of Identity (Ginsberg 1996), 221n8

Paucatuck Eastern Pequot Tribe (Connecticut), 157

Pennsylvania, and self-identified Cherokee organizations, 199

performance, and identity making by race shifters, 45–46, 178, 222n4

Perry, Pamela, 233n13

physical appearance: and Cherokee identity, 59–60, *173*, 228n8; race shifting and categorization of, 220n4; and "white Indians," 95–96

place, race shifters and sense of, 100–101

Playing Indian (Deloria 1998), 87, 183–184, 213n6

politics: Cherokee neotribalism as contempo-

rary form of, 85; and culture in discourses of race shifting, 143–144; indigenous reclamation as act of, 87–88. *See also* neoliberalism; Red Power movement; sovereignty

popular culture, and Cherokee identity, 59

population: growth in Cherokee since 1970, 15, 16; growth in Native American between 1960 and 2000, 5, 184, 214–215n14. *See also* census

Portraits of the "Whiteman": Linguistic Play and Cultural Symbols among the Western Apache (Basso 1979), 224n4

Poteete, Troy Wayne, 17, 96, 99–100, 104, 106, 117–118, 119, 225n14, 232n5

power: American Indian spiritual redemption and symbolic, 105–109; and redemptive of Cherokee identity, 115

Powers, William K., 224n5

powwow(s), 47–50, 223n7, 224n5, 226n20

Powwow (Ellis, Lassiter, & Dunham 2005), 223n7

Putnam, Robert, 84

"queering," of Cherokee discourses and identities, 45

race. *See* African Americans; multiracialism; Native Americans; race shifting; racism; whiteness

Race Changes: White Skin, Black Face in American Culture (Gubar 1997), 221n8

race shifting: ancestral callings and racial essentialism of, 40–44; and Black Dutch, 35–36; Cherokee Nation Task Force on, 166–171, 231–232n3–4, 232n6–7; and Cherokee neotribalism, 15–20; and descriptions of "coming out," 44–46; and documentation of descent, 117–145; explanations for in recent literature, 6–7; increase in Native American population and changes in racial self-identification on census, 5; methodology of study on, 20–27; as narrative act, 33–34; narratives of conversion and Cherokee neotribalism, 63–88; and new racial alchemy in twenty-first century, 183–192; opposing interpretations of as reclamation or appropriation, 172–174; passing and interpretations of, 174–178; and perceptions of race shifters by citizen Cherokees, 94–115; racial "being" and cultural "doing" in, 139–145, 179–183; racial persecution and narratives of victimization in, 37–38; recognition of tribes and debate on political rights, 147–164; and subversion of racial classifications and hierarchies, 38–40; summaries of motivations for, 5–6, 8–9; use of term, 215n16; whiteness and authenticity of Indianness as issues in, 9–14; whiteness and racial choices in, 47–61

racism: and essentialist understandings of blood kinship, 43; and neoliberalism, 188–189, 233n17; reclamation of Cherokee identity and legacy of, 54

Reagan, Ronald, 188

Real American Dream: A Meditation on Hope, The (Delbanco 1999), 83–84

reclamation: of indigenous identity as political act, 87–88; interpretations of race shifting as appropriation or, 172–174, 179; and race shifting as quest for meaningful difference, 61

Red Power movement (1970s), 38, 152, 184, 214n14, 233n16

Reenchantment of the World, The (Berman 1981), 221n11

Reinhart, Christopher, 157, 230n13

relocation, and federal Indian policies, 184

removal, and federal Indian policies, 218–219n5, 219n7. *See also* Trail of Tears

Resnick, Judith, 230n12

Rhoades, Teri, 232n5

Ritzer, George, 221n11

Roberts, Kathleen Glenister, 226n20

Roediger, David, 189–190, 232n10

Rogers, Dan, 149

Rose, Wendy, 226n17

Ross, Daniel, 205, 206

Ross, John, 96, 99, 154, 228n13

Roth, George, 230n9

Rottenberg, Catherine, 178, 232–233n11

Schaghticoke Tribe of Kent, Connecticut, Inc. v. Potter (1991), 158

Schroedl, Gerald F., 219n8

Sedgwick, Eve Kosofsky, 45, 214n9

segregation, and documentation of descent claims from South, 122

selective assimilation, 177

self: contemporary American culture and neoliberalism, 84; racial conversion and new narrative of, 74

Sequoyah (George Guess), 224n1

sexuality, and "Cherokee Princess" ancestry claims, 114

Shades of White: White Kids and Racial Identities in High School (Perry 2002), 233n13

Sharing the Journey: Support Groups and America's New Quest for Community (Wuthnow 1994), 77

Sheffield, Gail K., 229n3

Shinnecock Indian Nation (New York), 229n3

Shohat, Ella, 191

"should-bes": and documentation of descent claims, 125–128; use of term, 120

Signs of Cherokee Culture: Sequoyah's Syllabary in Eastern Cherokee Life (Bender 2002), 213n1

slavery, and Cherokees during Civil War, 133

Smith, Chadwick, 162

Smithsonian Institution, 126

Snipp, C. Matthew, 214n12, 227n6, 229n2

Snow, David A., 65, 74, 222n4

Sober, Nancy Hope, 227n4

social movements, and intersection of race and class in race shifting, 10

social networks, and Cherokee neotribalism, 70, 79–83

sociology, and "deprivation-ideology" models of conversion, 66

Souls of Black Folks, The (DuBois 1903), 182–183

South: Cherokee Tribe of Northeast Alabama powwow and cultural symbols of, 49–50;

race shifters and desire for distance from white culture of, 221n7; racial classification and hierarchies in narratives of race shifters from, 40; segregation and documentation of descent claims from, 122. *See also* Southeast; *specific states*

South Carolina: and self-identified Cherokee organizations, 199; and state-recognized tribes, 203

Southeast, and Cherokee neotribalism, 18

Southeastern Cherokee Confederacy (Georgia), 51, 135

Southern Cherokee Nation (Oklahoma), 12, 31, 37, 59–60, 117–118, 119, 133–135, 137–138, 227n1

Sovereign Cherokee Nation of Tejas, 6

sovereignty: implications of citizenship status for, 218n40; race shifting and debate on tribal recognition and political rights, 147–164, 181–182; understandings of in scholarly literature, 229n4. *See also* politics; tribe(s)

spatial metaphors, and perception of race shifters by citizen Cherokees, 100–101

spirituality: and cultural fulfillment through race shifting, 56; and diversity of Native American religions, 223n11; and narratives of racial conversion, 67–73; and perceptions of race shifters by citizen Cherokees, 105–109

Spruhan, Paul, 227n6

Stark, Rodney, 79

state-recognized tribes: controversy on tribal sovereignty and, 150–151, 162–163, 164, 230n12; discussion of in text, 26; economic impact of on federally recognized tribes, 166–167; inclusion of in research study, 23–24; and legal decisions of state courts, 157–158; list of, 201–204; and varieties of recognition, 152–156, 229n3, 230n10. *See also* neotribalism

State v. Sebastian (1997), 157, 158

State of Sequoyah Conference. *See* Great State of Sequoyah Commission

stereotypes: Cherokees and cultural forms of, 16–17; and encounters between citizen

Cherokees and race shifters, 94; and reinvention of Indianness by race shifters, 57; of spirituality and community as part of Indianness, 56, 75; and "Thindians," 132; of "wannabes" in conversations of citizen Cherokees, 95

Stone, Willard, 126

Stonewall riots (New York City 1969), 214n11

Stromberg, Peter G., 74

Studi, Wes, 149

Sturm, Circe, 16, 182, 213n2, 217n32, 227n5, 228n1

support groups, and new tribal communities, 77, 84

surveys, and research methodology, 21, 25, 26, 207

sweat lodge, 92, 93

Tahlequah Daily Press, 166, 169, 170–171, 232n8–9

talking circles, 69

Tallige Fire Cherokee Nation (Ohio), 2–5, 44, 213n6–7

Taylor, Jonathon, 224n5

Tennessee: and Cherokee neotribalism, 18; and self-identified Cherokee organizations, 199; and state-recognized tribes, 203

Tennessee Commission for Indian Affairs, 153

Tennessee River Band of Chickamaugan Cherokees, 81

termination, and federal Indian policies, 184

Texas: and self-identified Cherokee organizations, 199–200; and state-recognized tribes, 23–24

"Thindians": and documentation of descent claims, 120; and negotiation of racial and cultural marginality, 128–132; use of term, 227n5

Thompson, Robert, 97, 100, 112, 140–141, 143–144

Thornton, Russell, 110, 214–215n14

time, in discourse of race shifting, 58

Tompkins Roll (1867), 227n1

Trail of Tears (1838), 18, 35, 38, 102–103,

128–129, 158, 219n5

transcendence, racial conversion as search for, 83–88

Travisano, Richard, 65

Treuer, David, 190, 234n21

tribal rolls, 125, 227n3. *See also* Baker Roll; Dawes Roll

tribe(s): federal and state recognition of and quest for political rights, 147–164; and tribal enrollment policies, 16, 59, 81, 111, 131–133, 138; use of term by anthropologists, 221–222n1; and use of term "nation," 182. *See also* federal recognition; neotribalism; state-recognized tribes

Truly Disadvantaged: The Inner City, the Underclass and Public Policy, The (Wilson 1987), 233n17

Tsalagi Nvdagi (Texas Cherokees), 11, 36

Twilight of Equality: Neoliberalism, Cultural Politics, and the Attack on Democracy, The (Duggen 2003), 187

Uhlan, Leslie Panchula, 159–161, 230–231n14–15

United Keetoowah Band of Cherokee Indians (Oklahoma), 15, 22, 25, 132, 162, 216–217n29–30, 217n34, 225n9, 228n8

United States: federalism and competing sovereignties of Cherokee-identified populations, 157–158; relocation and termination as federal policies, 184. *See also* Bureau of Indian Affairs; census; federal recognition; Office of Federal Acknowledgment

U.S. Fish and Wildlife Service, 220n2

universalism, and racial politics of neoliberalism, 187–188

University of Oklahoma, 22, 23

Utah, and self-identified Cherokee organizations, 200

value: assignment of to different racial identities, 12, 189, 190; and conversations about race shifting by citizen Cherokees, 98–101

Vermont, and self-identified Cherokee organizations, 200

Virginia: and self-identified Cherokee organizations, 200; and state recognition of tribes, 153, 156, 203–204, 229n3

vision quests, 64

voluntary associations, 84

voting rights, and "should-bes," 126

Wages of Whiteness: Race and the Making of the American Working Class, The (Roediger 1991), 189–190

Wald, Gayle, 221n8

Walker Blanchard, Jessica, 23, 24, 49, 71, 133–134, 219n1

wannabes: and ceremonial events, 107; and "Cherokee princess" ancestor claims, 110; citizen Cherokees and perception of race shifters as, 91, 94–101, 115; and narratives of victimization, 102–103; and New Age phenomenon, 105–106; and "outalucks," 125; and racial identity of Cherokee Freedmen, 225n10; use of term, 9, 215n17, 225n7–8

Washington, and self-identified Cherokee organizations, 200

Waters, Mary C., 189

Watie, Stand, 227n1

Webber Falls (Oklahoma), 117

Weber, Max, 221n11

Weismantel, Mary, 177

Wesho-Bauer, Kathleen, 232n5

West Virginia, and self-identified Cherokee organizations, 200

"white Indians": and documentation of descent claims, 120, 129; use of term, 227n5

White Man's Indian, The (Berkhofer 1979), 94

whiteness: authenticity and migration away from in racial shifting, 9–14; citizen Cherokee perceptions of, 94; and motivations for racial choices of race shifters, 47–61; narratives of racial conversion and experience of contemporary, 87, 186, 189; and racial passing, 175–177; and subversion of racial classifications and hierarchies by race shifters, 38–40. *See also* physical appearance

Whiteness: A Critical Reader (Hill 1997),
    215n19
"white shamanism," 106–108
White Trash: Race and Class in America (Wray
    and Newitz 1996), 215n19
White Women, Race Matters: The Social
    Construction of Whiteness (Frankenberg
    1993), 220n3
Wilkins, David E., 233n15
Willard, William, 229n4
Williams, Raymond, 178

Williams, Tonia, 232n5
Wilson, William J., 233n17
Winant, Howard, 187
Wisconsin, and self-identified Cherokee
    organizations, 200
Withoft, John, 214n8
Wray, Matt, 215n19
Wuthnow, Robert, 77

YMCA, and Y-Indian Princess program, 111

Circe Sturm is a cultural anthropologist who has spent most of her career exploring how individuals and societies come to understand and use categories of sameness and difference, self and other, and how these in turn shape our lived experiences. Most of her research has been based on work with indigenous people in the United States. Her first book, *Blood Politics: Race, Culture and Identity in the Cherokee Nation of Oklahoma* (2002), explores issues of racial and cultural difference in Indian Country, particularly as they are expressed through the idiom of "blood." Recently, Sturm has turned her attention to related debates about indigenous reclamation, tribal recognition, and sovereignty. She has also co-produced her first ethnographic film, *Texas Tavola: A Taste of Sicily in the Lone Star State* (2007), a portrait of Sicilian American women in Texas. Currently, she teaches at the University of Texas at Austin, where she is an associate professor of anthropology, and is also involved in the campus-wide Indigenous Studies Initiative.

CPSIA information can be obtained
at www.ICGtesting.com
Printed in the USA
LVHW102056300621
691582LV00012B/701